FIRST PEOPLES IN CANADA

Third UPDATED and REVISED edition of *Native Peoples and Cultures of Canada*

FIRST PEOPLES
IN CANADA

ALAN D. McMILLAN
ELDON YELLOWHORN

DOUGLAS & McINTYRE
Vancouver/Toronto

Douglas & McIntyre
2323 Quebec Street, Suite 201
Vancouver, British Columbia
V5T 4S7
www.douglas-mcintyre.com

National Library of Canada Cataloguing in Publication Data
McMillan, Alan D. (Alan Daniel), 1945–
    First peoples in Canada / Alan D. McMillan and Eldon Yellowhorn.
    — 3rd ed.

Previous eds. published under title: Native peoples and cultures of Canada.
Includes bibliographical references and index.

ISBN-13: 978-1-55365-053-9 · ISBN-10: 1-55365-053-0

    1. Native peoples—Canada—History. 2. Native peoples—Canada.
I. Yellowhorn, Eldon, 1956– II. McMillan, Alan D. (Alan Daniel), 1945– .
Native peoples and cultures of Canada. III. Title.

E78.C2M32 2004   971.004'97   C2004-902588-0

Editing by Lucy Kenward (third edition)
Copy-editing by Pam Robertson
Cover and text design by Jessica Sullivan
Cover photo by © Galen Rowell/CORBIS/MAGMA
Maps by Dennis and Struthers Visual Communications Inc.
Printed and bound in Canada by Friesens
Printed on paper that is forest friendly (100% post-consumer recycled paper)
and has been processed chlorine free.

Every attempt has been made to trace accurate ownership of copyrighted
visual material in this book. Errors and omissions will be corrected in subsequent editions, provided notification is sent to the publisher.

The publisher gratefully acknowledges the financial support of the Canada
Council for the Arts, the British Columbia Arts Council, the Province of
British Columbia through the Book Publishing Tax Credit, and the Govern-
ment of Canada through the Book Publishing Industry Development Program
(BPIDP) for its publishing activities.

C O N T E N T S

Photograph Credits

All photographs are credited in the captions. Some institutions are identified by their initials:

CMC: Canadian Museum of Civilization
NAC: National Archives of Canada
PABC: Provincial Archives of British Columbia
RBCM: Royal British Columbia Museum
ROM: Royal Ontario Museum

PREFACE

· · · · · ·

MUCH HAS HAPPENED since the first version of this book appeared in
1988. Land claims agreements establishing Aboriginal governments
have been completed across much of Canada's north, and the Inuit aspirations for a self-governed homeland have been achieved through the creation
of Nunavut. Canadian court decisions continue to clarify and expand the nature
of Aboriginal rights recognized in the constitution. Aboriginal issues are featured
prominently in the media, and talented Aboriginal individuals enrich Canadian
society through their contributions in fields such as the arts. Despite great successes, there are still major areas of grievance and unrest, as the violent outbreaks
at Oka (Quebec), Ipperwash (Ontario) and Gustafson Lake (British Columbia) in
the 1990s amply demonstrate. In this book we examine the evolving relationship
between Canada and the Aboriginal communities that exist within its borders. In
addition, recent academic research has substantially added to our knowledge of
the Aboriginal past, providing new perspectives on such topics as the initial arrival and settlement of First Peoples in Canada.

For this re-titled new edition I am pleased to welcome my friend and colleague
Eldon Yellowhorn as co-author. Eldon brings to this task a wealth of knowledge
from his Blackfoot heritage and his extensive experience in First Nations Studies.
His involvement helps to ensure that an academic approach to Aboriginal studies
is not incompatible with a First Nations perspective.

In writing a book of this nature, we have incurred more intellectual debts than
could ever be acknowledged. Many anthropologists, archaeologists, historians,
Aboriginal scholars and others have provided perspectives and knowledge that

have been incorporated in this book. Some kindly responded to my requests for illustrations or information, while others I know only from their published works. We are grateful to all. We also offer our thanks to the people at Douglas & McIntyre, particularly our editor, Lucy Kenward, for keeping the project running smoothly. Finally, as always, I am indebted to my wife, Gillian, for her unwavering support.

Alan McMillan

I was delighted to be asked to co-author this volume. Anthropology has contributed substance to Native Studies, and the two disciplines share many research objectives concerning Aboriginal People. In the following chapters I add a perspective that begins with my interest in archaeology. Examining ancient times can provide us with some insights to explain present conditions and also to imagine the lessons we can apply to plan our future. As yet, few Aboriginal students have pursued this area of study, but that will change in the years to come. A scientific perspective of antiquity may challenge traditional interpretations, but it also opens exciting possibilities for imagining the past. Readers of this volume will find that antiquity still presents intriguing insights, no matter how it is perceived.

Like many Aboriginal scholars, I am concerned with the current conditions of our communities and I am motivated by a desire to understand them and to make a difference. Aboriginal People have experienced the loss of much of their culture, and I know that examining the past can help us make some connections that are no longer apparent. Certainly my own studies have helped me to appreciate my cultural heritage in a new way. Since I can imagine the lived experiences of my Blackfoot ancestors far into the past, I can muse on the future trajectory of current affairs and envision a larger destiny for all Aboriginal People. Studying ancient times has given me a greater context in which to help find the explanations I seek about the present. Somehow, this gives me hope for the future.

Eldon Yellowhorn

CHAPTER 1

Anthropological Research
and Aboriginal People

. . . . .

EPIC NARRATIVES are stories we tell ourselves to explain our society, its nature and its institutions. Anthropology is embroiled in one such narrative, which contains all the elements of a good story. It has an enigmatic beginning, intricate and compelling plot development and intriguing personalities. Of course there is no conclusion in this case, but the debates and dialogue do keep it interesting. Since it is an epic narrative, the plot may take centuries to unfold, and many generations will participate in the drama.

Anthropological inquiry began in the mid-nineteenth century and continues into the present. The characters include generations of scholars who have devoted their careers to this project. Some of the personalities whose work inspired the search include Charles Darwin, a naturalist whose discoveries provided an alternative to religious thought, and Lewis Henry Morgan, who attempted to emulate the Darwinian approach for cultural systems. They were succeeded in the twentieth century by a new cast of characters, led by Franz Boas, who rejected earlier ethnocentric evolutionary schemes and took the discipline in the direction of cultural relativism (the view that each culture is unique and must be understood on its own terms). Their objective was nothing less than deciphering the enigma of culture and tracing the untold story of humankind to its opening sentences.

Revealing those unwritten chapters was made possible by the development of the anthropological methods discussed below. Following these methods allows researchers to delve into the cultures of Aboriginal Peoples to gain insights about their ways of life. In pursuit of such objectives, anthropologists conduct research in such areas as linguistics, ethnography, archaeology and human biology. During the discipline's fledgling days, scholars could engage in research that contributed new knowledge across the sub-disciplines. As the years, decades and centuries went by, the data generated by this research accrued to such an extent that specialization became the rule rather than the exception. Nineteenth-century researchers emphasized comparative ethnography and philology (structure, history and relationship of language), whereas the twentieth century brought new methods in archaeology, linguistics and physical anthropology. Presently, research is identifying new lines of evidence in ever-more technical and specialized fields such as paleoanthropology and molecular archaeology. Each contributes to a clearer understanding of humanity's common heritage. As these sub-disciplines developed in North America, much of the research focussed on Aboriginal Peoples, and anthropologists rushed to document Aboriginal cultures and traditions, which seemed to be disappearing.

One important chapter of this narrative concerns the origins and antiquity of humans in the Americas. Multiple accounts of the past exist among Aboriginal Peoples, most of which explain specific cultural origins in supernatural terms. Although these origin myths are of anthropological interest, anthropology works within a secular world view. Thus, when looking for the origins of humans, the search begins with paleoanthropologists scouring the fossil record because they accept the Darwinian theory that biological evolution is a natural process. Combing through the myriad strata of sediments that eons of geological processes have deposited, they have pieced together a story that begins in Africa and ultimately unfolds around the world. Their chapter in the anthropological narrative tells about the hominids that lived long ago and attempts to position them in a sequence that leads to modern humans.

The long history of humans and their ancestors is revealed as the atomic theories of physicists provide a bundle of methods that allow antiquity to be measured in absolute years. Anthropologists can thus infer the span of time for evolution to proceed from our earliest to our most immediate ancestors. Molecular archaeologists employ the discoveries of geneticists and molecular biologists to determine the connections between human populations. Such research reveals ancient genetic relationships that may not be evident at the physical level. The story that is unfolding leads anthropologists to speculate about the Asian origin of Aboriginal People because an equivalent fossil sequence is not discernible in the Americas, where the earliest human remains recovered possess fully modern traits. The anthropological perspective draws on archaeological evidence to unravel that mystery. By examining the cultural strata that contain the artifacts, features and remains of ancient humans they attempt to learn the details of a story that has been obscured by millennia.

What is known from the archaeological record is that once people became established on the continent, there was a great era of exploration and colonization during which cultures proliferated and diversified. Each distinct culture followed its own path based on a combination of factors that emanated from the environment, technology and economy of its particular era. There was never any homogeneous mass of humanity known as Indians; that is a historical misconception. Instead there existed a perplexing mix of cultures and language families that transcended geographical and environmental boundaries. Each chapter in this volume explores the material and intellectual cultures that developed in this matrix. The anthropological taxonomies of culture areas and language families, which are explained below, are used to organize the diverse Aboriginal cultures to be discussed.

ABORIGINAL PEOPLES WITHIN CANADA

Every narrative benefits from the presence of intriguing characters whose actions move the story along. This volume presents a portrait of the cultures of Aboriginal Peoples whose homelands exist parallel to Canada. Of course, labels such as "Aboriginal People" necessarily homogenize a collage of people and imply sameness where there is none. The prologue to the story of Canada, for example, alludes to the Indians, Inuit and Métis, all of whom comprise categories recognized as Aboriginal Peoples in section 35 of the Constitution Act of 1982. However, finer distinctions only become evident when we consider in greater detail the characteristics that distinguish people from their neighbours. The following definitions, categories and phrases deal with this cultural complexity.

Although many Aboriginal cultures continue to be recognizable today, they cannot escape the sameness that Canada has created. "Aborigine" is itself a noun derived from the Latin phrase *ab origine* which means "from the beginning." In this instance, "aboriginal" is an adjective that modifies "people," a noun, to produce the phrase "Aboriginal People." In one context it may adequately acknowledge the people who were present from the beginning of history. However, such a reference may become imbued with ambiguity because of the priority given to one perspective of history. It encompasses too many diverse cultures to have more than a very general utility.

If the term "Aboriginal People" seems problematic, phrases such as "Native People" or "Indigenous People" are no clearer. "Native" typically denotes a condition of birth. People are native to the culture, city or nation of their birth, therefore anyone born in Canada is native Canadian. "Indigenous People" is the phrase usually associated with international discussions and protocol agreements. Unfortunately, it is often lumped in with words that sound like cognates but are not; a quick glance at the dictionary reveals that "indigene" and all things "indigenous" are nestled too comfortably between "indigence" and "indigent." "Indigenous People" may quickly come to mean the impoverished people of the undeveloped world. As general categories go, neither is better or worse than the other. Like all generic phrases, they invariably disguise diversity for the sake of convenience.

Legal terms are particularly powerful because they directly affect public policy and therefore people's lives. Owing to its fiduciary role, the federal government in

Canada delivers services to Aboriginal Peoples, and for administrative purposes it must determine eligibility. Thus, the government defines who qualifies for "Indian" status and denies some people their Aboriginal identity. Furthermore, Aboriginal People possess Aboriginal and treaty rights that were recognized and affirmed in the Constitution Act of 1982. Vague though they are, these rights continue to be the subject of an ongoing legal contest. In its search for a clearer idea of the heirs to these rights, the federal government accepted Aboriginal Peoples to be Indians, Inuit and Métis. Although it is an artifact of the Canadian constitution, this understanding has become common in public and academic discourse.

Since Canada's birth, successive governments have inherited a fiduciary relationship with Aboriginal People. To manage this responsibility, the federal government created the Indian Act in 1876, which was basically an administrative document. It defined such things as "Indians, and lands reserved for Indians"; initially, Indians were adult males, and any wives or children were considered the dependants of such males, as was the legal convention among Canadians then. Although Canadian laws evolved to accept women as persons, the Indian Act remained frozen in the nineteenth century. Its definition of "Indian" expanded—often in inexplicable ways—so that at one point the legal definition of Indian included Inuit but excluded many Indians. Thus the category of non-status Indians was created.

Although successive Canadian governments acknowledged their fiduciary relationship with Indians and Inuit, they only formally included the Métis in 1982. Métis people had emerged with the fur trade, but from the beginning their identity has been clouded with tension and controversy. Neither Indian nor white, they nonetheless look to both as their progenitors. Identity may transcend biology, but it is complicated by culture. Thus, not every person of mixed-race ancestry can claim Métis heritage. Their unsettled history with Canada has further shrouded the core of Métis identity and the government has been slow to recognize them. Before the British government repatriated the British North America Act (the Constitution Act of 1867) to Canada, only the Alberta government had formally acknowledged Métis people, when it identified lands for settlements in 1938. Métis status, however, was not equivalent to Indian status because it resided with a province, rather than the federal government, and it did not extend beyond Alberta.

The word "Indians," which is entrenched in the Indian Act and the constitution, continues to cause confusion. Not only is this term historically inappropriate, it also masks the diversity of Native languages and cultures across Canada. "First Nations" is the preferred term today because it implies many separate, formerly sovereign entities. This term is not legally recognized, however, and refers only to those individuals and groups defined as "Indian" under the Indian Act.

Legal definitions may determine the beneficiaries of government services, but they are less effective for interpreting intangible characteristics such as culture and identity. Although identity is internally constructed, culture is manifested in ways that can be studied anthropologically. Researchers have devised analytical tools to sort the many disparate groups by the traits they hold in common. Among these taxonomies are language families, which place related languages in one category, and culture areas, which organize groups primarily by geography and material culture traits.

LANGUAGE FAMILIES

Linguistic differences give some idea of cultural diversity. Exactly how many Aboriginal languages were spoken in Canada on the verge of the global era will never be known, since some disappeared early in the historic period without ever being recorded. Others exist in a wide range of dialects, which confuses attempts to classify them. Distinguishing between two closely related languages and two dialects of the same language is a somewhat subjective task, which is further complicated by the passage of time and loss of traditional knowledge of the languages. Approximately fifty-three distinct Aboriginal languages survive in Canada. These can be classified into eleven language families, with differences between them as great as those between English and Arabic. They range from large families containing many separate languages to language isolates with no close relatives. Linguistic diversity is greatest in the west, with six families occurring in British Columbia. The eleven language families are listed below, roughly in order of size.

By far the largest and most widespread language family in Canada is **Algonquian**. This family contains such well-known individual languages as Cree, spoken from northern Quebec to the Rockies, and Ojibwa, spoken from southern Ontario to Saskatchewan. Other Algonquian languages include Mi'kmaq and Maliseet in the Maritime provinces, Innu (Montagnais-Naskapi) in northern Quebec and Labrador, and Blackfoot in Alberta. The now-extinct Beothuk of Newfoundland may have belonged in this category; however, lack of information leads some linguists to classify it as a twelfth language family.

Northern **Athapaskan** languages are distributed from the Alaskan interior to Hudson Bay. Athapaskans occupy the Western Subarctic, with several groups stretching into the Plateau and Plains. Individual Athapaskan languages include Gwich'in, Hare, Dogrib, Han, Tutchone, Chipewyan, Slavey, Beaver, Kaska, Sekani, Tahltan, Carrier, Chilcotin and Sarcee.

The original **Iroquoian** languages in Canada, such as Huron, are now extinct. All Iroquoian languages surviving today in southern Ontario and Quebec are those of the famous "Six Nations" or "League of the Iroquois," originally from northern New York State. Mohawk is the dominant language among Canadian Iroquoians, while others (Cayuga, Oneida, Onondaga, Seneca and Tuscarora) are endangered.

Aboriginal language families in Canada, showing approximate locations of traditional homelands.

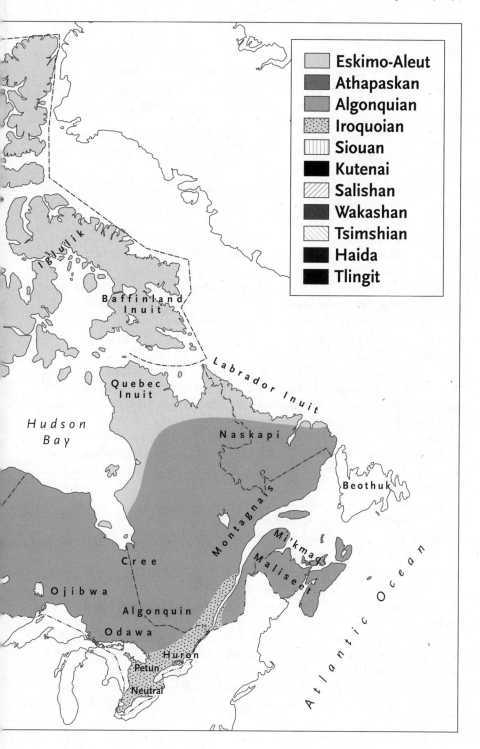

Legend:
- Eskimo-Aleut
- Athapaskan
- Algonquian
- Iroquoian
- Siouan
- Kutenai
- Salishan
- Wakashan
- Tsimshian
- Haida
- Tlingit

Iglulik

Baffinland
Inuit

Quebec
Inuit

Labrador Inuit

Hudson
Bay

Naskapi

Beothuk

Montagnais

Mi'kmaq

Maliseet

Cree

Atlantic Ocean

Ojibwa

Algonquin

Odawa

Huron

Petun

Neutral

Languages in the **Salishan** family occur throughout southern coastal British Columbia, both on the mainland and on eastern Vancouver Island, with Nuxalk (Bella Coola) an isolated example on the central coast. They are also the dominant languages of the adjacent Plateau, in British Columbia's southern interior. Coastal languages include Nuxalk, Comox, Sechelt, Squamish, Halkomelem and Straits, and those in the Plateau consist of Stl'atl'imx (Lillooet), Nlaka'pamux (Thompson), Secwepemc (Shuswap) and Okanagan.

Although several **Eskimo-Aleut** languages exist in Alaska and Siberia, the Canadian Inuit speak dialects of a single language, known as Inuktitut. The Inuit of Greenland also use this language.

People converse in several closely related **Tsimshian** languages on the northern coast of British Columbia. The Nisga'a in the Nass River valley and the Gitksan along the Skeena River speak distinct dialects of one Tsimshian language. The Coastal Tsimshian of the lower Skeena and offshore islands and the Southern Tsimshian of the outer islands to the south speak dialects of a second language.

Members of the **Wakashan** family occupy the central mainland coast of British Columbia and the northern and western portions of Vancouver Island. The northern groups, once erroneously referred to as the "Kwakiutl," are the Haisla, Heiltsuk and Kwakwaka'wakw. The southern Wakashans, along the west coast of Vancouver Island, were historically called the "Nootka," though they are the Nuu-chah-nulth today.

The **Siouan** language family in Canada consists of one language with two major dialects, Dakota and Nakota. Both occur in the southern portions of the three Prairie provinces. The Dakota proper, who settled in Saskatchewan and Manitoba in the nineteenth century, speak Dakota, and the Assiniboine in Saskatchewan and Manitoba and the Stoney in southern Alberta speak Nakota.

The **Haida** occupy Haida Gwaii (also known as the Queen Charlotte Islands), off the northern coast of British Columbia. Their language is an isolate and has no demonstrated ties to any other language.

Most **Tlingit** live in the southeastern Alaskan archipelago. Their distribution, however, extends into extreme northwestern British Columbia and the southern Yukon. Some linguists consider the Tlingit language to be distantly related to Athapaskan, but this remains speculative.

The small **Kutenai** (**Ktunaxa**) language group is restricted to southeastern British Columbia. This language has fascinated linguists, as it has no close relatives. Inconclusive attempts have been made to link it to Algonquian and Salishan, but it remains a linguistic isolate.

The names for Aboriginal languages (and political groups) are in flux today. Many names in common use were assigned by outsiders (both Native and non-Native), and they are occasionally even derogatory. Aboriginal groups continue to reclaim the names by which they wish to be known, and although this may cause considerable confusion, it is a natural response to inappropriate labels.

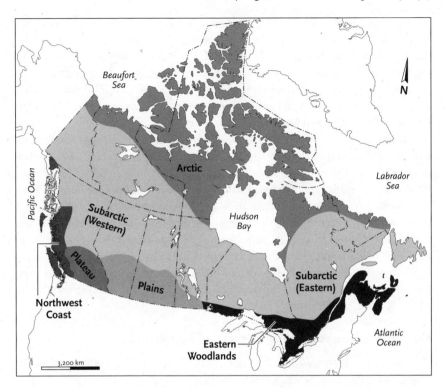

ABOVE *Aboriginal culture areas of Canada*

Like legal definitions, language families try to account for cultural diversity by researching the threads that bind cultures to each other. They are convenient groupings, but they do not elucidate identity. No one self-identifies as Wakashan or Algonquian; these categories are merely linguistic conventions that indicate past relationships.

CULTURE AREAS

As language families classify speech, culture areas order by geography. Similar patterns of culture tend to exist within broad environmental zones. The classifications employed by anthropologists were first developed by Clark Wissler in 1922 to organize the material culture collection at the American Museum of Natural History. His anthropological colleagues then extended these culture areas beyond the storage shelves at the museum and envisioned geographical regions where those cultural traits prevailed. Wissler found that most occupants of an area based their economies on the same essential resources, such as bison on the Plains and salmon on the Northwest Coast. He also noted that cultural borrowing took place between adjacent groups.

In Canada, anthropologists recognize six such culture areas, though none are contained exclusively in this country. The **Arctic**, that tundra land of Canada's far north, and the **Subarctic**, the vast land of northern forests, cover most of the country. The latter is usually divided into Eastern and Western, to distinguish between its Algonquian and Athapaskan occupants. Coastal British Columbia encompasses much of the **Northwest Coast** culture area. Only the northern portions of the **Plateau, Plains** and **Eastern Woodlands** fall within Canada.

Culture areas are somewhat artificial divisions that are imposed for descriptive and analytical convenience. Although they provide a convenient way to classify groups, and they allow anthropologists to refer in general to "the Plains tribes" or "the cultures of the Northwest Coast," such concepts are limited. They mask variations within the culture areas and they ignore broad ties of trade and religious thought that linked Aboriginal Peoples across the continent. They also cannot capture such fluid concepts as Native identity. The Cree who moved onto the Plains from their Subarctic homeland early in the historic period did not cease to be Cree, though they did adopt certain traits useful in their new surroundings. Nor did Aboriginal People find accommodation in Euro-Canadian society by adopting its material culture.

ANTHROPOLOGISTS AND ABORIGINAL PEOPLES

"Indians have been cursed above all other people in history. Indians have anthropologists." Vine Deloria Jr. in *Custer Died For Your Sins*

The above quotation from an American Dakota author illustrates the tension often felt between Aboriginal Peoples and anthropologists. Many Natives have charged that anthropologists, as members of a colonizing race, are involved in exploitation, removing what they need (information, stories, songs) but providing little or no benefit to the Native people they study. The additional role of many nineteenth- and early-twentieth-century anthropologists as collectors of artifacts, transporting the remaining treasures of Native communities to distant museums, added greatly to this perception. Today, however, much anthropological research is applied work, done in co-operation with Native communities. This work ranges from linguists preparing instructional materials for teaching Aboriginal languages to archaeologists and ethnohistorians gathering data to be used in legal battles over Aboriginal land claims. Government administration and public policy have become fields of study for some anthropologists, who act as advocates on Aboriginal issues. Mutual benefit is a requirement for most modern First Nations research.

Anthropology is literally "the study of humans." In North America, however, most research has focussed on Aboriginal Peoples. Considering the uneasy historical dialogue between academics and Aboriginal People, the surprise is that signs of rapprochement are emerging. Applied anthropology has many advocates who regularly launch research projects in co-operation with Aboriginal People.

Conversely, Aboriginal students do not turn their backs on anthropology and its sub-fields once they enter academia. Instead, many enroll in undergraduate anthropology courses, and some declare it their major and even earn advanced degrees. Aboriginal scholars trained as anthropologists now populate the academic discipline of Native Studies.

The current state of affairs is exactly opposite to the condition that Deloria would have predicted. Indeed, rather than shunning anthropology, Aboriginal scholars are embracing its methods on their own terms and appropriating them to understand their own cultures better. As scholars, they draw on anthropological methods to provide new knowledge that emanates from their internal dialogue with their culture. Aboriginal scholars have challenged the hegemony of the non-Native anthropological voice, and they provide new perspectives and contest established beliefs about Aboriginal history and cultural reconstructions. No longer is anthropology the instrument of oppression of a colonial power; in the minds of many Aboriginal participants it has become a mode of liberation.

Anthropology has a number of sub-fields, each of which contributes unique information about the ancient and recent histories of Aboriginal Peoples. The anthropological endeavour encompasses such diverse activities as documenting oral traditions, recovering material items from the ground that can tell of lifeways in the remote past, and assessing relationships between individuals and populations through DNA analysis of blood samples. Each of the major sub-fields is briefly discussed below.

Ethnography, the descriptive recording of specific cultures, fits the popular image of the anthropologist, as a researcher observing and recording the way of life of a different society. Early ethnographers in North America attempted to integrate themselves into cultures, to understand and record the people's lifestyle and beliefs. Later, as traditional cultures became increasingly changed through Euro-Canadian contact, ethnographers began to rely more heavily on knowledgeable Native informants who could describe aspects of cultures no longer being practised.

The heyday of ethnography in Canada was the last two decades of the nineteenth century and the first few decades of the twentieth. This was the brief period between when anthropology emerged as a separate discipline, with fieldwork being done by trained professionals, and when many traditional Aboriginal practices disappeared. Although observers gathered extensive information on many Native groups, they were far too late for others. For example, the Huron and other Canadian Iroquoians, so important in Canada's early history, had been extinct or dispersed for centuries before ethnographers arrived. Other groups, though still surviving, had gone through immense cultural change. The Mi'kmaq, for example, had been in contact with Europeans for almost 400 years before being studied early in the twentieth century. In more remote regions, however, such as the central Canadian Arctic, relatively complete ethnographic data on traditional cultures could be obtained well into the twentieth century.

Franz Boas (at upper right) with George Hunt (back row) and his family, Fort Rupert, ca. 1894. Courtesy American Philosophical Society, Philadelphia.

One of the earliest and most important ethnographers working in Canada was Franz Boas (1858–1942). Trained in his native Germany as a geographer, Boas joined a scientific expedition to the Canadian Arctic in 1883–84. His account of the Inuit of Baffin Island, published as *The Central Eskimo* in 1888, was his first major contribution to ethnography. He became fascinated with the cultures of the Northwest Coast and in 1886 began field research that continued throughout the rest of his life.

Boas was an indefatigable fieldworker and a prolific writer, who was concerned with fully documenting Native life by amassing great quantities of descriptive information on groups all along the Northwest Coast and into the interior of

TOP *Anthropologist T.F. McIlwraith (on left) with group of Nuxalk, all in ceremonial dance regalia, at Bella Coola, 1922.* CMC 56872. BOTTOM LEFT *Diamond Jenness in the Arctic as part of the Canadian Arctic Expedition of 1913–18.* CMC 50806. TOP RIGHT *Marius Barbeau transcribing Native songs from a phonograph.* CMC J4840.

British Columbia. Most of his writing was on the Kwakwaka'wakw (who he termed "Kwakiutl"), particularly the group at Fort Rupert on northern Vancouver Island. His volumes of descriptive data, produced in collaboration with George Hunt, a Native resident of Fort Rupert, make the Kwakwaka'wakw among the best-documented Aboriginal People in Canada. Boas and Hunt also published volumes of myths and other oral traditions in Kwakwala, the language of the Kwakwaka'wakw people. By the end of his life, Boas had become the dominant figure in American anthropology, leaving the field stamped with his insistence on rigorous empirical data collection.

Boas also coordinated the Jesup North Pacific Expedition, a massive research and publication project dealing with Aboriginal People on both sides of Bering Strait. The *Jesup* series included important volumes by Boas and Hunt but also by other researchers supported and encouraged by Boas. These publications include John Swanton's early study of the Haida and James Teit's major ethnographies on the Interior Salish.

Perhaps the most distinguished of the early Canadian ethnographers was Diamond Jenness (1886–1969). Born in New Zealand and educated at Oxford, he came to Canada to participate in the Canadian Arctic Expedition of 1913–18. His study of the Copper Inuit in the central Arctic resulted in the major ethnographic source for these people, *The Life of the Copper Eskimos* (1922). In addition to his detailed ethnographic studies, Jenness made major contributions to Arctic archaeology and applied anthropology, the latter through his five-volume *Eskimo Administration* series, in which he assessed government policy across the Arctic, from Alaska to Labrador and Greenland. He also did fieldwork among the Coast Salish, the Carrier and Sekani of the western Subarctic, the Sarcee of the Plains and the Ojibwa of the Eastern Woodlands. His knowledge of Aboriginal groups across Canada is clearly shown in his best-known work, *The Indians of Canada* (1932).

Another prominent Canadian ethnographer, a contemporary and associate of Jenness, was Marius Barbeau (1883–1969). Born in Quebec, he eventually studied at Oxford, where he became intrigued by the new field of anthropology. Barbeau was captivated by the Aboriginal cultures of the Northwest Coast, particularly the Tsimshian, and he began extensive research among them. He was greatly aided in this work by William Beynon, a local resident of Tsimshian descent, who gathered much of the ethnographic data. Barbeau is best known for his writings on art, such as *Totem Poles* (1950), which records these monuments along the entire west coast of Canada. However, his greatest interest was in the myths, stories and music. Taking a phonograph into the field, he recorded hundreds of songs and legends.

Many other anthropological pioneers conducted important research. In the east, Frank Speck's study of the Naskapi is an ethnographic classic, as is Wilson and Ruth Wallis's account of the Mi'kmaq; Ruth Landes and Frances Densmore provide the major studies of the Ojibwa. On the Plains, important early ethnographic research includes that of Clark Wissler on the Blackfoot, Robert Lowie on the Assiniboine, David Mandelbaum on the Plains Cree and Wilson Wallis on the Canadian Dakota. Many researchers have added to our knowledge of Northwest Coast cultures, but particularly important ethnographic works include John Swanton's description of the Haida, Homer Barnett's study of the Coast Salish, Philip Drucker's account of the Nuu-chah-nulth and Tom McIlwraith's work among the Nuxalk. In the Arctic, such pioneers as Knud Rasmussen, Kaj Birket-Smith and Therkel Mathiassen made substantial contributions with their ethnographic studies.

Quite aside from the professional academic researchers were amateur ethnographers, whose connections to Aboriginal cultures came through marriage, friendship or family. For example, James Teit, a rancher in the southern interior of British Columbia, was married to a Thompson woman. She introduced him to people who related their customary lifeways and intellectual culture, which allowed him, with support from Franz Boas, to produce several volumes on the Interior Salish that are now considered classics of the genre. Another neophyte ethnographer was Walter McClintock, whose career began when he decided to spend some time among the Piikani (Peigan) in Montana and Alberta in the early 1900s. Often Aboriginal informants recruited these interested amateurs because of the literary skills they possessed. The spiritual leader Mad Wolf, for example, insisted that Walter McClintock record his knowledge of Piikani lore so he could leave a legacy for future generations.

Thus, credit for the knowledge gathered and published by both professional and amateur researchers belongs largely to their Aboriginal colleagues. These people were the repositories of their cultures' traditions, and we are greatly indebted to them for sharing their knowledge with anthropologists. Many clearly went well beyond the passive role the term "informant" implies and could better be described as collaborators and colleagues. Certainly George Hunt played that role with Franz Boas, as did William Beynon with Marius Barbeau and David Duvall with Clark Wissler. Today, Aboriginal scholars routinely consult this literature, knowing that their ancestors were the original sources who narrated their stories to the anthropologists. Just as Mad Wolf had hoped, the stories, myths and rituals were transmitted via the written word to a generation of Piikani who never knew him.

The major period of traditional Canadian ethnography has passed, but there is still much to learn. Some modern researchers are documenting Native life in its present complex situation. Good examples come from the writings of anthropologist Hugh Brody. In *The People's Land* (1975), dealing with the Inuit of the eastern Arctic, and *Maps and Dreams* (1981), on the Dunne-za (or Beaver) of northeastern British Columbia, Brody writes about the modern realities of Aboriginal life. These include the nature of relationships with Euro-Canadians, the persistent struggle to maintain Native identity and beliefs, and the constant threat to Native lands and the animals upon which Native cultures depend. Brody's works and similar studies offer insights into how Aboriginal cultures are adapting to new conditions, and they provide a context for understanding modern Native grievances.

Ethnohistory, a mixture of anthropology and history, looks at Aboriginal cultures through written documents. Source material includes the journals and correspondence of explorers, fur traders, missionaries, early settlers and government administrators. Ethnohistorians use techniques of historical research to study Aboriginal cultures at the time of European contact and subsequent changes. As ethnohistory is restricted to writings left by Europeans, a considerable time lag exists from east to west, corresponding to the rate of European expansion. Thus, almost two and a half centuries separate the early observations of Jacques Cartier on the St. Lawrence Iroquoians in 1535 and those of Captain James Cook on the Nuu-chah-nulth of western Vancouver Island in 1778.

One outstanding example of ethnohistoric documentation is the insight into Huron life provided by the *Jesuit Relations*. From their bases in Huronia from about 1634 to 1650, Jesuit priests sent voluminous correspondence, describing their work and the people they were attempting to convert, to their superiors in Quebec. There the documents were compiled and sent to Paris, where they were published as the *Jesuit Relations*, providing colourful descriptions of this new land and its people for European readers. As the Huron were dispersed and their society nearly destroyed by 1650, our knowledge of them comes almost entirely from the writings of a few early observers, supplemented by archaeological research.

As vital as this ethnohistoric documentation is, it also has major weaknesses and limitations. The explorers, missionaries and government agents who left these records were not trained academics, nor could they be objective about practices they were attempting to eradicate. The documents present Native life as seen through the eyes of outsiders, who often had little comprehension of what they were viewing. In addition, their accounts of Native life are often woefully incomplete, or based on very brief visits. Even the important description of Nuu-chah-nulth life provided by Cook was based upon a stay among them of slightly less than one month, an insufficient time, as Cook himself lamented, to gather data on many aspects of their culture. Modern ethnohistorians working with these biased and incomplete records must assess what valid information and insights they contain and then integrate data from various sources to create a coherent picture.

Linguistics includes the scientific study of the nature and structure of languages; the evolution of languages over time, including tracing historical relationships between languages; and the interrelationship between language and thought. In early work in Canada, linguists were conscious that traditional knowledge and many Aboriginal languages were being lost, so they dedicated much of their effort to recording songs, myths and other oral traditions in the local languages. As Aboriginal languages include many phonemes (the smallest units of sound in a language) not found in English, attempts to write these languages with the English alphabet proved unsatisfactory. Accordingly, linguists devised several different orthographies (writing systems) to record Aboriginal languages, usually employing a combination of symbols and English letters to represent all phonemes. Although a number of such orthographies are now in use across Canada, the International Phonetic Alphabet is a common standard.

Around 1840, before such orthographies were developed, James Evans, a missionary at Norway House in Manitoba, invented a system of syllabics for writing Cree. Syllabic writing has one character per whole syllable (minimally, a consonant and vowel combination). Once this system was established for Cree, it spread to the neighbouring Ojibwa and Montagnais and was adapted later for writing Inuktitut and several Athapaskan languages. It is still widely used.

Linguistic analysis also traces historical relationships between languages. Closely related languages are classified into language families and are assumed to have a common origin. When an individual language is located at some distance from all others in its family (such as Sarcee on the Plains), linguists trace past population movements. In addition, some scholars have attempted to link various language families into even larger linguistic units, which suggest ancient connections. These larger groupings, however, are often highly controversial.

One of the most distinguished linguists to work on such problems was Edward Sapir (1884–1939), who pioneered studies of language and culture and of the psychology of culture. During a period of residence in Canada he conducted fieldwork on a number of Aboriginal languages, most extensively with the Nuu-chah-nulth of western Vancouver Island. He not only collected data on the structure of the language but amassed a large body of myths, stories and accounts of traditional life. Sapir is also well known for his attempts to classify Aboriginal language families into a small number of "super-stocks," which share a remote common ancestry. For example, he grouped the Wakashan and Salishan languages together in a category termed "Mosan." He then placed Mosan into one large super-stock with the Kutenai and Algonquian languages. These suggestions of distant past relationships are provocative, but they cannot be demonstrated conclusively, and most linguists regard them with suspicion. Even more controversial is the American linguist Joseph Greenberg's classification, which places all the above languages and many others in a single category (see chapter 2).

Today, much linguistic work is applied, rather than purely academic. Linguists work with Aboriginal communities across Canada, developing writing systems and helping to prepare curriculum materials for teaching Aboriginal languages. The threatened state of many Aboriginal languages makes this work all the more pressing. Some (notably Cree, Ojibwa and Inuktitut) remain vibrant, whereas others are spoken by so few people that they are all but moribund. Many Aboriginal languages share the precarious conditions of Haida, Squamish, Sekani and Sarcee and are in imminent danger of going silent. Despite valiant efforts, such as the Inuit use of modern broadcast media to promote Inuktitut, most languages are endangered because they are spoken only in small areas, often single communities. Most Aboriginal People are ultraminorities whose populations may simply fall below the critical mass of speakers necessary to keep languages active. Moreover, English is the *lingua franca* of the modern world, and the proliferation of media means that all non-English languages feel this pressure to some degree. Even in Quebec, where French prevails in most places, many Aboriginal communities have adopted English to participate in national organizations such as the Assembly of First Nations. Like linguistic islands in a sea of English, Aboriginal People appear to be on the verge of being inundated by a rising tide of unilingual anglophonism.

Physical (or biological) anthropology, unlike the other sub-fields that study cultural (or learned) behaviour, deals with inherited human physical characteristics. Although it is largely a biological study, such cultural factors as marriage rules and dietary practices affect biology and must be taken into account. Physical anthropologists study variations in human populations, the environmental and hereditary bases of that diversity and the evolution of humanity to modern form. Both living and skeletal populations provide information.

Researchers have long studied the physical characteristics of living populations in Canada. Franz Boas, for example, measured and recorded such physical attributes as height and head shape during his fieldwork with Northwest Coast populations. More recently, scientists have investigated such topics as how Aboriginal groups in the Canadian north adapt physiologically to the cold climate and how social practices such as marriage help shape the genetic profiles of human populations.

Physical anthropologists often work with archaeologists to examine human skeletal remains recovered by accidental disturbance or through controlled excavation. They have found evidence of a wide range of burial practices in Aboriginal Canada, from single interments to large communal burial pits to placing the dead in caves, in trees or on scaffolds. Although researchers study burial practices through the contexts in which skeletal remains are found, physical anthropologists can also investigate many details by analyzing the bones in the lab. They can reconstruct general morphology, such as height and body build. They can also gain some insight into diet and cultural practices. One good example, from the coast of British Columbia, is the intentional flattening of the forehead through binding during infancy, which produced a shape consistent with cultural ideals of beauty or status. Skeletons can show evidence of disease, injury or violent death, from which we can speculate about the hazards of life at that time. The high incidence of violent death visible on Iroquoian skeletal remains, for example, demonstrates that internecine warfare was prevalent. Physical anthropologists also examine the demography (vital statistics) of past populations to determine the age and sex compositions, average life expectancies and rates of infant mortality. New techniques in DNA analysis allow researchers to assess how individuals in any given population were related.

Skeletal recovery poses ethical issues. Many Aboriginal People oppose any project that disturbs their dead. Nevertheless, construction projects, erosion and archaeological research occasionally expose human skeletal remains. Agreements between First Nations and anthropologists are required for any research on Native burials. The potential for conflict over this issue is well illustrated by past events. In 2000, a largely intact Aboriginal cemetery in Midland, Ontario, was discovered when it was disturbed by a housing development, bringing Aboriginal elders and archaeologists together to salvage and to bless the site. In such cases, archaeologists must approach the First Nation that has traditional ties to the land and consult with band representatives on the proper way to treat human remains. Often the First Nation will help to remove their ancestors, monitor the research conducted on them and perform rituals before they are reburied. These protocols ensure that burial sites are treated with respect and sensitivity, and today the collaboration between Aboriginal People and scientists appears to be beneficial to both groups. This is in stark contrast to a 1972 case in which the Union of Ontario Indians was so incensed at not being consulted that it attempted to charge an archaeologist for failing to comply with the Cemeteries Act. Work on that site was abruptly halted while legal, moral and political issues were debated. In a similar vein, protests by irate Saskatchewan Natives forced the Royal Saskatchewan Museum in Regina to remove its displays with human skeletons.

Historically, some physical anthropologists did not follow the most ethical methods in their research and this has tainted relations with Aboriginal People. Franz Boas, for example, robbed graves while on a collecting expedition to British Columbia. In his journal he wrote about his anxiety and troubled sleep over his actions, but he placated his conscience by reminding himself of his duty as a scientist. Such disrespectful practices have given Aboriginal People a poor view of physical anthropology. However, as in other sub-fields of anthropology, Aboriginal students have not shied away from researching the hard questions that bring them into contact with burials. They have identified ways to show respect for the dead, such as smudging the deceased with sweetgrass, and they bring such practices into the research milieu.

There are now more examples of co-operation for mutual benefit than protests. When ancient cemeteries have been disturbed, many First Nations have worked with physical anthropologists and archaeologists to ensure that the bones are gathered with respect and that the information available is collected. They know that their ancestors still have lessons about the past to impart to modern generations. One of a number of physical anthropologists active in such co-operative research is Jerry Cybulski, of the Canadian Museum of Civilization, who has worked primarily in British Columbia. In some cases collaboration was initiated due to First Nations concern about an increase in vandalism and loss at their historic burial caves or cemetery areas. In other cases modern construction activities that accidentally disturbed burial sites provided the stimulus. Although Cybulski and his academic team supervise the recovery of skeletons and conduct the laboratory analyses that follow their removal, control of each project remains with the First Nation. The Aboriginal People decide what in-field proto-cols will be followed and what level of analysis will be permitted on the bones. After the laboratory studies are completed, the researchers return all human remains to the First Nation involved for reburial. However, some physical anthropologists find such co-operative solutions unacceptable because repatria-tion and reburial prevent potential future studies.

The exhumation and investigation of ancient human remains is no longer sim-ply an ethical dilemma debated among academics. Laws now specify what must happen at every stage from excavation to reburial. In the United States, the Native American Graves Protection and Repatriation Act (NAGPRA) has been most influential. Museums that receive public funding are compelled to inventory their collections and accept repatriation requests from Native American tribes. In Canada, modern treaties negotiated across the north and in British Columbia in-clude clauses that specify the protocol for when burials are encountered. Modern protocols came into effect when the well-preserved body of an ancient hunter was found frozen in the ice of a glacier near the British Columbia–Yukon border in 1999, over five centuries after his death. He was subsequently given the name Kwaday Dan Ts'inchi ("Long Ago Person Found") by the Aishihik-Champagne First Nations. Scientists were allowed to study his remains for a specific time, after which he was cremated and his ashes scattered on the glacier where he was found. The local Native community then held a farewell feast involving all participants in the project.

Archaeology is the study of past human behaviour through material remains, which are generally recovered from the ground through excavation. Archaeolo-gists attempt to understand the ways of life of societies that existed in the past, to document cultural change that occurred over time and to explain how and why such change took place. With the exception of the last few centuries, the lengthy heritage of Aboriginal Peoples in Canada can be studied only through physical objects that have survived the passage of time. Archaeologists can also investigate more recent Aboriginal cultures to provide information that is lacking in the written records. What we know about the Huron and Neutral peoples of southern Ontario, for example, comes from both ethnohistoric and archaeological research.

The word "prehistory" was coined to distinguish the period before writ-ten records. However, in oral traditions such a concept is meaningless. This terminology implicitly denies the long history that Aboriginal Peoples hold in their oral narratives. As more Aboriginal People enter the field of archaeology they will bring changes to the way archaeologists organize the past. They, like many historians, have become sensitive to the semantics of classifying antiquity and they reject the division into "prehistoric" and "historic" eras based on when Europeans arrived with their writing systems. Archaeology appeals to many Aboriginal People because, like their oral narratives, it can extract history from unwritten sources.

Although archaeological sites such as pictographs (red ochre paintings on rock surfaces), petroglyphs (carvings into rock surfaces) and fish traps can be studied only through remains on the surface, other site types, such as ancient villages, contain buried deposits that can be excavated. Modern archaeologists are conscious that excavation is a destructive data-gathering technique, and that they must recover as much information as possible. To reconstruct the way of life of the people who lived on a site, researchers study not only artifacts but also traces of houses or shelters, other features such as cooking and storage pits, and food refuse such as animal bones. Modern archaeologists, often in collaboration with specialists from other disciplines, bring a variety of new scientific techniques to the excavation and analysis of archaeological sites.

There are limitations to how much these techniques can reconstruct past ways of life. As archaeologists depend upon the material remains of past cultures, we know a lot about those past behaviours that produced the most evidence. Technology and diet, for example, are well represented in the archaeological record. Other important components of past cultures, such as kinship patterns and political systems, leave fewer discernible traces. Also, not all elements of material culture survive to be recovered archaeologically. While stone and ceramic objects last under virtually all conditions, organic materials fare much more poorly. Bone and antler persist only in non-acidic soils, such as the shell middens on both coasts, whereas wood, bark, hide and sinew are preserved only under rare circumstances. In areas of poor preservation, archaeologists must attempt to reconstruct the past using only small portions of the material culture.

Some conditions favour exceptional preservation of organic materials. Waterlogging will keep wood and bark indefinitely, but not hide, flesh or sinew. Several waterlogged sites excavated along the British Columbia coast have yielded objects of wood and bark, such as baskets, fish hooks and line, and cordage, that would usually have disintegrated. These sites are particularly important, as wood and bark were the dominant raw materials on the Northwest Coast. In addition, at some Arctic sites, where remains have been kept continually frozen, organic materials have stayed virtually intact. Excavating an Inuit house ruin can be an unforgettable experience as centuries-old whale oil and food refuse thaws! In contrast, most sites in the vast Subarctic contain only stone tools, though in areas near the Great Lakes there may be other imperishable objects such as ceramic sherds or implements of native copper.

Archaeological research draws heavily upon certain discoveries from the physical sciences. By far the most important has been radiocarbon (or carbon-14)

dating, a technique that allows actual dates to be assigned to archaeological discoveries. Atmospheric carbon dioxide contains three carbon isotopes (^{12}C, ^{13}C and
^{14}C), of which the first two are stable and the last—which occurs only in a minute
amount—is unstable, or radioactive. All living plants and animals contain the
same ratio of ^{14}C to ^{12}C as is found in the atmosphere. When an organism dies, no
further radiocarbon can be incorporated and the radioactive isotope already present continues to decay at a constant rate. The rate of decay is measured in terms
of the "half-life," the length of time in which one half of the radioactive isotope
will have disappeared, which in the case of ^{14}C is about 5730 years. The amount of
^{14}C still present in the organism's remains can be measured and compared with
the known rate of decay to calculate how much time has elapsed since it died.
Only organic substances, such as wood, bone, shell, seeds or charcoal, can be dated
using this method. Samples are carefully collected and their exact positions in the
site noted, since the samples' ages are used to date the various strata.

A later refinement of radiocarbon dating is known as AMS (for "accelerator
mass spectrometry") dating. This technique can be used to analyze much smaller
samples, such as a tiny sliver of bone from an ancient artifact, than is possible
with the conventional method. Another more recent development, called "cali-
bration," uses known-age wood samples to correct for inaccuracies in dating that
result from fluctuating ^{14}C ratios in the atmosphere over time. Although calibrated dates can be considerably different from radiocarbon years, particularly for
the earliest period of Canada's past, most archaeologists still think and write in radiocarbon years, as is the case in this book. Despite radiocarbon's limitations, the
period before written records in Canada is dated almost entirely by this method.

Heritage conservation is a major concern of Canadian archaeologists and First
Nations today. Native village sites and other remains are being destroyed at an
alarming rate, and Canadian archaeology is being forced to shift from purely academic research to applied management. Urban and industrial construction, highways, flooding of large areas for hydroelectric developments and plowing for
agriculture all take a huge toll on archaeological sites. Even in the Canadian
north, which was formerly spared from such disruptions, southern demands for
energy supplies are threatening heritage sites. A conservation and management
ethic has linked archaeologists, First Nations and environmentalists in attempts
to protect Canada's cultural and natural legacy.

Many recent field projects in Canada have been conducted in consultation or
co-operation with local Aboriginal communities. Archaeology can provide information and objects for Native education programs and it can document traditional use of the land for legal claims based on Aboriginal title. For these reasons,
many Aboriginal groups across the country, from the Nuu-chah-nulth of Vancouver Island to the Mi'kmaq of southern Newfoundland, have hired archaeologists, funded their projects or solicited their expertise.

Archaeologists, however, may hold quite a different view of the past than do
the First Nations with whom they work. Trained as they are in the European

ABOVE *Archaeological excavation on the Kamloops Reserve, British Columbia, 1992. John Jules (in foreground) of the Kamloops First Nation trained in archaeology and is now his band's cultural resources manager. Photo by George Nicholas*

scientific tradition and concerned with collecting empirical data, such researchers have tended to discount Native traditions as unscientific folklore. Aboriginal People, on the other hand, accept that their oral histories are founded on lived experience. They accept their oral traditions as adequate explanations for features on the landscape and origins of the people. Such oral accounts document a rich and lengthy history, full of momentous events, migrations and battles, struggles and victories, heroes and sages. Retelling stories generation after generation allows people to engage in a dialogue with their ancestors. Myths allow people to come to terms with their environment by telling of powerful transformers, whose ancient actions resulted in the present appearance of the land and the animals. Myths also stress the fundamental unity of humans, animals and supernatural beings, in a manner that allows people to account for the natural phenomena of their world. Archaeologists have much to learn from these traditions, since scientific reconstructions of the past based solely on material remains lack the richness and human dimension of the oral histories. Both systems of knowledge make important contributions to understanding the Aboriginal past.

ABORIGINAL STUDENTS and scholars are bringing fresh, new perspectives to the study of anthropology. Some have specialized in the traditional sub-fields and have contributed meaningful perspectives that continue to foment debate, while

LEFT *Cree archaeologist Eva Linklater holds a replica spear and spear thrower in front of a display on Aboriginal heritage that she organized at the Manitoba Museum. Photo by Leigh Syms*

others have become leaders in newer avenues of research. Medical anthropology is one such field, in which the study of fetal alcohol syndrome in Native communities by Métis academic Caroline Tait is one example. Aboriginal scholars have successfully appropriated the methods of their self-selected careers and used them in their struggle to overcome the conditions that oppress them. By using anthropological methods they have made a difference in their communities.

Although Aboriginal Peoples tend to be blended in a homogenizing paradigm, they still possess a remarkable ability to express diversity. Even within broad culture areas, language families and political units there are individual perspectives that add more intrigue to the characters of this narrative. For example, Beatrice Medicine and her cousin Vine Deloria Jr. are both Sioux, from the Lakota and Dakota Nations respectively. Although Vine Deloria Jr. has been a hostile critic of anthropology, Beatrice Medicine embraced anthropology as a fulfilling occupation, beginning her career just after World War Two. She has demonstrated to the present generation that appropriating the methods of anthropology does not dilute one's Aboriginal identity.

Terra Nullius: The Land
that Was Empty

. . . . .

"IT IS COMMONLY accepted that the first Aboriginal people of North America came from Siberia, over the Bering terrestrial bridge, some 12,000 years ago. They found a *terra nullius* and gradually began to explore and populate the territory." So wrote Justice Claire L'Heureux-Dubé in her dissenting opinion in the Aboriginal rights case known as *Regina v. Van der Peet*. *Terra nullius* is a Latin phrase meaning "empty land," and there was a time when this continent was *terra nullius*. This portion of the epic narrative is about the first humans who discovered an empty land at the end of the last Ice Age. When those early explorers first laid eyes on this continent they saw a world primeval awaiting sentient life. For millennia after the Ice Age, when new lands were becoming evident, there existed a great age of exploration and discovery. The first people exercised the rights that flow from discovering new lands that have never known human footprints. Simply by naming the features on the land and establishing their settlements they could claim it as theirs. At first there was a great continent and few people, but eventually every part of it was occupied.

Millennia later, when Europeans first sailed along this land's eastern coast they called it Vinland. The Vikings treated it as *terra nullius* despite the Aboriginal People around them. They established a settlement, but eventually abandoned it and went home. When other Europeans voyaged to this land they would call it America. Like their Viking cousins, they too asserted they had discovered a *terra nullius*. They saw only a mysterious, empty land casually inhabited by Native People but essentially unclaimed. One white man, such as Alexander Mackenzie, walking over Indian country was enough to obliterate the land tenure of a whole nation. Although *terra nullius* now seems a curious intellectual artifact, this legal fiction was once a powerful instrument that legitimated the European claim to land already held by Aboriginal People.

When Europeans arrived in North America they were conditioned to see the world through the Bible, so they associated the Native People they encountered with such historically known seafaring groups as the Egyptians and Phoenicians, or with the "lost tribes" of Israel. However, several early writers recognized a physical similarity between the Aboriginal Peoples of the Americas and Asia and assumed that an early migration of Asiatic hunters had taken place. Later, when anthropology emerged as a discipline, research seemed to confirm the Asiatic origin of North American Natives, across what is today the Bering Strait, and this became scientific orthodoxy.

Many Aboriginal People, however, reject this anthropological explanation of migration from Asia because it conflicts with their own religious beliefs and perceptions of their past. Oral traditions often place Native groups in their ancestral territory from "the beginning of time," a point clearly expressed in the "Declaration of First Nations," prepared by the Assembly of First Nations:

We the Original Peoples of this Land know the Creator put us here. . . .

The Creator gave us our spiritual beliefs, our Languages, our culture, and a place on Mother Earth. . . . We have maintained our Freedom, our Languages, and our traditions from time immemorial.

Although the belief in Asian origins brings anthropologists into conflict with some Aboriginal People, agreement exists that the First Nations have an ancient heritage in Canada. From the vantage point of our own brief lives, the thousands of years documented by archaeologists and "time immemorial" are essentially the same. Furthermore, only over a great period of time could so many languages and cultures have developed among the many separate Aboriginal groups before the global era. Thus, Aboriginal communities can justifiably claim to have emerged "in place" over the thousands of years that followed their initial settlement.

Paleoanthropologists rely on the fossil record to trace the human story that began when our ancient, remote ancestors first left Africa. Unlike on that continent, in the Americas there have been no fossil discoveries of pre-modern humans. No fossil has been found that might be the equivalent of the Neanderthal in Europe or the earlier *Homo erectus* in Africa, Europe and Asia. The first humans to enter North America were biologically modern populations (*Homo sapiens sapiens*). Paleoanthropologists infer that two branches of humanity parted ways after they left Africa and became strangers to each other. One branch led to Europe and the other to Asia, with the latter ultimately populating the Americas as well.

Thousands of generations would pass before these two groups met again. That seminal moment occurred on the west coast of Greenland approximately 1000 years ago. They did not know it then, but, from that day when a seasoned Inuk sealer first spied the sail of a Viking ship beyond the bow of his kayak, humanity had entered a new era.

PLEISTOCENE ENVIRONMENTS AND THE FIRST PEOPLE

The anthropological narrative begins with human arrival in the Americas during the glacial conditions of the late Pleistocene. During much of the Wisconsinan, the final glaciation of the Pleistocene era, most of Canada was deeply buried under huge ice sheets. Glaciation was not static, however, and ice fronts continually advanced and retreated as temperatures fluctuated. During times of maximum glacial extent a vast amount of the earth's water supply would have been locked up as ice, and worldwide sea levels would have dropped by as much as a hundred metres. This would have joined the islands of Japan to the adjacent mainland, for example, and exposed large areas of continental shelf off the western coast of Canada. One of the most dramatic effects would have been the emergence of a land surface more than 1000 kilometres wide joining Asia and North America in the area now covered by the shallow waters of the Bering Sea. Although commonly called the "Bering Strait land bridge," an inappropriate term for such a large land mass, scientists know this huge sweep of unglaciated land, stretching from Siberia to the Alaskan interior and into the Yukon, as "Beringia."

The cold, dry steppe and tundra environment provided habitat for herds of large game animals. Mammoth, horse, bison, caribou and musk-oxen occupying Beringia may have led human hunters gradually eastward. If these early people followed the game herds into new lands they would have brought with them such skills essential to survival in harsh northern conditions as the ability to make warm tailored clothing of hide and fur, to construct shelters that could withstand extreme cold and to hunt such large and formidable beasts as the woolly mammoth.

Although fur-clad mammoth hunters have featured prominently in the traditional anthropological narrative about the initial peopling of the continent, many writers now propose a very different view. They note that the southern coastline of Beringia in the late Wisconsinan would have been a suitable habitat for maritime-adapted people. Fishing and hunting sea mammals may have been the major economic activities, as they were for later cultures in the region. Some form of watercraft, such as the hide-covered vessels used historically, would have been required and would not have been beyond the technological capabilities of that time. Since the Beringian platform was flooded at the end of the Pleistocene, however, there is no archaeological evidence for such early adaptations.

A major issue concerning these early human populations is how and when they moved southward, ultimately to occupy two continents. Hunters could have crossed the unglaciated steppeland into eastern Beringia, as far as what is now the Yukon, but their routes beyond are uncertain. If the initial movement was during the glacial conditions of the late Wisconsinan, massive ice sheets might have presented formidable obstacles to southward travel. Two major hypotheses concerning this migration have been advanced.

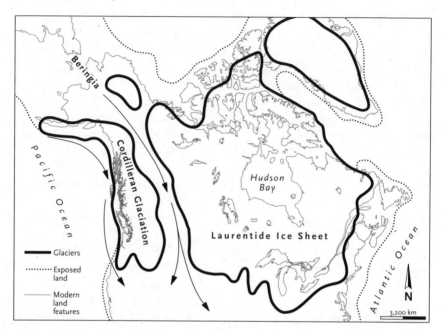

ABOVE *North America near the end of the Wisconsinan glaciation, showing both the "ice-free corridor" and possible coastal migration routes for human entry*

The traditional scenario focusses on what has been termed the "ice-free corridor," which extended along the eastern slope of the Rocky Mountains. In this view, North America was initially peopled by way of this unglaciated strip of land between the Cordilleran glacier over the Rockies and the huge Laurentide glacier covering much of northeastern North America. Rather than a single unbroken ice mass existing over most of Canada throughout the late Wisconsinan, geological studies suggest that there were periods when the ice sheets did not coalesce. Many archaeologists seized upon this geological evidence as showing a logical route out of Beringia for early North American populations, even though there are no archaeological discoveries in the corridor of sufficient age to support this view. Also, critics of this hypothesis have pointed out that the corridor would have provided extremely inhospitable conditions for human survival: a cold climate, harsh winds and a landscape of barren rubble, large lakes and turbulent meltwater rivers. In addition, as is discussed below, recent geological studies indicate that the corridor was not fully open for human travel until the very late Pleistocene, at a time too late to account for early archaeological sites farther south. The ice-free corridor theory is suspiciously similar to that other infamous shortcut, the Northwest Passage, and both may be illusions brought on by the desire to see something for more than what it is.

The alternate migration hypothesis involves a coastal route, which is an idea most vigorously advocated by Canadian archaeologist Knut Fladmark. He points out that most researchers have focussed on an interior hunting way of life for early arrivals and ignored the possibility of a coastal adaptation by people possessing some form of watercraft. Although the rugged British Columbia coastline today presents major obstacles to travel, during the late Wisconsinan lowered sea levels would have exposed large areas of the continental shelf. Archaeologists once thought that massive glaciation would have blocked travel south along the coast, but recent geological studies indicate that the coast was largely ice-free by about 16,000 years ago, and that it supported large animals such as bears, whose ancient skeletons have been found in a number of caves. Detailed underwater studies along the continental shelf show that large open areas of dry land, capable of supporting plant and animal life, existed off the British Columbia coast at the end of the Pleistocene. This now-submerged landscape may be reflected in certain Aboriginal oral traditions, which refer to a time before trees covered the land or to land where none now exists. Fishing and sea-mammal hunting could have supplied enough food for early coastal travellers. However, as people moving by watercraft would have left little evidence of their passing, and archaeological sites along the shore would now be submerged, this hypothesis lacks direct archaeological support. Further knowledge will have to wait until new and more effective technologies for undersea archaeological investigation are developed.

Not only the route but also the timing of any such arrival has been vigorously debated. The standard archaeological belief has been that big-game hunters traversed Beringia and discovered the ice-free corridor by 12,000 years ago. Once through the corridor they expanded rapidly across the continent, preying on large game such as mammoth and leaving behind the distinctive spearpoints and other implements that archaeologists have termed "Clovis," after the town in New Mexico where the original site was discovered. Clovis tools have been found across the continent south of the ice sheets. All such discoveries fall within a narrow time span beginning about 11,500 years ago, which suggests that an empty land was rapidly settled. The great majority of archaeologists accepted this theory, yet claims for pre-Clovis sites continued to emerge. Few such claims withstood prolonged scrutiny and scholars who championed the argument for much earlier arrival were relegated to the fringes of the discipline.

Lately, however, the "Clovis-first" model has suffered major, if not lethal, wounds. Although there are a considerable number of sites with reasonable claims to pre-Clovis age, only one has been widely, if often grudgingly, accepted. At Monte Verde, far to the south in Chile, American archaeologist Tom Dillehay and his team excavated extensive remains sealed under a layer of peat. The waterlogged conditions preserved wooden and hide remnants of what were interpreted as shelters, wooden and stone artifacts, remains of edible plants and the bones of several mastodons. Radiocarbon dates place this occupation at 12,500 years ago, or, because radiocarbon and calibrated dates differ significantly for this period, about 15,000 calendar years ago. In either case, this is significantly before Clovis. Other sites in South America offer suggestions of even greater ages. With the "Clovis barrier" thus broken, archaeologists are carefully examining the North American record. As yet, no additional sites have reached the level of acceptance held by Monte Verde.

Recent geological analysis and dating of a series of glacial erratics at the south end of the ice-free corridor have also raised new questions about the timing of the first peoples' arrival on this continent. These large stone blocks were carried eastward from what is now Mount Edith Cavell in Jasper National Park during a major advance of the Cordilleran glacier. When the ice lobe exited the mountain front it encountered the massive Laurentide glacier and was deflected southward. Even after the coalesced ice sheet reached its maximum, the erratics encased in the ice were transported farther south, perhaps in icebergs that floated in proglacial lakes, to near the modern international boundary. Today, these boulders form the Foothills Erratics Train that runs parallel to the eastern side of the Rocky Mountain front. Researchers from the Geological Survey of Canada tested a new radiometric dating technique on these erratics, and the results indicate that the corridor would not have been completely open for human occupation until about 11,000 or 11,500 years ago—which is possibly just old enough to have allowed Clovis ancestors to enter and spread rapidly, but not old enough to account for the early occupants of Monte Verde.

With their long-established view thrown into question, archaeologists can advance other possibilities about how and when the Americas were peopled. Multiple origins and movements of people, rather than a single founding event, are also highly possible. The coastal route has attracted particular attention as the front-runner for the earliest entry scenario. People with watercraft could have moved swiftly down the west coast of North America, arriving as far south as Chile sometime before the occupation at Monte Verde. Such maritime-adapted cultures would have tended to settle along the coast, and only later, when population growth began to put pressure on resources, would they have extended inland. Paleoenvironmental evidence suggests that travel along the northern coastline would not have been feasible until after about 16,000 years ago, and there is no evidence of human occupation in western Beringia (northeastern Siberia today) much earlier than that. Many archaeologists are now most comfortable with the view that the first peoples skirted the coastal margin to arrive south of the glacial sheets perhaps 13,000 to 15,000 radiocarbon years ago.

Replacing one popular narrative of the first peopling with another does not end the debate. Some archaeologists still argue strongly for a much earlier arrival, but their claims are based on sites where the interpretations are disputed;

either the dates are suspect or the "tools" in question may have been produced by natural forces rather than humans. Studies in other anthropological fields, such as linguistics and biological anthropology, have also failed to reach consensus on the timing of the initial occupations.

INSIGHTS FROM LANGUAGES AND HUMAN BIOLOGY

The debate over the earliest arrivals in North America has moved from the purely archaeological domain to one which involves linguists, physical anthropologists, geneticists and molecular biologists. By studying living Native populations, these specialists hope to determine historical and evolutionary relationships that have a bearing on the nature, number and timing of migrations into North America.

Joseph Greenberg, an American linguist, put forward a wide-sweeping and influential argument in the 1980s. He outraged many of his critics by maintaining that the great linguistic diversity of the Americas can be reduced to three large families, which indicate three separate waves of migration from Asia. His Eskimo-Aleut family is the least contentious of the three. More debatable is his Na-Dene category, which comprises all Athapaskan languages plus Tlingit and (more distantly) Haida. Greenberg argued that all other Aboriginal languages of North and South America shared a common origin and he places them in his third category, termed Amerind. This huge grouping has drawn the most fire from opponents.

According to Greenberg, the ancestors of the Amerind stock entered North America first. He favoured a relatively late date, about 12,000 years ago, which fit well with the view many archaeologists held at the time. The Na-Dene migration came next, finally followed by the Eskimo-Aleut. Some writers have claimed three different routes for these migrations—the Amerinds travelling down the ice-free corridor, the Na-Dene down the coast before expanding inland and the Eskimo-Aleut across the northern reaches of the Arctic.

This model, though it sharply focussed debate, remains highly controversial. Although many archaeologists accepted them, most linguists disagreed with Greenberg's conclusions when they were published. To believe in many unrelated language families, however, necessarily assumes either multiple migrations into North America or an early arrival with subsequent extensive divergence over time. Both require a much longer period of time than Greenberg's model allows. Linguist Johanna Nichols, for example, argues that to account for the diversity of Aboriginal languages the first peoples must have entered more than 20,000 years ago, and 35,000 years is more likely.

The three-migration model has received support from fields other than linguistics. Christie Turner, a physical anthropologist who studies teeth, has conducted a detailed analysis of dental traits based on the remains of thousands of individuals. Teeth have numerous variables, which are primarily genetically determined and change slowly. He has concluded that all Aboriginal Peoples of

North and South America, along with those in Siberia, Mongolia and northern China, share a dental pattern he terms "Sinodont." He has further divided the American Sinodonts into three groups, which correspond closely to Greenberg's three linguistic categories. Turner also interprets his findings as evidence for three separate migrations into North America. His estimate for the timing of the initial arrival, based on the rate of dental change, is similar to Greenberg's, and he associates these early migrants with the Clovis culture.

In genetics, some researchers have turned to the study of mitochondrial DNA (mtDNA), the DNA in the cell outside the nucleus in living populations. As mtDNA is transmitted only through the mother, it avoids the genetic shuffling that nuclear DNA undergoes each generation. It also has a relatively rapid mutation rate, which means that genetic differences between populations emerge more quickly. One major study of global mtDNA variation independently supported three divisions of Aboriginal Peoples in the Americas, roughly corresponding to Greenberg's linguistic stocks, and again concluded that Amerind was the oldest. Some newer research argues that the first peoples arrived in a single wave of migration, which was followed by *in situ* differentiation. Attempts to date the genetic divergence of various groups have been inconclusive, however, and the estimates differ wildly. Several Amerind populations tested, such as the Nuu-chah-nulth of Vancouver Island, showed such a high level of mtDNA diversity that researchers had to conclude the diversity originated in Asia and that the first migrants to the Americas were already genetically varied.

ARCHAEOLOGICAL EVIDENCE FOR EARLY PEOPLES

In 1926, near the small town of Folsom, New Mexico, archaeologists unearthed stone tools in the same level as bones of a species of giant bison. Continued work on the site exposed a number of projectile points of a distinctive type, one of which was lodged between two bison ribs. It was the first clear evidence that human hunters had preyed on these large, long-extinct animals. This conclusion was further strengthened in the 1930s, when excavations in Colorado and New Mexico yielded stone projectile points of a somewhat different type associated with the remains of several mammoths. Although these discoveries occurred several decades before the development of radiocarbon dating techniques, the Aboriginal sites were clearly of considerable age.

"Paleo-Indian" was one of several terms coined to identify the early hunters of large, now-extinct herd animals. As most of the archaeological discoveries have been at places where animals were killed, we know of these early cultures primarily through the distinctive projectile points they employed to bring down their prey, as well as other stone tools used to skin and butcher the animals. The projectile points were hafted on thrusting spears or on short spears that were hurled with a spear thrower. However, only the points remain for study today. Variations in projectile point styles have led to the definition of several Paleo-Indian cultures, the best known of which are Clovis, Folsom and Plano.

ABOVE *Early Paleo-Indian projectile points with associated prey species. Left, Clovis point with mammoth; right, Folsom point with giant bison*

The earliest well-known archaeological culture in North America is Clovis. Its traces are widespread across the continent south of the Pleistocene glacial limit. In Canada, Clovis or Clovis-like points have been found from northeastern British Columbia to Nova Scotia. The culture's heartland, though, seems to have been in the Great Plains and the American Southwest. Radiocarbon dates for Clovis sites tend to cluster in the brief period between 11,500 and 10,900 years ago.

Archaeologists in the past tended to view the Clovis people as specialized hunters of large game, particularly mammoth. This was a bias induced by the highly visible and spectacular nature of several excavated mammoth kill sites. Actually, such kills were probably relatively rare, and the Clovis people likely had a more generalized hunting and gathering economy. The known mammoth kill sites, however, indicate that these people had developed communal hunting techniques to prey on large and formidable herd animals.

The distinctive Clovis point, along with the Folsom, is described as a "fluted" point. After carefully flaking the object almost to its final form, the Aboriginal flintknapper removed long flakes from each side with deft blows to the base. The channel that resulted on the lower surface of each side almost certainly facilitated hafting to a wooden shaft. "Fluting" is a very distinctive feature, which is found only on the earliest spearpoint types.

The Clovis culture figures prominently in many arguments concerning the appearance of humans in North America at the end of the Pleistocene. Proponents of the "late arrival" school of thought see the Clovis people or their immediate ancestors as the first to leave significant archaeological traces. Even if earlier discoveries are made along the west coast, Clovis may represent the founding population across much of the continent. In this view, Clovis hunters entered a landscape teeming with mammoth, mastodon, giant bison, ground sloth and the American horse and camel. The extinction of all of these animals by the end of the Pleistocene has frequently been attributed to the activities of human hunters.

This "Pleistocene extinctions" or "prehistoric overkill" hypothesis was proposed by a number of writers but it was put in fullest form in the 1960s by archaeologist Paul Martin. In Martin's scenario, small groups of hunters traversed the corridor between the Cordilleran and Laurentide glaciers, arriving near what is today Edmonton around 11,500 years ago. From there they spread explosively to the south, into an unpopulated and biologically rich environment. As the human "front" advanced, population densities became sufficiently large to overkill much of their prey. The front then moved on, leaving behind a lower population density. In this way, according to Martin, humans swept across this empty land, reaching the tip of South America in only 1000 years and leaving numerous animal extinctions in their wake.

The prehistoric overkill hypothesis has been criticized on a number of grounds. The changing climate at the end of the Pleistocene might also have spelled doom for those species highly adapted to glacial conditions. Also, the extinctions did not all occur at once. Horses and camels appear to have preceded the mammoths into oblivion, whereas the giant bison survived for centuries longer. However, the evidence of Clovis points with mammoth kills and the fact that mammoths were extinct by the end of the Clovis period implies that Clovis hunters contributed to the animals' demise. Perhaps the "overkill" scenario was inspired by the green politics and environmentalism of the 1960s as a parable of the tragedy that befalls us when we are indifferent to our shared natural legacy.

The earliest cultural stage following Clovis is termed Folsom, after the town in New Mexico where the original site was discovered. Folsom points, which are smaller and more delicate than Clovis examples, are characterized by extreme fluting that extends over most of the surface of each face. They have a more restricted distribution than Clovis points but are found from the southern Canadian Prairies to Texas. Radiocarbon dates indicate an age of 11,000 to 10,000 years. By this time the mammoth was extinct, and Folsom people seem to have been relatively specialized hunters of giant bison (*Bison antiquus*). Folsom hunters appear to have been the first to drive bison into natural traps where they could be killed easily, and most of our knowledge of these people comes from such kill sites.

Much of Canada would have been covered by glacial ice during this early era of human occupation. One possibly very early site lies in the unglaciated land of easternmost Beringia, today the northern Yukon. The Bluefish Caves locality has yielded a meagre sample of stone tools, including microblades and waste flakes from tool manufacture, with the bones of horses and other late Pleistocene animals in deposits dated between about 25,000 and 10,000 years ago. Unfortunately, the bone beds could have accumulated through natural processes and the complex nature of the deposits hinders attempts to place the stone tools precisely within the radiocarbon age span. Claims for human presence as early as 25,000 years ago are based on alleged modifications to animal bones, though these are far from conclusive. Although the evidence is weak, Bluefish Caves remains a candidate for one of the earliest sites in Canada. However, its location in eastern Beringia means that it casts little light on settlement south of the ice sheets.

Most early sites discovered in Canada are associated with the southern margins of the retreating glaciers, indicating they were settled from the south as the land became available. Numerous surface discoveries of fluted points along the shores of glacial lakes attest to human presence. Only a few sites, however, have been excavated or firmly dated.

One discovery in southern Alberta has yielded dramatic new insights into human and animal life at the end of the Pleistocene. The Wally's Beach site, which had been inundated by the St. Mary Reservoir, was exposed during a recent period of low water. Subsequent wind erosion revealed a wide range of paleontological and archaeological remains. These included the bones of late glacial fauna, such as extinct horses, bison, musk-oxen and caribou. Well-preserved prints forming trackways indicated that mammoths, camels and horses regularly tramped through the coulees, perhaps on their way to drink from the river. A complete suite of projectile points, from classic Clovis points to the diminutive arrowheads of much later times, were also found at this site. Four radiocarbon dates on bones from extinct animals cluster between 11,000 and 11,350 years ago. Although these dates cannot be directly associated with the Clovis points, which could be somewhat later, they are exactly what would be expected for known Clovis sites farther south. Of great interest is the fact that all three Clovis points found at the site contained traces of animal protein. When the residue from the points was analyzed, scientists discovered that two had been used to kill or butcher horses, and that the third had been used on a bovid, presumably either a bison or a musk-ox. This is one of the few demonstrated associations of horses and ancient hunters in North America. The researchers, from the University of Calgary, argued that humans may have played a role in the extinction of horses in North America. The mammoth trackways, which showed relatively few traces of juvenile animals, led paleontologists to consider this a population under stress.

One of the few Canadian sites to have yielded fluted points in their original context and with firm radiocarbon dates is near the east coast. At Debert, in central Nova Scotia, excavation in the 1960s uncovered a large collection of stone tools, including more than a hundred fluted points. Several closely resemble the classic Clovis form. Although no animal remains were preserved in the region's acidic soils, reconstructions of the past environment led archaeologists to suggest that caribou was most likely the major prey animal. Recent blood residue tests on several scraping implements from Debert have confirmed this theory. Radiocarbon dates indicate that Debert was occupied about 10,600 years ago, a time when glacial ice was only a short distance away.

A small excavation at the nearby Belmont site in 1990 produced an assemblage of stone tools nearly identical to those from Debert. In addition, Clovis-like fluted points have been discovered on the ground surface at locations in all three Maritime provinces. The people who left these tools would have lived on a larger

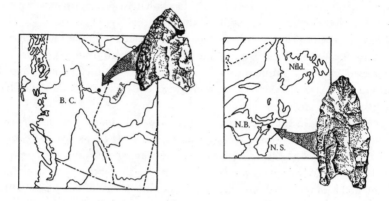

ABOVE *Two Canadian fluted point discoveries, showing site locations. Left, Charlie Lake Cave, British Colum-bia; right, Debert, Nova Scotia*

land mass than exists today due to lower sea levels that linked Prince Edward Island to the mainland.

Fluted points and other stone tools resembling those from Debert and dating to about the same time were uncovered at the Vail site, in northwestern Maine near the Quebec border. Once again, there were no faunal remains, but the major prey animal was likely caribou. Such sites show that early humans were moving into the area shortly after deglaciation and that a hunting economy was widespread across the northeast during this time.

One of the few other Canadian sites with a firmly dated fluted point is Charlie Lake Cave, in northeastern British Columbia. Located between two sandstone outcrops, the site probably once faced out over glacial Lake Peace. It was excavated in 1983, and again in the early 1990s, and revealed a long history of human use. Found at the lowest level of the site were stone artifacts, including a short, extensively resharpened fluted point, and the bones of an extinct form of bison, some still bearing marks of ancient butchering. Radiocarbon dates for this level indicate an age of 10,500 years.

Although Charlie Lake Cave is situated within the ice-free corridor region, it was occupied at least a millennium too late to provide evidence of initial entry. It was more likely settled from the south after final deglaciation. Other sites along the corridor are of similar age. Several fragmentary fluted points, similar to the one from Charlie Lake Cave, were excavated at Sibbald Creek, west of Calgary, Alberta, though no acceptable radiocarbon dates were obtained. The Vermilion Lakes site in Banff National Park, with initial dates of about 10,700 years, provided a considerable number of stone flakes and tools, but no diagnostic artifacts such as fluted points at the earliest levels. The pattern of artifacts, animal remains and features at this site suggest that ancient people constructed open-air shelters at temporary camps while they hunted mountain sheep nearby. Also at Banff, only a short distance away, is the Lake Minnewanka site, which has yielded un-dated Clovis points in disturbed contexts on the lakeshore, and intact archaeolog-ical remains below a radiocarbon date of 10,000 years. Undated surface discoveries of fluted points, many resembling the Charlie Lake Cave example, have been made throughout much of the corridor, from southwestern Alberta to the Yukon.

Other fluted points have been reported from undated sites or surface discover-ies across much of southern Canada. Clovis-like points are relatively common in southern Ontario, where they may date to as much as 11,000 years ago. The first Clovis-like points from Quebec were recently discovered at a site east of Mon-treal, near the border with Maine. Many fluted point sites have been found along the surface of ancient glacial lake shorelines, leading one Ontario study to sug-gest an age of 10,700 to 10,400 years based on the known geological history. At the Parkhill site, near London, Ontario, excavation revealed a large sample of fluted points and other stone tools. Although this site cannot be directly dated, projectile point styles suggest that it may be placed in the 10,800 to 10,500 year range. It was interpreted as a temporary camp, used on a number of separate occa-sions by people who were hunting caribou and other game beside a former lake that extended from Lake Huron.

Due to the nature of archaeological discoveries, we tend to know these ancient people primarily by the stone tools they made, in particular the distinctive pro-jectile points. Frequently, archaeology can provide evidence of the animals they hunted, their pattern of settlement across the landscape, and what long-distance trade or travel they undertook to procure the high-quality stone used to manu-facture their tools. In rare cases, we also have glimpses into past beliefs or ritual practices. A considerable number of Clovis "caches," some associated with burials but others thought to be ritual offerings, are now known. One of the best exam-ples is the East Wenatchee, or Richey-Roberts, site, in Washington State near the border with British Columbia. An array of very large, exquisitely crafted Clovis points, some bearing traces of red ochre, was found in a pit with other well-made stone tools and bone rods with bevelled and cross-hatched ends. Volcanic ash on the underside of one point has been correlated with a known eruption of 11,250 years ago, which suggests the cache should date to some time shortly after. Be-cause there is no evident burial associated, and the large points are distinct from anything found in kill or camp sites, this cache has been interpreted as a possible ritual offering. In southern Ontario, at the Crowfield site, excavators found a pit containing numerous stone tools, including fluted points that had been shattered by heat, again possibly as a ritual offering. Nearby, the early-Holocene Caradoc site shows signs that stone tools were purposefully broken and deposited.

Other possibly ritual remains allude to the relationship between people and animals. For example, Folsom-period people at a kill site in Oklahoma placed a bison skull painted with red lightning bolts in an arroyo where bison were driven. This offering may have been to draw the bison into the traps, as historic

Plains bison-hunting cultures used similar practices. Two intact raven skeletons, apparently associated with stone tools, were recovered from the earliest layers of Charlie Lake Cave in British Columbia. Jon Driver, an archaeologist at Simon Fraser University, argued that they were intentionally buried as part of ritual activity and noted the significant role that ravens play in Aboriginal belief systems across the Canadian west.

Following Folsom-age sites are archaeological cultures collectively referred to as Plano, which range in age from about 10,000 to 7500 years. A variety of styles of large unfluted projectile points are characteristic of this period. As the last of the large animals, or megafauna, disappeared, Plano hunters preyed on more modern species. On the Plains, bison gradually decreased in size, from the giant bison of the Folsom period to a medium-sized form (*Bison occidentalis*) associated with early Plano sites, and finally to the modern form (*Bison bison*) by late Plano times. Communal hunting techniques for taking large numbers of bison, such as driving them over "jumps" or into narrow canyons, appear to have been well developed.

In Canada, Plano points are widespread. Although concentrated on the Plains, they are also found in western and southern Ontario, east as far as the Gaspé Peninsula of Quebec (with only rare examples from the Maritimes) and north to northeastern British Columbia and southern regions of the Yukon and Northwest Territories. Common variants of Plano on the Canadian Plains include the related Eden and Scottsbluff points, with their fine "ripple" flaking; Alberta points, a broad stemmed variant characteristic of the northwestern Plains; and Agate Basin points, an early lanceolate version with a wide distribution. To the east, in western Ontario around Thunder Bay, the "Lakehead Complex" refers to a number of sites that yielded large lanceolate projectile points.

Once again, most Canadian examples are either surface discoveries or from excavated sites that did not yield suitable organic material for radiocarbon dating. Fortunately there are some exceptions. The Fletcher site, a bison kill site in southern Alberta associated with Scottsbluff and Alberta points, could not be reliably dated through the original excavation in the 1960s. Later archaeological work at this location, specifically designed to obtain material for dating, uncovered a layer of seeds directly below the bison bone bed. These were dated to 9300 years ago, indicating that the animals were killed only shortly after. In southern Saskatchewan, the Heron Eden site has yielded a number of Eden-Scottsbluff points associated with bison bones dating to about 9000 years ago, and a radiocarbon date of 8000 years has been obtained from the Sinnock site, a Plano bison kill location in southeastern Manitoba. In addition, the Cummins site, part of the Lakehead Complex of sites around Thunder Bay, has produced a date of almost 8500 years on fragmentary remains of a cremation burial. In Quebec, excavation at the Rimouski site documented a Plano occupation that yielded a radiocarbon date of 8100 years, well within the range considered typical of the Plano period.

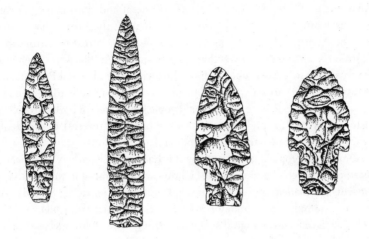

ABOVE *Examples of Plano points. All are surface finds from Saskatchewan. Left to right: Agate Basin, Eden, Scottsbluff, Alberta*

During the time Plano hunters stalked the big-game herds east of the Rockies, apparently quite different early cultures occupied the west coast. However, the coastline today differs markedly from that of the Pleistocene, so evidence of the region's earliest arrivals may now be submerged. Radiocarbon dates as early as 9700 years ago come from the lowest levels at the Namu site on the central coast, where leaf-shaped projectile points and simple stone chopping tools indicate a generalized coastal way of life. At Kilgii Gwaay, on the Queen Charlotte Islands, Parks Canada and Haida archaeologists worked in the modern intertidal zone to recover archaeological remains that had been deposited as the sea transgressed the land 9400 years ago. They found stone and bone tools, discarded animal bones and shells, and even wooden objects preserved by waterlogging. The animal bones indicate a fully maritime way of life, with people relying on a suite of fish, sea mammals and shellfish that differs little from that of more recent Haida villages. (The early cultures of the west coast are discussed in greater detail in chapter 8.)

AFTER THE ICE AGE

Archaeologists have had a difficult time devising appropriate taxonomies to encompass the accelerated pace of cultural change during the Holocene, and the terms in common use seem awkward and misleading. Scholars typically place Holocene cultures within either the Archaic or the Middle and Late Prehistoric periods. The Archaic is basically a material culture inventory that became a quasi-cultural, quasi-chronological unit of analysis for archaeologists. This loosely conceived stage encompasses the long period between the late Pleistocene big-game hunters and the advent of settled agricultural societies. However, as agriculture was absent across much of Aboriginal Canada the term has been extended to span the Holocene, up to the point when objects of metal and cloth mark Aboriginal Peoples' entry into the global economy. Unfortunately, the Archaic has tended to characterize Aboriginal cultures as unprogressive in contrast to European cultures. Similarly, although many archaeologists still use it, the term "prehistoric" completely disregards Aboriginal Peoples' histories. The idea of a Prehistoric period reduces antiquity to little more than an overly long prelude to the era of European historiography. Hence, Aboriginal People have rejected both "Archaic" and ".Prehistoric," on the grounds that they serve only the interest of archaeology while they perpetuate negative stereotypes and assumptions.

As Aboriginal People appropriate the methods of archaeology to investigate their past, they are challenging the discipline's assumptions and finding that certain concepts are inadequate for their goals. Traditional knowledge provides alternatives. For example, Eva Linklater, a Cree archaeologist from Nelson House, Manitoba, devised a chronological sequence through the Holocene based on Cree traditions. Now that a fledgling corps of Aboriginal archaeologists has arrived, they are attempting to syncretize their cultural traditions with archaeological methods. They accept that oral narratives are inspired by lived experience and can be organized temporally. Folk taxonomies, such as the Blackfoot distinction between the Dog Days and the Horse Days, have begun to influence mainstream archaeological thought.

In this volume we avoid referring to the Archaic as much as possible. In its place we use the Holocene as the chronological backdrop to our discussion of Aboriginal People. We have also tried to avoid schemes that measure time in units either before or after Europeans arrived, to avoid making this event the paramount defining moment in a long Aboriginal heritage. Accordingly, we do not use terms such as "prehistoric" and "precontact." Instead of the traditional Early, Middle and Late classifications, which unintentionally but unfortunately reduce the Aboriginal past to merely the prologue to a European presence, we examine trends that leave their signature in the archaeological record. Introducing untried terms is not necessary to our purposes here, and rejecting biased terms does not constrain our discussion.

After the glaciers retreated, the warmer climate of the Holocene placed severe environmental pressure on extant cultures to adapt. Ice that had buried vast regions gradually melted to reveal these hidden lands, which triggered an extended period of exploration during which the first peoples exercised their rights of discovery. Animal species that had provided the essentials of life went extinct, and new lifeways proliferated as people invaded and colonized new lands and environments. Hunting and gathering cultures that had their genesis in the Pleistocene continued to flourish in the Holocene and diversified when new resources were discovered. Habitual plant gathering eventually introduced people to a new economy that liberated them from the uncertainties associated with hunting and gathering wild species of animals and plants ("country foods"). People embraced new ways of living and invented new technologies throughout the Holocene.

Since these practices proved successful, though not always sustainable, most persisted well into the global era.

Early Holocene environments were dynamic and prone to fluctuations before they came to approximate those of the present. In general, however, the climate grew warmer and people adapted their material culture to the changing environment. In the continental heartland, country foods, which people obtained from exploiting a wide range of resources, continued to support the resident cultures. Yet they did tend to focus on particular game animals that were most abundant in specific regions, such as bison on the Plains, caribou in the boreal forest and deer in the Eastern Woodlands. Hunters often stalked their game, or drove the herds toward a trap where the animals could be ambushed by waiting hunters.

Such mobile lifeways required tools and lodging that were easily portable and effectively used local materials. Hide-covered tipis provided shelter on the Plains, whereas in the woodlands people built similar conical structures which they covered with sheets of birchbark. Several neighbouring bands often coordinated their schedules to intercept the herds. Although hunting cultures pursuing terrestrial game were often on the move, the sea-mammal hunters of the west coast were more sedentary. The abundant coastal resources allowed these peoples to develop complex societies, with permanent villages of large wooden houses, on a hunting-fishing-gathering economic base.

If the west coast provided the entry route for the first people who discovered this continent, the people moving along its shores would have been maritime adapted. On the east coast, the artifacts recovered from the Debert site in Nova Scotia indicate that Ice Age hunters had already occupied this land by the end of the Pleistocene. The early Holocene warming directly affected both coastlines when the melting glaciers emptied into the sea. Around the world sea levels rose, but in formerly glaciated areas the land also rebounded when it was finally freed from the glaciers' weight. Resident populations had to adapt to rapidly changing conditions. The gradual slope of the continental shelf on the east coast meant that even a slight rise in sea level could inundate large regions.

The coastlines did not stabilize until after about 5000 years ago, by which time people had long since discovered the resources available in the littoral zone and had invented the technology to exploit them effectively. Those who established their settlements on the west coast faced the uncertainty that comes with living in a tectonically active region. Oral histories recount the devastation great earthquakes and tsunamis occasionally wrought on coastal communities. However, such events were rare and the rewards from harvesting abundant marine resources more than offset the dangers.

Across the top of the world lay an empty land that stayed unclaimed when almost all other places on earth were occupied. For millennia it abided the weight of glaciers and remained frozen long after the rest of the world had thawed. By mid-Holocene times, about 6000 years ago, when the Ice Age abated even in the Arctic, fragile plant communities supported sparse herds of caribou and musk-oxen.

They were enough to encourage people to explore the possibility of living there. Over 4000 years ago, the first people to lay claim to the high Arctic lands moved eastward from the area around Bering Strait and discovered the land between the treeline and the coast that was the calving grounds for caribou. Some turned north following the musk-oxen and occupied the archipelago that brought them near the north pole and ultimately to the northern coast of Greenland. These people were the Tuniit of Inuit oral narratives. They were resourceful people who could transform the limited local raw materials into the tools they needed. With their bows and arrows they hunted musk-oxen and caribou and tailored the hides into insulated clothing. They shot birds in flight, they speared fish at the weirs they built, they snared small mammals and they even hunted polar bears. The ancestors of the Inuit, whose culture was more oriented to the ocean, followed the Tuniit into the Arctic. These people set out in hide-covered boats to pursue whales, and hunted walrus and seals with harpoons from the edge of the ice. The Inuit encounter with the Vikings as the latter were expanding the frontiers of their known world was the first contact that set the stage for the global era.

Aboriginal lifeways that depend on a hunting economy go back to the first people who colonized the continental heartland at the end of the Pleistocene. Food preserving and storing techniques brought some security to mobile cultures, but they were still subject to the fluctuations of nature. By mid-Holocene the first harbingers of change were emerging, as people in the Eastern Woodlands began to embrace a new lifestyle based on producing their own food. These Aboriginal farmers did not entirely abandon country foods, nor did they ignore the riverine resources adjacent to their villages. However, their diet consisted mainly of their own food crops.

By controlling food production, farmers secured a stable food supply but they had to make major changes to their lifestyle. Gone was the luxury of mobility, and in its place was a practice that demanded stability and commitment in exchange for security. Settled village life allowed farmers to produce surplus food and store it for the lean times. With farming came a higher standard of living and the ability to connect with trade networks that brought exotic material across the continent. Villages and towns, the seeds of urban culture, grew in a network that supported the new polities that emerged from the alliances between kin groups. As society grew more complex, new social institutions became necessary to maintain stability. Effective organization of the food supply, for example, required social controls to direct production and labour, especially at the northern edges of corn agriculture where scheduling was most important.

People began to gather plants intensively before 5000 years ago, initially concentrating on species such as sumpweed and sunflowers. By deliberately manipulating the local environment, they created the conditions favourable for target species, which in turn led to full-blown plant cultivation. Farming was already an ancient practice in the Eastern Woodlands by 2000 years ago when Aboriginal farmers imported their first exotic food crops. Thereafter, local cultigens grew alongside the imported corn, beans and squash. Although they became staples for Aboriginal gardens in the Eastern Woodlands, these plants were carried north from the tropical regions where they were first domesticated. These imported plants transformed the agricultural economy of the Eastern Woodlands, and about 1200 years ago corn came to be the most important food crop in their gardens. The vital role corn, beans and squash played in their lives inspired Aboriginal farmers to incorporate these staple plants into their mythic traditions as the "three sisters."

Farming left a very different signature in the archaeological record than hunting or fishing, though the tools needed to prepare the soil for cultivation were largely ephemeral. Fire, for example, was essential for clearing the land, but it is impossible to distinguish the traces of this practice from natural forest fires. The basic implement for tilling the soil was a wooden digging stick. Ungulate ribs and scapulae were salvaged from the hunt to make picks and hoes to break up clumps of dirt. Planting and harvesting was done by hand. Baskets woven from plant fibres were used to carry the produce, but the organic raw material did not preserve well. Even the facilities in which farmers stored their surpluses did not persist long in the soil.

Processing the crops for meals, however, required special technology. As beans, for example, must be soaked before cooking, their preparation demanded a vessel that could hold water long enough to soften them. Basketry was not efficient for that task, but pottery provided a solution. Earthenware dishes also facilitated cooking because they could be placed directly on the fire. Using the paddle and anvil technique, artisans formed pots to a desired shape. When dry the medium is brittle, but firing it makes an impermeable, albeit fragile, vessel. When pottery breaks, the sherds remain in the ground indefinitely. Broken pieces of ceramic vessels are among the most conspicuous remnants of farming communities in the archaeological record.

Sometime near the end of the Pleistocene the ancestors of modern Aboriginal People had discovered a *terra nullius*; however by the mid-Holocene it existed no more. There was no land left to be discovered or explored because that task was complete. With wood, stone, bones and antlers for their tools and with hunting, gathering and farming economies fully developed, the first peoples filled the land. They had adapted their cultures to the warmer conditions of the Holocene and thrived on the land they had claimed by right of discovery. Every biome on the continent bore the signs of human occupation. Amid this matrix, the cultures of modern Aboriginal People took form.

The following chapters introduce the diverse Native Peoples who encountered the world when globalization began. They chronicle the archaeological roots of Aboriginal cultures and examine the changes wrought upon them as they adapted to an integrated world system. They also describe some of the challenges that confront traditional cultures in the modern world. Finally, the closing chapter reflects on the querulous dialogue and tense relations between Aboriginal People and Canada and the potential trajectory into the future.

CHAPTER 3

The Atlantic
Provinces

. . . . .

T HE FIRST NATIONS of Canada's Atlantic coast—the region consisting of Nova
Scotia, New Brunswick, Prince Edward Island, the Gaspé Peninsula and north
shore of the St. Lawrence in Quebec, the island of Newfoundland and southern coastal Labrador—shared numerous cultural traits, despite considerable environmental differences from south to north. All along the Atlantic coastline
Aboriginal groups relied heavily on the resources of the sea. In the historic period
all spoke Algonquian languages, though the early demise of the Beothuk in Newfoundland has left too little information to be certain of their affiliation.

The first peoples came to this area at the end of the Pleistocene, when the
gradual retreat of the glaciers opened these lands to human occupation. The distinctive fluted spearpoints found at the Debert archaeological site in Nova Scotia
indicate that early hunters had reached the east coast by 10,600 years ago. However, it appears that several millennia elapsed before human populations felt
sufficiently pressured to continue north, where they eventually reached the island of Newfoundland. The landscape that greeted those early arrivals would
have been quite different from the region today: lower sea levels at the end of the
Pleistocene exposed extensive areas of coast, joining Prince Edward Island to New
Brunswick and Nova Scotia in a large region known as Northumbria. Over this
newly uncovered land spread plants, animals and people. As the climate changed,
rising sea levels gradually drowned much of the land on which these early
hunters might have lived. The tundra-like landscape of Pleistocene times gave
way to a boreal forest of spruce and pine, and later to mixed hardwood forests
that characterized the area historically.

RIGHT *Distinctive fluted points, found in all three Maritime provinces, mark the early presence of the Paleo-Indians. Courtesy D. Keenleyside, CMC*

Today the Maritime provinces, plus the Gaspé Peninsula, can be classified as the northeastern extent of the Eastern Woodlands culture area. Southern regions of New Brunswick and Nova Scotia are covered primarily by deciduous forests common to the Eastern Woodlands, whereas more rugged northern regions, such as Cape Breton Island and the Gaspé, are transitional to more northerly environments. Newfoundland and much of the Labrador coast are considered part of the Subarctic, and are characterized by igneous rock outcrops of the Canadian Shield and vast coniferous forests. In the north, the Labrador coast grades into the true Arctic. Overall, the topography of Atlantic Canada is provided by the highly eroded northern reaches of the Appalachian Mountains.

EARLY CULTURES OF THE HOLOCENE

Changing sea levels have obscured the archaeological picture in the Maritime provinces. After deglaciation, large areas once open to human occupation were submerged by rising seas. In fact, archaeologists in the Maritimes refer to the "Great Hiatus" between 10,000 and 5000 years ago, a period lacking any evidence of human presence. Some early Holocene sites have certainly been lost to the rising waters. Coastal submergence was largely complete by about 5000 years ago, though sea levels continue to rise slowly. Even relatively recent sites are being actively eroded by wave action. In contrast, the coastline north of the Gulf of St. Lawrence is slowly emerging relative to the sea, and sites from early periods may be located at some distance inland. As a result, the major discoveries dating to the early Holocene have been made in Newfoundland and Labrador.

Many such sites, dated at about 7500 to 3000 years ago, have been recorded along the Atlantic coast, but two are particularly well known. Both are burial sites, revealing the importance of burial ceremonialism as far north as Labrador.

The array of artifact types left with the dead gives a dramatic view of the religious beliefs and subsistence practices of these early coastal dwellers.

The earliest of these sites is L'Anse Amour, located on the southern Labrador coast. This low burial mound, capped by about 300 boulders, was located and excavated by Canadian archaeologists James Tuck and Robert McGhee. Slightly less than two metres below the top of the mound, in a large pit dug into the sand, was the skeleton of a child of about twelve years of age, lying face down with a large flat rock on his back. The sand surrounding the skeleton was stained red with ochre, and on each side of the body were concentrations of charcoal, showing where fires had been built on the bottom of the original pit. Charcoal from one of the fires, submitted for radiocarbon dating, indicated that this remarkable burial took place about 7500 years ago. This site provides our earliest glimpse of life and death in the early Holocene.

Particularly significant are the many objects left with this unfortunate youth. An ivory walrus tusk, certainly a valuable trade item, was placed by the face. Around the head were piles of knives or spearpoints of chipped stone and polished bone, a decorated bone pendant and a whistle or flute of bird bone. Near the waist were two graphite pebbles and a small concentration of ochre (the two can be mixed to form a metallic red pigment), along with a small antler pestle, possibly for grinding the pigment. One harpoon head of caribou antler is of the toggling type; that is, after being driven into an animal, it holds in place by turning sideways (or "toggling"). It may be the oldest such harpoon head yet discovered anywhere on earth and indicates, along with the walrus tusk, that a sophisticated technology for hunting sea mammals had developed by this early date.

The abundance of artifacts with the skeleton, the presence of red ochre and the graveside fires, as well as the considerable effort required to dig the pit and pile boulders on top, indicate that this was a special burial. Certainly no hunting community in this environment could afford the labour or materials to make this type of burial a common practice. Logically such special treatment would be reserved for a chief, shaman or other person of great importance in the community, yet here was a child being interred in an elaborate burial. The prostrate position of the skeleton, the heavy rock on its back and the apparent rituals have eluded our understanding, but explanation is not required for us to appreciate these ancient mysteries. L'Anse Amour demonstrates that elaborate burial ceremonies were taking place on these northern shores in very early time periods.

The second important burial site is Port au Choix, located on the western shore of Newfoundland's Great Northern Peninsula, a short distance from L'Anse Amour across the Strait of Belle Isle. Construction activities at this small fishing village exposed a mass of human bones and artifacts covered in red ochre, and led to an archaeological excavation directed by James Tuck. The fine sand of the ancient beach in which the people and artifacts were interred is extremely alkaline, which preserved the bone. Skeletal remains of more than one hundred individuals were excavated, along with numerous burial objects. The site appears to have been a cemetery, in use from about 4400 to 3200 years ago. In recognition of the significance of this discovery, it was declared a National Historic Park, the first such status given to an ancient Aboriginal site.

The excavated human remains include both sexes and all ages, from infants to individuals more than sixty years of age. Most of the adults were buried in a flexed position; that is, the knees were drawn up to the chest and the hands were near the face. Often the skeletons were incomplete or simply bundles of bones, which means they were placed in the site after the flesh had decayed. This may indicate that the people had died during the winter and could not be buried until the ground thawed. It also suggests that Port au Choix was a special location, and that groups away hunting caribou during the winter transported their dead back to the coast. The presence of red ochre in all the graves and the abundant grave offerings attest to the importance of burial ceremonies.

Many of the objects placed with the dead were functional. Harpoon heads, both barbed and toggling, along with harpoon foreshafts of whalebone, show the importance of sea-mammal hunting. A number of large "bayonet" points, ground to shape from slate or bone, were probably once mounted on lances to kill land or sea mammals. Smaller barbed antler and bone points were probably parts of fish spears. Bone implements used to prepare animal hides, such as scraping tools, awls and needles, are well represented. Although wood was not preserved, many graves contained woodworking tools: stone axes and gouges, small knives made from beaver incisors and several large adzes of walrus ivory.

Other burial goods might be classified as decorative items or, with considerable caution, objects of magico-religious significance. Shell beads, perhaps originally sewn to clothing, appear in large quantities. Bone and antler combs, pendants and pins were carved to represent birds' heads. Bear and wolf teeth, seal claws and the bills of such birds as loons and the great auk may have been worn as decorations or as amulets to aid the hunter. Similarly, numerous white quartz pebbles, as well as crystals of quartz, calcite and amethyst, may have had both decorative and magical functions. Various unusually shaped stones, some slightly altered to resemble birds or animals, may have had special meaning. Particularly striking are two large stone objects apparently representing killer whales. To people who were hunters of sea mammals, the killer whale, the ultimate predator of the sea, must have seemed an animal worthy of respect and possibly fear.

Evidence of mid-Holocene burial ceremonialism had long been available from sites to the south of L'Anse Amour and Port au Choix. However, the acidic soil at the sites, which are distributed from Maine to Newfoundland, had destroyed all organic remains. These could be described as "boneless cemeteries," where only the grave inclusions made of stone have survived the passage of time. The common occurrence of red ochre, however, indicates that burial ceremonialism was practised, giving rise to the popular term "the Red Paint People."

Perhaps the most important of such sites in the Maritime provinces is Cow Point, located in south-central New Brunswick. Archaeologists who use the

Archaic as a cultural construct disagree over whether to classify this site as "Maritime Archaic," a term that recognizes numerous traits shared by coastal peoples and artifacts from Labrador to Maine, or include it with the "Laurentian Archaic" extending from the St. Lawrence River valley of southern Ontario and Quebec. Excavation revealed about sixty oval red ochre stains marking where burials had once been. Although only stone objects have been preserved in the acidic soil, many of these were carefully crafted. Particularly distinctive are long slender points, or "bayonets," reminiscent of those from Port au Choix, made of polished slate. They range from smaller utilitarian examples to very long and slender implements decorated with incised designs, which possibly were made specifically as grave offerings. Polished stone gouges, used as woodworking tools, were also found at this cemetery. Radiocarbon dates indicate that this site was in use about 3800 years ago, at the same time as Port au Choix.

The dramatic nature of these burials and the elaborate grave offerings found with them have attracted the most archaeological attention. Other sites of similar provenance give insight into the everyday lives of ordinary people. Once again, rising sea levels in the Maritime provinces have obliterated the majority of such sites, so that most information comes from Newfoundland and Labrador. A recent intensive search for a habitation site associated with the burial area at Port au Choix has led to the discovery of hearths and artifacts, including two ground stone gouges, dating to the same time as the nearby cemetery. In addition, the Beaches site in northeastern Newfoundland has yielded numerous stone tools, most of which were chipped to shape. The finely made ground stone tools characteristic of the cemetery sites are much rarer but not unknown. The Beaches site even yielded a fragmentary ground slate point with an incised design similar to the ones found at Cow Point.

On the central Labrador coast at Hamilton Inlet, Smithsonian Institution archaeologist William Fitzhugh has documented a series of artifact assemblages dating from about 6000 to 3700 years ago. The most recent and best known is the Rattlers Bight Complex, whose occupation sites are characterized by abundant chipped stone tools, a smaller number of tools ground from stone and large rectangular house remains. Also found at the Rattlers Bight site was a cemetery, identified by the typical red ochre stains common to burials in the mid-Holocene. Although no bone was preserved, many grave offerings of stone were found: chipped and ground points, gouges, and imported materials such as mica and native copper. Interestingly, the chipped stone tools were made exclusively of an easily flaked translucent grey stone termed "Ramah chert," which comes from outcrops near Saglek Bay in northern Labrador.

The Ramah chert quarries may have been the reason people spread far up the Labrador coast, where they reached Saglek Bay, well north of the treeline, by 5000 years ago. Such northern outposts are characterized by abundant tools flaked from this distinctive stone, which would have been an important trade commodity. Ramah chert appears in archaeological sites as far south as the Maritime provinces and Maine, indicating cultural ties linking all of Atlantic Canada through the mid-Holocene.

From this archaeological evidence, a subsistence economy can be partially reconstructed. Several species of seals were hunted, as were walrus, which were plentiful as far south as the Gulf of St. Lawrence. A variety of fish species, including the large swordfish taken by more southerly groups, contributed to the diet. In addition, vast numbers of migratory waterfowl were seasonally available. Over 200 bills of the great auk, a large now-extinct flightless sea bird, were found with one burial at Port au Choix. However, most archaeological remains are of species that were available from spring to fall. James Tuck and others have speculated, at least for the groups north of the Gulf of St. Lawrence, that with the first snows of winter the people moved inland to intercept migrating caribou herds. After spending the winter hunting in the interior forests, their seasonal round would take them back to the coast in early spring, when seals could be easily hunted on the pack ice. Social groups would have consisted of small bands, moving with the seasons.

Other aspects of Holocene life in Atlantic Canada have left few archaeological traces. Except for the rectangular stone remains in central and northern Labrador, we know little of the housing. People living as far north as Labrador obviously needed warm and waterproof clothing, but there is little direct evidence. A double row of shell beads over the skull of one of the Port au Choix burials, suggesting the hood of a parka, is a rare example of indirect evidence for clothing styles. However, the practice of elaborate burial ceremonialism, particularly evident at L'Anse Amour and Port au Choix, provides dramatic insight into the beliefs and activities of early to mid-Holocene people.

LATER HOLOCENE CULTURES

About 4000 years ago a new group of people appeared in northern Labrador, eventually replacing earlier occupants who had abandoned the entire coastline south as far as Newfoundland. Physically and culturally dissimilar to their predecessors, these were Arctic people, who reached the Atlantic coast as part of an expansion across Canada's north. They are known as the Tuniit (or "Paleo-Eskimo") to distinguish them from the later Inuit.

There were several regional variants of the Tuniit, particularly on the Labrador coast. The first to settle on the island of Newfoundland is a group known as Groswater, after Groswater Bay in central Labrador. A large Groswater site near Port au Choix dates from about 2800 to 2000 years ago. The harp seal, which hauls out on the ice of the Gulf of St. Lawrence to mate and give birth, was one major resource that would have sustained these people.

The Dorset, who got their name from Cape Dorset on Baffin Island, are the final and best-known Tuniit group to have reached the island of Newfoundland, arriving over 2000 years ago. Typically a coastal people, the Dorset left sites encircling Newfoundland but did not penetrate far inland. The abundance of sea mammals allowed the Dorset to settle in fairly large villages. At one such site, near Port au Choix, more than thirty-five rectangular depressions mark where houses once stood. Each house had sod walls, with timber rafters supporting a roof covered with sod, and was dug slightly into the ground. At another site in northern Newfoundland, the Dorset people quarried a soapstone cliff to carve their distinctive bowls and rectangular lamps. These soapstone vessels meant that they did not depend on wood for fuel, and they could burn seal oil for heat and light in their confined homes. Burial remains from several small caves indicate the people were physically similar to the historic Inuit of the Arctic, and quite distinct from the Indian populations of Atlantic Canada.

Across the Arctic, more recent arrivals, the Thule, the direct ancestors of the historic Inuit, gradually replaced the Dorset. The Thule settled only as far south as northern Labrador, and the reasons why the Dorset disappeared from the Atlantic coast, after occupying it for about a millennium, are unknown. (The Dorset way of life is discussed further in chapter 10.)

To the south, in the Maritime provinces, the Ceramic (or Woodland) period began about 2500 years ago when finely made pottery was introduced, probably through contact with southern cultures. The early pottery is well made and carefully decorated with patterns pressed into the lips and necks of the pots. Occasionally the entire body was impressed with patterns from a cord-wrapped stick. Such earthenware pots could be set directly over a fire to cook food or boil water, whereas stones had to be heated to red-hot and added to vessels of wood or bark. Pottery containers are heavy and fragile, however, and they are far less suited to a mobile lifestyle than those of bark, hide or wood. As a result, the ceramic industry that archaeologists associate with this period declined over time and did not survive into the global era.

In coastal regions shell middens mark many Ceramic era sites. As people began to rely on clams and other shellfish as part of their diet, discarded shells accumulated beside their houses. Since the shell deposits helped to neutralize the acidic soil, these sites also contain a range of bone and antler tools, in addition to

RIGHT *Ceramic vessels from the Maritimes, dating between about 2100 and 1700 years ago. Courtesy D. Keenleyside, CMC*

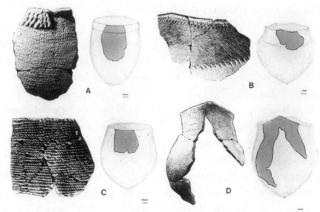

ABOVE *Excavation at the Augustine Mound, New Brunswick. Courtesy D. Keenleyside,* CMC

the more commonly found implements of stone and sherds of pottery. Once again, however, coastal erosion has removed much of the archaeological evidence, even from this late period.

Although most early Ceramic era sites document everyday life, one remarkable discovery in northeastern New Brunswick indicates that the people were in contact with religious ideas and ceremonial practices from far to the south. Excavation in the mid-1970s of the Augustine Mound, long a location important to the Mi'kmaq of the Red Bank Indian Reserve on which it is situated, revealed that the low mound, about eleven metres in diameter, had been raised over a large central burial pit and ten smaller pits. The latter contained both cremated burials and "secondary burials"—disarticulated remains brought from earlier locations for ceremonial reburial. Radiocarbon dates from one of the pits place the mound's construction at about 2300 years ago. Stone artifacts interred with the dead include large finely flaked points and knives, gorgets (flat polished stone objects, perforated for wearing at the throat or on the chest) and pipes. Many wealth goods were made of raw materials not available locally. The most numerous of these were thousands of rolled beads and other implements of native copper, a raw material obtained from the western Great Lakes region. The copper in the mound altered the chemical composition of the soil, resulting in excellent preservation of organic materials, such as fragments of woven fabrics, matting and basketry. The Augustine Mound is the only site in eastern Canada with preserved organic fragments such as these.

Another excavated mound, near Halifax, is known as the Skora site. Evidence from this location shows that preparation for interment began with cremation. A large pit was dug into a hilltop, where the remains and associated artifacts were placed. Afterward, construction of the mound began. Radiocarbon dates show that this site was being used at the same time as the Augustine Mound.

The practice of building burial mounds and the types of associated artifacts indicate some contact with cultures farther south, particularly the Adena in the Ohio River valley. As ideas spread with trade contacts, religious influences from the south would have made their way north. These beliefs were then expressed as ritual practices that can be seen in the archaeological record.

Developments in the Maritimes during the late Holocene led directly to the Mi'kmaq and Maliseet cultures of historic times. Their lifeways are well documented at sites located along coastal saltwater lagoons and sheltered tidal estuaries, where fish, shellfish and waterfowl abound. Most coastal shell middens date to this late period. Although found in all three Maritime provinces, the middens are particularly common in coastal Nova Scotia and southern New Brunswick, where they are concentrated in areas such as Passamaquoddy Bay. Large fish weirs were constructed near some sites, especially those on estuaries where spawning species such as salmon and eels could be taken. Bones of seals and walrus in midden sites indicate that sea mammals were also hunted. Although no remains of watercraft have been preserved, bark-working tools found in the middens suggest that canoes and houses were covered with this material, as was the case in historic times. Artifacts from the Oxbow site, a seasonal salmon-fishing location along a tributary of the Miramichi River in New Brunswick, show how Mi'kmaq culture evolved over the last 2500 years.

Farther north, in Newfoundland and Labrador, archaeologists use the category "Recent Indian" to refer to the period beginning about 2000 years ago. Archaeological sites from this time yield meagre traces of past activities, and consist primarily of chipped-stone tools such as projectile points and scrapers. In central Labrador, where such assemblages are referred to as the Point Revenge Complex, the most common raw material is Ramah chert, which shows that contact continued with the north. Rocks forming oval tent rings with central hearths hint at the style of housing, and one Point Revenge site yielded the remains of a collapsed wooden tent frame, preserved by charring. On the island of Newfoundland, several late Holocene cultural complexes exist, with similar tools made from locally available stone. Tiny arrowpoints dating to the eve of the global era identify the Little Passage Complex. These Little Passage artifacts almost certainly belonged to people who became the historic Beothuk, but the lineage of the Point Revenge people is less clear. They may have been the ancestors of the historic Innu of the region, or they may have become extinct in the very early historic period.

Although Beothuk culture can be seen in late Holocene archaeological remains in Newfoundland, this group's origin is uncertain. The Beothuk's ancestors, in one view, arrived relatively late from the mainland. If this is the case, they probably spoke a language in the Central Algonquian stock and were closely related to the Innu. James Tuck argues a competing view, which stresses lengthy cultural continuity. He points to archaeological evidence that Paleo-Eskimos and Indians might have been contemporaneous in Newfoundland and southern

Labrador. If so, it means Beothuk culture developed in the same place over a long period of time, possibly extending back as far as the mid-Holocene.

These "Recent Indian" groups may have been the Aboriginal People who encountered Norse colonists, as the latter explored to the south and west from their settlements in Greenland. These voyages, described in the Norse sagas, took them along the Atlantic coast where they repeatedly met Aboriginal Peoples: both Eskimoan (Dorset and Thule) groups in the north, and Indian (Point Revenge and ancestral Beothuk) peoples farther south. The Norse made no distinction, referring to them all as *skraelings* (or "savages"). Archaeological evidence of Norse colonization comes from L'Anse aux Meadows in northern Newfoundland, where remains of sod-walled houses indicate a settlement at about AD 1000. Their interaction with Native People of the area was hostile, and Norse attempts to occupy the land seem to have been frustrated by the Native defence of their territory. This experience forestalled European colonization for another five centuries.

Throughout this long period, the Aboriginal cultures of Atlantic Canada depended, at least during most of the year, upon the sea. This coastal adaptation continued into the historic period with the Mi'kmaq, Maliseet and Beothuk. In Labrador, however, the historic Innu led a way of life that relied more upon hunting in the interior. (They are discussed with the other Subarctic Algonquians in chapter 5.)

THE BEOTHUK

The Beothuk were the Aboriginal People who bore the brunt of early sustained contact with Europeans. Their ultimate extinction at the hands of the new arrivals is a tragic chapter in the history of uneasy encounters between the races.

The Beothuk were the original "Red Indians," a term later mistakenly applied to all other North American Native Peoples. The term refers not to the colour of their skin but to the practice of smearing red paint, made from powdered ochre mixed with oil or grease, over their bodies and hair, as well as on their clothing and utensils. Although the use of paint made from red ochre is common throughout Aboriginal America, no other group used it as extensively as the Beothuk. Liberally smearing the body with this greasy paint may have partly protected them from the cold and from the hordes of biting insects that plague animals and humans in this environment. Its widespread use throughout Beothuk culture, however, argues for a more deeply rooted meaning. Beothuk burials, in which the corpse and all objects interred with the dead were covered with red ochre, suggest that this colouring may have had a ceremonial or religious association, and that these beliefs had their roots in the cultures of the early Holocene. The striking appearance of these people is evident from an early seventeenth-century description:

> They are of a reasonable stature, of an ordinary middle size, they goe bareheaded, wearing their hair somewhat long but round: they have no beards; behind they haue a great locke of haire platted with feathers, like a hawke's lure,

with a feather in it standing upright by the crowne of the head and a small lock platted before, a short gown made of stags' skins, the furre innermost, that raune down to the middle of their legges, with sleeues to the middle of their arme, and a beuer skin about their necke, was all their apparell, saue that one of them had shooes and mittens, so that all went bare-legged and most bare-foote. They are full-eyed, of a blacke colour; the colour of their hair was divers, some blacke, some browne, and some yellow, and their faces something flat and broad, red with oker, as all their apparell is, and the rest of their body. *Howley 1915: 17*

Most of our knowledge of the Beothuk comes from eighteenth- and early-nineteenth-century descriptions. By this time, European and Mi'kmaq encroachments had reduced Beothuk territory to its historically known core along Red Indian Lake and the Exploits River of central Newfoundland. Because the population had declined and most coastal resources were lost, only an impoverished remnant of Beothuk culture was observed. The full extent of their lives before explorer John Cabot arrived at Newfoundland in 1497 remains largely unknown.

The Beothuk population at the time of European contact has been estimated at anywhere from about 500 to several thousand. Beothuk social groups were small bands of closely related families even before their numbers were reduced.

For much of the year the Beothuk were a coastal people who lived by fishing, collecting shellfish and hunting both land and sea mammals. Men ventured out in their bark canoes to harpoon seals and even the occasional small whale. Collecting birds' eggs was an important activity, and the Beothuk travelled as far as Funk Island, a trip of about sixty-five kilometres across the rough waters of the North Atlantic, to find them. The eggs were hard-boiled for later use or, according to one early description, mixed with seal or caribou fat and sun-dried to form a staple food. A sketch by Shanawdithit, the last of the Beothuk, shows that such traditional foods as dried meat, dried salmon, pieces of seal fat on the skin and long strings of dried lobster tails were stored.

The Beothuk spent autumn and winter in the interior, where the economy centred almost entirely on caribou. They built long "deer fences" of felled trees, branches and posts to channel the caribou herds to where hunters waited with spears or bows and arrows. Hunters had to take and preserve enough meat by freezing or smoking it to last through the long winter. Historic descriptions of the Beothuk as primarily interior hunters, however, reflect only their final declining years when they had been largely excluded from important coastal resources.

Most of the year the Beothuks preferred to travel by water, using birchbark canoes on inland lakes and rivers as well as along the coast. The shape of Beothuk canoes was distinctive, with a sharply pointed prow and stern and a high peak at mid-length. For ocean travel the canoes had to be ballasted with large rocks for stability. The Beothuk were confident mariners, venturing far from land in these frail craft. In winter, they travelled through the interior on foot, using snowshoes and pulling heavy loads on sleds.

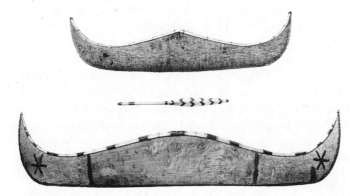

LEFT *Beothuk model canoes.* CMC 67232

A typical Beothuk dwelling was a conical structure of poles covered with birchbark, referred to as a *mamateek*. A winter mamateek might have several layers of bark, separated by dried moss to provide insulation. Earth banked against the lower portion of the structure also helped keep out the winter cold. A distinctive feature was the presence of sleeping hollows in the ground around the central fireplace.

Many surviving material objects of Beothuk culture were recovered in the nineteenth century from burial sites. The body, wrapped in birchbark and covered in red ochre, was left in a wooden box placed on a scaffold or in a crevice in the rocks. Objects placed with the dead include wooden dolls, models of birchbark canoes and distinctive bone pendants incised with geometric designs which might once have been sewn to clothing.

So little evidence has been documented for Beothuk culture that we have to turn to archaeological research for more information. A good example is the Boyd's Cove site in northeastern Newfoundland, occupied by the Beothuk from about AD 1650 to 1720 and excavated by Memorial University archaeologists in the 1980s. Eleven circular depressions on the site's surface show that the Beothuk had constructed their houses, which were apparently occupied from early spring until fall, over shallow pits. The site's occupants feasted primarily on caribou and harbour seal, though other mammals, birds, fish and shellfish were part of their diet as well. Considering the date of occupation, these people possessed relatively few European goods. The major exception is a large number of nails, which the Beothuk were hammering out and shaping into arrowpoints. The Beothuk also manufactured such objects as tiny chipped-stone arrowpoints and several distinctive bone pendants with incised designs, similar to those placed in graves.

The final years of Beothuk culture must have been ones of great deprivation. Increasingly cut off from the coast by English and French settlement, the Beothuk were forced to rely on the limited resources of the interior. Unlike elsewhere in Canada, where initial relations centred on the fur trade, the Europeans in Newfoundland were interested in fish, not furs. Since the Beothuk lacked access to items of European manufacture through trade, they instead salvaged such objects from the unoccupied fishing stations. The hostility this created led to retaliatory raids on Beothuk encampments, and many were killed. With populations plummeting due to introduced diseases and hostile encounters with outsiders, it appears they had difficulty even carrying out the traditional caribou hunt. In addition, the Mi'kmaq were crossing over to Newfoundland from the mainland, searching for new sources of furs for trade. The Beothuk were increasingly pushed into the centre of the island, where the impoverished remnants of the group, plagued by tuberculosis and malnutrition, were described in the early nineteenth-century accounts. As Newfoundland historian Frederick Rowe points out in his book *Extinction*, this tragic story certainly does not need the dramatic exaggerations of huge massacres and wanton hunting of Beothuks for sport which have been presented by some writers.

Details on the final years of the Beothuk come from nineteenth-century captives. In bungling attempts to establish communications, English colonists took a number of Beothuk prisoners, the most famous being Demasduit (better known to history as Mary March, after the month of her capture in 1819) and Shanawdithit, captured in 1823. Although a few individuals may have fled the island and mixed with neighbouring groups, Shanawdithit is considered to have been the last of the Beothuk. Her death of tuberculosis in 1829 marks the date of their extinction.

THE MI'KMAQ AND MALISEET (WOLASTOQIYIK)

Traditional Mi'kmaq (this spelling, adopted by the Mi'kmaq Grand Council, has almost totally replaced the earlier "Micmac") territory consists of the Gaspé Peninsula of Quebec, northern and eastern New Brunswick, and all of Nova Scotia and Prince Edward Island. Early in the historic era, they expanded their territory to include southern Newfoundland. Closely related to them are the neighbouring Maliseet (or Malecite) along the St. John River of western New Brunswick and extending just into Quebec. The name Maliseet is derived from a term the Mi'kmaq used for their neighbours; today many Maliseet prefer the self-designation Wolastoqiyik, which comes from their name for the land along the St. John River. Speaking a dialect of the same language as the Maliseet are the Passamaquoddy, today residents of Maine, whose historic territory extends a short distance into southwestern New Brunswick around Passamaquoddy Bay. Although all these groups were similar, the Mi'kmaq were more of a coastal people, whereas the Maliseet emphasized interior resources and historically cultivated small plots of corn. Early descriptions of Native life refer mainly to the Mi'kmaq, since the Maliseet and Passamaquoddy were further removed from areas of early European exploration and settlement.

Most of our knowledge of the Mi'kmaq comes from ethnohistory. Several seventeenth-century writers left extensive observations on Native life. These accounts are incomplete and frequently contradictory, but they paint a picture of Mi'kmaq culture that can be supplemented with later ethnographic data. The people they describe, however, had been familiar with Europeans and their trade goods for over a century.

Early in the seventeenth century the Mi'kmaq population was estimated at about 3500, and the Maliseet numbered about 1000. Both groups had already suffered many deaths due to the epidemic diseases that inevitably followed European contact. Also, French trade in alcohol and new food items was detrimental to Native health. Early observer Nicolas Denys praised the traditional diet of meat, animal fat and fish, which allowed the Mi'kmaq to "live long and multiply much," and commented on the poorer health and greater susceptibility to disease caused by the change in diet.

The size of social groups varied with the seasons. Winter camps were typically small groups of several related families, whereas in the summer more abundant resources allowed bands of several hundred individuals to form. Each had a chief, referred to as a *sagamore*, who held limited power over the group. Although power seems to have passed often from father to eldest son, ability and personality were paramount considerations. The sagamore's duties were primarily to provide leadership and advice, which allowed individuals a great deal of independence. The role of the sagamore in the early seventeenth century is described by the Jesuit Father Biard:

> All the young people of the family are at his table and in his retinue; it is also his duty to provide dogs for the chase, canoes for transportation, provisions and reserves for bad weather and expeditions. The young people flatter him, hunt, and serve their apprenticeship under him, not being allowed to have anything before they are married ... all that the young men capture belongs to the Sagamore; but the married ones give him only a part, and if these leave him, as they often do for the sake of the chase and supplies, returning afterwards, they pay their dues and homage in skins and like gifts. Thwaites, *Jesuit Relations 3: 87–89*

That this authority was limited is made clear by the observations of Father LeClercq:

> The most prominent chief is followed by several young warriors and by several hunters, who act as his escort, and who fall in under arms when this ruler wishes particular distinction upon some special occasion. But, in fact, all his power and authority are based only upon the good will of those of his nation, who execute his orders just in so far as it pleases them. *LeClercq 1910: 234*

The Mi'kmaq, though lacking overall political unification, perceived themselves as a common people and paid nominal allegiance to a "Grand Chief," traditionally located at the Mi'kmaq "head district" of Cape Breton Island. One of the duties of this Grand Chief was to call council meetings of Mi'kmaq leaders to discuss issues of common concern. The famed seventeenth-century sagamore

RIGHT *Mi'kmaq fishing camp, Restigouche, Quebec.* NAC C16436

Membertou held this role, combining abilities as political leader, warrior and shaman to strengthen his power among the Mi'kmaq.

Mi'kmaq economic life shifted with the seasons as people moved between coast and interior to take advantage of various resources. The seasonal round was described by Father Biard at Port Royal in 1616:

> In January they have the seal hunting. . . . In the month of February and until the middle of March, is the great hunt for Beavers, otters, moose, bears (which are very good), and for the caribou. . . . If the weather is then favorable, they live in great abundance, and are as haughty as Princes and Kings, but if it is against them, they are greatly to be pitied and often die of starvation. . . . In the middle of March, fish begin to spawn, and to come up from the sea into certain streams, often so abundantly that everything swarms with them. . . . Among these fish the smelt is the first . . . after the smelt comes the herring at the end of April; at the same time bustards [Canada geese] . . . sturgeon, and salmon, and the great search through the Islets for [waterfowl] eggs. . . . From the month of May up to the middle of September, they are free from all anxiety about their food; for the cod are upon the coast, and all kinds of fish and shellfish . . . our savages in the middle of September withdraw from the sea, beyond the reach of the tide, to the little rivers, where the eels spawn, of which they lay in a supply. . . . In October and November comes the second hunt for elks [moose] and beavers; and then in December comes a fish called by them ponamo [tomcod], which spawns under the ice. Thwaites, *Jesuit Relations* 3: 79–83

Although the coast, rivers and forests all played a part in the Mi'kmaq economy, as much as 90 per cent of their diet came from the sea. They took fish by hook and line, by harpoon or in weirs and traps. Nicolas Denys described spearing fish by torchlight, and he stated that 150 to 200 salmon could be caught in a single night by this method. The Mi'kmaq collected shellfish and lobsters, and they harpooned sea mammals, including the occasional small whale, from canoes. And, as mentioned by Biard, waterfowl and their eggs were available in great quantities during seasonal migrations.

Hunting in the interior occupied far less time and provided far less of the diet, but it was a more prestigious activity than fishing. Every young man aspired to become a great hunter. The Mi'kmaq hunted animals with bows and arrows, or took them with snares set across game paths. They used dogs in the hunt, but dogs could occasionally become the main dish at a feast. Meat was prepared by roasting or by boiling it with red-hot stones in large wooden troughs carved from fallen trees (later these were replaced by copper kettles, which were highly desired trade items since they could be carried by the Mi'kmaq on their travels). Hunting was a precarious activity, and, as mentioned by Biard, people would starve if poor weather affected the hunt.

Transportation also varied with the seasons. The lightweight birchbark canoe was indispensable to Mi'kmaq life. Father Biard described the craft as "so capacious that a single one of them will hold an entire household of five or six persons, with all their dogs, sacks, skins, kettles, and other heavy baggage" (Thwaites, *Jesuit Relations* 3: 83). The use of sails, apparently adopted by the Mi'kmaq in the seventeenth century from European examples, greatly increased the speed of coastal travel. Equally indispensable were snowshoes, allowing winter travel and hunting over deep drifts. The Mi'kmaq also had both the sled and the toboggan (the latter owing its English name to the Mi'kmaq word *taba'gan*).

Mi'kmaq housing reflected the need for seasonal mobility. Father LeClercq described bark-covered wigwams as being "so light and portable that our Indians roll them up like a piece of paper, and carry them thus upon their backs wherever it pleases them, very much like the tortoises which carry their own houses" (LeClercq 1910: 100). The houses varied in size and floor plan, as described by Nicolas Denys:

> If the family is a large one they make it long enough for two fires; otherwise they make it round, just like military tents, with only this difference that in place of canvas they are of barks of Birch. These are so well fitted that it never rains into their wigwams. The round kind holds ten to twelve persons, the long twice as many. The fires are made in the middle of the round kind, and at the two ends of the long sort. *Denys 1908: 405–406*

Father LeClercq also noted brightly coloured designs painted by women on the bark coverings. Inside, the floor was covered with fir branches, with hides placed over these for beds. Although most seventeenth-century accounts favourably describe Mi'kmaq habitations, they also refer to the constant smoke in the dwellings, the stench of fish and animals being prepared and the danger of severe burns from sleeping too near the fire on a cold winter night.

The basic item of clothing for men was the loincloth. In colder weather, they added a loose robe of furs or hide, worn with leggings and moccasins. Women

ABOVE *Ornately decorated nineteenth-century Mi'kmaq coat.* CMC 77-6557. RIGHT *This Mi'kmaq woman and her son display traditional nineteenth-century clothing. Taken in Halifax, ca. 1864–74. Public Archives of Nova Scotia, Halifax*

wore a similar robe. According to Denys (1908: 407), "the girls were very modest . . . always clothed with a well-dressed Moose skin which descended below the knees." This clothing was decorated by painting or with dyed porcupine quills, and people further enhanced their appearance by oiling their hair and painting their faces. By the eighteenth century, however, fur and hide had almost totally given way to cloth, decorated in a distinctive Mi'kmaq style with beads, ribbons and embroidery. The women's traditional high-peaked caps, of beaded and embroidered dark blue cloth, belong to this later period.

Birchbark was a particularly important raw material for making utensils as it was readily available, light, and relatively waterproof and rot resistant. Boxes, bowls and baskets of this material were ideally suited to mobile people. Even in the seventeenth century these were decorated with porcupine quills, and later these developed into the elaborately quilled birchbark baskets for which the Mi'kmaq are known. Although metal tools eventually replaced most traditional Mi'kmaq implements of wood, stone and bone in the years that followed contact with Europeans, basket making not only continued but expanded into a major craft for sale.

The Mi'kmaq shared with other Algonquians the concept of a supreme being. Several early sources state that the Mi'kmaq identified this creator as the sun, to which they prayed twice daily. Lesser deities included some that were human in

LEFT *Mi'kmaq basket,
decorated with porcupine
quills.* CMC J3332

form but were immortal and had supernatural powers. By far the most prominent of these among both the Mi'kmaq and Maliseet was the culture hero named Glooscap. Many myths tell how he transformed the animals into their present shapes and how distinctive features of the landscape resulted from his activities. After teaching humans how to make tools and weapons, he departed, promising to return in times of need. At the lowest level of the pantheon were supernatural races, ranging from giants to the forest-dwelling "little people."

Shamans were individuals with power to intercede directly with the realm of the supernatural. Shamanic powers included curing the sick, predicting the future and providing supernatural aid in warfare and the hunt. The healing rituals were particularly dramatic, involving dancing and singing around the patient to exorcise the malevolent force, and blowing on the afflicted part of the body to drive out the disease. Some individuals became so successful and received so many goods for their services that they became full-time religious practitioners. However, shamans were also feared, for they had the power to cause disease and injury as well as to cure.

Important in Mi'kmaq social life were feasts held on numerous occasions. Marriages and funerals required feasting, but LeClercq writes that there were also "feasts of health, of farewell, of hunting, of peace, of war, of thanks." To ensure success in the hunt, they held an "eat-all" feast, during which those present gorged themselves until they consumed every scrap of available food—certainly inducing them to do well on the next hunt. Feasts included lengthy speeches, by which family traditions and genealogies were maintained. Songs and dances paid tribute to the host. Such social occasions also provided an opportunity to play *waltes*, a favourite gambling game played by flipping bone dice in a wooden bowl.

Warfare was also important among the Mi'kmaq and Maliseet, and was one route to prestige for a young man. Raids were conducted against other Algonquian groups, such as the Montagnais. However, the most bitter hostilities were with the Iroquois, particularly the Mohawk. This trend intensified, with disastrous consequences for the Mi'kmaq during the warfare of the early historic period.

The Mi'kmaq seem to have admirably adapted to their environment, and the seventeenth-century observers, though very much products of their own European backgrounds, all grudgingly praise Native lifeways. Although privation did exist, particularly in the lean months of February and March, for much of the year food was plentiful and easy to obtain. Warfare might have caused hardships, but it was also a path to glory and political advancement. As befitting a mobile people, their material wants were few. However, this way of life was to change dramatically with increased European contact.

INTO THE GLOBAL ERA

Contact with European fishermen likely took place shortly after Christopher Columbus crossed the Atlantic Ocean. Such encounters would have been fleeting, and as these Europeans were generally illiterate we have almost no record of this period. However, when Jacques Cartier sailed by Chaleur Bay in 1534, the Mi'kmaq loudly hailed the ship and waved furs on sticks to signal their desire to trade, suggesting that such relationships had been established for some time. Cartier reports that the Natives were so eager for European knives and other iron goods that they traded the furs off their backs and had to return naked to their camp.

The French began to colonize intensively early in the seventeenth century, and the Mi'kmaq and Maliseet became loyal allies of the French and partners with them in the fur trade. Despite the strong Mi'kmaq sense of self-worth and their skepticism of claims that France was the superior nation, when the French seemed so eager to leave it to voyage to Mi'kmaq lands, Aboriginal People adopted many European traits. As European trade items, particularly those of metal and cloth, were introduced, much of the former Aboriginal material culture was lost. The need to obtain furs for trade brought changes in traditional economic patterns, and their acceptance of European foods, generally nutritionally inferior to those in the traditional diet, was detrimental to Native health. Traders introduced alcohol, with devastating results. Epidemics continued to reduce the Native population, contributing to demoralization and loss of faith in the shamans, who could not deal with these new afflictions. From the beginning of French settlement, the priests enthusiastically tried to convert Aboriginal People to Christianity.

The alliance of the Mi'kmaq and Maliseet with the French inevitably drew them into conflict with the English and their Iroquois allies. Territorial squabbles between these two European nations came to a temporary halt with the Treaty of Utrecht in 1713, by the terms of which French possessions in Atlantic Canada were reduced to Île St. Jean (Prince Edward Island) and Île Royale (Cape Breton Island). Shortly afterward the French began to construct the fortress of Louisbourg on the latter. From this base, the French encouraged the Mi'kmaq to continue hostilities against the English. Mi'kmaq raids on English ships and settlements escalated the warfare and led to an English campaign of attempted genocide against the Mi'kmaq. The English even sought the assistance of their Mohawk allies, assuming they would be more efficient in Aboriginal warfare. After the English established the settlement of Halifax, the new governor placed a bounty on Mi'kmaq scalps. Hostilities continued until French power in Atlantic Canada came to an end shortly after the fall of Louisbourg in 1758, forcing the Mi'kmaq to make peace with the English.

The pressures of continuous warfare, particularly with the Iroquois, caused the northeastern Algonquians to form the Wabanaki Confederacy. Although these groups had earlier been allied against the Iroquois and the English, their organization into a confederacy probably dates to the middle of the eighteenth century. The confederacy centred on the Penobscot of Maine, with the Mi'kmaq and Maliseet being "younger brothers." This confederacy was in turn joined with the Ottawa and with the Catholicized Mohawk in Quebec, bringing together the major French allies for council meetings. Election of chiefs and use of wampum were Iroquoian traits incorporated into Algonquian cultures through this confederacy.

Historically, the Mi'kmaq were also well established in Newfoundland. It is possible that they first reached this island before the English, as the Newfoundland Mi'kmaq maintain today, though there is no archaeological evidence of this. Historic records show they were present by the early 1600s. After 1760, however, when the English replaced the French on Cape Breton Island, large numbers of Mi'kmaq sought new lands on southern and western Newfoundland. Sources of furs for trade provided the major incentive. According to anthropologist Frank Speck's informants, in early times crossing the Cabot Strait from Cape Breton Island was done by canoe at night, when the sea was calmer and the paddlers might be guided by a light from the cliffs of southern Newfoundland, kindled by experienced men who had gone ahead of the main body. In later times, the Mi'kmaq used shallops, small European sailing vessels, to make this dangerous crossing. Relations with the Beothuk appear to have been unfriendly, causing that group to gradually withdraw from the southern portion of the island. After the Beothuk extinction, the Mi'kmaq remained as the only Aboriginal People on the island of Newfoundland.

The late eighteenth and early nineteenth centuries were difficult times for the Mi'kmaq and Maliseet. More English settlers poured into the area, particularly after the American Revolutionary War, displacing Native People from the most desirable locations and reducing them to squatters on their own land. As the fur trade declined and traditional lands for hunting and fishing were lost, many starved or died as the epidemic outbreaks of disease continued.

After Confederation, when the Crown colonies of Nova Scotia, New Brunswick and Prince Edward Island became provinces of Canada, administrative responsibility for Aboriginal People shifted to the federal government in Ottawa.

The new nation, however, was looking westward for its future, and its administrators were preoccupied with subjugating the Plains tribes and opening the west
to non-Native settlers. The Mi'kmaq and Maliseet, reduced in numbers and already dispossessed from most of their land, received little attention. Natives in
the Maritimes were left to eke out a living by various forms of labour and craft
production through this long period of neglect.

THE MI'KMAQ AND MALISEET TODAY

Today over 26,000 Mi'kmaq live in Canada's five easternmost provinces. They are
divided into twenty-eight bands, the largest being Restigouche (now known as
Listuguj Mi'gmaq First Nation) in Quebec, Eskasoni and Shubenacadie in Nova
Scotia, and Big Cove in New Brunswick. The Maliseet population of about 6000
people is divided into seven bands, the largest and best-known of which is
Tobique in New Brunswick. These are the registered populations, those who
carry status cards recognized by the federal government under the Indian Act.
Other people claim Mi'kmaq or Maliseet heritage but have been denied such
recognition.

The Mi'kmaq of Newfoundland have had a long struggle to be recognized as
Canadian Indians. Isolated on the island's south coast, the Mi'kmaq at the Conne
River settlement, after a lengthy battle with the provincial and federal governments, were finally legally established in 1984 as the Miawpukek First Nation. A
few years later their community lands were registered as a reserve under the federal system. Other Newfoundlanders of Mi'kmaq origin, particularly on the west
coast, are still seeking equivalent status.

One other group of northeastern Algonquians extends into Canada today. The
Abenaki speak a language closely related to Mi'kmaq and Maliseet and were allied to these peoples in the Wabanaki Confederacy. During the historic wars, their
ties to the French led many to leave their New England homeland, settling in
Quebec by the late seventeenth century. Today there are two Abenaki First Nations in Quebec, with a total population of about 2000. However, the Abenaki language is all but extinct, and few traits distinguish their reserves from
surrounding French-speaking villages. Maintaining their language and cultural
identity is a vital concern of these communities.

One of the pressing problems confronting Mi'kmaq, Maliseet and Abenaki
First Nations today is providing a livelihood for reserve residents. Many men
find work in the lumber industry. Fishing and lobster trapping have been important occupations on some reserves, though the general decline in the Atlantic
fishery has brought tough economic times to Native and non-Native communities alike. Manufacturing baskets, from the finely quilled tourist baskets to more
utilitarian splint baskets, is still an important source of income for many. In
recent years band councils, aided by new federal funding programs, have introduced a number of Native-run enterprises, such as an oyster farm at Eskasoni

and a sawmill at Shubenacadie, to employ band members. Unemployment rates, however, remain high.

Due to the lack of jobs, many Mi'kmaq and Maliseet have moved to large urban centres in the American northeast, particularly Boston. Like the Mohawk before them, the Mi'kmaq discovered that high-steel construction work can be well-paying and psychologically satisfying. Although some band members moved permanently to the city, many remain transients, often returning to the reserve. The Mi'kmaq population in Boston is now substantially larger than many of the Mi'kmaq reserve communities in Canada.

The Union of Nova Scotia Indians and the Union of New Brunswick Indians are political organizations representing Mi'kmaq and Maliseet people. The "peace and friendship" treaties of the eighteenth century, designed to end hostilities be-tween the Mi'kmaq and Maliseet and the British, did not involve cession of land or surrender of Aboriginal rights. As a result, land claims have emerged as a major political issue, along with asserting Aboriginal rights to natural resources.

The 1999 *Marshall* decision in the Supreme Court of Canada focussed griev-ances concerning Aboriginal and treaty rights in the Maritimes. Donald Marshall Jr., a member of the Membertou First Nation in Nova Scotia, was charged with il-legally catching and selling eels, without a licence and in a closed season. His de-fence was based on the eighteenth-century treaties, which provided for Mi'kmaq fishing and hunting rights. Although he was convicted in provincial court, the Supreme Court overturned this verdict. The Supreme Court justices ruled that the acquittal was required to uphold the "honour and integrity of the Crown" in respect to its treaty obligations, and that, as the treaties covered the commercial use of resources, the Mi'kmaq people were entitled to earn a "moderate living" (that phrase was not defined) from their traditional resource harvests. Although this case involves catching eels, the ruling has clear implications for all traditional economic resources. These rights, however, are not unlimited but are subject to government regulation for purposes such as conservation.

A storm of controversy followed this decision. Many Mi'kmaq were jubilant that their treaty rights had been recognized in Canada's highest court. They assumed these rights had priority over fisheries regulations, whereas non-Native fishers were frustrated by the decision and concerned about their livelihood. When some Mi'kmaq began trapping lobsters well before the season opened, vio-lent protests ensued. A major clash occurred at the Mi'kmaq community of Burnt Church in New Brunswick, where non-Native fishers destroyed hundreds of Native lobster traps and damaged nearby fish plants that had been buying lob-sters from the Mi'kmaq. Although most Mi'kmaq communities agreed to a federal request for a fishing moratorium to ease the tensions, Burnt Church rejected the idea of government interference in the fishery. Government attempts to limit the number of traps led to further outbreaks in the summer of 2000. Raids on Mi'kmaq fisheries resulted in confrontations on the water, arrests, and seizure or destruction of traps and boats, and the Mi'kmaq retaliated by blocking a major highway nearby. Subsequent negotiations have somewhat eased the tensions, but the Mi'kmaq at Burnt Church maintain that acknowledging government authority over the fishery would infringe on the Aboriginal rights recognized by the *Marshall* decision.

The Mi'kmaq in Newfoundland are also pressing for a land claims settlement. In 1981 the Federation of Newfoundland Indians and the Mi'kmaq at Conne River launched a comprehensive land claim to the southwestern third of the island. Their claim was rejected, at least partially because they were deemed "recent" arrivals in Newfoundland. Occupancy since "time immemorial," however, had never been required in earlier agreements, such as the treaties on the Prairies. Brian Peckford, then premier of Newfoundland, dismissed the Mi'kmaq as just one of several immigrant groups, like the Irish or the English. In a similar vein, the Newfoundland and Labrador Supreme Court in 2003 denied the Conne River Mi'kmaq special fishing, hunting or trapping rights because they were said to have arrived too recently for these practices to qualify as Aboriginal rights. The Mi'kmaq at Conne River are preparing to take their case for Aboriginal land rights to court, and the Federation of Newfoundland Indians, which represents those individuals not legally recognized as Indians, continues to fight for "status" for its members and recognition of their rights to the land.

After almost five centuries of contact, Mi'kmaq and Maliseet life has changed extensively and accommodated outside forces. Intermarriage with outsiders has been common since the seventeenth century, and many reserve communities differ little from their non-Native neighbours. The vast majority of Mi'kmaq and Maliseet maintain the Catholic faith, a legacy of their past alliance with the French. The Mi'kmaq language is still widely used in many reserve communities, though many younger people do not speak the language. Despite the pressures upon them, the Mi'kmaq and Maliseet have maintained their Aboriginal identities, and their cultures today integrate traditional values with those of the larger society that surrounds them.

CHAPTER 4

The Iroquoians of the
Eastern Woodlands

.   .   .   .   .

THE IROQUOIS feature prominently in Canadian history. Events of the early historic period have left them indelibly stamped in the public mind as warriors, yet they were also skilled politicians and diplomats. The political alliance known as the League of the Iroquois is one of their enduring achievements.

The terms "Iroquois" and "Iroquoian" are distinct. The former is usually restricted to the groups that allied as the League of the Iroquois. The original five nations of the league (the Seneca, Cayuga, Onondaga, Oneida and Mohawk) were later joined by the Tuscarora from the south, forming the historic Six Nations. Although the homeland of the league was in New York State, today all six groups have communities in Canada. The term Iroquoian refers to the entire language family. People speaking related Iroquoian languages include the Huron and the now-extinct Petun, Neutral and St. Lawrence Iroquoians, who occupied the land east from the Great Lakes toward the Atlantic when they first encountered Europeans. All the peoples speaking Iroquoian languages shared a common cultural pattern that differed only in minor aspects, which can also be referred to by the general term Iroquoian.

Northern Iroquoian nations held a large block of land around the eastern Great Lakes. Far to the south, the Cherokee and Tuscarora also spoke Iroquoian languages. The northern Iroquoians occupied the land from Georgian Bay off Lake Huron south to Lake Erie and Lake Ontario, and east along the St. Lawrence River past modern Quebec City. This is the Lower Great Lakes–St. Lawrence Lowlands, an environment covered with predominantly hardwood forests. Its soils and climate were conducive to indigenous agriculture. At the beginning of the global era these were the only societies of Aboriginal People practising agriculture within what is today Canada. Their farming economy and denser population distinguished them from their Algonquian neighbours of the boreal forests to the north.

Throughout the area the ethnographic pattern was one of relatively sedentary village life. Corn, beans and squash, grown in fields near the villages, were the dietary staples. Hunting (particularly for deer), fishing and gathering wild plant foods also contributed to the diet. Villages were clusters of bark-covered longhouses, each sheltering several families, and were generally surrounded by palisades for defence. Desirable village locations were those with good soils and a creek or stream for fresh water, but away from any navigable rivers to avoid being surprised by canoes bearing enemy warriors.

HOLOCENE CULTURAL DEVELOPMENTS

The Lower Great Lakes–St. Lawrence Lowlands area was initially occupied shortly after the glaciers retreated. Stone spearpoints left by these early people, including distinctive fluted forms, have been found at a number of sites. Such evidence suggests that humans were present by perhaps as early as 11,000 years ago. The disturbed context and lack of organic materials at these sites, however, means that this early presence cannot be securely dated.

The Holocene developments that led to the Iroquoian cultures are complex and the archaeological record is incomplete. As well, there is considerable controversy about how to interpret various discoveries. Archaeologists have used several different schemes to classify cultural developments; a simplified overview that divides Holocene cultural development into three broad stages—the Laurentian, the Early Ceramic and the Late Ceramic—is presented here. At the end of this sequence the Iroquoians encountered outsiders and the global economy. Although we are fortunate to have extensive early descriptions of Huron life, the neighbouring Iroquoians were poorly documented. As these cultures are extinct today, much of our knowledge continues to come from archaeological research.

The late glacial landscape that sustained the earliest occupants gradually gave way, during the early Holocene, to environmental conditions resembling those of today. A variety of hunting, fishing and collecting activities, depending on the availability and abundance of local resources, supported a diverse range of cultures across northeastern North America. In southern Ontario and Quebec the best-known of these cultures is termed the **Laurentian**, which dates from about 7000 to 3000 years ago. Discarded food remains from Laurentian sites show that these people lived primarily by hunting, with deer, elk, bear and beaver as the most common prey. Fishing also provided a large part of the diet. Wild plant foods leave far less evidence in the archaeological record, but clearly such activities as berry picking and nut gathering would have been important seasonal sources of food.

Typical Laurentian artifacts include a variety of stone tools, both chipped and ground to shape. Projectile points once armed spears, which were hurled with a spear thrower. Distinctively shaped weights of polished stone were attached to the spear throwers to increase their propulsive force. Polished stone gouges appear to have been efficient woodworking tools. In addition, Laurentian sites contain relatively abundant implements of native copper, including projectile points, knives, fish hooks, awls, pendants and beads. The raw material for these objects came from the copper deposits of western Lake Superior, indicating that trade was well established in southern Ontario by this period.

Many of the Laurentian artifacts come from burial sites, which provide glimpses into the religious beliefs of these people. Red ochre found sprinkled over the bodies and objects uncovered in the graves indicates that ceremonial burials took place. Over time the grave goods become more lavish and abundant. Exotic goods placed with the dead include copper ornaments, beads of shell from the Atlantic coast, pendants of conch shell from the Gulf of Mexico and tools of stone from various distant locations. Extensive trade networks were required to maintain these burial practices.

Human remains also reflect the dark side of Laurentian life. The occasional projectile point lodged in bones or the chest cavity, skull fractures and decapitation all indicate violent death. Warfare, that common feature of later Iroquoian life, was endemic in this area in early times.

No abrupt change in Native lifeways marks the introduction of the **Early Ceramic** period, which lasted from about 3000 to 1100 years ago. Instead, life appears to have continued as it did during the Laurentian period, with one major addition—pottery. Although ceramic vessels may not have drastically changed Native life, they are very important to the archaeologist. The broken sherds are abundant and virtually indestructible. Stylistic variations in form and decoration allow archaeologists to isolate cultural groups and time periods. Pottery vessels were decorated before firing, often by pressing a cord-wrapped stick or a notched implement into the still-damp clay.

Another feature of the Early Ceramic period is that burial ceremonies became more elaborate, and burial mounds were constructed. The idea of expressing religious concepts in mortuary rites appears to have entered from the south, particularly from the Adena and Hopewell cultures of the Ohio River valley, which favoured large burial mounds containing many wealth goods placed with the dead. However, burial mounds are not particularly common in the Canadian Iroquoian area, and are restricted to the southern margins of Ontario.

One of the earliest and most widely distributed of the Early Ceramic cultures is Point Peninsula. Sites of this culture, known for its distinctive pottery, are found throughout southern Quebec and in southern Ontario north of Toronto. Ceramic vessels were decorated with notched or toothed implements and, in later periods, had added collars. Soapstone pipes were also found in these sites. As the burial mounds demonstrate, southern ideas and goods were entering Point Peninsula culture.

RIGHT *Serpent Mound on Rice Lake, Ontario.* Photo by A. McMillan

Perhaps the most famous of these sites is Serpent Mounds, located on a point overlooking Rice Lake, near Peterborough, Ontario. The largest mound has a sinuous elongated shape about sixty metres long and up to two metres high. Although commonly known as Serpent Mound, whether it was actually intended to represent a serpent is unclear. Eight smaller mounds cluster around it. Excavation has revealed numerous burials, both complete and partial. High-status individuals were apparently interred in sub-mound pits, whereas others were scattered throughout the mound fill. Associated objects were relatively few, but they included cut wolf and bear jaws, fossils, and beads of shell, copper and silver. The copper is from western Lake Superior (a distance of about 1000 kilometres), the silver is from deposits in northern Ontario (about 370 kilometres) and the conch shell had to come from the Gulf of Mexico (about 1500 kilometres), indicating that trade networks were extensive. Radiocarbon dates show that this site was used from about 1900 to 1700 years ago. The decline in the use of burial mounds and exotic grave goods after this period coincides with the beginning of Hopewell collapse further south.

Coexisting with Point Peninsula was another Early Ceramic culture, termed Saugeen, which was distributed throughout southwestern Ontario. Most excavated sites are along rapids, at creek or river mouths, or in other good fishing locations. Fish bones, particularly sturgeon, pickerel and drum, dominate food remains from these sites, which represent seasonal villages where large populations could gather. Evidence of rectangular houses is visible in the pattern of small dark circular stains (termed "post moulds") that mark where wooden posts (long since decayed) stood, along with the presence of hearths. Saugeen pottery is generally similar to Point Peninsula, but there are recognizable stylistic differences. Although they do not seem to have constructed burial mounds, Saugeen people shared other elements of Hopewellian burial practices. A small cemetery excavated at the Donaldson site, on the Saugeen River near its mouth on Lake

Huron, revealed such Hopewell-related objects placed with the dead as two copper panpipe covers, a stone earspool, three sheets of cut mica and a modified timber-wolf jaw.

In the final centuries of the Early Ceramic period, Princess Point culture replaced Saugeen in southernmost Ontario. New and distinct pottery styles identify the archaeological remains, though whether this means the arrival of new people or simply new ideas on how to decorate pots is difficult to say. Also, corn agriculture first appears in southern Ontario during this stage. From crops domesticated in Mexico thousands of years earlier, agriculture gradually spread northward as new strains became adapted to cooler climates and the shorter growing season. This set the stage for a population explosion and the full development of Iroquoian cultures in the following period. Many archaeologists, pointing to discontinuities with earlier cultures, argue that Princess Point culture represents a movement of Iroquois speakers from the south into southern Ontario. Others, however, trace Iroquoian origins further back in time, arguing for a long continuity. Most agree that Princess Point culture is directly ancestral to later Iroquoian cultures.

The disturbed burial site of an adult male, found on the north side of Lake Erie, provides information on religious beliefs of the time. This individual lived about 1100 years ago, right at the end of this stage or the beginning of the next. Objects placed in his grave include a number of presumably ritual items, such as the mandibles of three bears (two cubs and one adult) with the ends cut off and polished, and four drilled bear phalanges. An otter mandible was directly associated with a bone tube, and several pebbles found together may have been inside a rattle. Archaeologist William Fox and physical anthropologist Eldon Molto, who analyzed and reported the discovery, interpret it as the grave of a bear shaman and speculate that an otter-skin medicine bag once held the ritual items, as was the practice in more recent times.

The **Late Ceramic** period, from about 1100 years ago until international trade rendered the local industry obsolete about 400 years ago, was when the specific Iroquoian cultures known historically emerged. The defining feature for this stage is the growth of villages of longhouses, traced archaeologically by the pattern of post moulds marking the outside walls and interior partitions, with interior hearths and storage pits down the centre. Frequently a single or double row of palisades encircled the houses. Two separate but related traditions exist within this period. In southern Ontario, the Late Ceramic developments leading to the historic Huron, Petun and Neutral peoples are referred to as the Ontario Iroquois tradition. In the St. Lawrence River valley of southern Quebec and adjacent Ontario, a separate development led to the St. Lawrence Iroquoians.

In its early centuries, the Ontario Iroquois tradition was separated into two geographic branches. The southern branch, with sites to the north of Lake Erie, was Glen Meyer, whereas to the north, from Lake Ontario to Georgian Bay, was Pickering. Although they differed in various features such as pottery styles, these two regional branches developed in similar ways. They may, in fact, represent a continuum of cultural variation rather than two distinct regional cultures. The economy was based on corn agriculture, supplemented by fishing and hunting. Small triangular stone arrowpoints show that the bow and arrow were in use by this time. Longhouses were clustered into small villages, which were frequently surrounded by palisades for defence. Pottery and tools of stone and bone were similar to later Iroquoian types. Burial practices included secondary burials (where the disarticulated bones of an individual who had been given an earlier interim burial in a shallow grave or on a scaffold were gathered and buried in a bundle) and small ossuaries (pits containing bundles of disarticulated bones from a number of individuals).

Around 700 years ago the Pickering branch appears to have expanded across southern Ontario. J.V. Wright attributes this to conquest, with the Glen Meyer people being dispersed and partially absorbed. There is no compelling evidence of widespread warfare, however, which has caused other archaeologists to be skeptical of this hypothesis. Whatever the cause, the following period was one of fairly homogenous culture across southern Ontario. During this time ossuary burial became common, and some pits contained the remains of hundreds of people. Numerous pipes of pottery and stone, some embellished with effigies of humans or animals, mark the introduction of the tobacco-smoking habit. From this common cultural base, the separate historic Iroquoian cultures emerged.

In the final stage before they encountered Europeans, two branches of Iroquoian culture developed in southern Ontario. The most northerly led to the historic Huron and Petun, whereas the other led to the Neutral of southernmost Ontario and their close kin, the Erie, in adjacent New York. Agriculture became more important when beans and squash were introduced, since corn and beans

ABOVE *Reconstruction of a Glen Meyer village (ca. AD 1000), based on archaeological evidence, near London, Ontario. Photo by A. McMillan*

are complementary in providing adequate nutrition. This broader agricultural economy promoted a sharp increase in population. Hunting played a lesser role in the economy than in earlier periods, in part because larger populations would have depleted game in the surrounding area. The larger size and greater number of villages and ossuaries show that the populations were growing significantly. Longhouses became progressively longer, and extensions were periodically added to one or both ends. Warfare was evidently widespread, with cut and burned human bones in village debris suggesting the fate of captured warriors. All the basic features of historic Ontario Iroquoian cultures as they became known in the early seventeenth century are present in these Late Ceramic sites.

The Draper site, located about thirty-five kilometres northeast of Toronto, is a large ancestral Huron village that was almost totally uncovered by a series of excavations. When the site was occupied around 500 years ago, populations were coalescing into larger villages, presumably for protection. Segments of the palisades were repeatedly torn down to make room for village expansions. The site eventually grew from a small cluster of seven longhouses to a large village, surrounded by up to four rows of palisades, containing at least thirty-seven houses sheltering nearly 2000 people.

Hostilities intensified in the years just prior to direct contact with Europeans, leading to the abandoning of many areas and the contraction of territories to those known historically. The Huron withdrew from the lands north of Lake Ontario to gather in their historic homeland near Georgian Bay, off Lake Huron. Similarly the Neutral abandoned much of southwestern Ontario, clustering around the western end of Lake Ontario and the Niagara Peninsula.

Along the St. Lawrence River valley, similar developments occurred throughout the Late Ceramic period. Although cultures in this area resembled those in southern Ontario, differences did exist. Pots and pipes were particularly finely made and differed stylistically from those of their western kin. Bone was especially important as a raw material for making tools. Rather than placing their dead in ossuaries, the St. Lawrence Iroquoians buried them in flexed positions throughout the villages. Remains of broken and charred human bones, as well as ornaments and tools made from human bone, indicate that warfare and ritual cannibalism were not uncommon. Judging from historic information, the victims were usually males taken captive. Large villages of longhouses, frequently palisaded for defence, were similar to those in southern Ontario and those described by early European observers.

THE ST. LAWRENCE IROQUOIANS

Our earliest historic descriptions of Iroquoians come from the voyages of Jacques Cartier. On his first journey in 1534, Cartier encountered a fishing party from the village of Stadacona off the Gaspé Peninsula and took two people, sons of the headman Donnacona, back to France. They served as guides for Cartier's larger expedition of 1535, leading him up the St. Lawrence River to Stadacona (located where Quebec City now stands), where he spent the winter. Both groups endured illnesses that winter. The Iroquoians provided medicine made from fronds of white cedar for the Europeans' scurvy, but the French could do nothing to alleviate the Natives' suffering from European diseases. Cartier also antagonized the Stadaconans by travelling upriver to Hochelaga (the site of modern Montreal) against their wishes and by kidnapping ten Native People, including Donnacona and his two sons, when he returned to France in 1536. All except a young girl died there before Cartier returned to Stadacona during his third voyage of 1541.

Cartier's descriptions of Stadacona are disappointingly brief. Stadacona was the largest of a cluster of about seven villages, all located on the north shore of the St. Lawrence. The south side may have remained uninhabited because of attacks by a hostile people known as the Toudaman, who were probably the Mi'kmaq or Maliseet. The French appear to have been unimpressed with these villages, which suggests that they were small. Unlike most Iroquoian villages, they were not protected by palisades.

Fortunately, Cartier left a fuller description of Hochelaga. On 3 October 1535, Cartier and his men marched through forests and cornfields to the village, read the Gospel to the Native inhabitants, and climbed Mount Royal to survey the surrounding land. From Mount Royal, Cartier could see the St. Lawrence and he noted the turbulent waters of the Lachine rapids that barred further travel upriver. The village itself was located well away from navigable water, presumably for defence, and was surrounded by vast fields of corn. A triple row of palisades, with ladders leading to platforms where defenders could stand during an attack, encircled about fifty bark-covered longhouses. This would indicate a population equivalent to the large Huron villages to the west that the French described a century later. Unfortunately, Hochelaga stands in the clear light of recorded history for only this one day. Cartier did not return to Hochelaga on his later trip up the St. Lawrence, and by the time other explorers reached the area over half a century later nothing remained of this important Iroquoian village..

Reminders that vestiges of the Native past lie beneath the concrete, glass and pavement of modern Montreal occasionally come to light. A good example is the Dawson site, located near McGill University. Construction in the late nineteenth century disturbed large quantities of Iroquoian pottery, other artifacts and human skeletons. Since then archaeologists have debated whether those are the remains of Hochelaga. In the end the question cannot be answered, but the Dawson site appears to be too small to fit Cartier's description and may have been a separate Hochelagan village.

The economies of the Hochelagans and Stadaconans clearly differed. The Hochelagans were typical Iroquoians, relying on crops of corn, beans and squash, supplemented by hunting and fishing. The Stadaconans, though also agriculturalists, lived in a marginal environment for growing corn and had to rely more heavily on hunting and fishing. During the winter, men travelled far inland in hunting parties. In the summer, fishing and catching eels were important activi-

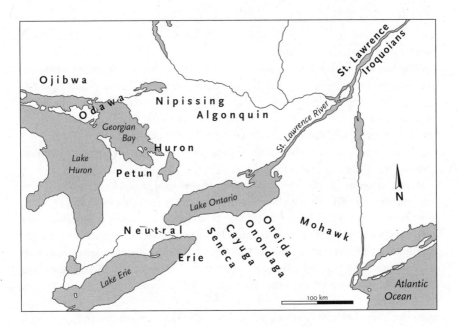

ABOVE *The Iroquoians and their neighbours at first contact with Europeans*

ties. Large groups of Stadaconans also travelled downriver to the mouth of the St. Lawrence to fish for mackerel and hunt sea mammals such as seals and small whales. The fishing party Cartier encountered during his 1534 voyage was one such group.

The term "St. Lawrence Iroquoians" is something of a catch-all phrase. They may not have been a single political group, despite the Hochelagan claim to rule all the tribes downstream. French accounts shed no light on whether the villages around Stadacona formed a single tribe or were politically autonomous. Present practice is to refer to the two clusters described by Cartier as Stadaconans and Hochelagans, and to recognize considerable differences between them. In fact, archaeological studies have isolated as many as five distinct clusters of Iroquoian villages on the St. Lawrence.

We do not even know if the two groups spoke the same language. Our only information comes from word lists collected from Cartier's Stadaconan captives. Linguistic analysis has indicated that these people spoke a distinct Iroquoian language that cannot be assigned to Huron or any of the Five Nations Iroquois languages as was once thought possible. Canada's name is derived from this language, from a word meaning "village" that was extended to refer to all the lands around Stadacona.

After Cartier's final departure, the St. Lawrence Iroquoians disappear from history. Samuel de Champlain, who arrived on the St. Lawrence in 1603, was the next chronicler to leave an impression of his visit there. By that time the Stadaconans and Hochelagans had vanished, leaving a vacant expanse travelled only by war parties of Algonquians and Five Nations Iroquois, who were locked in bitter conflict over the vital waterway.

The fate that befell the St. Lawrence Iroquoians remains a mystery. Epidemic diseases, beginning as early as their first encounter with Cartier, may have decreased their numbers. Crop failures may also have played a role, since the lower St. Lawrence River valley was a precarious environment for Aboriginal agriculture. However, their most probable fate was annihilation through warfare. As early as 1535 the Stadaconans were trying to prevent Cartier from proceeding upriver, in order to have a monopoly on French trade goods. The desire to obtain access to European goods or to gain control of the trade would have provided motivation for warfare, though the identity of the aggressors is unknown. J.V. Wright has made a convincing argument that the St. Lawrence Iroquoians were destroyed in warfare with the Huron. He points to the presence of typical St. Lawrence Iroquoian pottery in late Huron sites as evidence that female captives were adopted into Huron society and continued to make pots in their accustomed fashion. Adult males, on the other hand, were killed, explaining the relative lack of St. Lawrence Iroquoian style pipes, which were a male craft. Other researchers, however, have concluded that the St. Lawrence pottery present in late Huron sites indicates a refugee population that fled destruction in its homeland at the hands of the Iroquois, particularly the Mohawk. The early-sixteenth-century formation

ABOVE *St. Lawrence Iroquoian pottery vessel.* CMC K75-1073.

RIGHT *Typical Huron-Petun artifacts: (a) pottery rim fragments; (b) small pot, possibly made by a child; (c) stone pipe bowl; (d) antler harpoon; (e) stone scraper; (f) netting needle; (g) stone turtle amulet; (h) stone and bone arrowheads; (i) pottery pipes; (j) dagger made from human bone.* CMC 73-7763

of the League of the Iroquois united the Five Nations as a powerful military force, one that other Iroquoian groups could not withstand. Whether aggressors or hosts in their relations with the St. Lawrence Iroquoians, the Huron and their neighbours were to suffer the same fate in less than a century.

THE HURON AND PETUN

These closely related neighbouring groups emerged from the same Late Ceramic cultural stratum. They were politically separate, though they spoke the same language and differed little in customs. The Petun were famed for their extensive cultivation and trade of tobacco (for which they were known as the "Tobacco Nation"). Although the Huron and Petun were closely allied during the seventeenth century, the Jesuits recorded that they had "formerly waged cruel wars against one another."

The Huron and Petun are known primarily through ethnohistoric documents. European chronicles describe the cultures of the Huron, Petun and Neutral for the first half of the seventeenth century, before these groups were destroyed or dispersed at the hands of the Iroquois. Yet for this brief period we have extensive written records, particularly about the Huron. Colonial policy combined with a lucrative fur trade and missionary zeal to draw the French into Huron country early in the seventeenth century. Samuel de Champlain was one of the first to travel through the Huron homeland, Huronia, in 1615–16, and he left a detailed account of his experiences. He requested that the Récollet order, a branch of the Franciscans, send a missionary to work with the Huron. Gabriel Sagard laboured among them from 1623 to 1624 and he too recorded his observations of Huron life. The most extensive source of information is the *Jesuit Relations*, the voluminous annual documents compiled by the Jesuits that chronicle their work among the Huron from 1634 to 1650. These accounts provide a wealth of information on the Huron (and to a lesser extent on the Petun and other neighbouring groups). Further details can now be obtained only through archaeology.

The French used the name Huron, from an old term for "boar's head," to describe the bristly hairstyles of the Iroquoians. More generally the word came to mean "ruffian" or "knave." The Huron referred to themselves as *Wendat*, meaning "islanders" or "dwellers on a peninsula," because their homeland was surrounded by water on three sides. This term survived as *Wyandot*, which was applied to the descendants of Huron-Petun refugees from the Iroquois wars. Similarly, the term "Petun" comes from a word the French used for tobacco. The Native name for the group is variously written as Tionontati or Khionontateronon, meaning "people of the hills."

By the early seventeenth century, Huronia was restricted to the region between Georgian Bay and Lake Simcoe. Its fertile soils lay immediately south of the rocky Canadian Shield. Much of Huronia was open land, since people had cleared and then abandoned their agricultural fields. Sagard describes it as "full of fine hills, open fields, very beautiful broad meadows bearing much excellent hay."

Early estimates suggest between eighteen and twenty-five Huron villages, of which perhaps six would have been large fortified villages containing numerous longhouses. The total population was estimated to be between 20,000 and 30,000. Epidemic diseases quickly reduced their numbers to about 9000 by 1640.

The Petun were located to the southwest of the Huron. Trails linked the Petun and Huron villages, requiring about a day's journey. The Petun also maintained close ties with Algonquian groups such as the Odawa to the west, with whom they traded. Champlain mentions eight villages in 1616, and the Jesuits list nine in 1639. Little information exists on the size of the population, though 8000 may be a reasonable estimate. Again, epidemic diseases caused the population to drop, to about 3000 by 1640.

Both the Huron and Petun were confederacies of separate tribes. Of the five groups that made up the Huron, the Attignawantan ("Bear Nation") was by far the largest, occupying the western portion of Huronia, including all of the Pene-tanguishene Peninsula. The others were the Arendarhonon ("Rock Nation"), At-tigneenongnahac (usually interpreted as "Cord Nation"), Tahontaenrat (possibly meaning "Deer Nation") and Ataronchronon (possibly "Nation Beyond the Silted Lake"). The latter group did not appear in the initial Jesuit lists, so it may have been a division of the Attignawantan. The Attignawantan and the Attigneenong-nahac were the original occupants of Huronia, with the others arriving, probably from near Lake Ontario, only a short time before the Jesuits. The Petun were di-vided into two groups, which the Jesuits called the "Nation of the Wolves" and the "Nation of the Deer."

Village locations were carefully chosen. The primary requirements were ac-cess to fresh water and arable soils, available firewood and a location that could be defended. Only larger villages and those on the frontier were strongly fortified, and the inhabitants of smaller centres fled to these strongholds in times of dan-ger. Palisades, constructed from long slender poles twisted into the ground, encir-cled the villages, frequently in several rows. Large sheets of bark strengthened the palisades, and ladders provided access to walkways where the defenders could stand. Sagard provides details:

> [They] are fortified by strong wooden palisades in three rows, interlaced into one another and reinforced within by large thick pieces of bark to a height of eight or nine feet, and at the bottom there are great trunks of trees placed lengthwise.... Then above these palisades there are galleries or watch-towers ... and these they stock with stones in war-time to hurl upon the enemy, and water to put out the fire that might be laid against their palisades. *Sagard 1939: 91–92*

Within the confines of the palisades the longhouses were arranged in seem-ingly random fashion, though the constant threat of fire required that they be spaced at least a short distance apart. Large villages contained up to 100 long-houses, sheltering 1500 to 2000 people. Champlain, however, estimated 200 "fairly large lodges" at the important village of Cahiague, a figure which has been

ABOVE *Reconstruction of a Huron village, Midland, Ontario. Photo by A. McMillan*

questioned by some writers. Due to the exhaustion of soils and firewood supplies, villages had to be moved every ten to fifteen years, and at such times the larger villages might split into two.

The longhouse was the basic unit of Iroquoian life. Large sheets of cedar, elm or ash bark were woven between arched poles to form a long structure with a vaulted roof and rounded ends. Each sheltered a number of families. Lengths varied widely according to the number of occupants, and shorter structures could be extended to accommodate new inhabitants. Both Champlain and Sagard described the longhouses as being twenty-five to thirty fathoms long (roughly forty-five to fifty-five metres) and six wide (about eleven metres), though sizes varied considerably. A central corridor running the length of the longhouse contained the hearths. Each hearth was shared by two families, living across the corridor from each other. Raised benches or sleeping platforms extended along each side of the house. According to Champlain and Sagard, however, these platforms were used for sleeping only in the summer, whereas winter cold forced the family to sleep on the floor near the fire. Food and firewood were stored in enclosed porches at each end and under the sleeping platforms. Fish and corn hung drying from the roof of the house. The Huron also hung personal belongings from the roof or buried them in storage pits dug into the house floor. Despite openings in the roof, smoke from the fires filled the houses and caused serious eye problems. Although the Huron no doubt appreciated the warmth and social interaction of their homes, the Jesuits described them as "a miniature picture of Hell," complaining of noise and lack of privacy, choking smoke, the stench of fish and urine, unrestrained rampages of dogs and small children, and infestations of fleas, flies and mice.

Residence within the longhouse tended to be matrilocal (that is, the man moved into the household of his wife), though this was likely an ideal rather than an inevitable rule. Often, a group of related adult women lived with their spouses and children in a longhouse. Divorce was simple, requiring only that the husband move out of the wife's house. Once the couple had children, however, marital breakdown was less common. Descent was matrilineal, meaning that all children belonged to their mother's clan. Young men could not inherit their father's property or position; these were passed down from their mother's brothers. In his old age a man counted more on his sister's children than on his own for support.

The Huron and Petun diet was overwhelmingly comprised of agricultural produce. Corn, along with beans, squash and pumpkins, made up at least three-quarters of all their food. To make flour, they dried and pounded corn kernels in a hollowed-out tree trunk, using a long wooden pole. Although the Huron and Petun devised many ingenious ways to prepare corn, most recipes were variations on a theme. The everyday meal was a corn soup (*sagamite*), often with pieces of fish, meat or squash. They might toss a whole small fish into the pot, remove it after boiling a short while and mash it, then return it to the pot without removing bones, scales or entrails. For feasts, they might serve a thick corn soup with some fat or oil on top. A bread of cornmeal, often mixed with deer fat or dried fruit to provide flavour, was baked under ashes. Placing small ears of corn in a stagnant pond to ferment for several months before eating made a "stinking corn" dish that delighted the Huron palate but revolted their Jesuit guests. Women raised the crops and cooked the food, and they also collected a wide variety of wild plants, such as nuts and berries, which were less important nutritionally but added flavour to their bland diet.

Men hunted and fished, though the Huron ate less game and fish than corn. Fishing was far more important than hunting and was possible through much of the year, though the spring and late fall spawning runs were peak periods. In the fall men travelled to the many islands of Georgian Bay to catch whitefish, trout and sturgeon, most commonly in nets. Inland, they sometimes built weirs along creeks and streams to block the fish runs. Once they were trapped, the fish could be speared or netted. Champlain described fish weirs along the full length of the narrows between Lake Simcoe and Lake Couchiching.

Hunting was less important for food, but was essential for obtaining hides for clothing. Although deer were the principal game animals, the Huron also sought bear and beaver. Since Huronia's dense population meant that game animals were scarce, hunters set out on lengthy expeditions to the south or east. They conducted communal drives, in which a line of hunters forced the deer between long converging fences of brush into an enclosure where they were speared or shot with arrows. Deer were also driven into lakes and killed from canoes. Dogs helped in the hunt but they also wound up in the stewpot, and Champlain and Sagard reported that tame bears were raised from cubs for the same purpose.

The Huron were led by two types of chiefs. Civil chiefs governed affairs of state and organized feasts, dances, games and funeral ceremonies, whereas war chiefs were concerned exclusively with military matters. In theory each clan segment had both a civil and a war chief, so that several of each would exist within larger villages. A combination of inheritance and personal abilities, such as wisdom, speaking skills and bravery, determined who would fill these positions. Two councils conducted village affairs; one composed of war chiefs and senior warriors, the other of civil chiefs and older adult males. All matters were supposed to be decided by consensus, with all present given an opportunity to express their views. In practice, according to the Jesuits, the chiefs and elders made the decisions, owing to their higher social standing and powers of oratory. Although no individual was bound by any ruling, failure to comply left one open to criticism or ridicule.

At least once a year the entire Huron Confederacy held a council. This brought together civil chiefs from throughout Huronia to reaffirm their friendship and discuss matters of common concern. The Attignawantan, by virtue of their numbers, seem to have dominated these meetings. Again, no decisions were binding on individual members, and the difficulty in establishing effective common action was a weakness when faced with the Iroquois onslaught.

The Huron and Petun communicated by sending messengers on foot over a network of narrow trails between villages. Even to the Neutral and beyond, most travel was overland. Because winter was a difficult time to get around, despite the use of both snowshoes and toboggans, the Iroquoians rarely set out on major trips during this season. Canoe travel seems to have been restricted to fishing expeditions, long distance trade and crossing Lake Ontario to attack the Iroquois. Birchbark from the forests of Huronia allowed the Huron to build lighter and more efficient canoes than the Iroquois and Neutral, who had to use the inferior elm bark. However, Huron canoes were not as well made as those of their Algonquian neighbours, nor did they play as large a role in their culture.

Deer hides and beaver pelts, which were hunted or traded from the Algonquians, were made into clothing. In warm weather men wore only a breechcloth of deerskin and a pair of moccasins. Women added only a skirt, leaving their upper bodies bare. In winter both sexes also wore a cloak, long sleeves and leggings, held in place by leather thongs. Clothing could be decorated with paint or trimmed with dyed porcupine quills. Both men and women wore necklaces and bracelets of shell beads, and suspended them from their ears as well. They also lavished considerable attention on their hair. Women wore a single tress that hung down the back and was tied with leather thongs, whereas men cut theirs in a variety of styles. Some shaved the sides of their heads, others cut their hair in ridges, and a few trimmed one side and allowed the other to grow long. Both sexes rubbed oil or grease on their hair and bodies, and for special occasions painted their faces and bodies as well. Tattooing, though rare among the Huron, was apparently common among the Petun and depicted, according to Sagard, snakes, lizards, squirrels and other animals.

Religious and mythological beliefs, along with associated feasts and dances, integrated Huron society. Certain old men were repositories of traditions and myths, which they recited publicly at feasts. In the Huron world, all things, whether animate or inanimate, had a soul or spirit. The more powerful of these were called *oki*, a term also extended to unusual individuals, such as shamans, witches, fierce warriors or even lunatics. The most important spirit was the sky, which determined weather, wind, waves and other natural forces affecting human life. Lesser spirits were associated with prominent features of the landscape. Although some were friendly and could be approached for assistance, others were malevolent, seeking to kill and devour humans, and had to be placated with tobacco and other offerings. Fish and animals also had spirits, and care had to be taken not to offend them. Their bones were never to be thrown into the fire or to the dogs, lest their souls be angered and the living animals no longer allowed themselves to be taken.

In the Huron creation story, the world came into being after Sky-Woman (known to the Huron as Aataentsic), one of the supernatural people who dwell on the upper surface of the visible sky, fell through a hole into the darkness below. The Great Turtle, swimming in the primordial sea, witnessed her descent and commanded the other ocean creatures to bring up mud from the bottom to pile on his back. The earth was formed in this manner and still moves about on the back of the Great Turtle. Several species of birds flew up toward Aataentsic and grabbed hold of her dress so that she landed gently on this newly formed land. She was pregnant when she fell, and she soon gave birth to a daughter. The daughter grew quickly and, becoming pregnant by the spirit of the Great Turtle, gave birth to twin boys, good and evil. Iouskeha, the good twin, was born in the usual fashion, whereas Tawiscaron, the evil-minded twin, burst forth from his mother's body, killing her in the process. Iouskeha, the good twin, made the world suitable for humans by creating lakes and rivers, making corn grow and releasing the animals from a great cave so that people could hunt them. Tawiscaron, the evil twin, became the favourite of his grandmother, but he tried to undo his brother's creations. After violent combat between the brothers, Tawiscaron was forced to flee. As blood from his injuries dropped on the ground it became the flint that humans use for arrowpoints and other tools. Iouskeha continues to assist humans, whereas Aataentsic, who decreed that all people must die, opposes him. The Huron identified Iouskeha with the sun and Aataentsic with the moon.

Every Huron had a soul, and these souls had desires which they communicated through dreams. Hurons who failed to fulfill their dreams and satisfy the soul could fall ill or die. If they dreamed of an object, they had to identify and obtain it. The owner of the object was obliged to make a gift of it. If a Huron dreamed of a feast or ceremony, he or she had to make every effort to recreate it in real life. Occasionally dreams were overtly sexual; for example, a person might request a ceremony for his or her recovery in which the young people of the village danced naked. Although such sexually expressive acts were usually prohibited, dreams were so important that they transgressed cultural restrictions. Dreams were sometimes ambiguous, requiring a shaman to interpret the soul's demands.

Illness could also be caused by natural factors or by witchcraft. Medicinal plants treated natural ailments, whereas a shaman was required to aid in removing a spell. If the witch could be identified, he or she might be killed. Some shamans also controlled the weather or predicted future events.

Feasts, dances and games brought together the social groups that made up Huron society. Feasts were held for a variety of occasions and were an important mechanism for gaining status. Great quantities of food were distributed, though the host was expected to eat little or nothing. Dances were usually performed to cure illness or celebrate a victory. Such social gatherings also provided opportunities for games. Lacrosse was the most popular, often played between teams from different villages. It was a rough sport, played by young men, and frequently resulted in injuries. A gambling game, in which marked fruit stones were tossed like dice in a wooden bowl, was passionately played and bets were heavy, some men losing all that they owned. Games also cured illness and could fulfill soul desires expressed in dreams. When epidemic diseases were spreading among the Huron, the shamans decided that the whole country was sick and they decreed that lacrosse should be played to cure it.

When a Huron died, inhabitants in the surrounding villages were notified so they could attend the funeral several days later. A feast was held, and gifts were presented to the grieving relatives. A scaffold erected in the village cemetery held the body, which was accompanied by offerings. Some individuals, such as those who drowned or were killed in battle, were interred and shrines were raised over their graves. For all except those who died violently, these arrangements were temporary, and the individual was not considered to have had final burial until the next Feast of the Dead.

The Feast of the Dead was the most important ceremony in Huron society. It was held every ten to twelve years, or whenever a large village shifted location. At this time people from a number of neighbouring villages gathered from their cemeteries the remains of all who had died since the last such ceremony and prepared them for reburial in a common grave. Sagard described how the women prepared the corpses of their relatives:

> The women who have to bring the bones of their relatives go to the cemeteries for them, and if the flesh is not entirely destroyed they clean it off and take away the bones. These they wash and wrap up in fine new beaver-skins, and with glass beads and wampum necklaces, which the relations and friends contribute and bring. . . . And putting them into a new bag they carry them on their backs, and also adorn the top of the bag with many little ornaments, with necklaces, bracelets, and other decorations. *Sagard 1939: 211–12*

After honouring the remains with feasts in their own villages, the Huron set out for the Feast of the Dead, the women carrying the bundles of bones. They met at a location where a large circular pit had been dug and a platform, from which the bags of bones and grave goods could be suspended, had been built. The pit was lined with beaver robes, and large offerings such as kettles were placed at the bottom. After several days of ceremonies and a final farewell to the deceased, each family threw the bones of their dead and the goods being offered into the burial pit. Several men went into the pit with long poles to arrange the bones, the effect being to mix together the bones of numerous individuals. At last the pit was filled and covered over, presents were distributed, and a final feast was held. Everyone could then return to their villages, secure in the knowledge that their dead relatives had been laid to final rest, and strengthened as a tribe by this shared ceremony. One excavated ossuary contained the remains of about one thousand individuals.

Before the fur trade, warfare among the Iroquoians was commonly to avenge previous deaths and acquire personal prestige. Most military expeditions took place during the summer, and they were usually organized by the war chiefs at the request of families that had suffered losses at the hands of the enemy—usually the Iroquois. Although groups of several hundred men might set out to attack an Iroquois village, more commonly they split into small groups, hiding along paths and in fields, hoping to surprise the enemy. Major weapons were the wooden club and the bow and arrow. Warriors wore armour of wooden slats covering much of the body and carried shields. The goal of these military campaigns was to capture or kill as many of the enemy as possible. Prisoners, along with heads or scalps as trophies of those killed, were taken back to the Huron villages.

Captives were distributed among those who had participated in the raid, and a decision was made on their fate. Some, particularly women and children, were adopted by the family to which they had been given, usually to replace members lost in previous warfare. They eventually became full members of this society, and the few adult males adopted in this manner might even have found themselves in battle against their former kin. More commonly adult males were tortured to death. This was a public spectacle in which the entire community participated. The victim's suffering might be prolonged over several days. After death finally came, his body was cut into pieces, which were cooked in a kettle and served at a feast. If the victim had been a particularly brave warrior, young men eagerly consumed his flesh and heart in the belief that they could acquire his courage.

Contact with the French in the early seventeenth century brought great changes to Huron life and in time led to their downfall. Initially, the exchange of beaver pelts and other furs for iron tools and other European goods was so profitable for both sides that the beaver were soon nearly exterminated within Huronia. The Huron were forced to turn to the Algonquians to the north for furs. As the principal trading partners of the French, the Huron were intermediaries, blocking the Petun and others from direct access to European trade. The Huron exchanged corn and European goods for large quantities of furs that they obtained from the Algonquians and took to French settlements on the St. Lawrence each year. However, such trips were dangerous, and attacks by the Iroquois became increasingly common.

As well as fur trade wealth, the French sought to save the souls of Native People. First the Récollets, then the Jesuits attempted to convert the Huron to Christianity. The Jesuits made the most sustained effort and had the greatest effect. After they established their central mission, Sainte-Marie, in 1639, the Jesuits had a permanent base among the Huron and converted many people. This undermined Huron society by dividing the people into Christian and traditional factions.

Also arriving with the French were European diseases, to which the Iroquoians had no immunity. Smallpox and measles took a huge toll, greatly weakening the Huron Confederacy. The smallpox epidemic of 1639 was particularly devastating. Diseases aided the Jesuits' proselytizing, as many Huron accepted baptism as a curing ritual; however, others opposed the Jesuits when they noticed that most of those who had been baptized soon died. The Jesuits were content to convert victims of disease so they could die as Christians.

The fur trade also altered the pattern of Iroquoian warfare, from blood feuds spurred by revenge to wars of extermination. The Iroquois, trading first with the Dutch and later with the English, desired access to the rich beaver country to the north, from which they were blocked by the Huron. The Iroquois soon had a major advantage in firearms, since the Jesuits forbade any French trade in muskets to the Huron except for trusted Christian converts. The western Iroquois, particularly the Seneca, began raiding far into Huron territory in large, well-organized armies bent on destroying entire villages. In the east, the Mohawk made any Huron attempt to get their furs to Quebec a very risky venture.

The Huron were unable to deal with this looming threat and became increasingly uncertain about their future. Thousands flocked to the fortifications of Sainte-Marie, greatly increasing the number of Christian converts. In 1648 the Iroquois launched determined attacks, destroying a number of eastern Huron villages. That winter an army of over 1000 men, mainly Seneca and Mohawk, secretly spent the winter camped north of Lake Ontario, so they could surprise the Huron before the snows melted in the spring. The Huron could not withstand this onslaught, which overran the villages around Sainte-Marie. The Iroquois captured the Jesuit Fathers Brébeuf and Lalemant and tortured them to death, according to Iroquoian custom. The surviving Huron—having decided that their situation was hopeless—abandoned their villages, torching them so they could not be used by the Iroquois.

Many refugees starved to death or were killed by marauding Iroquois war parties. Others, particularly the Attignawantan, sought refuge among the Petun, but were slaughtered or dispersed when the Iroquois turned on the Petun and destroyed their villages by the end of 1649. Some fled to the Neutral, who dropped their neutrality after the Huron defeat and subjected these fugitives to a harsh captivity. Many of both the Huron and Petun were absorbed into Iroquois communities, adopted by their conquerors to replace members lost in warfare. Although the smallest Huron tribe, the Tahontaenrat, with some of the Arendarhonon, were allowed to build a separate town in Seneca territory, all eventually lost their own cultural identity and adopted that of their conquerors.

One large group of Petun and Huron refugees fled to the upper Great Lakes region and allied with such Algonquian groups as the Odawa and Potawatomi. They became known as the Wyandot, the corruption of the Huron name for themselves. After several moves they settled near Detroit. In the nineteenth century, the American policy of removing Indians to settlements west of the Mississippi forced the Wyandot to Kansas and Oklahoma, where their descendants remain. Their language is extinct, though it was still spoken into the twentieth century.

Another large group of Huron fled to Gahendoe (Christian) Island, a short distance from the shores of Huronia in Georgian Bay. After the Jesuits burned and abandoned Sainte-Marie, they established a new fortress among these Huron and spent the winter of 1649–50 there. This was a time of extreme hardship, when provisions ran out early in the winter and fishing through the ice proved unusually unproductive. Bands of Iroquois roamed the shores of Georgian Bay, preventing any attempt to hunt on the mainland. Hunger led people to eat moss and bark, and eventually to cannibalism. Many Huron died of starvation or contagious diseases over the winter. Others were killed or captured by the Iroquois as they attempted to leave the island. Finally, in June of 1650, the Jesuits and about three hundred Huron survivors began the final retreat to Quebec.

After 1650, few if any Huron remained in Huronia. The Iroquois had no interest in permanently settling this territory, travelling through it only on occasional hunting and trading expeditions. Only charred poles remained where the villages had stood, and weeds overgrew the cornfields which had once supported the dense population of now-abandoned Huronia.

Descendants of the Huron who fled with the Jesuits still live at the Village-des-Hurons, just outside Quebec City. Once known as the Huron of Lorette, they now refer to themselves as the Nation Huronne Wendat. As is typical of Quebec villages in this region, they are Catholic and francophone. Numbering almost 3000 people, this is the only Huron population in Canada today. The Huron language, however, is extinct.

THE NEUTRAL

Although similar in culture to the Huron and Petun, the Neutral, along with the Erie across the lake which bears their name, emerged from a slightly divergent Late Ceramic branch. The Neutral language resembled Huron, and the two groups referred to each other as the Attiwandaronk, meaning "people whose speech is a little different." The French used the term "Neutral" to describe a people who were determined to avoid being dragged into the destructive wars between the Huron and the League of the Iroquois. The Neutral, however, were embroiled in long-standing warfare with other groups, particularly the "Fire Nation" (the Algonquian-speaking Mascouten, in what is now Michigan).

Neutral lifeways did not survive long into the global era and thus are poorly known. Both the Récollets and the Jesuits travelled into Neutral territory but neither established permanent bases among them. The Jesuits noted that the Neutral regarded their missionaries as "sorcerers who carried death and misfortune everywhere." As a result, modern researchers depend much more upon archaeological evidence to discern Neutral life in the early seventeenth century than they do for the Huron.

The Neutral occupied southwestern Ontario, primarily between the Grand and Niagara Rivers, and most of their villages were situated west of Lake Ontario. The climate of this area was slightly more benign than Huronia, and the hardwood forests sheltered more game animals. About forty Neutral villages existed in the early seventeenth century. Although population estimates vary considerably, perhaps 30,000 to 35,000 people lived in Neutral territory, making them the largest group of northeastern Iroquoians. Smallpox epidemics, however, particularly between 1638 and 1640, drastically reduced their numbers.

Like the Huron and Petun, the Neutral were organized as a confederacy of separate tribes. Ethnohistorical and archaeological evidence suggests between five and ten separate tribes made up the Neutral, but we have too little information to draw up even a full list of their names.

The Neutral way of life closely resembled that of the Huron. They lived in palisaded villages of longhouses, occupied by people related through the female line. They practised corn agriculture, supplemented by hunting and fishing. However, game was more abundant in their territory and therefore made up more of the Neutral diet. The Neutral were less adept canoeists, so they did not set out on long journeys by water. Like the Petun but unlike the Huron, the Neutral tattooed their bodies and grew tobacco, which was an important trade commodity.

The Jesuits also noted differences in burial customs. Father Lalemant contrasted Huron and Neutral practices:

> Our Hurons immediately after death carry the bodies to the burying ground and take them away from it only for the feast of the Dead. Those of the Neutral Nation carry the bodies to the burying ground only at the very latest moment possible when decomposition has rendered them insupportable; for this reason, the dead bodies often remain during the entire winter in their cabins; and, having once put them outside upon a scaffold that they may decay, they take away the bones as soon as is possible, and expose them to view, arranged here and there in their cabins, until the feast of the Dead. Thwaites, *Jesuit Relations 21: 199*

Although both groups held a Feast of the Dead, involving communal reburial in an ossuary, some differences existed. Excavation of the Grimsby site, an historic

Neutral ossuary, indicates that they took care to maintain the integrity of separate burials, in contrast to the deliberate mixing of disarticulated bones from many individuals in the larger Huron ossuaries.

Several writers have argued that by about 1615 the Neutral had developed politically from a tribal confederacy to a chiefdom, under the leadership of the powerful war chief Tsouharissen who ruled throughout Neutral territory. Father Daillon, a Récollet priest, commented on Tsouharissen in 1627: "This man is the chief of the greatest credit and authority that has ever been in all these nations, because he is not only chief of his town, but of all those of his nation. . . . It is unexampled in the other nations to have a chief so absolute. He acquired this honour and power by his courage, and by having been many times at war" (Noble 1985: 133). Whether the chiefdom would have continued after Tsouharissen remains a question that cannot be answered. The Iroquois destruction of Neutral society put an end to this political experiment after less than four decades of existence.

Seneca expansion westward began to threaten their Neutral neighbours. Even after the Seneca attacked and burned an eastern Neutral town in 1647, the Neutral did not retaliate, vainly hoping to stay out of the conflict. However, once the Huron and Petun villages had fallen, the full force of the League of the Iroquois turned against the Neutral. Iroquois attacks in 1650 and 1651 weakened the Neutral resolve and caused the confederacy to collapse. Those living in villages not yet attacked abandoned their lands and fled. A Jesuit account describes their dispersal:

> Great was the carnage, especially among the old people and the children, who would not have been able to follow the Iroquois to their country. The number of captives was exceedingly large,—especially of young women, whom they reserve, in order to keep up the population of their own villages. This loss was very great, and entailed the complete ruin and desolation of the Neutral nation; the inhabitants of their other villages, which were more distant from the enemy, took fright; abandoned their houses, their property, and their country; and condemned themselves to voluntary exile, to escape still further from the fury and cruelty of the conquerors. Famine pursues these poor fugitives everywhere.
> Thwaites, *Jesuit Relations 36: 177*

Many of the Neutral survived as captives of the Iroquois, particularly the Seneca. Others were scattered as refugee populations or absorbed into other groups. The dispersal of 1651, however, marked the end of the Neutral as a separate cultural or political entity.

THE HAUDENOSAUNEE (LEAGUE OF THE IROQUOIS)

The famed League of the Iroquois united five separate nations (from west to east, the Seneca, Cayuga, Onondaga, Oneida and Mohawk) into a single confederacy. The league was established shortly before European contact, during the late fifteenth or sixteenth century. Anthropologist Dean Snow argues that the process had been completed by about 1525. Iroquois oral traditions credit Deganawidah, a supernaturally powerful individual from Huron country to the north, with founding this alliance to promote peace among the five quarrelling groups, a task in which he was aided by his Onondaga convert Hiawatha. He established the Great Law of Peace, which still serves as the constitution of the league. The warring factions buried their weapons under the roots of a great white pine, the Tree of Peace, which is a symbol of the confederacy. The Iroquois visualized their league as a longhouse, with the Seneca and Mohawk the western and eastern doors respectively, and the Onondaga the central "keepers of the fire." Accordingly, the Onondaga were responsible for calling and hosting council meetings of the confederacy. League members refer to themselves as the Haudenosaunee, "the People of the Longhouse." The more common term, "Iroquois," comes from a French version of a word, adopted by the Algonquians from the Basques on the east coast, meaning "killer people." As unsuitable as this term is, it is so widely used, by both Natives and non-Natives, that it is generally retained here.

Although the league was a political and military alliance, its members maintained considerable autonomy, and often acted independently. The Seneca, for example, pursued most vigorously the wars with the Huron and Neutral, while the Mohawk harassed the Algonquian tribes along the St. Lawrence. When the French finally won a truce with the Mohawk, they still found themselves assailed by war parties of Onondaga and Seneca. Over a century later, during the American Revolutionary War, most of the League members supported the British, whereas the Oneida entered the war on the American side.

ABOVE *Eighteenth-century engraving of an Iroquois warrior.* NAC C-3164

Later in Iroquois history, long after the Huron, Petun and Neutral were destroyed, an additional member joined the league. The Tuscarora were a southern Iroquoian group, whose homeland was in what is today North Carolina. They were displaced from their lands by Europeans, which led to the Tuscarora Wars of 1711–13. After their defeat, the Tuscarora fled north to take refuge among the Iroquois. Around 1722 the league formally adopted the Tuscarora as "little brothers," after which it became known as the Six Nations.

The league was governed by a council of fifty chiefs (called *sachems*), among whom the principal Onondaga chief held the position of honour. Each new chief assumed the name of his predecessor, thus perpetuating the council list from when the league was formed. When a chief died, the senior woman in his clan chose his successor from the males eligible for the position. The council attempted to achieve unanimous decisions before taking any action. If lengthy orations and debate failed to produce a consensus, each group was free to follow its own course.

Although there is less ethnohistoric information on the seventeenth-century Iroquois than on the Huron, the Haudenosaunee have survived into modern times. The ethnohistoric and archaeological data are augmented by invaluable nineteenth- and twentieth-century ethnographic studies of the Iroquois, and by the writings of more recent scholars of Iroquois descent. These studies give insights into Iroquoian beliefs and other aspects of their lives not recorded for other Iroquoian groups.

The basic pattern of Iroquois life in the early contact period closely resembled that of the Ontario Iroquoians. They lived in villages of bark-covered longhouses, each sheltering several families related through the women. Society was divided into clans, and membership was transmitted through the female line. They were farmers, growing corn, beans and squash as the basis of the diet, but they also hunted, fished and gathered a variety of wild plant foods. Ceremonies related to planting, ripening of the green corn and beans, and harvest gave structure to lives attuned to the agricultural cycle. They held a Feast of the Dead but did not practise ossuary burial. The Haudenosaunee shared with other Iroquoians the origin story of Sky-Woman and the good and evil twins, with the earth being formed on the back of the Great Turtle. Today, Turtle Island is a much-loved emblem of pan-Indianism.

One well-known aspect of historic Iroquois life was the use of wampum. Wampum beads of white and purple shell were woven into belts, which were given as gifts at all major occasions. Any treaties or other agreements, whether with other Aboriginal groups or Europeans, required that wampum be publicly presented. The Onondaga became the "wampum keepers" of the league, that is, the keepers of the public archives. The use of wampum, however, was fairly recent, probably originating in the fur trade period. Europeans established wampum "factories" on the Atlantic coast to make enough to trade to the Iroquois for beaver pelts. Although wampum was once a form of currency among Europeans, the Iroquois saw it only as a valuable commodity that could be traded or publicly given to mark important events.

European arrival greatly upset the balance of power among the Aboriginal polities. From the beginning of their contact with Europeans, the Iroquois were drawn into war with the French, and this caused massive disruptions in civil life. To strengthen the French alliance with Aboriginal groups who lived along the vital St. Lawrence waterway, Champlain turned his military force against their traditional enemies, the Iroquois. In 1609 and 1610 he actively aided the Montagnais and others in raids against the Mohawk, Champlain himself killing several Mohawk war chiefs who had not yet learned the power of European muskets. To extend French trade into Huronia, Champlain accompanied the Huron and their

Algonquian allies on a raid against an Onondaga town in 1615. Thus French colonial policy intensified traditional warfare and forced the Iroquois to look east for their trade alliances, first with the Dutch, then with the English.

The twin spectres of war and disease greatly weakened the Iroquois in this period. As elsewhere, European explorers and colonists brought with them epidemic diseases to which Native People had no immunity. Early records describe the death and despair that accompanied major outbreaks. In addition, warfare, which was endemic among the Iroquoians from ancient times, was expanded and made more deadly by European alliances and the quest for furs. This stimulated further warfare, as rapidly declining populations sought war captives to replace their losses. The Jesuits stated in 1668 that the Oneida were about two-thirds Huron and Algonquian ex-captives, and that the Seneca were really a medley of Huron, Neutral, Erie and other defeated groups, with only a small core of the original Iroquois population.

Such historic forces led many Iroquois to move northward into what is today Canada. Three waves of arrival had different motivations. In the first, small groups of converts to Catholicism, primarily Mohawk and Oneida, settled near the Jesuit missionaries on the St. Lawrence as early as 1667. During the 1670s, their numbers swelled, as many Mohawk moved north to join this colony. The Jesuits boasted that more Mohawk lived among them than remained in their homeland. As Catholic converts settled among the French, they were soon drawn into conflict with the league Iroquois who remained hostile to the French. After several moves, they established Kahnawake (meaning "at the rapids," the name of one of the original Mohawk villages). Another group of Mohawk, along with many Algonquians, settled a short distance away at Oka, where the community became known as Kanesatake. Although they remained agriculturalists, the Kanesatake Mohawk also shared with the Algonquians the rich hunting grounds to the north. Both settlements exist today as Mohawk communities near Montreal.

Two additional reserve communities later emerged from this first wave of arrivals. In the middle of the eighteenth century, a group split from Kahnawake and moved upriver to establish a settlement known as Akwesasne ("where the partridge drums" in Mohawk). When the international boundary was drawn later in the century, it cut through the middle of Akwesasne. As a result, the modern reserve, near Cornwall, Ontario, has portions in Ontario, Quebec and New York State. In the late nineteenth century, many people left Kanesatake after disputes over land ownership and founded the Gibson Reserve in ancient Huronia, near Georgian Bay in Ontario. These people are now known as the Wahta Mohawk.

The second and largest wave of Iroquois to move into the British territories arrived after the American Revolutionary War. The Mohawk had been the staunchest British allies, though the Seneca, Cayuga and Onondaga eventually also entered the war on the British side. After the war they could not return to their traditional lands in New York State. In reward for their loyalty, one group of

Mohawk under John Deserontyon (or Deseronto) was given land on the north side of Lake Ontario at the Bay of Quinte in 1783. This group is known today as the Mohawks of the Bay of Quinte and their reserve as Tyendinaga. In the following year a larger group, under the famed Mohawk war leader Joseph Brant (Thayendanegea), moved into southern Ontario to lands purchased for them along the Grand River, near what is today Brantford. The nearly two thousand Loyalists who arrived with Brant were mainly Mohawk, Cayuga and Onondaga but also included some Seneca, Oneida and Tuscarora, as well as Delaware and other Algonquian groups who had lost their homelands and sought refuge in the League of the Iroquois. Each established a separate tribal village of log cabins along the Grand River.

The original grant gave the Iroquois all land to a depth of six miles on each side of the Grand River from its mouth to its source. Problems soon developed, however. Brant, an ardent supporter of Iroquois sovereignty, maintained that the land was an unconditional grant as restitution for lands lost in the war, and that the Iroquois could do as they wished with the land, including leasing and selling it to outsiders. Since hunting was unproductive and traditional farming could not support the Iroquois, Brant negotiated numerous land sales to finance a transition to European-style agriculture. This policy brought him into conflict with government officials, who maintained that the land was not alienable and that the Crown had to approve all such transactions. The Iroquois rejected what they considered to be government interference in their affairs and continued to lease and sell land. Not until 1841 was the land surrendered to the Crown to be established as an Indian reserve, and by this time only a small portion of the original land grant remained. This community, containing members of all six Iroquois groups, is today known as the Six Nations of the Grand River.

The council fire of the League of the Iroquois was rekindled among the Six Nations of the Grand River. The fire had been extinguished in their New York homeland during the American Revolutionary War, when no common decision could be reached. The Six Nations in Ontario found themselves with the largest Iroquois population and reinstituted the league in an attempt to establish traditional political patterns in their new land. Once again the Onondaga held the council meetings, and all six Iroquois nations, plus some smaller dependent groups, participated as separate units. However, their decisions were now restricted to a single reserve, and the council acted much like a municipal government. Nevertheless, traditions of separate tribal membership remain strong among the Six Nations.

The third wave of Iroquois moved into the British territory when several hundred Oneida settled north of Lake Erie in the early 1840s. After the American Revolutionary War, the Oneida lost their lands and American relocation policies forced one large group to move to Wisconsin. Another group, wishing to be reunited with the other members of the league, purchased land along the Thames River of southern Ontario, near modern London. Soon after they arrived, they were readmitted to the league and sent their chiefs to council meetings among the Six Nations. Today this group is officially known as the Oneida Nation of the Thames.

In addition to the Iroquois, several Algonquian groups moved into southern Ontario from the American northeast during this resettlement period. Three communities of Delaware now reside in Canada. The first arrived with Joseph Brant in 1784, maintaining a separate Delaware community among the Six Nations. Two other groups, one led by Moravian missionaries, followed in the 1790s, settling on the Thames River near London. The Delaware language, however, is nearly extinct today. Later, mainly between 1835 and 1845, several thousand Potawatomi from the American Great Lakes area entered southern Ontario. Lacking claim to land or treaty rights, most of the Potawatomi settled on reserves of Ojibwa and Odawa bands along western Lake Huron and Georgian Bay. Only two Canadian bands are legally recognized as Potawatomi today (one of these, Walpole Island near Windsor, is listed as mixed Ojibwa/Potawatomi), and few Canadian Potawatomi still speak the language. In addition to these movements from the south, various Ojibwa bands, in a process beginning as early as the late seventeenth century, were filtering from the north into the ancient territories of the Huron, Petun and Neutral, forcefully displacing any Iroquois occupying this area. When the British settled Joseph Brant's Iroquois Loyalists along the Grand River, they had to buy the land from an Ojibwa group known as the Mississauga.

Their spirit of adventure and the rapid westward expansion of the fur trade lured some Iroquois far to the west. These were predominantly the Quebec Mohawk from Kahnawake, Kanesatake and Akwesasne, who were voyageurs and trappers in the fur trade, first for the North West Company and later for the Hudson's Bay Company. By the 1790s small groups of Iroquois were scattered across the plains and into the Rockies in the service of the fur trade companies. In one of the largest movements, a group of about 250 Iroquois accompanied a North West Company expedition to Fort Augustus, near modern Edmonton, in 1798. Many of the men stayed, marrying local Cree women. This mixed population was eventually established as Michel's Band and assigned a reserve. In 1958, by a majority vote, the members of Michel's Band used a provision of the Indian Act to surrender their Indian status and ceased to exist as an Indian band. Their descendants still live in the area, though few traditions of their partial Iroquois heritage remain.

THE CANADIAN IROQUOIS IN THE MODERN ERA

Eight Iroquoian reserve communities exist today in southern Ontario and Quebec. One is Huron (the Nation Huronne Wendat), five are Mohawk, one is Oneida and the largest, Six Nations, contains all six league members, plus several other groups such as the Delaware. All except the Huron moved northward in response to historic political events. By far the most populous Indian band in Canada is Six Nations of the Grand River, and Akwesasne, Kahnawake and

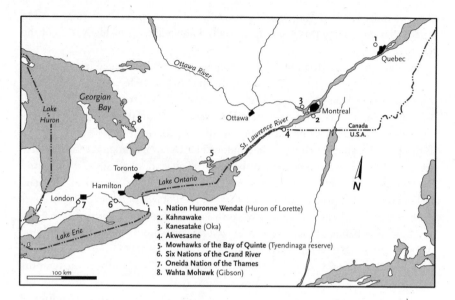

1. Nation Huronne Wendat (Huron of Lorette)
2. Kahnawake
3. Kanesatake (Oka)
4. Akwesasne
5. Mowhawks of the Bay of Quinte (Tyendinaga reserve)
6. Six Nations of the Grand River
7. Oneida Nation of the Thames
8. Wahta Mohawk (Gibson)

ABOVE *Modern Iroquoian communities in Canada*

Mohawks of the Bay of Quinte are the second-, fourth- and eighth-largest respectively. Their total population is almost 60,000 people, more than now live in their American homeland. The Mohawk account for about two-thirds of the total number, and Mohawk is the only Iroquoian language which is not highly endangered in Canada.

In the modern reserve economy, agriculture has played a declining role. The reserve lands under cultivation today are mostly leased to non-Native farmers who have the capital to make modern farming viable. Since few employment opportunities exist on their reserves, most Iroquois commute or relocate to find work in such nearby cities as Montreal, Cornwall, London and Brantford.

Many Iroquois, particularly the Mohawk, work in high-steel construction. Mohawk steelworkers date from 1886, when many men from the reserve constructed a bridge across the St. Lawrence at Kahnawake. The Mohawk were so good at this work that they were sought for similar projects. Today high-steel work continues to be a high-paying and high-status occupation. Although most maintain ties with their home reserve and eventually return there, the demands of their work have meant that Mohawk enclaves have developed in New York, Detroit and other large North American cities.

Contemporary Iroquois artists have adapted traditional forms to meet new market demands. This is particularly true on the Six Nations Reserve, where carving false face masks and making pottery, using modern techniques to produce traditional styles, have been major activities. Handicrafts are also an important source of income for the Huron community in Quebec. Today, Iroquois artists are best known for a recent innovation: detailed carvings sculpted in soft brown soapstone. Perhaps the best-known artist working in this medium is Joe Jacobs, a Cayuga from Six Nations, whose recognition as a major Canadian sculptor has opened the door for a new, distinctly Iroquois art form. Although some younger artists now carve abstract and modern pieces, Jacobs and others continue to carve figures inspired from Iroquois myths and legends.

In religion, the descendants of the first wave of Mohawk settlement remain primarily Catholic. The Mohawks of the Bay of Quinte, the Oneida of the Thames and the Six Nations communities are largely Protestant. At Six Nations, however, much of the population follows the Longhouse religion, and this traditional faction has spread in the twentieth century to Akwesasne, Kahnawake, Kanesatake and the Oneida.

The Longhouse religion is based on traditional Iroquois practices and beliefs. In its most widespread version today, however, it is modified by revelations that the prophet Handsome Lake made among the Seneca in western New York in 1799. He declared that social problems besetting the Iroquois were due to evils introduced by whites; these had to be abandoned and Iroquois ceremonies and values restored. Consequently his visions defined a new moral code, outlawing drunkenness, witchcraft, promiscuity, quarrelling and gambling, and he announced that the world would be destroyed by fire if the Iroquois failed to reform. This message was sufficiently compelling that the new religion and moral code quickly spread to the Six Nations Reserve.

The restored Iroquois ceremonial life takes place in modern longhouses, which now exist on most Iroquois reserves. The ceremonies are essentially rites of thanksgiving, at which speeches and offerings are made and feasts held for all participants. Important ceremonies include Midwinter (or New Year, the longest of the ceremonies), Seed Planting, Bean (held when the green beans are mature), Green Corn (when the first corn is ripe) and Harvest. Also important are the rites of the medicine societies. Particularly well known are the False Face Society and the Husk Face Society, whose members wear masks as part of their curing rituals. The wooden masks of the False Face Society, with their distorted carved faces, flowing horse hair and brass eye plates, depict the humanoid beings seen in the forest or in dreams. The Husk Face Society masks are braided of corn husks and represent agricultural spirits. Both give their wearers extraordinary powers, such as the ability to handle hot coals without being burned, as well as to cure illness. Dreams continue to play an important role in Iroquois religious life, helping to determine the steps one should follow to maintain health and harmony, or the rituals that should be carried out to cure illnesses.

Iroquois society, particularly at Six Nations, is split into two factions. Those in the conservative or traditional faction participate in the Longhouse religion, uphold the code of Handsome Lake, often speak an Iroquois language, tend to emphasize matrilineal descent and recognize clan affiliations, and support the council of hereditary chiefs as the only legitimate government. Non-traditionalists

ABOVE LEFT *Iroquois false face mask.* CMC 74-7172. ABOVE RIGHT *Iroquois false face dancer with turtle-shell rattle, Six Nations Reserve.* CMC J3031

belong to a Christian church (usually Anglican or Baptist at Six Nations), tend not to recognize clan distinctions, deal with the federal government through the elected band council and generally speak English as their main or only language. Both groups highly value their Iroquois heritage, but the larger non-traditionalist faction participates more fully in the broader world around them.

A divisive event occurred at Six Nations in 1924. Members of the traditionalist hereditary council, in accordance with their view of Iroquois sovereignty, followed a policy of non-cooperation with Canadian government officials. They also alienated many of their own people, who viewed them as too conservative and inefficient; because tradition required that they reach unanimity in their deliberations, they were unable to reach decisions on many matters. The Royal Canadian Mounted Police (RCMP) moved in and locked the hereditary council out of the council house, and an elected council was established in its place. Since then, the Canadian government has recognized only this band council. The hereditary council, however, continued to hold regular meetings in the Onondaga longhouse, and it focussed the discontent of the traditionalist faction. Continued unrest led to an uprising in 1959, when a group of traditionalists seized the council house, reinstating the hereditary council and rejecting the Indian Act, before the faction was suppressed by the RCMP. Today both the elected and hereditary councils exist at Six Nations, as well as at Kahnawake and Akwesasne, and traditionalists still see the hereditary chiefs as the only legitimate government.

ABOVE *Upper Cayuga longhouse, Six Nations Reserve. Photo by A. McMillan*

The underlying issue concerns Iroquois sovereignty. From the time of Joseph Brant, the Iroquois at Six Nations have maintained that they are a sovereign people. Today, they espouse their role as loyal allies of the British Crown to assert sovereignty. They continue to reject the policies of the Canadian government, which treats them as dependants, as interference with their internal affairs. Accordingly, they have strongly opposed the Indian Act, which allows little in the way of autonomous decisions, because they assert that they are a separate nation with their own political constitution. Many of the provisions of the Indian Act, such as the insistence on tracing band membership through the father, have run counter to Iroquois practices. In the early 1920s the Six Nations chiefs issued their own passports and sent several of their members to Europe, though they were unsuccessful in their attempt to present their grievance before the League of Nations in Geneva. Later, when federal voting privileges were extended to all Canadian Indians in 1960, many Iroquois opposed this change because they felt their status as a separate nation would be endangered by voting in Canadian elections.

Other contentious issues strengthen the distrust many Iroquois feel for the Canadian government. Particularly galling for the Mohawk of Akwesasne, who live astride the international boundary, is the Canadian government's failure to recognize the Jay Treaty of 1794. One clause in this treaty, signed between Britain and the new American government, promised "nor shall any Indians passing or repassing with their own proper goods and effects of whatever nature, pay for the same any impost or duty whatever." However, the Supreme Court of Canada has ruled that the Customs Act takes precedence, so any reserve residents moving their goods north across the border must pay duties. The Mohawk have protested this issue by blocking the busy international bridge crossing the St. Lawrence River from their reserve. The Akwesasne Mohawk continue to challenge the Canadian government in court cases involving their right to transport goods across the border.

Other specific issues continue to cause discontent. For example, during the construction of the St. Lawrence Seaway, Kahnawake lands were lost to flooding. The Mohawk protested vigorously but lost their legal battle against expropriation. This loss of historic riverfront property led to resentment against the Canadian government and caused the traditionalist faction to grow.

Since the Iroquois see themselves as a separate nation within Canada, they have had few common political ties with other First Nations. For the traditionalists, the most important goal is to re-establish ties between all the Haudenosaunee, on both sides of the border, to recreate the political structure and institutions of the League of the Iroquois and its Great Law of Peace.

In spite of the political turbulence that surrounds them, the People of the Longhouse have retained much of their traditional culture. Most schools at Six Nations today offer instruction in at least one Iroquois language. However, only a small portion of the population speaks their native tongue, and only Mohawk has a good chance at long-term survival. Initiatives such as a Mohawk immersion school program at Kahnawake are helping to reverse the gradual decline in the use of the Mohawk language. Wampum still plays an important role in Iroquois cultural and political identity. Some institutions, such as the Royal Ontario Museum in Toronto, have complied with Iroquois demands and returned wampum belts and false face masks so these items can be used in revitalized Iroquois ceremonies. The longhouse is still the focus of spiritual life for many of the Haudenosaunee.

TENSION AND VIOLENCE IN MOHAWK COUNTRY: THE EVENTS AT AKWESASNE, KAHNAWAKE AND OKA

Violent confrontations troubled all three Quebec Mohawk communities in 1990. The basic issue was discontent around Mohawk self-determination. The Warrior Society emerged among embittered young Mohawk as a voice for Mohawk Nation sovereignty. A tenuous alliance between the Warrior Society and the traditionalists of the longhouse often pitted them against the elected band officials.

Akwesasne, with its unique geographic situation, is where many of the tensions first developed. As both an international and a provincial border slice through this community, two federal and three provincial or state governments all claim jurisdiction. The Mohawk position is that they do not recognize these borders. Three separate Mohawk governments also exist on this reserve: the elected Mohawk Council of Akwesasne on the Canadian side, the St. Regis Tribal Council on the American side and the Mohawk Nation Council of traditional chiefs, which is opposed to the elected councils and rejects the divisions caused by international borders. Eight governmental entities claiming overlapping jurisdictions make Akwesasne an administrative nightmare.

Akwesasne is ideally located for moving goods across the international border without being detected by Canadian authorities. Cigarettes are a major commodity, but alcohol, drugs and firearms are also part of the trans-border traffic. Canadian cigarettes exported to the United States avoid Canada's high taxes on tobacco products, and are transported back across the border at Akwesasne and sold on the Kahnawake Reserve. Although the government brands this movement as smuggling and considers it a criminal activity, many Mohawk argue that it is an exercise in free trade, a right under the Jay Treaty and an expression of Mohawk sovereignty. Large-scale police raids at both Akwesasne and Kahnawake in 1988 failed to stop this enterprise and actually radicalized Mohawk who might otherwise have been moderates. In retaliation, the Kahnawake Mohawk briefly blocked the busy Mercier Bridge into Montreal.

Even more disruptive was the arrival of high-stakes gambling at Akwesasne. A strip of casinos built along the highway on the New York side of the reserve soon served a growing, primarily Canadian, non-Aboriginal clientele. The casinos brought wealth to a few Mohawk and provided employment opportunities in a community where few other jobs were available. The Warrior Society rose to prominence by positioning themselves as the defenders of the casinos (from external or internal opposition) and maintaining that Mohawk sovereignty was at stake. Other Mohawk, however, opposed the unregulated casinos. Early in the struggle, the three Mohawk councils reached agreement that the gambling should stop but they lacked the power to enforce this resolution. The people at Akwesasne became increasingly polarized into pro-gambling and anti-gambling factions.

With considerable money at stake, violence soon flared between these factions. The office of the *Akwesasne Notes* editor, who had used this Mohawk newspaper to argue against gambling, was firebombed. Police cars belonging to the Mohawk Council of Akwesasne, which strongly opposed the casinos, were rammed or shot at. Blockades, erected by anti-gambling forces to deter the busloads of casino patrons, became scenes of increasingly violent confrontations with the Warriors and casino employees. The well-armed Warriors, who were not sanctioned by any tribal authority, were denounced by the Mohawk Nation Council of traditional chiefs as a "lawless and terrorist cult." By early 1990 the slide into what has been called the "Mohawk civil war" was well underway. In April, numerous shootings, beatings and arsons led the Mohawk Council of Akwesasne to begin to evacuate the Canadian side of the reserve, eventually moving several thousand people to temporary lodgings in Cornwall. On May 1 a gunfire battle resulted in the deaths of two Mohawk, whose bodies were found on the Quebec portion of the reserve. The Canadian and American governments, which had refused to intervene in an "internal matter" on the reserve, were forced into action. Hundreds of officers from the RCMP, the Ontario Provincial Police, the Sûreté du Québec and the New York State Police were dispatched to Akwesasne, quelling the violence and closing the casinos.

At the same time, events leading to a new outbreak of violence were taking place at Oka, just west of Montreal. This incident grabbed public attention far more than the situation at Akwesasne, and the Warriors were able to improve their image, from defenders of gambling and smuggling to defenders of Aboriginal land rights.

The land dispute at Oka had been brewing for more than two centuries. In the eighteenth century, the French Crown granted land to the Seminary of St. Sulpice to settle and provide religious instruction to the Mohawk, Algonquin and others under their care. Disputes over land title arose repeatedly in the following centuries. The Sulpicians argued that the Native occupants had no legal rights to the land, and they proceeded to sell off large portions of the original land grant. The Algonquins and some Mohawk moved to other settlements as a result of these disputes. Conflict and legal battles over Sulpician land sales continued until 1945, when the federal government purchased the remaining lands. By this time the area was an ethnic checkerboard: the Mohawk community of Kanesatake occupied small scattered plots of land within and beside the white municipality of Oka. Furthermore, the lands were never legally transferred as an Indian reserve under the Indian Act, which made Mohawk rights to the land they occupied tenuous.

The Kanesatake Mohawk tried repeatedly to resolve their land dispute. In 1961 they attempted, without success, to have their lands formally declared a reserve. In the early 1970s the three Quebec Mohawk communities used the newly established comprehensive claims process to assert Aboriginal title over their territories, but their claim was rejected because they could not demonstrate occupancy since "time immemorial." The Kanesatake Mohawk then initiated a specific claim, based on the principle of federal "lawful obligation," which was also rejected.

For the residents of Kanesatake the final straw was a proposed expansion of the municipal golf course at Oka into the disputed lands. The existing course, with its clubhouse directly adjacent to an historic Mohawk cemetery, already occupied lands the Mohawk considered theirs. On 11 March 1990 a group of Kanesatake Mohawk set up a barricade in the wooded area slated for development. Armed Warriors from Akwesasne and Kahnawake later joined the local residents at the barricade, setting the stage for the conflict to come.

Early in the morning of 11 July 1990 more than one hundred Sûreté du Québec police officers, armed with assault rifles, concussion grenades and tear gas, attacked the Mohawk barricades. In the ensuing shootout one officer was killed and the police were forced to retreat. The police then set up roadblocks around Kanesatake, and the Mohawk erected barricades on the highway, using police vehicles abandoned after the failed raid. At the same time the Mohawk at

Kahnawake blockaded all approaches through their reserve to the Mercier Bridge, the major traffic artery from the south-shore communities to the centre of Montreal. What followed was a tense seventy-eight-day standoff, a time of protracted negotiations and intense media coverage. Six Nations Iroquois Confederacy chiefs mediated the negotiations. In August, the Canadian government sent more than 2000 soldiers to the scene, the first time that Canadian troops had been called out against Aboriginal Peoples since Riel's Northwest Rebellion of 1885. The Kahnawake blockades were finally dismantled and the Mercier Bridge reopened on September 6, but a small group of Warriors and their supporters held out at Kanesatake until September 26.

These events poisoned relations between the Mohawk and surrounding non-Native communities, leading to some ugly racist riots. Citizens of south-shore Montreal communities battled police and burned effigy figures of Mohawk. When women, children and the elderly were evacuated from Kahnawake, police did little to stop the mob that gathered to throw stones and bottles at their vehicles. One elderly Mohawk man suffered a fatal heart attack after this incident.

This protracted conflict was not simply a local outbreak of Native discontent. Most of the Warriors at Oka were from the more populous and militant communities of Akwesasne and Kahnawake, and they viewed their actions as defence of the Mohawk Nation. They were joined at the barricades by people from various First Nations across Canada. First Nations communities in Ontario, the Prairie provinces and British Columbia blockaded highways and railways crossing their reserves to show support for the Mohawk at Oka and to press for settlement of their own land grievances.

The incident at Oka is over but the issues are far from resolved. The federal government has purchased much of the disputed land to create a land base for the Mohawk at Kanesatake. The Warrior Society remains strong at Kahnawake and Akwesasne. The Mohawk continue to assert their right to run their own affairs. An agreement between the federal government and the Mohawk Council of Kahnawake turned jurisdiction for policing, health, social services, education and other cultural matters over to the local council. The Mohawk at Kanesatake also assumed responsibility for running their own police force. A heightened sense of community and Mohawk identity has been one of the legacies of the Oka crisis.

The long troubled "Indian Summer" of 1990 brought Native discontent to wide public attention, across Canada and abroad. Pro-Mohawk demonstrators in many cities around the world denounced Canada's treatment of its First Nations. A South African official publicly rejected Canada's right to criticize other nations for human rights abuses. For a brief period these violent clashes moved First Nations issues to the front of the national agenda, though little in the way of lasting gains resulted.

CHAPTER 5

The Algonquians of the Eastern Woodlands and Eastern Subarctic

· · · · ·

ALL OF NORTHEASTERN North America, except for a wedge along the eastern Great Lakes and St. Lawrence River occupied by Iroquoians, is the traditional territory of the Algonquian First Nations. In Canada, Algonquian languages are spoken from the Atlantic Ocean to the Rocky Mountains. This chapter deals with those of the upper Great Lakes to Hudson Bay, including subarctic Quebec, Ontario and Manitoba. Although known to history by a bewildering array of regional names, they can be classified by language into the broad divisions of Ojibwa, Cree and Innu, each with a number of major dialects.

No firm boundary can be drawn between the Eastern Woodlands and Eastern Subarctic culture areas. The mixed forests of the Woodlands gradually give way to the northern coniferous forests. Strong ties to the Eastern Woodlands are evident from the northern shores of the Great Lakes to southeastern Manitoba. Construction of burial mounds and manufacture of pottery are archaeological traits which link this area with early Eastern Woodlands cultures far to the south. At the beginning of the global era some Algonquian groups practised marginal corn agriculture or traded with the Huron for agricultural produce. These Algonquians also obtained such rituals as the Feast of the Dead from their Iroquoian neighbours. For these reasons, much of the territory the Ojibwa occupied could be included in the Eastern Woodlands culture area rather than the Subarctic. However, the Ojibwa shared the basic fabric of their life with their Algonquian kin to the north.

There is much linguistic confusion concerning the Algonquians, most of which comes from trying to equate languages and social groups. The Algonquians lived in small independent bands, shifting in territory over time, speaking a continuum of mutually intelligible dialects. Among the best-known groups speaking variants of Ojibwa are the Saulteaux, Odawa, Nipissing, Mississauga and Algonquin. In the north, dialects of Cree are spoken from northern Quebec to northern Alberta. Closely related to the Cree are the Innu in Quebec and Labrador.

Anthropologists and others distinguish between the terms Algonquian and Algonquin. Algonquian (or Algonkian) refers to the entire language family, by far the largest in Canada. This broad classification takes its name from the Algonquin, referring to those groups with their traditional lands centred on the Ottawa Valley, along what is today the border between Ontario and Quebec.

Physiographically, the area is dominated by the Canadian Shield, a low, rolling land of forest, rock outcrops and muskeg, with innumerable lakes, ponds and rivers. The climate is continental, characterized by long, extremely cold winters and brief summers. Landforms and resource availability vary markedly from north to south. The more southerly territory of the Ojibwa, in the northern reaches of the mixed forests, provided excellent fishing locations and plentiful wild plant foods such as berries and wild rice. To the north, the boreal forests of the northern Ojibwa and Cree offered fewer plant resources, requiring greater emphasis on hunting. The Algonquians, though they shared many cultural traits, differed considerably throughout the area, and each local community made decisions that best suited its environment.

HOLOCENE CULTURAL DEVELOPMENTS

The Canadian Shield environment poses major challenges and limitations to archaeological reconstruction. The highly acidic soils have destroyed all bone and other organic materials, leaving only stone tools to provide glimpses into how people lived in the distant past. Although some sites may also contain fragments of pottery vessels and occasional tools of copper, the artifact inventory from most is meagre. Small mobile communities of hunters and fishers left few material traces of their passing.

The northern regions were still under thick sheets of glacial ice when small groups of hunters first moved into the southern margins. Large, finely flaked spearpoints identify Plano cultures, the early Holocene hunters who followed the fluted-point makers across much of North America. Although these surface discoveries cannot be directly dated, similar tools found elsewhere are as much as 9000 years old. A unique Plano-era cremation burial site near Thunder Bay gives some insight into their funerary practices and provides a radiocarbon date of almost 8500 years ago. In addition, several Plano quarry sites have been investigated, the best known being Sheguiandah, on Manitoulin Island. Here Plano and later peoples obtained fine-grained quartzite which they chipped into their distinctive tools, leaving the ground strewn with waste flakes, broken artifacts and other debris.

As the glacial sheets retreated northward and boreal forest gradually covered the land, people moved into what is today northern Ontario and Quebec. These cultures, which may have developed directly out of Plano, pursued their livelihood over much of the Eastern Subarctic for thousands of years. This long-lived adaptation to the northern forests is appropriately termed the **Shield culture** (or "Shield Archaic," by many archaeologists). Many Shield culture sites are located at narrows on lakes and rivers where the caribou herds could cross. Fish and caribou would have been the essential resources, though bear, beaver, hare and waterfowl would also have been important. However, because no bone has been preserved, the Aboriginal diet cannot be precisely determined. The sites yield only chipped-stone tools, almost all of which can be classified as either scrapers, knives or projectile points, plus the occasional implement of native copper from western Lake Superior. Sites on islands and along waterways suggest that the birchbark canoe was already an essential part of Aboriginal life, and the same logic assumes that these people had snowshoes for winter travel.

In northern areas, this long-lived cultural pattern gave rise directly to such historic people as the Cree. Shield culture sites persist into the global era, when objects of iron and brass, obtained from the trade in furs, were added to the indigenous tool kit. Modern Cree communities in the northern forests can claim an ancient heritage, extending throughout the Holocene. Although they may not use the same terms as archaeologists, the Cree hold extensive knowledge of their ancient past, which they see expressed in the features of their landscape.

In southern regions, as among the neighbouring Iroquoians, the introduction of pottery marks a new stage—the Ceramic (or Woodland) period. The **Early Ceramic** variant in the central Algonquian area is called the Laurel culture, dated from about 2200 to 1000 years ago. Except for the ceramic technology, no great cultural break is evident from the preceding Shield culture. Laurel sites are distributed in Canada from east-central Saskatchewan through the lakes country of central Manitoba to Lake Superior, possibly extending into northeastern Ontario. The heartland appears to be the Rainy River–Lake of the Woods region of westernmost Ontario, where Laurel sites have their earliest and latest dates and where their most impressive burial monuments are located. In more northerly Ontario, most of subarctic Quebec and in Labrador, however, Aboriginal People never adopted the pottery technology which marks this stage.

In addition to pottery sherds and stone tools, the latter strongly resembling the Shield culture forms from which they developed, many Laurel sites contain such native copper implements as knives, chisels and beads. At Heron Bay, on the north shore of Lake Superior, archaeologist J. V. Wright also found abundant bone tools and refuse. Wood ash from ancient campfires had neutralized soil acidity, and bone artifacts such as harpoon heads, awls, netting needles, beads and beaver-tooth knives, as well as the bones of such food animals as moose and beaver, were preserved. This still provides only a limited view of their material culture, since nothing remains of the wooden, bark and hide objects that would have made up the larger part of their technology.

Important information on long-distance trade connections also comes from the Heron Bay site. Wright's excavation revealed such exotic goods as obsidian from Wyoming (a distance of about 1850 kilometres), shell from southern Manitoba (740 kilometres) and pottery from the Saugeen culture of southern Ontario (580 kilometres). Native copper from Lake Superior was almost certainly the major item being exported. This emphasis on trade along the southern margins of the Shield is shared with Eastern Woodlands groups to the south. In contrast, excavated sites further north in subarctic Ontario and Quebec show little or no evidence of long-distance trade.

Excavation at the Ballynacree site in Kenora exposed an entire late Laurel village. Patterns of dark-stained post moulds suggest that this village consisted of three oval-shaped houses, sheltering about thirty people. The houses appear to have been large domed lodges of bent saplings covered with bark, similar to historic Algonquian structures. The way of life in this community would have seemed familiar to the historic Ojibwa of the area.

Large burial mounds, which would have been important centres of religious life, also characterize Laurel culture; examples from this period occur in Ontario between Lake Superior and the Manitoba border. Particularly well known is a cluster of mounds along the Rainy River. One of these, about thirty-five metres in diameter and seven metres high, is the largest burial mound in Canada. Excavation at a smaller one of the cluster, the Armstrong Mound, revealed that it was built about 1000 years ago, near the end of the Laurel period. Remains of thirteen individuals—most disarticulated bone bundles, liberally covered with red ochre—were unearthed there, indicating that skeletal remains had been collected from elsewhere and ceremonially reburied. The inspiration for mound burials and elaborate mortuary rites lies well to the south, in somewhat earlier cultures such as Hopewell in the central Eastern Woodlands. One stone platform pipe from the Armstrong Mound is typically Hopewell in style.

In the **Late Ceramic** period, which began somewhat over 1000 years ago, regional differences developed out of the relatively uniform Laurel base. There is no sharp distinction between the periods, though new pottery styles appear. Because this stage lasted into the global era, some sites can be attributed, with reasonable assurance, to known ethnic groups. This allows archaeologists to work back in time from historically documented cultures to reconstruct earlier Aboriginal lifeways.

The Late Ceramic culture found from northern Lake Superior to southeastern Manitoba is termed Blackduck. Its distribution straddles the boundary between the Eastern Woodlands and the Subarctic. Blackduck is known primarily by a distinctive pottery style, which may have developed out of the Laurel culture. The well-made globular pots are decorated with cord-wrapped-stick impressions around the neck and rim, frequently with a row of incised punctate elements.

RIGHT Western Algonquian artifacts: (a) fragments of Blackduck pottery vessels; (b) small pottery vessel made for placement in burial mounds; (c) stone pipe; (d) stone amulet in the form of a beaver; (e) stone arrowheads; (f) stone scrapers; (g) stone knife; (h) antler harpoons; (i) gambling disk made from a pottery fragment. CMC 74-18216

However, Blackduck pottery is often found mixed with other styles, suggesting that women, who were the potters in historic times, joined their husbands' bands at marriage. If groups from considerable distances intermarried, a single social group could produce many different styles. Stone tools, along with those of bone where they are preserved, are similar to those of the earlier Laurel culture. Small triangular and side-notched arrowpoints also appear in Blackduck assemblages, as do relatively numerous knives, awls, fish hooks and beads made of native copper, which show that the people had access to the copper deposits of western Lake Superior. The addition of European trade goods to artifacts of Aboriginal manufacture ushered in the global era. Some authorities attribute this complex to the Siouan-speaking Assiniboine, who were living in the area when they were first mentioned in historic documents. The general similarity with surrounding cultures, however, suggests that Algonquian speakers such as the Ojibwa left these remains.

Blackduck people also constructed burial mounds, though these were smaller than their Laurel precedents. The low Blackduck mounds are interspersed with the larger Laurel mounds along the Rainy River, and are also found in southern Manitoba. The mounds show that complex mortuary rites continued into the later period. Archaeologists have found bundled bones covered in red ochre, and on some of the skulls the eye sockets were filled with clay and shell beads inserted. Small pottery vessels were frequently placed with the dead.

To the northwest, a similar culture has been termed Selkirk. This group ranged from northwestern Ontario, across the Shield country of Manitoba and into northeastern Saskatchewan. Archaeological sites of this culture contain distinctive fabric-impressed pottery and a limited variety of stone tools. Occasionally, Selkirk and Blackduck pottery types are found at the same site, which suggests that individuals from considerable distances intermarried and any one social group contained women from several regions. The Selkirk culture is considered to be ancestral Cree in that region. In other locations, however, archaeological cultures identified as Cree did not manufacture pottery.

Similar pottery styles extend only into the westernmost portions of Quebec, though typical St. Lawrence Iroquoian pottery has been unearthed in Algonquian sites along the entire north shore of the St. Lawrence. In interior subarctic Quebec and Labrador, the complete absence of pottery places the entire Holocene sequence in the Shield culture. From their work in the Mistassini region of central Quebec, C.A. Martijn and E.S. Rogers have divided the cultural history into two complexes: the Wenopsk, a regional variant of the Shield culture, which survived with little change from around 6000 years ago to the global era, and the Mistassini, which reflects the historic Cree of the Mistassini area with their abundance of European trade items. Few outside influences seem to have disturbed this long-lived and stable adaptation.

One fascinating though enigmatic type of archaeological site is the red ochre pictograph. Lively depictions of humans, animals and mythological beings adorn rock faces along the waterways of the western regions, from around the northern Great Lakes to the Shield country of northeastern Saskatchewan. They are very

ABOVE *Pictographs at Agawa Rock, Lake Superior, showing Mishipisu (the "horned panther"), serpents and men in canoes. Photo by A. McMillan*

rare in Quebec and the more northerly Shield country in Ontario. The practice of painting these images on rocks almost certainly dates to ancient times, but most surviving examples are relatively recent. Some, depicting horses, rifles and other introduced items, are obviously from the contact period. Occasionally, we can recognize familiar figures from Ojibwa mythology, such as Thunderbird and Mishipisu, the "Great Lynx" or "Horned Panther," a dangerous supernatural creature of the turbulent waters. Similar images appear on the bark scrolls that were part of Ojibwa religious life. Although many pictographs cannot easily be identified or interpreted, they give us unparalleled glimpses into the religious beliefs and practices of the early Ojibwa and their neighbours.

THE ANISHINABEG (OJIBWA-ODAWA-ALGONQUIN)

The Ojibwa (variants include Ojibway, Ochipwe and Chippewa) were originally named for one group north of modern Sault Ste. Marie. The term was later extended to other groups in the upper Great Lakes area that shared the same culture and language. At the beginning of the global era their homeland appears to have been along the northern shores of Lakes Huron and Superior, and its centre was the major fishery at the rapids of Sault Ste. Marie. From this broad base the Ojibwa expanded their territory dramatically, as new opportunities arose. Some moved to the southeast, into lands in southern Ontario made available by Iroquoian dispersal in the seventeenth century. Others pushed south into Wisconsin and Minnesota, displacing, often forcefully, the Dakota. The lucrative fur trade lured many far to the north and west, into the Shield country of northern Ontario and Manitoba, in search of new trapping grounds. Some spread out onto the Plains, becoming the Plains Ojibwa of southern Manitoba and Saskatchewan. As

ABOVE *Ojibwa camp on Lake Huron, a painting by Paul Kane, 1845.* ROM 86 ETH58/912.1.8

the Ojibwa dispersed across a range of environments, significant cultural differences emerged.

When these people first encountered European fur traders there were many similar but politically autonomous groups, which gradually became collectively known as the Ojibwa. Many of the original names are still in use. The term "Saulteaux" comes from the French Saulteurs, or "people of the rapids," and refers to their origins at Sault Ste. Marie. Although used as a near-synonym for Ojibwa, Saulteaux is more commonly applied to western groups, such as those around Lake Winnipeg in Manitoba and Lake of the Woods in Ontario. The American Ojibwa, along with those of southern Ontario, are generally known today as the Chippewa. The Mississauga originally occupied Manitoulin Island and the northern end of Lake Huron, then moved into southern Ontario as early as the seventeenth century. The Nipissing held the land around Lake Nipissing, to the north of the Huron between the Ojibwa and Algonquin. No strongly held common identity existed between these different groups, yet one is emerging today. Many Ojibwa people prefer to be known as Anishinabeg, a term meaning "First People," and the concept of an Anishinabeg Nation now links speakers of the Ojibwa language.

The Odawa (or Ottawa) occupied much of the north shore of Georgian Bay and Manitoulin Island, as well as the Bruce Peninsula, where they bordered on the Huron and Petun. Their role as intermediaries in the trade with these Iroquoian groups gave rise to their name ("traders"). Their lifestyle and language closely resembled the neighbouring Ojibwa and the Potawatomi of lower Lake Michigan. Indeed, these three groups shared a belief in a common origin and remained allied throughout the contact era in a loose confederacy known as the Council of the Three Fires. Several modern reserve communities in Ontario trace their ancestry to all three groups. The Algonquin inhabited the Ottawa Valley and adjacent regions in the early contact period. Linguists have classified Ojibwa, Odawa and Algonquin as a single language with numerous dialects. Thus the terms Anishinabeg and Ojibwa today often include the Odawa and Algonquin, though these both survive as separate designations for First Nations.

The numerous politically independent bands that made up the Ojibwa people were linked by intermarriage and common traditions. Each had its own chief and hunting territories. Bands dispersed into family hunting units much of the year, assembling in greater numbers only during late spring and summer. Leadership positions were informal, and chiefs held power by virtue of their prowess in hunting, warfare or shamanism. No single leader united the Ojibwa people or could speak for more than his small band.

Ojibwa society was divided into clans, each identified by a clan symbol or totem. William Warren, the mid-nineteenth-century half-Ojibwa chronicler of their traditions, stated that they "are divided into several grand families or clans, each of which is known and perpetuated by a symbol of some bird, animal, fish, or reptile which they denominate the Totem or Do-daim (as the Ojibways pronounce it)" (1885: 34). Warren lists twenty-one totems, of which the most important were the crane, catfish, bear, marten, wolf and loon. The living totem animals were not worshipped, and clan members did not refrain from killing them for food, though a certain respect had to be shown. Clan membership was patrilineal; that is, children inherited their totem animal from their fathers. Persons sharing the same totem were considered to be close kin, and intermarriage was forbidden, even if they came from widely separated bands.

Ojibwa subsistence was based on an annual round of hunting, fishing and plant collecting. Men took great pride in their prowess as hunters and devoted the winter to the pursuit of moose, deer, bear and other game. However, by the mid-seventeenth century beaver was the most sought-after animal due to the demands of the fur trade.

In spring, families returned from their hunting camps to rejoin others at their major fishing sites. Pickerel, pike and suckers could be taken throughout the summer, and autumn spawning brought whitefish, trout and sturgeon close to shore. The Ojibwa netted or speared great quantities of fish, and the fisheries were centres of community life. Particularly good fishing locations attracted large concentrations of people. We know from the writings of the Jesuits that during the mid-seventeenth century up to 2000 individuals might congregate at the rapids of Sault Ste. Marie. A 1670 account indicates that the local Saulteurs at the rapids played host to nine other groups, including some visiting Cree from the north.

Plant foods played an important role in the Ojibwa economy. They tapped maple trees in early spring and collected the sweet sap in buckets. Boiled down to

ABOVE *Ojibwa fishermen at the Sault Ste. Marie rapids, a painting by William Armstrong, 1869.*
NAC C-114501

a coarse maple sugar, it seasoned a wide range of foods. In summer large stores of berries were collected. Wild rice (not a true rice but a cereal grass), which grows in the shallow water around the edges of lakes, ripened in late summer. Harvesters worked in groups of two, often a husband and wife. While the man poled the canoe through the beds, the woman bent stalks over the canoe and knocked off kernels with a stick, continuing until the canoe was full. The kernels were then dried in the sun, parched over a slow fire, pounded and winnowed to remove the husk, and stored. This plant was a staple food for the many Ojibwa fortunate enough to live in areas where it abounded.

The western Ojibwa did not practise agriculture, but those groups in contact with the Huron raised some crops. The Odawa relied considerably on their crops of corn, beans and squash. The Nipissing and Algonquin, though they cultivated small plots of corn around their summer camps, could not depend on horticulture due to poor soil and uncertain weather. As a result, they traded furs and fish to the Huron to obtain much of their agricultural food. A good description of the Nipissing annual round, showing the importance of trade in their economy, was given by the Jesuit Father Lalemant in 1641:

> They seem to have as many abodes as the year has seasons,—in the Spring a part of them remain for fishing, where they consider it the best; a part go away to trade with the tribes which gather on the shore of the North or icy sea.... In summer, they all gather together ... on the border of a large lake which bears their name.... About the middle of Autumn, they begin to approach our Hurons, upon whose lands they generally spend the winter; but, before reaching them, they catch as many fish as possible, which they dry. This is the ordinary money with which they buy their main stock of corn, although they come supplied with all other goods.... They cultivate a little land near their Summer dwellings; but it is more for pleasure, and that they may have fresh food to eat, than for their support. Thwaites, *Jesuit Relations 21: 239–41*

Food was roasted or boiled. Although some Odawa and other southern groups used clay pots for cooking, birchbark vessels were far more popular, being more suitable for a highly mobile people. A typical meal might include meat and fish cooked with boiled wild rice or corn and sweetened with berries or maple sugar.

To move efficiently between their hunting and fishing grounds, wild rice fields and maple tree groves, the Ojibwa paddled birchbark canoes, which were ideal in this land of rivers and lakes. Canoes were made of large sheets of bark, easily peeled from the birch trees of the northern forests, then sewn with spruce root over a wooden frame. Seams were sealed with spruce or pine gum. Tough yet lightweight, the canoe could be portaged easily between waterways. In winter, canoes were cached and people travelled on foot, using snowshoes and hauling their belongings on toboggans.

Since they moved often, the Ojibwa designed housing that was easily constructed and largely removable. They built several styles of dwelling, though the

ABOVE *Ojibwa camp on Lake Winnipeg, 1884, showing two types of birchbark lodges.* CMC 594

principal form was the dome-shaped structure known throughout northeastern North America by the Algonquian term "wigwam." To make one, they drove saplings into the ground in a circular or elliptical pattern, then bent the poles over and tied them together at the top. Sheets of birchbark covered the structure. Rush mats sometimes formed the sides, but durable and water-resistant birchbark was required for the roof. Several layers of bark, separated by moss for insulation, might be used on winter houses. A flap of matting or hide covered the entryway, and a hole in the top allowed smoke to escape. In addition to the dome-shaped wigwam, a conical or tipi-shaped structure, also covered with sheets of bark, was common. Most structures sheltered only one family, though several related families might occupy the larger elliptical forms.

Women stitched together tanned hides of deer or moose using thread of nettle fibre or sinew to make clothing. A woman would wear moccasins, leggings and a deerhide dress belted at the waist, whereas a man's outfit consisted of breechcloth, hip-high leggings and moccasins. A heavy coat, generally of thick moosehide, was added in winter. Cold weather clothing might also include caps and mittens of beaver or other fur, and moccasins lined with rabbit skin. Dyes and porcupine-quill embroidery added decoration. When the traders' beads became available, Ojibwa women decorated moccasins, pouches and other clothing with elaborate beadwork. They also took care with their hair, which was generally worn long and braided by both sexes, and was kept shiny and in place by rubbing in bear grease or deer tallow. Faces were often greased and painted.

Numerous opportunities existed for social interaction. A child's naming required a small ceremony and a feast. The Ojibwa celebrated a boy's first kill, even if no larger than a rabbit or bird, with a feast at which all present sampled the meat and praised the boy's efforts. In the summer camps the larger social groups feasted, danced, played lacrosse and gambled with bone dice. Young people looked for prospective mates at these events, since the preferred marriage partner was a cross-cousin (that is, the offspring of the father's sister or mother's brother, who would belong to a different clan).

On cold and dark winter evenings, as people sat around the fires in their wigwams, they listened to tales told by the elders. Ojibwa mythology both instructed and entertained. The rich oral traditions were filled with supernatural humans and animals, one of the most prominent being the culture hero Nanabush (or Nanabozho). Known as Glooscap among the Mi'kmaq and Wisakedjak among the Cree, this supernatural figure occupied a central place in Ojibwa beliefs. Nanabush, the old stories say, put the earth and the animals into their present form and his actions are responsible for the many prominent features of the landscape today. He played an ambiguous role as both a benefactor to humans and a self-indulgent and occasionally obscene trickster.

The most terrifying of the legendary figures was the Windigo, a supernatural giant with an insatiable hunger for human flesh. He haunted the forests during the dark and cold months of winter, retreating to the north when warmer weather arrived. His size and supernatural strength made him a dreaded foe who could not be killed by ordinary weapons. Only a powerful shaman could destroy a Windigo. Any unexplained disappearance, such as a hunter's failure to return from the forest, was taken to mean that he had fallen prey to the Windigo. This monster was particularly feared, as conditions of near starvation (which were not uncommon during the later months of winter) could transform an ordinary human into a Windigo. Hunger might become a craving for human flesh, causing an individual to commit real or imagined acts of cannibalism, and then to metamorphose into the dreaded monster. Anyone suspected of becoming a Windigo could be put to death immediately, and those who, in extremes of hunger, began to lust for human flesh might request their own execution.

Many other powerful supernatural beings inhabited the Ojibwa world. Thunderbirds, who controlled the weather, lived in nests of stones on high mountaintops constantly shrouded in clouds. Lightning flashed from their eyes, and the flapping of their wings caused thunder. The power they could bestow made them particularly sought after as guardian spirits. Their mortal enemies and the main targets of their lightning bolts were the generally malevolent denizens of the waters, such as the Great Serpent and Mishipisu, a large and dangerous horned feline.

Lesser spirits also filled the Ojibwa world. Every animal, bird and plant, as well as some inanimate objects, had a power that could either help or hinder humans. Such a power or supernatural force was called *manitou*. The Jesuit Father Allouez, travelling among the "Outaouacs" (Odawa) in the mid-1660s, described their beliefs:

> The Savages of these regions recognize no sovereign master of Heaven and Earth, but believe there are many spirits—some of whom are beneficent, as the Sun, the Moon, the Lake, Rivers, and Woods; others malevolent, as the adder, the

dragon, cold, and storms. And, in general, whatever seems to them either helpful or hurtful they call a Manitou, and pay it . . . worship and veneration. Thwaites, *Jesuit Relations 50: 285*

Manitous could be beseeched or placated by offerings of tobacco, or occasionally by the sacrifice of a dog.

The most sacred force was Kitchi Manitou ("Great Spirit"), often identified as the sun. He was the ultimate source of all power, but was remote and had little to do with everyday human affairs. Although he played a prominent role in more recent Ojibwa religious thought, Kitchi Manitou did not appear in the early historic accounts (such as that of Father Allouez) and may be a fusion of introduced Christian concepts and traditional Native beliefs.

When young people reached adolescence, they sought the assistance of supernatural beings through a vision quest. Children, particularly boys, secluded themselves in the forest, refraining from food, drink and sleep until a vision appeared. This vision revealed their guardian spirit, and they learned the particular powers they were to receive later in life. Whether they would be successful in hunting, in warfare or in shamanism depended upon the guardian spirit they acquired at this time. Many of the rock paintings depicting humans, animals and supernatural beings were created as part of such quests for supernatural power.

The Ojibwa were widely respected for their shamanic abilities. Shamans could cure illness, see into the future and provide charms or potions to ensure success in love or on the hunt. One well-known ritual was the Shaking Tent, in which a shaman summoned his spirit helpers to a small lodge by drumming and singing. The sudden violent shaking of the tent and the babble of voices emanating from it announced the spirits' arrival. Other shamans used their powers for malevolent purposes. Unexplained illnesses and deaths were considered the work of evil sorcerers.

Although they shared their religious beliefs and practices with the other central Algonquians, the Ojibwa developed a unique formal organization of shamans. This was the famous Midewiwin (literally "mystic doings") or Grand Medicine Society. As well as its primary role in curing illness, the Midewiwin became the main expression of Ojibwa religious concepts. It was a structured hierarchy with a number of distinct levels, and was open to both men and women. Prolonged periods of instruction into the secret lore and rituals, along with a substantial payment, preceded each initiation to a higher level. Members used birchbark scrolls incised with pictures to teach ritual songs and other lore required for each initiation. Nineteenth-century accounts describe four successive levels; however, when Ruth Landes did her ethnographic fieldwork in Ontario and Minnesota in the 1930s, there were eight—the first four called earth grades and the second four called sky grades. Few people progressed beyond the lower levels, due to the great costs and fear of the sorcery involved in the higher levels. Each initiate had a medicine bag, which held the herbal remedies used in curing, and the *migis*, a small white shell that was ceremonially "shot" into new members, infusing them with spirit power. Because of extensive training Midewiwin members became the repositories of traditional religious knowledge.

Ethnohistoric accounts of this society, lacking in the seventeenth-century *Jesuit Relations*, first appear early in the eighteenth century. The Midewiwin seems to have originated after Christian missionaries impressed elements of their religion into traditional Ojibwa beliefs. In response to European pressure to change their culture, Native people may have established the organization to preserve their traditions. As such it parallels other nativistic movements, such as the Longhouse religion of the Iroquois and the Ghost Dance that emerged much later among Plains tribes.

Some Ojibwa groups practised the Huron Feast of the Dead, which was apparently introduced through the Nipissing, who were major trading partners of the Huron. Father Lalemant described such a ceremony among the Nipissing in 1641. He noted that about 2000 people attended, including some Huron and Ojibwa from as far away as the rapids of Sault Ste. Marie. The display and exchange of valuable gifts featured prominently at this gathering. As well as a communal reburial of the dead, the ceremony publicly installed new chiefs and renewed alliances, both between Algonquian groups and with the Huron. However, the Feast of the Dead appears to have disappeared from Algonquian culture after the Huron dispersal and the establishment of French missions later in the seventeenth century.

Alliances were essential in organizing war parties, especially against their hated enemies, the Iroquois and Dakota. War parties set out to avenge previous deaths and to provide young men with opportunities for glory. Warriors armed themselves with bows and arrows, spears, knobbed wooden clubs and moosehide shields. Typically they stealthily approached the enemy camp, then rushed in and killed as many of the foe as possible. Scalps were taken, and later stretched over wooden hoops and placed on poles to be carried during a victory dance.

In the period covered by early historic documents, the eastern Ojibwa were embroiled in warfare with the Iroquois. After dispersing the Huron and Petun, the Iroquois turned their military might against the Algonquin, Nipissing and Odawa. Their raids took them as far as Sault Ste. Marie and farther north. The Nipissing and the Odawa were driven far to the west, and were not able to return to their homelands for several decades. They were not simply on the defensive, however, as we know from Jesuit accounts that an alliance of Algonquians ambushed and destroyed a sizable Mohawk and Oneida war party near Sault Ste. Marie in 1662. By the end of the seventeenth century, as Iroquois power waned and beaver became scarce, the Ojibwa embarked on expansion, ultimately to occupy the vast area they inhabit today.

THE CREE

The term "Cree" is a contraction of Kristinaux, Kiristinon or a host of other variants by which one group speaking this language was known to early French explorers. A Jesuit account of 1640 refers to the "Kiristinon, who live on the shores of the North sea [James Bay] whither the Nipisiriniens [Nipissings] go to trade" (Thwaites, *Jesuit Relations* 18: 229).

The distribution of Cree speakers at European contact is difficult to determine. However, they seem to have occupied the lands surrounding James Bay, including far into what is today the interior of Quebec. Their territory appears to have extended north almost to the Churchill River along the western shores of Hudson Bay, west at least as far as Lake Winnipeg and south to Lake Nipigon. Seventeenth-century accounts indicate that they frequently visited the northern shores of Lake Superior, and on a number of occasions they were reported to be fishing at Sault Ste. Marie as guests of the Ojibwa.

The Cree obtained firearms early on through the fur trade on Hudson Bay, and they used these arms to increase their territory dramatically. Lured by profits from furs, the Cree expanded far to the west, eventually living in southern portions of the Western Subarctic as far as the Peace River of Alberta. Many groups pushed out onto the Plains, allying with the Assiniboine against their enemies and adapting their culture to become Plains warriors and bison hunters. By the early nineteenth century Cree speakers occupied the largest geographic area of any Aboriginal group in Canada, reaching from the interior of Quebec to the Rockies.

Although a single language was spoken throughout this vast area, dialectal differences meant that only neighbouring groups could converse easily. Linguistic studies have isolated nine major dialects: Plains Cree (spoken on the Plains and in the western woodlands), Woods Cree (spoken in the woodlands of central Saskatchewan and Manitoba), West and East Swampy Cree (two dialects spoken in the lowlands to the west of Hudson and James Bays), Moose Cree (spoken south of James Bay), East Cree (spoken through a large area of subarctic Quebec east of James Bay), Attikamek or Tête de Boule (spoken in the upper Saint-Maurice River region of Quebec), and Naskapi and Montagnais (spoken in eastern Quebec and Labrador). Groups speaking the latter two dialects are better known as the Innu today. They have maintained a distinct separate identity and are treated separately here, though many linguists place their language in the Cree continuum.

Throughout their Subarctic environment (the Plains Cree are discussed in chapter 6), the Cree were primarily hunters. Moose, caribou, bear and beaver were the main prey. When they failed to take big game, smaller but more plentiful animals such as hare became crucial for survival. Geese and other waterfowl were also seasonally important, particularly for the Swampy Cree of the Hudson Bay Lowlands. Snares and deadfall traps were widely used, as were bows and arrows. Fishing, though not as highly valued, was important socially, as it brought together larger groups. Although they enjoyed berries in the summer, plant foods played a limited role in their diet.

In general, the environment in which the Cree lived was less bountiful than the Ojibwa lands to the south. Winter conditions were harsh, with extremely cold temperatures, heavy snowfall and short periods of daylight. When strong winds coincided with low temperatures, hunters could freeze to death. In summer, though the climate was pleasant, innumerable ponds and bogs made travel more difficult, and people were tormented by swarms of mosquitoes and blackflies. As well, resources were scarce. Many of the plant foods collected by the Ojibwa did not grow in the northern forests of the Cree, and even good fishing locations were relatively rare. Since the Cree hunted solitary forest animals that were scattered thinly across the land, people lived in small social groups and were often on the move. Winter starvation was always a possibility, and survival cannibalism, though abhorrent, was not unknown. The spectre of the Windigo was never far from their winter camps.

Cree material culture was similar to that of the Ojibwa. Before winter freeze-up the Cree crossed their land of waterways in light birchbark canoes. During the winter they travelled on snowshoes, toboggans and sleds. Housing was the conical wigwam, usually covered with caribou or moose hides rather than birchbark, which was not common in the northern forests. In some areas winter houses were constructed of sod and earth over closely spaced poles. Clothing, predominantly of tanned caribou or moose hides, resembled that of the Ojibwa. It was frequently embellished with quillwork, which was replaced in later times by beadwork and coloured threads in floral designs. An early Jesuit description of ceremonial finery comes from a 1671 encounter with East Cree men "with painted faces, and adorned with all their costliest ornaments,—such as high head-dresses and porcelain collars, belts, and bracelets" (Thwaites, *Jesuit Relations* 56: 173).

The Cree had several levels of social organization: the nuclear family, the hunting group (or local band) and the community (or regional band). Individuals tended to wed at an early age, and one was not considered an adult until married. Although the Cree preferred cross-cousin marriage, this was far from an inevitable rule. Most marriages were monogamous, but a good hunter might take several wives, who were often sisters. Three to five nuclear families, usually related though sometimes linked only by bonds of friendship, made up the hunting group, and they lived and travelled together throughout much of the year. The community, the largest social aggregate, consisted of all those who gathered at one location during the summer months, generally at a favoured fishing locale on the shore of a lake, where breezes kept away annoying insects. Later, trading posts became centres of such gatherings. Although it did not function as an economic unit, this larger group provided opportunities for social interaction and for young people to search for spouses. The structure was highly flexible, and any family that was dissatisfied could join relatives in other groups.

At hunting camps labour was divided based on sex. Males hunted and trapped. Small groups of men worked together, often leaving the base camp for days at a time while they travelled great distances in search of game. They butchered their kills and hauled back meat from the hunt. Men also did the heavy work: they transported supplies and set up camp, and they manufactured most wooden articles, such as toboggans, sleds and snowshoe frames. Women performed their tasks near the base camp. They caught fish with set lines and hunted or trapped small game such as hare and ptarmigan. In the camp women also gathered and split firewood, replaced conifer-bough flooring, cooked meals, prepared hides and pelts, and constantly manufactured and mended moccasins, mittens and other apparel. Adolescent daughters aided in these tasks and in the care of younger children.

Hunting involved far more than simply tracking and killing animals. To the Cree, hunting was a religious activity and only through proper ceremonial acts could humans wrest from nature their means of livelihood. A successful kill was brought about not just by the skill of the hunter but was also a "gift" from the animal. If the hunter did not show respect, the animal would not allow itself to be taken in the future. The bear commanded particular consideration, but caribou, beaver and other animals also had to be respected. The hunter thanked the animal he had killed and offered it tobacco. When larger animals were taken, the hunter held a feast, to which all members of the hunting group were invited. Small portions of meat were placed in the fire as offerings to ensure future successful hunts, and the bones were handled carefully so the animals would not be offended. Bear and beaver skulls might be suspended from trees, whereas other bones were laid on special platforms to keep them out of reach of camp dogs. Dogs were fed only the meat or bones of abundant and less-valued species, such as hare and fish.

Other rituals involved divination, to locate the animals or to predict the outcome of the hunt. Scapulimancy was one such practice. A caribou scapula (shoulder blade) was placed on hot coals, and the resultant cracks and scorch marks were read to determine trails and the location of game. In addition, a shaman might perform the Shaking Tent ritual to summon spirit assistance and direct hunters to the animals they sought.

THE INNU (MONTAGNAIS AND NASKAPI)

The Montagnais (French for "mountaineers," due to the rugged topography of their land) and Naskapi (of uncertain derivation, but thought to be from a derogatory term meaning "uncivilized people" applied to the more northerly bands) occupy eastern Quebec and Labrador. The Naskapi inhabit the northern, largely barren-ground environment of the interior of Quebec east of Hudson Bay to the central Labrador coast, whereas the Montagnais dwell in the forested country to the south, which extends to the northern shores of the Gulf of St. Lawrence and the lower St. Lawrence River. They differ little in language and culture, except where they have adapted to somewhat different environments. Today they

ABOVE *Innu camp, Labrador.* CMC 54584

refer to themselves as Innu (or "person"), though many of the Quebec groups retain the term Montagnais.

In the north, the Naskapi subsisted mostly on the herds of barren-ground caribou. During autumn migrations, caribou were speared from canoes as they crossed rivers or lakes. In winter, hunters on snowshoes drove caribou into deep snow and shot them with bows and arrows while the animals floundered in the drifts. During the summer some Naskapi moved to the Labrador coast to fish, whereas others remained inland to fish in lakes and rivers and to hunt small game.

The Montagnais had access to a wider range of resources. They took mostly moose and woodland caribou, though they also hunted and trapped a variety of smaller forest animals. Coastal resources along the Gulf of St. Lawrence were also important. Fish played a prominent role in the diet, and large numbers of eels were taken in weirs during the early autumn. Seals could be hunted by canoe or clubbed on the rocky beaches. Edible roots and berries were present, and maple trees could be tapped for sap. In addition, those closest to the Huron traded moosehides for corn and tobacco.

Innu social groups varied with the seasons. Winter hunting camps consisted of several, usually related, nuclear families. Successful hunters, those who had "power" over animals, became leaders, but they led by example only and no person held authority over another. Groups were not permanent, and new combinations of families could be formed in successive winters. In summer, small groups emerged from the mosquito-infested woods to gather on the shores of large interior lakes or at the mouths of rivers. These summer camps were the largest social groupings, and they provided the major opportunities for social interaction and festivities.

Material culture was similar to that of neighbouring Algonquians. The birchbark canoe, snowshoes and toboggan were all essential to seasonal movements. Housing was usually the conical wigwam, covered with birchbark among the Montagnais and caribou hide among the Naskapi. Most clothing was made from caribou hide. Among the best-known examples of Innu material culture in museum collections today are the long, tailored, finely crafted caribou-hide coats produced by Innu women. The motifs of the intricate geometric patterns painted on the coats appeared to the hunters in dreams and helped ensure success in the hunts for caribou.

ABOVE *Labrador Innu, ca. 1880.*
CMC J-6541

Innu religion was intensely personal. If individuals respected the animals and "lived the right life," they acquired increasing powers of communication with the spirit world. Those who made a particular effort to obtain spirit power could become shamans and hold the Shaking Tent ritual or interpret the cracks on burnt animal bones to determine the location of game. The Innu made offerings to the spirits of animals they had killed, and carefully placed the bones, especially skulls of bears and beavers, in trees or on platforms. A successful hunt required a feast—especially following a caribou kill, when hunters ritually consumed marrow from the long bones. Following the feast, each hunter played the drum and sang hunting songs given to him by the spirits.

During the period of early contact with Europeans, the Montagnais were embroiled in bitter conflict with the Iroquois. The Montagnais also fought with the Mi'kmaq and the Inuit, but the Iroquois were their most hated foes. In the early contact period trade rivalries along the St. Lawrence intensified these traditional enmities. Champlain allied himself with the Montagnais and nearby Algonquians, accompanying them on raids deep into Iroquois territory. One war party assembled at the mouth of the Saguenay River numbered 1000 warriors. By the late seventeenth century, however, the Montagnais were greatly weakened by warfare, European diseases, depletion of game and displacement from their lands along the St. Lawrence.

IMPACT OF THE FUR TRADE

When European explorers and traders arrived in the early seventeenth century, the Algonquians of the St. Lawrence found themselves drawn into a new pattern of social and economic relations. With the newcomers greedy for furs, and the more distant Native groups eager to obtain European metal and cloth, the Montagnais, Algonquin, Nipissing and Odawa were ideally situated as intermediaries in the early fur trade along the St. Lawrence River. Iron knives and hatchets, copper kettles and other European items were traded for large quantities of furs, which could be taken down the river to Quebec and exchanged at great profit. As early as the 1630s one French observer commented that European clothing had largely replaced traditional garb, and that copper kettles were so widely used that cooking vessels of bark were only a memory. The St. Lawrence was a route to riches, and the Algonquians had to contend with an Iroquois bid for its control. To the north, the Cree also entered this trade relationship when the newly formed Hudson's Bay Company started to establish trading posts on the shores of Hudson and James Bays after 1670. Groups living far inland began to make annual journeys down to salt water to exchange their accumulated furs for coveted European wares.

Seeking new trapping lands for beaver and other fur-bearing animals, the Ojibwa and Cree expanded westward before the end of the seventeenth century, and continued doing so through most of the eighteenth. The Ojibwa pushed west to Lake Winnipeg and north far into territory formerly held by the Cree. By the mid-eighteenth century large groups of Ojibwa were making trading trips to Fort Albany, a Hudson's Bay Company post on James Bay. The northern Ojibwa intermingled with the Cree, abandoning such southern traditions as the Midewiwin and totemic clans, and living in small, scattered hunting and fishing bands identical to the Cree. Today several northern Ojibwa bands consider themselves to be (and are officially designated as) Cree, whereas others in northern Ontario and Manitoba are listed as "mixed" Ojibwa-Cree. "Oji-Cree" emerged as a distinct language, and is still widely spoken in northern Ontario and Manitoba.

Until the late eighteenth century, Hudson's Bay Company employees were content to remain in their coastal "factories" (major trading posts), waiting for the Algonquians to arrive with furs. Such posts as York Factory, Fort Albany and Moose Factory on Hudson and James Bays drew Native traders from great distances inland. Competition developed from the generally French, Montreal-based trade along the Great Lakes–St. Lawrence River system. Rather than waiting for Native groups in a few fixed locations, the French spread far into Algonquian lands to pursue trade, often settling there and taking Native wives. The Algonquians quickly realized that this competition could be used to demand greater returns for their furs.

After the fall of New France in 1760, merchants of English and Highland Scots descent took over the trade through Montreal, and the North West Company was eventually established. This was a time of intense competition, which finally disturbed the Hudson's Bay Company's long complacency in the north and required its traders to set up posts inland. These two great rival companies pushed westward, struggling for control of the trade, each attempting to establish posts in the most advantageous locations. This period of "taking the trade to the Indians" lasted until 1821, when the North West Company was finally absorbed by its competitor. Although the price of goods rose and many posts were closed, the Hudson's Bay Company continued the fur trade among the northern Algonquians into modern times.

The fur trade had a great impact on Aboriginal life. Many indigenous implements of stone, bone, wood and hide were quickly replaced by purchased objects of iron, copper and cloth. As a Montagnais chief joked: "The Beaver does everything perfectly well, it makes kettles, hatchets, swords, knives, bread; and, in short, it makes everything" (Thwaites, *Jesuit Relations* 6: 297). Traders' firearms made hunting more efficient but forced hunters to rely on the posts for ammunition. Many Algonquian groups began to emphasize trapping fur-bearing animals over hunting food animals, and this required a shift in their diet to European foodstuffs. Such staples as flour, lard, sugar and tea, as well as tobacco, became necessities, tying Native groups to the trading posts for supplies. Liquor was also widely distributed, with devastating impact, by traders. The overall effect was to destroy Native self-sufficiency, making the Algonquians at least partially dependent upon the traders, and many bands began to establish their summer camps around the posts. Some Cree bands became the "Home Guard Indians," settling around the posts and provisioning the traders.

Social changes also resulted from the fur trade. The socially prominent Native men who bargained with the traders on behalf of their bands became known as "captains." They received presents, including food and tobacco, to be distributed among their people, in exchange for ensuring that their groups returned to the same post the following year. This new leadership position, however, was as limited as traditional roles; authority lasted only as long as the trading expedition.

Another trade change in Algonquian culture was the system of land tenure. Early in the twentieth century, Frank Speck documented well-defined family hunting territories among the Algonquians and concluded that this was a fundamental feature of Algonquian life that had survived years of cultural change. Later anthropologists, however, viewed this as another adaptation to the fur trade. Since food was shared, access to hunting lands was originally open to all. However, taking animals for furs was an individual act for private profit. Accordingly, individuals attempted to keep others from what they regarded as "their" resources. The distinction between food and furs is clear in Eleanor Leacock's study of the Montagnais, in which she states that a man could kill a beaver on another's land if it was needed for food but not to obtain the fur for sale.

The beaver and other fur-bearing animals could not withstand such sustained pressures. In traditional hunting, the Algonquians practised conservation measures, since there was no advantage in having an overabundance of meat. During the fur trade, firearms and steel traps became available and an apparently limitless market for furs allowed the Algonquin to purchase the European goods on which they had become dependent. Along the St. Lawrence, beaver were already scarce by the mid-seventeenth century, and by the early nineteenth century they were depleted from all but the most remote regions. With game stocks also largely eliminated, many Native groups found themselves hard pressed to avoid starvation. Their plight is described by explorer and fur trader David Thompson at the end of the eighteenth century:

> The Nepissings, the Algonquins and Iroquois Indians having exhausted their own countries, now spread themselves over these countries, and as they destroyed the Beaver, moved forwards to the northward and westward; the Natives, the Nahathaways [Cree], did not in the least molest them.... For several years all these Indians were rich, the Women and Children, as well as the Men, were covered with silver brooches, Ear Rings, Wampum, Beads and other trinkets. Their mantles were of fine scarlet cloth, and all was finery and dress. The Canoes of the Furr Traders were loaded with packs of Beaver.... Every intelligent Man saw the poverty that would follow the destruction of the Beaver, but there were no Chiefs to controul it ... almost the whole of these extensive countries were denuded of Beaver, the Natives became poor, and with difficulty procured the first necessities of life.... *Tyrell 1916: 205*

In his controversial book *Keepers of the Game*, American historian Calvin Martin contended that hunting was traditionally a "holy occupation," based on respect and understanding between humans and animals. Spiritual reprisal, which could take the form of illness, would follow any wanton slaughter of game. Martin argued that the introduction of European diseases, in some areas before Europeans themselves had arrived, broke this mutual compact. Blaming the animals for the illness and death that beset them, Native People were no longer bound by traditions of respect and could literally "make war upon the animals." Equipped with European technology, lured by European commodities and unrestrained by the old taboos the Algonquians proceeded to overkill the game. Anthropologists, however, have strongly challenged Martin's thesis. The link between disease and animals is tenuous, and some historic references clearly indicate that Aboriginal People rightly perceived Europeans as the cause of their afflictions. Others point out that, far from disappearing, Native traditions of spiritual relationships with the animals they hunt continue to the present.

THE CENTRAL ALGONQUIANS IN THE MODERN ERA

Like the fur trade period, the modern era did not begin at a single time or have a common impact throughout the vast Ojibwa-Cree-Innu distribution. Hunting and trapping declined, forcing Native people to rely on wage labour and government assistance for support. This shift took place much earlier among the southern Ojibwa than in the north. One band of Innu was still living a mobile hunting life on the land until the 1950s, when it was relocated to the new mining town of Schefferville in Quebec in an attempt to integrate band members into the global economy. In general, the modern era has removed economic self-sufficiency, marginalized Aboriginal populations in their own lands, and continually encroached on these lands for logging, mining and hydroelectric developments.

In the south, many Ojibwa are located near urban centres, such as Thunder Bay and Winnipeg, that offer opportunities for employment and all the amenities of city life. Winnipeg has a very large Native population, a good portion of which is drawn from nearby Ojibwa (Saulteaux) reserves. Their lives differ little from other urban Aboriginal People in Canada. In reserve communities, many people earn money fishing commercially, gathering wild rice (particularly around Lake of the Woods) and producing handicrafts.

In more isolated areas to the north, Cree and northern Ojibwa settlements, often located at former trading posts, have become larger, more centralized and more permanent. Although such communities may be predominantly Native, there are invariably Euro-Canadian administrators, teachers, missionaries, merchants and medical personnel. Facilities run by non-Natives, such as churches, schools and stores, have become centres of community life. Band government has shifted from traditional informal leadership to the system of elected chief and councillors stipulated in the Indian Act. On many reserves the band government is the major employer, though some individuals work seasonally in construction, logging, tourist guiding, commercial fishing, tree planting or forest-fire fighting. In northern Quebec, treaty settlement has allowed on-reserve enterprises to develop and employ some residents. Improved health services have decreased infant mortality and stemmed the spread of infectious diseases. Most communities have their own schools, and educational levels are rising. As during the fur trade period, the trading posts are central to the community, though they have become retail stores with a cash economy. The Hudson's Bay Company continues to be the largest trade and retail organization, yet most communities now contain smaller independent stores operated by Native residents.

Introduced elements of Euro-Canadian culture continue to change Native life. High-powered rifles and steel traps have replaced traditional methods of taking game. Commercially manufactured boats, often powered by outboard motors, have replaced the birchbark canoe. Snowmobiles are widely used for winter travel and hunting. Long-distance trips are by airplane or, for those communities with road access, by automobile. Yet the overall impact has been to reduce mobility. Outboard motors, snowmobiles and chainsaws make life on the land easier but require fuel and parts from stores. Children's education and government welfare and family allowance payments also tend to keep people in the community throughout much of the year.

Nevertheless, in many northern communities a substantial number of families go into the bush to hunt, trap and fish for part of the year. Such activities are not just a way to obtain food and furs; they also reaffirm traditional beliefs and values. Accordingly, some parents withdraw their children from school to educate them in "bush skills" they need to survive as Cree.

Throughout Ontario and Manitoba the Cree and Ojibwa signed treaties with the government. This process began as early as 1850, with the surrender of Ojibwa territory to the north of Lakes Superior and Huron, and continued to 1905, when Treaty 9 extinguished Aboriginal title across northern Ontario. In Quebec and Labrador, however, Native People were not required to sign away their lands. The Grand Council of the Crees and the Conseil des Attikamek et des Montagnais in Quebec and the Innu Nation in Labrador were formed to demand settlement of the land claims issue.

The unresolved land issue became a crisis in 1971, when the Quebec government launched a massive hydroelectric project, involving damming and diverting rivers flowing into James Bay. The Cree were threatened with extensive flooding of traditional hunting and trapping areas and the need to relocate at least one of their villages. The Quebec government did not recognize any Aboriginal claim to the land until the Cree obtained a legal injunction that temporarily halted the huge project. Finally, in 1975 the governments of Canada and Quebec and the Cree and Inuit of northern Quebec signed the first land claims agreement in recent Canadian history. In return for surrendering their land claim, the Cree and Inuit received $225 million to be paid over a twenty-year period, rights to the lands around their communities and exclusive hunting, fishing and trapping rights over much larger areas. Although stung by charges from other Aboriginal groups that the deal was a "sellout," the Cree under Chief Billy Diamond maintained that this was the best deal possible under the threat of imminent development and that it ensured the continuation of Native lifeways in northern Quebec. The Naskapi of Schefferville signed a similar agreement in 1978. The principle of local self-government for the communities covered by these agreements was consolidated in the Cree-Naskapi (of Quebec) Act in 1984.

The Quebec Cree today run their own school board and other administrative structures. Settlement money has financed Cree-run industries, such as a company that manufactures fibreglass canoes through a partnership with Yamaha. The Cree operate their own airline (Air Creebec), which links their formerly isolated communities. Cree villages have new houses and schools, electricity and running water.

At the same time, much has been lost. Old village sites and valued fishing locations at river rapids were flooded under reservoirs or left dry as river water was diverted. Flooding of the forests has released an organic mercury into the reservoirs. Although the total amount of mercury is small, it is concentrated in fish and poses a significant health hazard for people who rely heavily upon fish in their diet. Furthermore, as the hydroelectric development opened up the Cree homeland to large numbers of outside workers, extensive social problems have plagued the Cree communities.

The Quebec government planned further assaults on the Cree homeland. It proposed additional dam construction to link much of northern Quebec in one huge hydroelectric project. When Quebec announced plans to flood the Great Whale River in 1988, however, the Cree were prepared through their previous experience. Young, articulate and politically astute leaders such as Matthew Coon Come (later to become National Chief of the Assembly of First Nations) thwarted Quebec's plans, forcing a halt to the project in 1994. Their tactics included taking their political battle to the northeastern American states to discourage any potential customers for Quebec's energy exports. Tense relations between Quebec and the Cree became even further strained during the 1995 Quebec sovereignty referendum, which the Cree effectively opposed. In their own referendum they voted overwhelmingly to keep their lands within the Canadian Confederation. In 2002, however, Quebec and the Cree reached an accord concerning hydroelectric development. In exchange for dropping their opposition, the Cree will receive substantial financial compensation, greater political autonomy, control of natural resources and assured employment opportunities in the project.

The Innu have had to contend with similar pressures on their traditional lands. Logging, mining and hydroelectric projects have all threatened the land and animals on which they still depend for food and identity. In addition, low-flying jet bombers on test runs from a nearby NATO training centre threaten the way of life of Innu hunters in Labrador. The sudden and deafening noise as the jets appear immediately overhead destroys the peace of the Innu camps and drives away the game. Innu protests in Labrador and St. John's have focussed considerable public attention on their plight.

Industrial wastes have polluted the waterways in many areas of the Cree and Ojibwa homeland. One well-known example is the English-Wabigoon River system in northwestern Ontario. Tests on fish taken from the river showed levels of mercury far above those considered safe for human consumption. The Ojibwa of the Grassy Narrows and Whitedog Reserves north of Kenora were suddenly confronted with the spectre of mercury poisoning, which can lead to irreversible damage to the brain and nervous system, blindness, paralysis and death. The government discouraged fish consumption even though the Ojibwa rely heavily on fish in their diet, and the collapse of the commercial and sport fisheries put many people out of work. After a lengthy legal battle, a 1985 settlement awarded the two bands $16.6 million in compensation and established a disability fund to aid band members whose health had been impaired by mercury poisoning.

Social problems have beset many Ojibwa, Cree and Innu communities in recent decades. Violence, suicide, family breakdown and alcohol abuse have reached alarming levels in some villages. At Davis Inlet, an Innu community in Labrador, the attempted suicides of six gas-sniffing children focussed media attention on the inadequate housing, extreme poverty and despair in the village. In a study of the Ojibwa at Grassy Narrows, Anastasia Shkilnyk traces social disintegration to their relocation from the old community, where they were isolated and relatively self-sufficient, to the new reserve, which is unsuited to traditional activities but is linked by road to Kenora and the modern economy. The poisoning of their water-

ABOVE *Painting of a moose by Ojibwa artist Norval Morrisseau.* CMC 81-13152

ways, loss of jobs and threat to their health were cumulatively devastating. She takes the title of her disturbing book, *A Poison Stronger Than Love,* from a statement by an anonymous resident of Grassy Narrows: "The only thing I know about alcohol is that alcohol is a stronger power than the love of children. It's a poison, and we are a broken people." Highly publicized cases have alerted many Canadians to the Third World living conditions endured by some First Nations in Canada. Such attention has stimulated government action; for example, the Davis Inlet community was relocated from an isolated island to a more suitable village site on the mainland. Both Innu communities in Labrador have recently been placed under federal jurisdiction as First Nations, and their lands have been designated as reserves under the Indian Act. However, whether these changes will make a difference to the ongoing social dysfunction remains to be seen.

A distinctive and widely acclaimed Cree-Ojibwa art style, usually referred to as "Woodlands art," has provided some Aboriginal artists with recognition and financial gain. The originator and foremost practitioner of this style is Norval Morrisseau, an Ojibwa from the Lake Nipigon area of northern Ontario. His inspiration came from the legends of his people, and from the images in rock paintings and birchbark scrolls. Morrisseau views himself as a shaman, signing his paintings with the Cree syllabics for "Copper Thunderbird," and his works often reflect shamanic themes. Bold and brilliantly coloured, with "x-ray vision" showing internal organs and undulating "power lines" connecting the figures, his style is instantly recognizable. Morrisseau's introduction to the Canadian art world in the 1960s brought rapid acclaim. Early contemporaries who helped shape the Woodlands style were Carl Ray, a Cree from Sandy Lake in northern Ontario, and Daphne Odjig, an Odawa from Manitoulin Island who developed a very distinctive and personal variant of the Woodlands style. Many younger Cree and Ojibwa artists emerged by the 1970s, and the style continues to evolve. The vigorous, colourful paintings illustrate the strength of the Algonquian oral traditions and are a new vehicle for Aboriginal identity.

Renowned writer, linguist and scholar Basil Johnston is among the Ojibwa people who have contributed to Canadian culture and literature. His work emanates from his personal and intimate knowledge of Ojibwa traditions. Complementing this genre of Aboriginal literature is work of the Cree writer and playwright Tomson Highway, who blends characters from spoken narratives into his modern plays, which often touch on the tragic and comic aspects of reserve life. Also contributing to the contemporary arts scene are Claude McKenzie and Florent Vollant, both Innu from northern Quebec. They formed the successful rock band Kashtin, which toured North America and Europe and released three best-selling CDs in the 1990s. Their success is all the more remarkable as the band's songs are primarily in the Innu language.

Cree and Ojibwa athletes have also figured prominently in Canada's official winter sport. Among the earliest personalities to demonstrate his hockey skills was Reggie Leach of Riverton, Manitoba, who spent much of his National Hockey League career with the Philadelphia Flyers and was inducted to the team's Hall of Fame. He paved the way for later players, including Ted Nolan from the Garden River Ojibwa First Nation near Sault Ste. Marie. After a brief career playing for the Detroit Red Wings, he became the first Aboriginal head coach in the NHL and was selected coach of the year in 1997. Chris Simon, from Wawa, Ontario, has also left a lasting impression in the NHL. He played on the Colorado Avalache team that won the Stanley Cup in 1996.

With the largest Aboriginal populations in Canada, the Cree and Ojibwa are in no danger of disappearing. Their languages, widely spoken over a large portion of Canada, are among the few Aboriginal languages in Canada that are not endangered. Courses in Cree, Ojibwa and Oji-Cree are offered at a number of educational institutions. The Cree, Innu and Ojibwa communities are increasingly taking control over issues that affect them. Despite centuries of contact and despite adopting many elements of Euro-Canadian life, the Algonquians have resisted assimilation and are determined that their cultures will survive.

The Plains

. . . . .

FEW CULTURES have captured the popular imagination as forcefully as the Aboriginal People of the Plains. For many people, even the word "Indian" automatically conjures up images of the historic Natives of the Plains—the mounted warriors and bison hunters bedecked in feathers and buckskin. Perhaps because they most dramatically resisted the juggernaut of globalization, these First Nations have been forever equated with the classic "Indian." Plains-style headdresses and buckskin clothing are among the most visible of their cultural exports. Plains dances and ceremonies symbolically nurture a pan-Indian identity and are practised far beyond their original distributions. Although Plains cultures were dynamic, the equestrian warrior with the feather headdress is the stereo-typical image that has been immortalized in frontier lore, Western movies, novels and motorcycles. Yet this stereotype is a recent and short-lived cultural ideal dis-tilled from a diluted reality of the nature of Aboriginal life and is foreign even to Plains cultures.

The Plains are the flat, semi-arid grasslands extending up from the United States across the southern portions of the three Prairie provinces, from the Rocky Mountains in the west to the woodlands of southeastern Manitoba in the east. Only the northern reaches of this vast land of sun, sky, wind and grass fall within Canada. The climate is continental, with hot, dry summers and long, cold winters. In the east is the tall-grass prairie, whereas the short grass of the "high plains" lies to the west. A broad belt of aspen parklands along the northern edge of the Plains marks a transition to the boreal forest of the Subarctic. The terrain varies from flat and featureless ancient lake beds to rolling and wooded uplands, such as

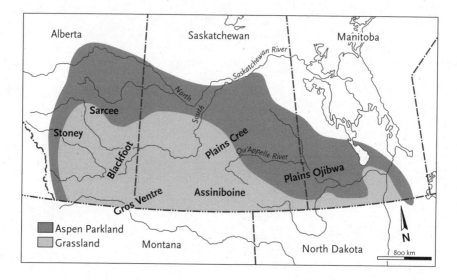

ABOVE *The Plains culture area, showing the division into grassland and aspen parkland and the nineteenth-century distribution of ethnographic groups.*

the Cypress Hills on the Alberta-Saskatchewan border. Deeply incised river valleys traditionally provided water, wood and shelter. The western Plains area has a more rugged topography, with cliffs and dry coulees that provided relief.

Vast herds of bison (popularly known as buffalo) sustained the hunting economy of Plains cultures. Once so numerous that they darkened the landscape, bison were the staff of life for the mobile Plains people until the herds were destroyed in the late nineteenth century. Not only did bison provide sustenance, but their hides were indispensable for shelter and clothing. The bones and horns were used for various tools, and bison skulls held deep symbolic value for rituals. Even dried dung was burned as fuel on the treeless Plains. In addition to the plentiful bison, resident cultures hunted a variety of fauna; pronghorn antelope once existed in great numbers, as did mule and white-tailed deer, elk, prairie chicken and other game. No diet of country foods would be complete without a full complement of edible plants. Many berries, fruits and tubers rounded out the daily requirements of vitamins and nutrients. Some eastern groups also ate fish, though this practice was taboo to other Plains groups such as the Blackfoot.

In the early historic period, most Plains dwellers spoke Algonquian languages. The main political entity was the powerful Blackfoot Confederacy, composed of the Siksika, Kainai (or Blood) and Piikani (or Peigan). These "raiders of the northwestern plains" epitomized the hunter-warrior culture of modern folklore. Their linguistic relatives and former allies, the Gros Ventre (or Atsina), once ventured far into the Saskatchewan River basin but they were subsequently expelled to the Missouri River basin, south of the Canadian border, when the alliance collapsed. Rivals of the Blackfoot were the Plains Cree and Plains Ojibwa to the east. In addition to these Algonquian speakers, the Athapaskan Sarcee became part of the Blackfoot Confederacy and the Siouan Assiniboine were closely allied and intermingled with the Plains Cree. Another member of the Siouan family, the Dakota, arrived from south of the border in the second half of the nineteenth century and witnessed the end of the horse-and-bison days in their adopted country.

The historic Plains Natives were highly mobile and ranged over great distances to hunt, trade or make war upon their enemies. Clearly defined territorial boundaries existed, and Aboriginal geographers were very conscious of the landmarks that constituted the edges of their homelands. Even when new groups surged onto the Plains, riding horses and armed with guns, they recognized the same landmarks. When these groups arrived, however, territories were contested and some groups were displaced. The dynamic history of Plains cultures has frustrated attempts to place neat labels on maps or to confidently assign archaeological remains to known ethnic groups.

DOG DAYS ON THE NORTHERN PLAINS

So engrained is the image of the equestrian Plains warrior that a Plains culture without horses seems to be unimaginable. Although the first people on the Plains may have hunted horses for food, the animal became extinct on this continent at the end of the late Pleistocene. Our ethnographic and historic accounts of Plains cultures refer only to the brief florescence after the horse was reintroduced in the mid-eighteenth century. For many millennia before that, Plains people successfully hunted bison herds on foot and used dogs to help carry their goods. The vast herds of bison are now gone from the Plains, but traces of those who pursued them—stone tools, camp sites, piles of bones left from a successful hunt—remain for archaeologists to interpret. When Plains Aboriginal People reflect on antiquity, they recognize two distinct periods: the Dog Days and the Horse Days. The Dog Days are the ancient, remote times on this side of the mythic past. The Horse Days commemorate the flourishing cultures in the dwindling days of antiquity before the reserve era dawned.

The **Ancient Dog Days** began when the first people arrived from the south just as the Ice Age was ending (see chapter 2). They brought with them their distinctive spearpoints with fluted channels on both faces. Fluted points have been discovered across all three Prairie provinces. Forms include classic Clovis and Folsom points, as well as a small triangular variant. However, none have been uncovered in a datable context. Many were plowed up by farmers or otherwise found on the surface, whereas a few, such as at the Sibbald Creek site west of Calgary, have been scientifically excavated but lack any clearly associated radiocarbon date. To estimate the age of these points, they are compared to similar dated discoveries farther south on the Plains. These place the early hunters on this landscape around 11,000 years ago.

Later populations also brought distinctive point types. They are collectively referred to as Plano and are widely distributed across the northern Plains. Plano points are large, lanceolate, unfluted points that conspicuously display the flint-knapper's skill. Projectile point types found on the Canadian Plains include those termed Plainview, Agate Basin, Hell Gap, Alberta and Eden-Scottsbluff. Once again most are surface discoveries; only a few have associated radiocarbon dates. Sites such as Fletcher in southern Alberta and Heron Eden in Saskatchewan show where Plano hunters using Eden-Scottsbluff points carried out mass bison kills about 9000 years ago.

For a short period after the Laurentide glacier retreated, large glacial lakes and tundra covered the northern Plains. This landscape was quickly followed by spruce forests and then by grasslands. Although the first people shared their environment with such Pleistocene fauna as the woolly mammoth and giant bison, by Plano times these animals had either become extinct or reached near-modern form. Herds of bison supported Plano cultures' big-game hunting lifestyles for thousands of years, and set the stage for all later cultural developments on the northern Plains.

Beginning about 7500 years ago medium-sized notched or stemmed points, presumably to facilitate hafting onto a wooden shaft, replaced the lanceolate points. Some researchers believe a different weapon system had emerged: the earlier lanceolate points are assumed to have been hafted to thrusting or throwing spears, whereas the notched points are thought to have been used on short spears or darts hurled by an atlatl (spear thrower). However, others argue that many of the earlier points also armed atlatl darts, and that the change in shape simply provided greater efficiency in hafting.

Projectile point types are key indicators of change. Although many elements of the material culture remained the same over long periods, shifts in the styles of projectile points have allowed archaeologists to distinguish different phases or cultures. Whether these actually correspond to different human populations, however, remains debatable.

In the Ancient Dog Days, the Plains entered a long, hot dry spell (the Altithermal or Atlantic period). Grasslands expanded considerably to the north and east at the expense of parklands and forest. Drought and limited water sources would have made survival difficult, but not impossible, for both humans and bison. At one time archaeologists posited a "cultural hiatus"—that the northern Plains were abandoned because of the adverse climate. More recent evidence indicates that the northern Plains were never entirely deserted; however, human populations were small, and few archaeological sites of this age remain. Moreover, the people of that era would have been accustomed to long periods during which resource availability fluctuated. They may have adjusted their seasonal round or looked farther afield for food sources. After several millennia, the climate shifted to essentially modern conditions and the grasslands covered roughly their present location.

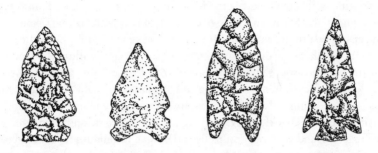

ABOVE *Projectile point types from the Ancient Dog Days. From left to right: Mummy Cave, Oxbow, McKean, Pelican Lake*

A number of early side-notched point types are collectively classified as the Mummy Cave series. The people who made these points hunted bison, elk and other large game with atlatls and they also took bison using "jumps"—driving the animals to their deaths over cliffs. Their distinctive projectile points are found at the earliest levels of the famous Head-Smashed-In bison jump in southern Alberta.

Perhaps the best-known and most widespread culture on the northern Plains during the Ancient Dog Days is Oxbow, named after the site excavated at Oxbow, Saskatchewan. Appearing somewhat before 5000 years ago, Oxbow points are found across the plains and parklands of all three Prairie provinces; later they extended north into the boreal forest. Oxbow points discovered with circles of stone that once held down tipi covers suggest hide-covered tipis were used at this time. At the Harder site in Saskatchewan, archaeologist Ian Dyck excavated six to eight round patches of packed earth which he interpreted as evidence for tipis, though he did not encounter any stone rings. He estimated that this Oxbow camp site, strewn with stone tools and butchered-bison bones, was occupied for a short period during the winter by about fifty people and their dogs.

Insights into Oxbow beliefs and ceremonial practices come from two nonresidential sites. One is the Majorville medicine wheel (a large ring of stones with a central cairn and radiating spokes) on the Bow River of southern Alberta. Archaeologists found Oxbow points at the lowest level of the cairn, demonstrating that the use of these enigmatic monuments goes back to at least this time. Also, an excavation at an Oxbow cemetery, the Gray site in Saskatchewan, revealed remains of more than 300 individuals. Although some are primary extended burials, most are incomplete bone bundles, which indicates that those who died at some distance from the site were defleshed and their bones taken back for burial. Extensive use of red ochre hints at funerary rituals, as does the placement of such exotic goods as marine shell ornaments and copper beads with some of the dead. Eagle talons and other animal remains possibly once were parts of medicine bundles, which suggests that the historic pattern of Plains religious practices was already in place.

Coexisting with late Oxbow is the McKean phase, which is divided into three related point styles. Many archaeologists maintain that McKean and Oxbow represent separate cultures, with the McKean influence emanating from the Great Basin to the south. Some even believe the stylistic variants within McKean indicate distinct ethnic groups, along the line of the historic Plains Cree and Assiniboine. Henry Kelsey stated in 1690 that the Assiniboine could distinguish their arrows (though admittedly looking at more than just the points) from those of the Plains Cree and Blackfoot, even though the Assiniboine and Cree lived and hunted together, and all three groups used the same techniques for taking bison. At the Cactus Flower site near Medicine Hat, all three McKean point variants were found. A tubular pipe indicates that smoking was already a well-established habit, though tobacco would not appear until much later. Artifacts interpreted as gaming pieces might well be from a popular hand game played by many Plains cultures. The stone circles associated with this site show that these people lived in tipis, the portable structures that are synonymous with the mobile Plains lifestyle. A cremation burial site near Saskatoon suggests that their mortuary practices differed from those of the Oxbow culture.

A later phase present on the Canadian Plains is termed Pelican Lake, after the site in Saskatchewan where it was first unearthed. Dating roughly between 3300 and 1800 years ago, the finely flaked corner-notched points of this phase are considered by many to have developed directly out of McKean. Camp sites follow the standard pattern evident from earlier times, but they are better represented in the archaeological record. The mobile people strategically located their seasonal camps near vital sources of food and water. Remains from the Head-Smashed-In and Old Women's bison jumps in southern Alberta show that the Pelican Lake people were adept at stampeding bison over cliffs. Fossil bacculites, which resemble small stone bison, have been found at their hunting camps. During the reserve era, ethnographers noted these small stone charms in medicine bundles. The Blackfoot people called them *iniskimiksi*, or "buffalo stones."

The people who left the Pelican Lake points buried their dead, often as secondary bundles, in pits dug into hilltops and covered with rock cairns. Red ochre in the graves and such wealth items as grizzly bear claw necklaces, decorated gorgets of shell from the Gulf of Mexico, dentalium shell beads from the Pacific coast and small pieces of copper from the western Great Lakes suggest rituals. Burial practices such as these persisted among Plains cultures into much later times. Even today, Blackfoot people say that every hilltop has a spirit. When they wish to pursue a vision quest, they go to an isolated butte and fast until the spirit shows its kindness.

The **Later Dog Days** began approximately 2000 years ago with an innovative approach to communal hunting. Earlier cultures had stalked animals, so local bands with a few hunters could adequately exploit a broad range of game animals sufficient to their needs. Besant people, named for the Besant Valley in south-central Saskatchewan, where the first excavations were conducted at the Mortlach site, coordinated the activities of many people and focussed significant energy toward hunting bison. Their sites are notable for the apparent ritualism associated with their bison hunts. At the Mortlach site, archaeologists found remnants of a structure that was remarkably similar in plan to the Sun Dance lodge of later times.

Blackfoot oral narratives provide clues to this new bison-hunting method. There is a story known as the Lost Boys that is commemorated by a cluster of circles adorning the smokeflaps of Blackfoot tipis. The upper part represents the sky country. The circles symbolize stars, specifically a constellation called the Lost Boys. Western folklore calls this cluster the Pleiades, and modern astronomers refer to object M45 in the Messier catalogue. When Blackfoot speakers observe this constellation it reminds them of the exploits of a group of young brothers one springtime ages ago. The boys coveted new clothes made from the hides of bison calves, but they were denied that luxury. They departed angry, saying they would seek refuge in the sky country. Every year when the bison calves were born, the boys disappeared from the sky country to remind their relatives of their stinginess. Coincidentally, object M45 disappears from the night sky in the northern hemisphere during the bison-calving season. For Plains cultures that dispersed for the winter, congregating at the right time and place to operate a successful bison drive was a major challenge. The Besant people used the Lost Boys constellation as their calendar: when the stars disappeared below the western horizon they left their winter camps and travelled to the cliff where the hunt would take place. This breakthrough discovery ensured the Besant people's success.

The spring hunt was critical because it replenished food supplies, which were exhausted by then. Coordinating the efforts of the many people needed to operate a buffalo jump brought a new degree of co-operation to communal hunting and greater group solidarity. Their management style of organizing people also relied more on rituals. Besant hunting sites are often the largest and most complex sites known to Plains archaeologists.

New materials and ideas were traded onto the Plains. Common use of a brown chalcedony ("Knife River flint") from a quarry in North Dakota exemplifies the long-distance trade networks that had been established. In the eastern Plains, burial mounds with exotic grave goods indicate that ideologies of the Eastern Woodlands cultures were imported to the Plains. Technological innovations also made their mark on the Plains bison-hunting cultures. Pottery and the bow and arrow became part of their traditional tool kit. Sherds of pottery appear in a few Besant sites but are not abundant; despite their fragile form, such vessels were valued domestic items for mobile Plains cultures because they could be placed directly on the fire. The bow and arrow rendered obsolete the atlatl and its side-notched projectile point, though the dart point likely influenced the design of the smaller side-notched points that tipped arrows.

Besant camp sites, where stone rings indicate use of hide-covered tipis, are distributed throughout the northern Plains. Bison kill sites include both jumps and

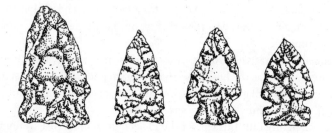

ABOVE *Projectile point types from the Later Dog Days. From left to right: Besant, Avonlea, Prairie Side-notched, Plains Side-notched*

"pounds," where the animals were driven into an enclosure. In addition, a series of burial mounds in the Missouri Valley of North and South Dakota (sometimes termed the Sonota Complex but considered part of Besant here) show their mortuary practices. Bison skulls and other remains buried in the mounds suggest rituals associated with the hunt, and a number of exotic goods placed with the dead indicate ties to the widespread Hopewell Complex, a mound-building culture of the central Eastern Woodlands with far-reaching trade connections.

Coexisting with Besant was the Avonlea phase, which began about 1800 years ago. Avonlea is characterized by small, delicately thin, notched points and is credited with introducing the bow and arrow to the Plains. Broken pieces of pottery frequently occur at Avonlea sites. Most of our knowledge comes from bison kill sites, and the Avonlea people seem to have emulated the efficiency of Besant hunters. At some sites, such as Head-Smashed-In in Alberta, they drove bison over cliffs. At others, such as Ramillies in Alberta or Waneskewin and Gull Lake in Saskatchewan, they drove bison into corrals or traps, often using natural features of the landscape to obscure the traps. Once inside, the trapped animals soon fell prey to the hunters' arrows, and the butchering could begin.

During the Later Dog Days on the northwestern Plains of Alberta and Saskatchewan, the popularity of the bow and arrow continued to expand. Whereas a hunter had to be close to the animal for dart points to be lethal, bows and arrows were more effective aimed at moving targets. A series of small, side-notched arrowpoints dominate the stone points recovered at bison kill sites. They can be grouped into two overlapping stages, termed Prairie Side-notched and Plains Side-notched. This late period is known as the Old Women's phase, after the bison jump near Cowley, Alberta, whose upper layers yielded abundant evidence that bison continued to be the mainstay of life. Pottery sherds at many of these sites show that a local ceramic industry persisted. The Old Women's phase extends into the Horse Days that followed, and Plains archaeologists consider it the ancestral culture of the Blackfoot and Gros Ventre.

In the northeastern Plains, small side-notched points also mark the Later Dog Days but more attention is focussed on the relatively abundant ceramics. The Blackduck pottery style of the Eastern Woodlands (discussed in chapter 5) spread into the parkland and plains of southern Manitoba. With a more diverse economy than their western contemporaries, people of the Blackduck culture hunted bison and smaller game, fished and collected a variety of plant foods. They also buried their dead in mounds. Although most archaeologists associate Blackduck with Algonquians, some argue the culture should be attributed to a Siouan group such as the Assiniboine.

Burial mounds of this late period are concentrated in southern Manitoba and adjacent North Dakota, with rare examples extending into eastern Saskatchewan. Manitoba archaeologist Leigh Syms has termed this the Devil's Lake–Sourisford Burial Complex. Burials, in pits under mounds, often contain grave goods. Finely made miniature pots, commonly decorated with spiral designs or with presumably sacred images of Thunderbirds, turtles and broken arrows, are thought to have been manufactured specifically as mortuary offerings. Similar motifs almost certainly once embellished tipi coverings, clothing and shields, but the mortuary offerings are the only remaining evidence. Other objects placed with the dead include engraved shell gorgets, incised stone tablets and tubular stone pipes. Widespread trade networks brought in catlinite (red pipestone) from Minnesota, copper from Lake Superior, obsidian from Wyoming and dentalium shell from the Pacific coast. This burial complex began about 1100 years ago and lasted for about five centuries, with some elements surviving into historic times.

ABOVE *Shell gorget from a burial mound in southwestern Manitoba. The raw material and the characteristic "weeping eye" motif suggest an origin far to the south.* ROM HK657

Ties clearly exist to the Mississippian culture of the lower Mississippi River valley, which was expanding its widespread influence even farther. An incised design on a shell gorget from a southwestern Manitoba mound, depicting a human face with forked lines around the eyes (the "weeping eye" motif), is very similar to common images in Mississippian art. Conch shells for such gorgets must have been traded up the Mississippi River from the Gulf of Mexico. Two similar shell gorgets with incised human faces have been discovered in a cave in the Sweetgrass Hills of Montana, near the Alberta border; just north of there the Milk River flows into the Mississippi River system. Syms speculates that the burial complex can be attributed to Siouan peoples who spread from the Eastern Woodlands into the northeastern Plains as part of the Mississippian expansion.

The spread of Mississippian influence northward was made possible by improvements in their agricultural economy, particularly the development of a hardy variety of corn which could mature in the short growing season of the northern Plains. Farming communities blossomed along the Middle Missouri area of North and South Dakota, eventually giving rise to such historic peoples as the Mandan and Hidatsa. Crops of corn, beans, squash and sunflowers grown in the river valleys supported substantial village populations. The Canadian Plains, however, were too far north for such economies to thrive. Horticultural practices on the Canadian Plains yielded only tobacco, though many groups traded for agricultural produce with their Mandan and Hidatsa neighbours to the south.

Archaeological evidence, however, shows that horticultural economies did reach as far north as southern Manitoba in times of warmer climate. The clearest picture comes from the Lochport site, on the Red River north of Winnipeg, at the northeastern edge of the Plains. As climatic conditions changed, the occupation at Lochport shifted from Plains bison hunters to Woodlands Laurel and Blackduck fishers, with a short-lived horticultural stage from about 800 to 500 years ago. Distinctive pottery, bison-scapula hoes and deep bell-shaped storage pits, all similar to those used by horticultural groups in the Middle Missouri area, plus charred kernels of corn found in the storage pits, provide the most convincing proof of Aboriginal horticulture. Similar evidence for horticultural lifeways comes from several sites in southwestern Manitoba, where Middle Missouri-style ceramics and scapula hoes have been found, though no preserved corn has been recovered.

Throughout the Later Dog Days, the people of the Plains led a stable existence, hunting bison on foot and using dogs as pack animals. Numerous camp sites attest to their mobility, and the variety of bison kill sites exhibits their hunting skills and ingenuity. Yet this way of life was to be rapidly and dramatically altered when the horse arrived and the global era began early in the eighteenth century.

ARCHAEOLOGICAL SITES ON THE PLAINS

Mobile Plains cultures and their ephemeral settlements left only a subtle, but indelible, signature in the archaeological record. Over thousands of years of manipulating the bison herds, they left the landscape littered with traces of their activities.

Bison kill sites reveal the most conspicuous signs of human activity. Both major types, jumps and pounds, required considerable preparation, including construction of long drive lines of piled rocks, wood or even dry bison dung to funnel the animals to the cliff or enclosure. Good locations were used repeatedly, providing a record of hunting techniques over time. The gathering basin would be set ablaze in the fall so that new grass would grow in the spring to attract the bison herds. Stealth was critical to the endeavour so under the cover of darkness, with

LEFT *The cliffs at Head-Smashed-In, a bison kill site in southern Alberta.* Photo by A. McMillan

only dim moonlight to guide their plans, the hunters set their lethal trap. A "buffalo runner" lured the herd toward the trap by imitating the anxious bleating of a lost bison calf. This tactic worked well in the spring since female herds usually congregated for the calving season. Enormous danger lay between the gathering basin and the trap, but the hunters' reward was a large harvest of their economic lifeblood. Typically more bison were killed than could be processed in the short time before the carcass became carrion, after which scavenging animals claimed their portion of the feast.

Head-Smashed-In Buffalo Jump in southern Alberta has gained particular fame since it was added to the prestigious list of UNESCO World Heritage Sites. An interpretation centre was funded by the Alberta government and staffed by people from the nearby Kainai and Piikani Reserves. The bluffs at this location were used repeatedly for nearly 6000 years, from early in the Dog Days to the historic era when the Piikani last pursued the declining herds. Similarly, people have used the nearby Old Women's site for the last 2000 years. Vast bison bone middens beneath the cliffs of these jumps attest to their efficiency. Artifacts are overwhelmingly projectile points for finishing off the wounded animals and butchering tools such as choppers and knives. The heavy work of butchering and processing the carcasses at nearby locations left huge numbers of archaeological features, such as boiling pits with fire-broken rock.

In areas lacking such suitable cliffs, bison were driven into a corral constructed of logs, or a natural enclosure finished with logs or brush. At the Ramillies site, north of Medicine Hat in Alberta, stone drive lines led to a natural depression that had been enlarged and closed off on the downslope side by an earthen wall topped with large rocks, a construction style apparently made necessary by the lack of nearby wood.

Various rock-feature sites are among the most common archaeological remains on the Plains. Cairns, medicine wheels, effigy figures, drive lanes, tipi rings and other arrangements of cobbles dot the surface of the Plains wherever they have escaped the plow and other disturbances. Although the function of some

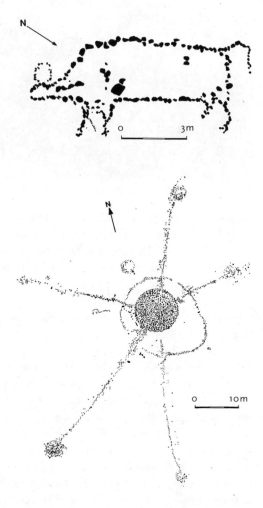

TOP LEFT AND RIGHT *Human and bison boulder effigy figures, southern Saskatchewan. Courtesy Saskatchewan Museum of Natural History.* RIGHT *Moose Mountain medicine wheel, southeastern Saskatchewan. Courtesy Saskatchewan Museum of Natural History*

seems clear, others are more difficult to interpret. Cairns may have been grave markers, food caches or landmarks. Ranging widely in size, they are found singly, in groups or in association with other boulder sites. For example, the large British Block Cairn in southeastern Alberta is in the centre of a medicine wheel, directly adjacent to a boulder effigy of a man and numerous tipi rings.

Medicine wheels are perhaps the most complex and enigmatic of the boulder sites. They generally consist of a large central cairn or circle, from which lines of stones radiate out like spokes, often with an outer stone circle and outlying cairns. A wide range of shapes, and presumably functions, is evident, leading Alberta archaeologist John Brumley to propose a classification with eight distinct subgroups. These structures are found only in the northwestern Plains, with their greatest concentration in Alberta. Although most are undated, excavation at the

Majorville site in Alberta revealed that the large central mound had been built up gradually, beginning about 5000 years ago. Others, however, are relatively recent and can be attributed to the efforts of the Blackfoot and their kin.

Ethnographic analogy contributes the most plausible explanation for at least some of these constructions. Blackfoot informants have reported to several anthropologists that these stone circles were memorials to warrior chiefs. As a few were constructed well into the twentieth century, specific details could be gathered. All such Blackfoot memorials share a common plan—a stone circle with lines of stones radiating outward. The central circle (perhaps a pre-existing tipi ring) marked the position of the burial lodge where the deceased chief was left, and the radiating spokes were added as signs of respect. Indeed, when John Brumley, then a consulting archaeologist in Alberta, excavated one such example, he exposed scattered human skeletal remains inside the central ring.

Other types of medicine wheels clearly had different functions. A major controversy erupted when astronomer John Eddy published his research on the Big Horn medicine wheel in northern Wyoming. According to Eddy, the Big Horn wheel, with its large central cairn and smaller cairns on the outer circle, was constructed for calendric purposes—specifically to mark the position of the summer solstice and the three brightest stars of the midsummer dawn. His search for further examples led him to the Moose Mountain medicine wheel in southeastern Saskatchewan. Although differing in many respects, the pattern of cairns is similar, leading Eddy and others to postulate the same astronomical significance. Astroarchaeological research at other Canadian sites, however, failed to turn up significant alignments, and some researchers have challenged those for Big Horn and Moose Mountain.

Other anthropologists relate the wheels to the primary religious ceremony of the Plains people, the Sun Dance, which was usually held around the time of the summer solstice. Some wheel types resemble an outline of the Sun Dance lodge—the outer circle being the wall of the lodge, the inner cairn representing the sacred central post and the spokes connecting them symbolizing the rafters. Whether or not medicine wheels were astronomical observatories, they certainly featured in the religious lives of Plains Natives. Discoveries of *iniskimiksi* ("buffalo stones") and other items in the central cairn at the Majorville site suggest that ritual offerings, possibly in the form of medicine bundles, were deposited there.

At other locations, boulders were carefully placed to form effigy figures. Humans and turtles were favourite themes, but Saskatchewan has one well-executed bison outline. Since these were constructed into historic times, some have specific events associated with them. Perhaps the best documented is on the Siksika reserve in Alberta, where a spread-eagled human figure lying along a trail of stones commemorates an 1872 duel between a Kainai man and a Siksika, the stones marking the paths each took and the spot at which the former fell dead.

The most common of the boulder arrangements, the stone circles usually referred to as tipi rings, are known as *mamma'pis* in Blackfoot. They were once placed around the edges of the tipis to hold down skin covers. They have been recognized for this use since the mid-nineteenth century, when the explorer Henry Y. Hind referred to "the remains of ancient encampments, where the Plains Crees, in the day of their power and pride, had erected large skin tents, and strengthened them with rings of stones placed around the base" (1971, 1: 338). In favourable locations for village sites they may occur in clusters of several hundred. Although some archaeologists have questioned this function, their sheer abundance seems to preclude anything other than domestic use. In fact, Blackfoot skywatchers designated one constellation *Mamma'pis* (known as Corona Borealis, the Northern Crown, to Western astronomers); each star in the crescent is said to represent one stone holding down the tipi of the Spiderman who lives there.

There are a few rock art sites, including both petroglyphs (incised designs) and pictographs (paintings), across the Plains. Petroglyphs are by far the most common, ranging from pictures lightly scratched on cliff faces to deeply pecked and grooved designs on large boulders. Humans and animals predominate, though the most common depictions at the St. Victor petroglyphs in southern Saskatchewan are a variety of animal footprints. The boulder petroglyph "ribstones," most common in Alberta, are covered with a pattern of grooves and pits, presumably representing bison.

The outstanding rock art site on the Canadian Plains is Writing-On-Stone (*Asinaip* in Blackfoot) in southern Alberta. The soft sandstone walls of the Milk River valley provided an excellent surface for Aboriginal artists to incise (and, much more rarely, paint) scenes of war and the hunt. Although these cliffs were no doubt used over a long period of time, erosion has removed all but the more recent glyphs. Still, several styles can be discerned. The presumably earlier depictions are carefully incised animal and human figures, the latter often hidden behind large round shields and associated with a bow-spear, a long bow tipped with a spearpoint like a bayonet. Possibly individuals attracted to this supernaturally charged area created these images while on vision quests. Later glyphs are often only lightly scratched into the soft cliffs and depict warriors on horseback. Images of equestrian warriors wearing long headdresses and holding rifles are clearly historic records of actual people. Several panels show complex battle scenes. These later glyphs mark the switch from ceremonial to biographic art created by the Blackfoot, who used the convenient cliffs to illustrate their war exploits.

Any unusual landmark could inspire veneration, and small offerings which were left at such locations might be all that would identify them to the archaeologist. Huge boulders, often weighing many tons, were carried from the north by Pleistocene glaciers, then dumped on the otherwise featureless prairie when the ice retreated. Such conspicuous objects were "medicine stones," considered sacred by the Plains First Nations. One boulder in Saskatchewan inspired several Cree legends because it resembled a huge recumbent bison. H.Y. Hind recorded in 1857 that Native People were leaving "offerings to Manitou," such as "beads, bits of to-

ABOVE *Native artists left numerous images in the soft sandstone cliffs at Writing-On-Stone, along the Milk River valley of southern Alberta (*TOP*), including shield-warriors with bows (*BOTTOM LEFT*) and a mounted hunter pursuing an animal (*BOTTOM RIGHT*). Photos by A. McMillan*

bacco, fragments of cloth, and other trifles" at such locations. In this way, mobile ritualists infused the landscape with a spiritual, if subtle, quality.

THE HORSE DAYS

When the horse arrived by the mid-eighteenth century, pedestrian hunters became the equestrian cultures of popular image. In many locations, the Horse Days began for Aboriginal cultures well before they directly encountered the Europeans who reintroduced this animal to the continent. Before their first direct contacts with the larger world, Aboriginal People had attached a patina of myth to horses by explaining their origins as supernatural; the Blackfoot, for example, credited the largesse of the Thunder Spirit for their acquisition of horses. The Horse Days cover the brief period of dramatic changes in Aboriginal cultures due to products of European introduction. Like horses, these imported wares were brought in by the extensive Aboriginal trade networks that criss-crossed the continent. The Horse Days chronicle the span of time between the Dog Days and the reserve era.

Horses were brought north along the axis of trade that originated in the Spanish settlements of the Southwest. As early as 1640 they were a feature of southern Plains life and scarcely a century later they were on the verge of revolutionizing life on the northern Plains. Although we lack specific information on when most tribes acquired horses, historic records give a reasonably clear picture for the Assiniboine. In 1738, when La Vérendrye accompanied an Assiniboine trading party, they lacked horses. When Anthony Henday travelled with a similar party sixteen years later, they had a few horses for packing goods but not for riding. In 1776, Alexander Henry described numerous horses among the Assiniboine and their use in mounted warfare. The Blackfoot were well provided with horses by the time of Henday's 1754 visit, though Henday's Cree companions had none since they had travelled to the Plains by canoe. Indeed, some Plains Cree bands remained "horse poor" well into the nineteenth century.

Within a generation Plains people had become skilled equestrians, riding as if the animal had always been part of their lives. No longer did they need to wait until bison approached the pounds; now hunters on their favourite mounts could ride among the shaggy beasts, selecting the animal to be felled with an arrow. Warriors and hunters ranged more widely across the Plains than had previously been possible, bringing them into greater conflict with other groups. Warfare became continuous, providing young men with opportunities for glory and excitement. Horse raiding was not considered theft but an act of bravery that could be proudly recounted, and it was an important way of obtaining additional mounts. Horses allowed Native People to accumulate wealth, since a horse could transport many more personal possessions than was possible with dogs. These new conditions fostered larger social groups and increased interactions with others, resulting in more elaborate political and religious institutions. Plains societies as they are historically known emerged during this brief cultural florescence.

Arriving about the same time as the horse were the rifle and other European trade goods. These items went west along the trade routes that Cree and Assiniboine maintained with the fur traders in the east. The Plains cultures were subjected to great upheavals during the Horse Days as constant war and population dislocations ensued. Smallpox and other European diseases also appeared, and periodic epidemics swept across the Plains at least as early as 1781. The smallpox epidemic of that year devastated all the Plains groups and greatly diminished their numbers.

Where the Plains tribes resided immediately before the horse and gun has been the subject of considerable debate. The Blackfoot appear to have the only claim to great antiquity on the northern Plains. Their oral narratives indicate their culture emerged far back in the Dog Days. Historic records also show they once ranged well to the northeast of their present location, to the parkland along the North Saskatchewan River. The Plains Cree, Plains Ojibwa, Assiniboine and

Sarcee all moved onto the Plains as the Horse Days commenced, displacing earlier occupants such as the Gros Ventre.

Other major population movements were taking place to the south as horticulturists abandoned their tedious tasks for the greater excitement of the equestrian lifestyle. Many of the Dakota (or Sioux) left their gardens and wild rice plots in Minnesota to move west and adopt all the trappings of Plains culture during the Horse Days. Along the Middle Missouri of North and South Dakota, people found the new attractions of Plains life compelling. Although the Mandan and Hidatsa maintained their horticultural economy and palisaded villages of earth-covered lodges well into the historic period, the Crow emerged during this period as an offshoot of the Hidatsa, moving west onto the high plains as equestrian warriors and hunters. Their new homeland was in the central Plains of the Missouri River basin, but their occasional forays north took them deep into the Saskatchewan River basin.

A few of the earthlodge villagers apparently established settlements far north of their kin. In 1801, Peter Fidler of the Hudson's Bay Company discovered three "Mud Houses" on the South Saskatchewan River. He estimated that they were about twenty years old, and stated that "they are said to have been built by a small war party from the Missouri River, who live in these kinds of habitations." The only major excavated archaeological example is the Blackfoot Crossing Fortified Village (formerly known as the Cluny site), along the Bow River on the modern Siksika Reserve. Here a large semicircular trench, ending along the riverbank, encloses eleven small pits and a palisade wall. The artifacts are predominantly pottery sherds of Middle Missouri style and reveal no evidence of agriculture. Despite the great effort required to dig the trench and construct the palisade, the site was apparently occupied only briefly around 1740. Its inhabitants may have been the Crow or another group, in the process of transition from earthlodge villagers to mobile high-plains hunters. Remains of several similar, but apparently much later, fortified encampments in southwestern Manitoba have been attributed to the Dakota's arrival in the 1860s.

THE ETHNOGRAPHIC CULTURES

The horse-and-bison days were long over by the time ethnographers began their studies of Plains cultures early in the twentieth century. The winter counts and memories of their oldest informants could reach back no farther than the mid-nineteenth century. Ethnographic descriptions refer to the few decades before the bison herds were finally destroyed in the early 1880s, as revealed through the writings of European observers and the "memory culture" of elderly informants who shared their knowledge with early anthropologists.

Throughout their entire history Plains Natives adapted their lives to intercept the bison herds. The hunting techniques described in the ethnographic accounts, however, differed somewhat from those employed for thousands of years previously.

Plains people continued to use both jumps and pounds long after the horse arrived. The Blackfoot occasionally drove bison over cliffs, such as at Head-Smashed-In, well into historic times. The Plains Cree and Assiniboine still relied heavily on pounds, particularly for the winter hunt. Long drive lines of stone or brush led to a stout corral, which was ringed with people holding hides to make the construction seem more substantial than it actually was. H.Y. Hind, who witnessed the scene in 1857, vividly described how the Cree used a pound:

> In hunting the buffalo they are wild with excitement, but no scene or incident seems to have such a maddening effect upon them as when the buffalo are successfully driven into a pound. Until the herd is brought in by the skilled hunters, the utmost silence is preserved around the fence of the pound: men, women, and children, with pent-up feelings, hold their robes so as to close every orifice through which the terrified animals might endeavour to escape. The herd once in the pound, a scene of diabolical butchery and excitement begins; men, women, and children climb on the fence, and shoot arrows or thrust spears at the bewildered buffalo, with shouts, screams, and yells horrible to hear. Hind 1971, 2: 142

Most of the time the Plains tribes preferred to hunt bison from horseback. Instead of constructing a corral and drive lines to direct a herd into it as their ancestors did, hunters ranged widely in search of the herds. Then groups of men might attempt to surround the animals or race down upon them in an organized charge. The hunters' skill in selecting and killing the beasts during a high-speed chase is shown in a 1792 eyewitness account by Peter Fidler:

> Men killed several Cows by running them upon Horseback & shooting them with arrows. They are so expert at this business that they will ride along side of

ABOVE *Cree buffalo pound near Fort Carlton, observed by artist Paul Kane in 1846.* ROM 86 ETH 83/912.1.33

ABOVE *Assiniboine hunters pursuing bison, painted by Paul Kane from his travels in the 1840s.* ROM 86 ETH 96/912.1.46

> the Cow they mean to kill & while at full gallop will shoot an arrow into her heart & kill her upon the spot. Sometimes when they happen to miss their proper aim (which is very seldom) they will ride close up to the Buffalo . . . at full gallop & draw the arrow out & again shoot with it. *Verbicky-Todd 1984: 144*

For this task, hunters preferred bows and arrows over the traders' guns, which were difficult to load on the gallop and scared the animals with their noise. Arrows were marked, so the hunters could later identify their kills.

The hunter's prize possession was his "buffalo horse," a swift and agile mount that was carefully trained. "Running buffalo" was a dangerous pursuit, and accidents were common in the noise, dust and confusion. The horses had to run alongside bison without stumbling on the uneven terrain or into the gopher holes that pockmarked the prairies. Occasional charges by enraged bulls were an additional menace. Any mistake could result in both horse and rider being gored or trampled.

Successful hunts required group discipline. A large communal hunt could be ruined if a few individuals dispersed the herd while taking provisions for themselves. Warriors formed police societies to enforce hunting restrictions. Offenders could be beaten or might have their weapons smashed, their clothes and tipi covers torn, and their dogs and horses killed. Harsh punishments were necessary so the actions of a few would not jeopardize the welfare of all. Blackfoot speakers called these police *iyinnakiikoan,* which alludes to their right to seize property.

Rituals also ensured success on the hunt. The Assiniboine and Plains Cree conducted an elaborate ceremony to dedicate each newly constructed pound and raised a "medicine pole" in the centre from which offerings were suspended. Before the Horse Days, when pounds were operated on foot, climbing the centre pole was a route of escape for the "buffalo runner." Singing and prayers were essential to draw the bison near.

Both men and women set to work after a successful hunt. Carcasses were stripped of their hides, which the women later laboriously transformed into clothing, tipi covers or other domestic items. Workers might satisfy their immediate hunger with bits of raw liver or kidney and the sweet fat from the hump. Tongues, a favoured delicacy, might be reserved for the pound owner, for the ritualist who claimed responsibility for the kills or for a communal feast. Meat was set aside, marrow extracted from the long bones and sinews saved for later use. One communal hunt could yield a large quantity of meat, and a great feast ensued at which all could sate themselves.

Meat was prepared in several ways. If it was to be eaten immediately, it was roasted over the fire. It could also be boiled in a pit lined with bison hide into which water and hot stones were placed. Some meat was cut into thin strips and dried for later consumption. It could also be made into pemmican by drying it, pounding it into a coarse powder and mixing it with melted fat; dried saskatoon berries or chokecherries could be added as well and the grease would preserve the vitamins in the berries. This mixture was cooled and sewn into bison-hide bags, where it would keep indefinitely, providing lightweight and nutritious supplies for warriors and hunters setting out on long journeys.

Bison were the mainstay of country food, but other animals were hunted. Elk and deer were available along the foothills and parklands, and pronghorn antelope existed in huge numbers across the grasslands. Their hides were particularly valued for making clothing.

Supplementing the country food diet was a large variety of consumable plants. Women worked near the camp, collecting berries and digging for edible roots. The most important root was the wild turnip, which was eaten raw, roasted, boiled or pounded into flour used for thickening soup. Other wild plants were collected for medicinal or other use.

The only historic example of plant cultivation on the Canadian Plains was the Blackfoot practice of maintaining small plots of tobacco. Seeds were kept in the medicine bags of ritualists and ceremonially planted in the spring. Then the small plots were abandoned to the care of the "little people" who lived in the woods. After a season of moving to their satellite camps, people returned to harvest their crop. Tobacco was mixed with the dried leaves of bearberry (kinnikinnick) and the cambium of red osier dogwood. This practice continued in later times when the Blackfoot blended their concoction with expensive trade tobacco.

Essential to the mobile lifestyle were the tipi and travois. When upright, the conical tipi featured a framework of poles fastened at the top, which supported a bison-hide cover. The cover, carefully prepared and sewn by the women, required between eight and twenty hides. When spread out it formed a half-circle, which was then folded in half before raising. When setting up a camp, the tipi poles were measured on the folded cover, at which point they were tied together and raised.

ABOVE *Assiniboine with painted tipi.* NAC C26461
LEFT *Inside a Piikani tipi.* NAC C24490

More poles were then added to the support frame; up to twenty poles might be used. The tipi cover was lashed to one pole and lifted into place, then unfurled around the frame until the two sides met where the door would be. Thin pegs were fitted into the prepared holes on the overlapping ends of the tipi cover above and below the door. In the past, rocks held down the edges and left behind a tipi ring; now pegs are inserted into loops around the fringe and driven into the ground. Two poles were slipped into flaps at the top to help control smoke from the central fire (though during the summer people preferred to cook outdoors). An inside liner insulated and protected the occupants from drafts. Clothing, weapons and bags of food were hung from the lodge poles, and sleeping robes were laid out around the walls, serving as couches during the day. The place of honour, reserved for the head of the family, was opposite the door flap. When the camp was set to move, the tipi could be taken down quickly and packed with other possessions on a travois, a framework of poles. Originally designed to be pulled by dogs, the travois was quickly adapted to the horse, allowing larger tipis and more numerous possessions.

RIGHT *A Blackfoot couple with horse-drawn travois.*
NAC C26182

All aspects of life, including social organization, were devised with mobility in mind. Each tribal group was divided into a number of independent bands, which were the basic social groups throughout most of the year. Band chiefs led by virtue of their wisdom or success in the hunt and required the support and respect of their people. Decisions were made by consensus, the chief hoping to persuade others through oratory and example rather than by direct orders. Good leaders might attract large followings, whereas those who lacked skill or experienced misfortune might find their band depleted as members drifted away to other camps. In addition to this political leader, each band had a war chief, who controlled military matters.

In contrast to the small, dispersed winter camps, tribes gathered routinely during the summer when people congregated in big, ephemeral tipi towns. This was when bison were concentrated in large herds. People might assemble to celebrate the major religious ceremony, the Sun Dance, which was also a timely convention for the military societies. These assemblies drew separate bands toward a common culture. Trade also brought many people together. Anthony Henday, during his 1754 trade mission to Blackfoot country, recorded his impressions of a large tipi town where people had gathered to exchange goods and noted that it disappeared after the negotiations concluded. The Blackfoot had the most fully developed tribal organization integrating the bands, whereas the Plains Cree, Plains Ojibwa and Assiniboine groups had fewer such ties.

Both popular and academic writing portray an overwhelmingly masculine image of Plains society. Men were the hunters and warriors in a society obsessed with bison and battles. Yet women played pivotal roles in the sacred and daily life of Plains cultures. They could quickly set up a camp and break it down. Although they spent much of the time in domestic toil, such as tanning hides to make clothing and tipi covers, women could own the hides and tipis. Men or women could own the designs that adorned tipis, and women were often sought for their artistic skills. Men were the undisputed heads of their households, but they heeded the subtle advice of their wives. A man would take several wives, often at the request of his senior wife, to ease the burden of household duties. Years of warfare during the Horse Days resulted in such a deficit of adult males that women encouraged polygamous arrangements. A quarrelsome wife could be sent back to her family, and an adulterous one could be killed, beaten or disfigured, typically by cutting off the end of her nose. Such threats governed social dynamics on the Plains, and several nineteenth-century observers noted that women with mutilated noses were not an uncommon sight. Virtuous women were highly respected and played central roles in important ceremonies.

Women's work kept the household functioning. Besides moving camp, they cooked all the meals, and they stitched the tailored-hide shirts, breechcloths, leggings and moccasins for their men, and long dresses, leggings and moccasins for themselves. They also prepared bison-hide robes and fur caps for their families to wear in winter. They spent their leisure time refining their aesthetic skills, and the better artisans were often commissioned to make special adornments. Warriors might request that trophy scalplocks be sewn to their shirts, and women might ask for rows of elk teeth for their dresses. They cut fringes and dyed porcupine quills to embroider onto their finest apparel. In later years they included beads, thimbles, coins and brass buttons imported through trade.

Both men and women painted their faces with a mixture of ochre and grease, usually as part of a religious ceremony. They greased their hair and arranged it in a variety of styles, but braiding was most popular for long hair. Young men in particular spent considerable time on this. The Plains Cree also tattooed their bodies: the men decorated their torsos, heads and arms, whereas the women were restricted to lines on the chin. In their hair they occasionally wore eagle feathers, and the association with military honours appears to have been traditional. Upright headdresses made with eagle feathers were worn among the Blackfoot on ritual occasions. However, the stereotypical long, trailing, eagle-feather headdresses were introduced very late, entering Canada with the Dakota near the end of the horse-and-bison days.

Many everyday items, such as folded rawhide containers (parfleche bags), were embellished with paint. Geometric designs were more popular with the Blackfoot, whereas Plains Cree and Plains Ojibwa preferred floral motifs commonly used in the Eastern Woodlands. Artistic talents and aesthetic products were often considered gifts from compassionate spirits and were thus imbued with a supernatural quality. Tipi designs were gifts received in dreams and were the property of the dreamer. Personal items, such as a warrior's shield, commonly depicted bison or other spirits encountered in visions. A group of warriors protected by a common companion spirit might form a society on that basis.

Warfare was a passion, and the only route to prestige for a young man. The honour of dying in battle was impressed upon boys from an early age. Times of peace were rare, and even then a chief had difficulty restraining young men from setting out on raids. Such expeditions ranged from small groups attempting to steal horses from enemy camps to large war parties organized to take booty (horses, guns, scalps) or revenge. Some groups became embroiled in warfare lasting generations, as each side sought revenge for previous losses. No male prisoners were taken, and each man fought to the death, attempting to inflict as much injury as possible on his foe. Women and children were often captured and adopted into families that had suffered losses during such wars.

War honours were based on the degree of courage displayed. Warriors tried to "count coup" on their enemies (from a French word, meaning "a blow"). Striking an enemy, with the fist, a club or a special coup stick, brought the greatest honours. Killing an enemy at a distance was not particularly meritorious; a warrior actually had to touch the body. Taking an enemy's gun or scalping a fallen foe bestowed honour, whereas stealing a horse was so common that it was considered a lesser achievement. Brave deeds were publicly recounted and often depicted on tipi covers. Such honours were essential if a young man aspired to chieftainship, or if he wished to win the admiration of his comrades and the attention of young women.

Blackfoot males were organized into a series of warrior societies based on age. As the young men in each group grew older, they sold their membership in that age level to a younger group and advanced to the next age level, eventually purchasing the regalia and learning the rituals of each successive society. The Plains Cree, on the other hand, had only a single society, to which entry was gained by a valorous deed. The societies kept order in the camp and on the hunt and guarded against enemy attack. Their rituals strengthened group solidarity and fostered a pride in military prowess. The Blackfoot Brave Dogs, for example, had to demonstrate bravery and contempt for death by never retreating from the enemy in battle. The Blackfoot also had a women's society, in which women represented bison in dances to honour the spirits of this essential animal.

Religion permeated everyday life. The universe was filled with supernatural beings, each with the power to help or harm. Manifestations of spiritual power, which could include any unusual object, such as a large rock or a strangely twisted tree, were termed *manitou* among the Algonquians and *wakan* among the Siouan speakers. A rite of passage into the adult world compelled young people to seek spiritual power by fasting and praying in secluded locations. In such circumstances a supernatural companion would come to them in a vision. Such helpers might bestow certain powers, present them with songs and demonstrate rituals to be performed, or

ABOVE *A Piikani warrior.* NAC C24487

LEFT *Sun Dance lodge frame on the Siksika Nation Reserve, 2003. Photo by E. Yellowhorn*

offer details of how to paint designs on tipis. If their instructions were followed, these companion beings provided life-long assistance and aid in the spirit world. Shamans received their power to cure through such spirit encounters.

Sacred objects, many representing gifts from supernatural encounters, were carefully wrapped in a medicine bundle whose contents might include skins of various animals, eagle feathers, braided sweetgrass used for incense, fossils or other supernaturally charged stones and a variety of other items whose significance was known only to the owner. Sacred pipestems were particularly important inclusions. Smoking was a way of communicating with the supernatural, so sacred pipestems were brought out to aid the sick, to settle quarrels or to bless those setting out on war parties. Like a portable shrine, the bundle could be hung outside on a tripod in fine weather. Opening the bundle or transferring it to a new owner required elaborate ceremonies, in which each object was reverently displayed while prayers and songs invoked the spiritual power associated with it. Friends or neighbours might vow to dance with the bundle to seek help from the spirit within it.

The most important religious festival of the Plains tribes was the Sun Dance (which is actually a misnomer since the ceremony was not directed to the Sun; the Cree called it the "Thirsting Dance"). It was held during the summer, when the tribes assembled in large encampments. All Plains groups shared the basic ritual, though the Sun Dance varied considerably between tribes. Among the Blackfoot (whose term for the Sun Dance is *Ookaan*) and Sarcee, a virtuous woman sponsored the ceremony to fulfill a vow she took at a time of crisis, as when illness threatened her family. Among the Plains Cree and Ojibwa, a man might pledge to hold a Sun Dance if he returned safely from a war expedition.

Sun Dance ceremonies began with the construction of the lodge. While the sponsor fasted, warriors cut down a tree suitable for the sacred central pole, counting coup on it as if it were a fallen foe. Erecting the centre pole at a Sun Dance brought together all the participants from the various societies in attendance. The Plains Cree and Ojibwa built a "Thunderbird nest" of branches at the top, and all groups hung cloth and other offerings from it. Painted or incised Thunderbirds, bison skulls or other vision images adorned the pole, and an altar with a painted bison skull and braided sweetgrass was placed near its base. Rafters from the central pole rested on the circle of posts and beams that made up the outer wall.

When the leafy branches forming the lodge wall were set in place, the dances and ceremonies could begin. The dancers were those who had made vows, and they often continued to perform, without food, water or sleep, for the several days of the ceremony. They danced in place, moving to the rhythm of chanted prayers, blowing on eagle-bone whistles and keeping their gaze fixed on the top of the central pole. During this time, young men who were fulfilling vows had the muscles of their chests pierced and wooden skewers pushed through. Ropes tied to the skewers were attached to the central pole. As they danced the young men leaned back on the ropes until they tore free. Sometimes the flesh of the back was also cut and threaded with wooden skewers on which hung heavy bison skulls. Men proudly bore the scars of such ordeals through the rest of their lives. The days together at the Sun Dance strengthened the common culture of the people as they observed their shared faith. Gathering at the Sun Dance also provided opportunities for such social activities as visiting friends, courting, gambling and horse racing. Since the Sun Dance, in its various forms, originated in myth, it was also a time for each group to cement its allegiance to the creator.

Myths explained the world, and the characters animating each story were archetypes culled from the Plains environment. One common persona was the trickster/transformer. The Plains Cree brought Wisakedjak from their original

ABOVE *Blackfoot Sun Dance, ca. 1887. Skewers through the flesh of the dancer's chest are attached by thongs to the central pole, while a shield is suspended by thongs from his back.* NAC C494766-16.

Subarctic homeland, telling of his actions that put the world in its present order. Among the Blackfoot, Naapi ("Old Man") was the major legendary figure. Although he is spoken of respectfully in some stories, such as those of creation, he is seen as foolish or spiteful in others. The basic Algonquian pattern is evident in myths from the Rocky Mountains to the Atlantic; the Sarcee and Assiniboine had similar stories due to close association with the Algonquians. The myths enlivened the cold winter evenings, as the occupants of the tipi sat around the central fire, listening to elders recount stories of ancient and mythic times.

When a person died, the body was placed in a tree or on a scaffold. Men of distinction, however, were left in their lodges with their valued possessions. Several of a man's favourite horses might be shot to accompany him into the spirit world. Mourners cut their hair and wore old clothes. A man might leave immediately on a war party, to ease his grief by striking at the enemy without regard for risk to his own life. A woman, in extremes of anguish for the loss of a husband or child, might gash her legs or chop off the end of a finger.

The Blackfoot believed the Sand Hills, a rather bleak sandy area on their eastern frontier, to be the entrance to the spirit world. Beyond the hills they imagined a pleasant country where their ancestors lived and practised customs much as they had in life. It was a wondrous place to behold, but it was guarded by a fearsome giant bison, which only let in the souls of dead people. Sometimes if a person was injured seriously and their soul wandered too close to the Sand Hills, the giant bison would sense their life and chase them back to their bodies. In death, near-death and in life, the bison sustained the ideologies and economies of cultures on the Plains.

THE BLACKFOOT AND THEIR ALLIES

At the height of their power the Blackfoot controlled a vast area from the North Saskatchewan River to the Missouri River, covering much of modern Alberta and Montana. Most of their territory was the short-grass high plains, though they also hunted in the foothills and into the Rocky Mountains. The Blackfoot valued bison far above any other game, referring to its flesh as "real meat." Populous and aggressive, the Blackfoot tribes were the major military force of the northwestern Plains.

The Blackfoot Nation comprised three tribes—the Siksika (literally "black foot," from a legend of walking across burned prairie), the Blood or Kainai (meaning "many chiefs"), and the Peigan or Piikani (meaning "scabby robes," from a legend in which the women had not properly prepared the hides). When Manchester House was hastily built in the fall of 1786 along the North Saskatchewan River, near Edmonton, Alberta, it was on the northern frontier of the Siksika. South of them, the South Saskatchewan and Red Deer Rivers defined the Kainai homeland. The Piikani regarded the Bow as the northern edge of their homeland, but they had also crossed into the Missouri River basin. Pressure from the Cree and Assiniboine, constant warfare, epidemic diseases and environmental catastrophes

ABOVE *Sarcee man and woman, near Calgary, 1921.*
CMC 53311

combined to reduce their population, and thus their ability to defend their customary lands.

Although the tribes shared the same language and customs and frequently intermarried, they remained three separate political entities, albeit closely allied for warfare. Despite occasional internal feuds, all three groups freely camped together. They formed their tipis into a large circle, and reserved various sections for different bands. · The name Blackfoot reflects only the fact that traders reached the northernmost group first; it does not correspond to any internal concept of unity.

The Blackfoot Confederacy included the Sarcee. This small Athapaskan tribe originated far to the north and ventured out onto the Plains not long before they encountered fur traders in the late eighteenth century. Traditions recount a common origin with the Beaver people of the Subarctic. In one legend, a feud between two chiefs divided the people. In another, as the original group attempted to cross a frozen river the ice broke; those who had already crossed became the Sarcee and those who remained behind were the Beaver. The Sarcee drifted south into the parklands and foothills at the edge of the Plains, eventually joining the Blackfoot and moving with them onto the high plains. They intermarried with the Blackfoot and adopted the military societies, religious practices and other customs of their allies, retaining only their separate identity and their Athapaskan language.

Also once considered part of the Blackfoot Confederacy were the Gros Ventre, or Atsina. Closely related to the Arapaho, Algonquian speakers inhabiting southern Wyoming and northern Colorado, they split off and moved north onto the Canadian Plains. The early fur traders met them in west-central Saskatchewan, by which point they were already firmly allied with the Blackfoot. A dispute over stolen horses in 1861 broke their friendly ties with the Blackfoot, and turned them into enemies. The Gros Ventre took the brunt of attacks from the Cree and Assiniboine, and were eventually forced south into Montana.

Hostile tribes surrounded the Blackfoot Confederacy. The Ktunaxa (Kutenai) forays onto the Plains from their Rocky Mountains homeland to hunt bison and trade brought them into conflict with the Blackfoot. In the early eighteenth century, the Blackfoot were on friendly terms with the Assiniboine and Plains Cree to the east, and sought their aid in driving the "Snakes" south. By the beginning of the nineteenth century, as the Cree and Assiniboine pushed west and encroached on Blackfoot lands, they became embroiled in bitter hostilities. Warfare became continual on the western Plains until the reserve period. The last major battle between the Blackfoot and Cree was fought near Fort Whoop-Up (near Lethbridge, Alberta) in 1870.

The fur trade affected the Blackfoot far less than the Cree and Assiniboine. Since their arid homeland supported few fur-bearing animals, there was little incentive for traders to establish posts among them. The Blackfoot were not interested in trapping and confined their trade with whites to bison robes and dried meat. In 1754 the Hudson's Bay Company sent Anthony Henday to persuade the western tribes to bring furs to York Factory on Hudson Bay. His trade mission failed when the Blackfoot told him that "it was far off, and they could not live without Buffalo flesh."

As declining bison herds brought the Horse Days to a close, the Blackfoot were obliged to sign Treaty 7 in 1877 and eventually to settle on reserves. The Siksika today occupy a reserve along the Bow River east of Calgary. The Kainai are to the south, on a large reserve along the Belly River, west of Lethbridge. The Piikani, originally the largest of the three tribes, became separated into two groups. The people of the northern division inhabit a small reserve straddling the Oldman River in southern Alberta, whereas the southern division occupies the Blackfeet Reservation in northern Montana. The small Sarcee tribe, now officially known as the Tsuu T'ina First Nation, originally received land on the Bow adjacent to the Siksika, but later moved to their present reserve, which adjoins the city of Calgary. The largest concentration of Blackfoot people in southern Alberta today is in the city of Calgary.

THE PLAINS CREE AND PLAINS OJIBWA

Much of eastern Canada, from the Great Lakes to Hudson Bay and northern Quebec, was dominated by the numerous bands of the Cree and Ojibwa people. When the fur trade expanded to the west, many moved onto the Plains and adopted a new lifestyle. In 1730, when La Vérendrye travelled through Manitoba, he encountered "Cree of the Mountains, Prairies and Rivers," which indicated that some bands were already established on the Plains. The western Ojibwa, termed Saulteaux or Bungi, moved there even later, searching for new lands where furs were plentiful. Eventually, armed with European weapons obtained in trade on Hudson Bay and allied with the Assiniboine, the Cree pushed across the northern Plains to the Rockies. Other groups were displaced in front of them until smallpox and the acquisition of firearms by their enemies finally halted their advance.

The Plains Cree, along with their Assiniboine allies, established themselves as intermediaries between the posts on Hudson Bay and the western tribes. They could make huge profits by taking furs to the posts and bringing back European

RIGHT "Kee-a-kee-ka-sa-coo-way," or "Man who gives the War-whoop," a Cree chief painted by Paul Kane, 1848. ROM 86 ETH 92/912.1.42

goods to trade to more distant groups. Later, when the companies set up posts across the Plains, the Cree and Ojibwa became major suppliers of pemmican and bison hides. Their close association with the fur trade led to the rise of the Métis, from unions between male fur traders and Cree or Ojibwa women.

Many of the Plains Cree and Ojibwa remained an "edge of the forest" people, preferring the parkland environment along the north and east of the Plains. From the shelter of the woods they could venture out onto the Plains in pursuit of bison. Some bands eventually became full-time residents of the open prairies.

Despite their Plains lifestyle, these people did not completely abandon their Woodlands heritage. Fish continued to be important in the diet of most groups, though those bands more fully adapted to Plains life began to develop the hunter's scorn of such food. They introduced the floral designs of the Woodlands to the art of the Plains, mixing it with older geometric patterns. They were regarded as particularly potent conjurers, and other tribes sought their medicines and "love charms." The Plains Ojibwa, in particular, retained many traits of their Woodlands life, including the curing rituals of the Midewiwin (see chapter 5). Despite their new surroundings, they kept their religion and folklore almost intact and blended it with such dramatic rituals as the Sun Dance. They also adapted their ideology to the Plains bison-hunting lifestyle.

When they dwelled in the woodlands, the Cree were closely tied to the Assiniboine. They brought that alliance to the Plains, with territories overlapping in what is today southern Saskatchewan. They camped together, hunted together and intermarried. Many people were bilingual. Some bands became so intermixed that they have been cited as examples of "fused ethnicity"—that is, they were neither Cree nor Assiniboine, but a new hybrid identity. Mid-nineteenth-century accounts describe large camps for bison hunts and the Sun Dance consisting of Assiniboine, Cree, Ojibwa and Métis.

Unlike the Blackfoot, the Plains Cree and Ojibwa lacked a strong tribal organization to tie together their numerous widespread bands. Today they are scattered in small reserves across all three Prairie provinces. The Plains Ojibwa tend to be concentrated in Manitoba and eastern Saskatchewan, whereas the Plains Cree are more numerous in Saskatchewan and Alberta. Cree reserves are frequently shared with the Assiniboine or Ojibwa.

THE ASSINIBOINE, STONEY AND DAKOTA

Today's Assiniboine speak a dialect of the Dakota language in the Siouan stock. Their speech is closest to the Yanktonai Dakota and they are believed to have separated from that group in the woodlands of Minnesota, moving north into what is today Canada. They first entered historic records as a distinct group in 1640, when they were mentioned in the *Jesuit Relations*.

In the mid-seventeenth century, they were a Woodlands people, occupying the area around Lake of the Woods and Lake Winnipeg. Already they were involved in the fur trade, supplying furs through Algonquian intermediaries for the French trade on the St. Lawrence. When the Hudson's Bay Company opened its northern posts later in the century, the Assiniboine, along with their Cree allies and trading partners, began long journeys to York Factory on Hudson Bay. As the trade moved west, the Assiniboine spread across the Plains, into Saskatchewan, Alberta and Montana. There they abandoned almost all vestiges of their Woodlands origins, becoming typical Plains warriors and bison hunters.

With their Plains Cree allies, the Assiniboine waged continual war against the tribes of the Blackfoot Confederacy to the west. To the south, the bitter enmity with their Dakota relatives simmered for centuries. War parties of Assiniboine, Plains Cree and Plains Ojibwa combined to do battle with these foes. At the end of the Horse Days the Assiniboine were distributed across southern Saskatchewan and northern Montana. Their reserves in Saskatchewan today are generally shared with the Cree.

Closely related to the Assiniboine are the Stoney, who split from the main group and established a separate identity, possibly in the eighteenth century. They pushed west to the Rockies, where they battled the Blackfoot for possession of the foothills and eastern mountain slopes. There they hunted bison on the Plains, and elk and other large game in the mountains, and they traded at posts such as Rocky Mountain House. They continued to hold this bountiful land, despite hostilities with the Blackfoot, until the Canadian government forced them and their former enemies to cede their land under Treaty 7. Today they occupy several reserves in the foothills country of western Alberta, the largest being at Morley, between Calgary and Banff.

The Sioux or Dakota remaining south of the border after the Assiniboine split also began to move west onto the Plains. However, not all abandoned their Woodlands heritage. Three large divisions, each containing several major political units, had emerged by historic times. The eastern groups, collectively called the Santee, remained in Minnesota, hunting, fishing, collecting wild rice and growing small plots of corn. From these traditional lands, they continued their age-old wars against the Ojibwa. The central groups, the Yankton and Yanktonai, lived on the edge of the Plains, hunting bison but also fishing and raising crops. On the west, in South Dakota, the Teton lived as typical Plains bison hunters and warriors. These were the people who brought Plains culture to its greatest elaboration, and who, under such famed nineteenth-century chiefs as Sitting Bull and Crazy Horse, became among the best-known of North American Indians.

The commonly used term "Sioux" comes from a French version of an Ojibwa word for "snakes" or, metaphorically, "enemies." Their own word "Dakota" ("allies") has been adopted by most anthropologists to avoid the pejorative term and to eliminate confusion with the larger Siouan linguistic stock. However, the language has three dialects and only the Santee called themselves Dakota. Among the central groups, from whom the Assiniboine emerged, the dialect replaces "d" with "n"; hence the self-designation "Nakota." Similarly, the Teton, whose dialect uses an "l," call themselves "Lakota."

Dakota hunters and war parties frequently ranged north into the Saskatchewan River basin. Alexander Henry's Plains Ojibwa travelling companions warned of constant danger from the Dakota. He recorded Dakota attacks against the Cree on the Red River in 1800 and the Plains Ojibwa at Portage la Prairie in 1806. These clashes were uncomfortably close to the new settlements on the Red River. However, decades passed before the Dakota arrived in large numbers, intending to stay.

The ill-fated Minnesota Uprising of 1862 led to the first large movement of American Dakota refugees into Canada. After their defeat by American soldiers, many Santee dispersed from their homeland. Some fled west to their Teton relatives, and several thousand drifted northwest into Manitoba. Initially, they clustered around Fort Garry, joining the Métis in their bison hunt and trying to avoid hostilities with their traditional enemies, the Plains Ojibwa. Later, many continued to the northwest, following the declining bison herds into Saskatchewan, and to the northern edge of the Plains.

The second wave of refugees to arrive were the Teton Lakota and their chief Sitting Bull. The Lakota signed a treaty with the American government in 1868 that gave them "forever" the land around their sacred Black Hills in South Dakota. The discovery of gold in the Black Hills in 1874 meant that forever lasted only six years. Realizing the futility of further negotiations, the Lakota and Cheyenne prepared for war. In perhaps the most famous battle of all North American Indian wars, the Lakota and Cheyenne annihilated George Armstrong Custer's U.S. Seventh Cavalry at Little Big Horn. Realizing they could not continue to hold out against American military might, the Lakota fled north, hoping the British would treat them more fairly. By the end of 1876, nearly three thousand Lakota were camped around the Cypress Hills and Wood Mountain in southwestern Saskatchewan, to be joined the following spring by Sitting Bull and remnants of his victorious army.

The presence of so many warriors on the border caused great consternation. Officials in Ottawa feared the Lakota would use Canada as a safe base to continue their war with the American military. They also worried about intertribal warfare as the Lakota competed with their former enemies—the Blackfoot, Cree and Assiniboine—for the dwindling bison herds. However, the newly formed North West Mounted Police maintained order and ascertained that the Lakota sought only sanctuary and a chance to settle peacefully in this new land.

Such an opportunity was to be denied them. Although the Santee Dakota had been allowed to remain in Canada only a decade before, much had changed in the intervening years. Canadian law had been imposed on the west, and the vanishing bison herds would no longer support the lifestyle of mobile hunters. Denied reserves and rations, the Lakota were eventually starved out. Sitting Bull stayed until 1881, when he reluctantly returned to the United States. Only a few families remained at Wood Mountain, determined to hold onto their new life in Canada.

Since the Canadian government regarded the Dakota as refugees without claim to lands in Canada, they were not included in the treaties signed with other Plains tribes. Eventually, however, they were assigned reserves. Today, there are ten Dakota First Nations in Manitoba and Saskatchewan. Most are descendants of the Santee Dakota who arrived in the 1860s; only the small community at Wood Mountain remains of the Lakota presence in Canada.

THE RESERVE ERA

The destruction of the bison herds undermined the very lifeblood of the Plains cultures that had existed since the Ice Age. Wanton slaughter by non-Natives for meat, hides and sport, plus the huge hunts organized by the Métis, left few animals for the First Nations of the Plains. The prairies were systematically cleared for European settlement and agriculture. The final disappearance of the herds by the early 1880s was the death knell for the traditional cultures of the Plains people.

Smallpox and other European diseases also took a great toll. Epidemics continued at periodic intervals until late in the nineteenth century. The terrible plague of 1781 is estimated to have killed half of the Blackfoot, and a subsequent outbreak in 1837 wiped out nearly two-thirds of those remaining. As late as 1869, a major smallpox epidemic devastated the Plains tribes, nearly exterminating the already-diminished Sarcee.

American whiskey traders arrived to prey upon the weakened and demoralized survivors. Fort Whoop-Up, established among the Blackfoot in 1870, was the earliest and most notorious of the whiskey posts. Although American law prohibited trade in alcohol to Native People, there was nothing to prevent traders from moving north of the border. Here they exchanged their foul brew for bison hides, dispensing a near-lethal concoction of watered-down alcohol mixed with chewing tobacco, molasses, pain-killer and anything else at hand. Drunken brawls and murders soon became commonplace, and Native People traded away all they owned to continue drinking. A priest among the Blackfoot in 1874 noted that where "formerly they had been the most opulent Indians in the country ... now they were clothed in rags, without horses and without guns" (Dempsey 1972: 76). The turmoil surrounding the whiskey trade was one of the reasons the North West Mounted Police was formed in 1873.

This lawlessness had its most brutal outburst in what became known as the Cypress Hills Massacre. In 1873, while a band of Assiniboine were camped near the traders, a party of white wolf hunters from Montana arrived. Relations between the "wolfers" and Native People had long been strained, and this group was seeking revenge for loss of their horses, apparently taken by Cree raiders. Although none of the horses were found in the Assiniboine camp, pent-up hostilities and heavy consumption of rot-gut liquor on both sides led to an eruption of violence. The better-armed wolfers poured volley after volley into the camp, killing men, women and children. The exact number of deaths is unknown, but estimates range from twenty to forty casualties. Despite Canadian government efforts to bring to justice those responsible for this atrocity, conflicting accounts led to acquittals.

When the bison disappeared, all vestiges of the mobile, autonomous Plains lifestyle eroded. European clothing replaced traditional garb of bison hide, and canvas covered the tipis. Metal tools and European firearms had long since replaced items of local manufacture. With their economy destroyed, destitute bands camped around the posts with nothing to trade.

Weakened by diseases and with their traditional way of life becoming unsustainable, the Plains tribes were in no position to resist government offers of assistance in exchange for signing treaties. Between 1871 and 1877, the First Nations of the Canadian Plains ceded by treaty all claims to their lands. The treaties allocated reserves and provided small payments of money and farm equipment. In only a few decades their fortunes had shifted from proud and self-sufficient hunters, riding freely across the Plains, to destitute and dependent groups, confined to small areas of land where they were forced to live in poverty.

The spectre of starvation soon hung over the new reserve settlements. Government policy encouraged all families to become self-sufficient farmers, and equipment and farm instructors were sent to the reserves to turn the Native hunters into peasant farmers. Log cabins replaced tipis, and garden crops of potatoes, turnips, wheat and barley supplanted traditional country foods. Not all, however, adopted this new lifestyle, and even those who made the transition to farming suffered crop failures and other hardships. Even in good years the crops could not sustain their population, and government rations of beef and flour were needed to supplement their meagre foods. Frequently the rations were inadequate, resulting in widespread hunger and starvation. The new life in small smoky cabins provided fertile ground for tuberculosis, influenza, whooping cough and other diseases. Once the Plains tribes resided permanently on their reserves, their traditional life was largely destroyed, and missionaries and government agents made major efforts to Christianize and acculturate them. Children were instructed in European ways in the newly created residential schools. There the missionaries taught that Aboriginal rites such as the Sun Dance were evil, and the agents actively suppressed such ceremonies. Many Aboriginal People came to believe that they were about to follow the bison into oblivion.

Outbreaks of violence were surprisingly rare. Tribal enmities and traditional values were still strong, and young men sought glory in horse raiding. Skirmishes between Blackfoot warriors and their Assiniboine or Gros Ventre enemies continued into the reserve period. However, the only uprising against agents of the Canadian government was the Northwest Rebellion of 1885 led by Louis Riel and the Métis (see chapter 11). Several Native groups, feeling hungry and betrayed by the government and chafing under the restrictions of reserve life, rose up in sympathy. Cree from One Arrow's reserve and Dakota led by White Cap fought beside the Métis at Batoche, while Cree and Assiniboine bands under Big Bear and Poundmaker took up arms to the west. Despite repeated entreaties, the Blackfoot refused to join the rebellion. One Kainai chief even offered his peoples' services to the government so that they might fight once more against their age-old enemies. The rebellion was short-lived and failed to win any consideration of Native grievances.

Repressive measures were imposed on the reserve residents after 1885. For several decades they needed passes to leave their reserves. Police regularly rounded up individuals who were absent without permission. Such measures isolated bands, preventing them from acting together on their shared grievances and hindering their traditional ceremonial life.

The late religious cults which swept the American Plains were largely ignored in Canada. In their demoralized state, Native Americans of the Plains welcomed such messianic movements as the Ghost Dance, which promised the bison would return and the whites disappear if the dances were faithfully performed. The Teton Lakota, starving and resentful over the loss of their beloved Black Hills, abandoned their small farms and danced, turning the new religion into military resistance. The massacre of one Teton group at Wounded Knee, in South Dakota in 1890, put an end to any further opposition movements on the Plains. In Canada, only a small number of Dakota in Saskatchewan adopted the Ghost Dance religion, and then without the militaristic interpretation of their American kin.

By the end of the nineteenth century the shift from tipis, horses and bison to log cabins, cattle and gardens was complete. Many bands produced substantial agricultural crops, despite outdated technology and inadequate areas of suitable land. Government policies, such as requiring an agent's permit to sell any produce grown on the reserve, undermined this success. The depression of the 1930s and the trend toward large-scale mechanized farming further discouraged such an economy. Lacking adequate capital to compete, many First Nations abandoned their agricultural efforts, often leasing land to non-Native farmers. In the west, the Blackfoot, Sarcee and Stoney were more successful with ranching.

THE MODERN ERA

The lack of economic security has been a chronic problem for Plains reserve communities. This is particularly true of the relatively small Cree reserves in Saskatchewan, where jobs as casual labourers on nearby farms have vanished due to increased mechanization. As a result, many people have relocated to cities such as Regina and Saskatoon in search of better economic opportunities. However, many have simply exchanged their rural poverty for urban despair. Although some people maintain strong ties with their reserves and have returned there eventually, others have settled permanently in the city.

Aboriginal People in Saskatchewan have initiated a successful experiment with urban reserves, which stem from modern land claims settlements, particularly where reserve lands entitled by treaty had never been fully allocated. These land holdings, in centres such as Saskatoon, Prince Albert and Yorkton, are typically used for commercial purposes. Businesses and service providers can lease office space from First Nations, or Aboriginal entrepreneurs can establish businesses on them to take advantage of the tax exemptions applicable on Indian reserves.

The generally larger reserves in western Alberta have offered greater opportunities. Ranching continues to be important to the Blackfoot tribes and the Stoney. A number of on-reserve industrial and commercial developments have also provided employment for band members. For example, the Kainai operate a successful factory constructing prefabricated homes. In addition, revenues from oil and gas have brought relative prosperity to the Stoney. The Piikani have initiated a project to install windmills on their land to produce electricity. Sarcee residents have benefitted from developing their land with recreational facilities, such as a golf course and a luxury resort. Their location adjacent to Calgary has been economically advantageous for the community.

Native traditions remain strong across the Plains. The sacred rituals of the Sun Dance, after a period of neglect, are being celebrated again on many reserves. Elaborate ceremonies are still required for the opening of medicine bundles, many of which have been repatriated to the reserves from museums. Many modern gatherings, however, are more secular and social. "Powwows" are a recent phenomenon and the most notable cultural export from the Plains. Participants can socialize, dance, gamble and reaffirm their Native identity in a modern context. Such events often feature prizes for the best traditional dancer or best jingle-dress dancer. Powwows foster pan-Indianism, a general sense of pride with all things Indian, and blur specific cultural differences between the Plains First Nations.

Rodeos also allow many of the Alberta groups to gather socially and affirm their identity as Native People. The Blackfoot, Sarcee and Stoney participate in

ABOVE *The Blackfoot tribes continue to present feather headdresses to accomplished individuals. A variety of achievements (rather than the traditional military deeds) merit this recognition today. The Piikani awarded Eldon Yellowhorn this headdress in 2004 for completing his Ph.D. at McGill University. Photo by Images Unlimited*

on-reserve rodeos and in larger events such as the Calgary Stampede. Several rodeo champions, including Tom Three Persons, have come from the Kainai community.

Plains First Nations have been very involved in the political battles of the last few decades. Through such provincial organizations as the Indian Association of Alberta, the Federation of Saskatchewan Indian Nations and the Assembly of Manitoba Chiefs, they have fought to settle treaty grievances, to restructure the Indian Act and to place Aboriginal rights in the constitution.

Many Plains First Nations have established cultural centres to preserve their languages and heritage. With the exception of Sarcee, their languages are healthy, though Blackfoot and Dakota are spoken mostly by the older people. The newly established First Nations University of Canada (formerly Saskatchewan Indian Federated College), with campuses in Regina, Saskatoon and Prince Albert, is a Native-run university-college with a range of offerings addressed at Aboriginal People. It offers language instruction in Cree, Assiniboine, Dakota and Ojibwa; Cree and other Aboriginal languages are also taught at several of the provincial universities. The Saskatchewan Indian Institute of Technologies, which provides a range of vocational and training programs, is an Aboriginal post-secondary institution with campuses in Regina, Saskatoon and several smaller centres. The Siksika operate Old Sun Community College (affiliated with Mount Royal College and University of Calgary) on their reserve, and the Kainai do the same with Red Crow Community College (affiliated with Lethbridge Community College). The First Nations of the Plains are increasingly assuming control of their own educational programs and administration, and are taking a prominent role in the nationwide drive for greater Aboriginal self-determination.

The Plateau

· · · · ·

T HE HIGH, generally arid Plateau region lies between the Rocky Mountains on the east and the Coast Mountains on the west. Roughly bisected by the international border, the Canadian portion falls within the southern interior of British Columbia. The northern boundary is less clear, as the Plateau grades into the forested environment of the Subarctic. The Plateau encompasses the territories of the Interior Salish, Ktunaxa (Kutenai) and Chilcotin people, plus a few bands of southern Carrier who pushed into the northern Plateau in relatively recent times.

The Plateau landscape consists of a diverse series of valleys, plateaus and mountain ranges, generally oriented on a north-south axis. The environment varies from sagebrush near-desert in the west to heavily forested mountain slopes in the east. The Fraser River, with its major tributary the Thompson, and the upper reaches of the Columbia River drain the Canadian Plateau. Long, dry, hot summers with cold winters characterize the climate.

The Plateau is also linguistically and culturally diverse. Speakers of four Interior Salish languages—Lillooet (Stl'atl'imx), Thompson (Nlaka'pamux), Okanagan and Shuswap (Secwepemc)—dominate the Canadian portion. The Ktunaxa (Kutenai), whose language is a linguistic isolate, are in the mountainous southeast of British Columbia. The Plateau Athapaskans consist of the now-extinct Nicola in the central Canadian Plateau and the Chilcotin (Tsilhqot'in) and southern Carrier in the north.

Sustained contact with Europeans came late to the Plateau. Nineteenth-century descriptions of Plateau cultures provide only meagre details, and the bulk

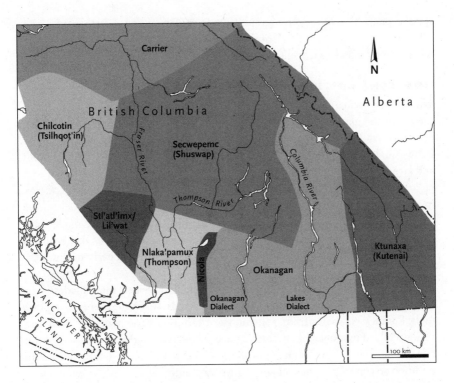

ABOVE *Ethnographic groups in the Canadian Plateau*

of our knowledge comes from ethnographic research conducted early in the twentieth century, particularly by James Teit. Such information is doubtless affected by the late date at which it was obtained.

Huge runs of salmon annually ascend the rivers, and were a major food resource throughout much of the Plateau. Vast quantities were caught and dried for later consumption. Not all Plateau groups, however, had access to salmon rivers, and throughout the Plateau other resources were important. People followed the seasons, hunting, fishing and gathering a wide range of foods.

On the east and west were the dynamic Plains and Northwest Coast culture areas, whose influences were strongly felt in the Plateau. An infusion of Plains traits appeared late in the Plateau, after the horse arrived and the historic Plains cultures were fully developed. Such traits as feather headdresses, tipis and warrior societies characterize this late Plains influence, being particularly marked among such eastern groups as the Ktunaxa. Northwest Coast influences lasted longer, especially along the Fraser and Thompson Rivers, where, because of a shared salmon-fishing economy, Plateau cultures evolved in parallel with those of the coast. Many carvings in stone and antler from archaeological sites on the Plateau closely resemble their coastal counterparts, as do elements of the ceremonies and social organization of the ethnographic western Plateau group. Rather than being a barrier between coast and interior, the Fraser Canyon seems to have been an area where goods and ideas travelled in both directions.

HOLOCENE CULTURAL DEVELOPMENTS

The earliest occupants of the Plateau entered from the south sometime after the retreat of the glaciers freed the land. Exactly when these hunters pursued their prey into what is now the interior of British Columbia is unknown, nor do we know much about how they lived. Undated surface discoveries of fluted points and large stemmed points indicate a way of life generally similar to that of early Holocene cultures on the Plains. Indeed, bison roamed the valleys of the Plateau in early post-glacial times, as did species more typical of the later Plateau such as deer and elk. The discovery of a cache of large, distinctive, finely made fluted points near Wenatchee, Washington, a short distance south of the Okanagan Valley in British Columbia, shows the Clovis culture was present early in the Pacific Northwest.

Several other sites, of post-Clovis origin, have revealed microblades, small razor-blade-like slivers of stone that were used as cutting edges in composite tools. Radiocarbon dates from a site on the Thompson River, where a small excavation yielded microblades and broken deer bones, shows that people were hunting in the Plateau by about 8400 years ago. This culture shared the mobile tradition so common to hunters of terrestrial mammals.

An incomplete skeleton of a young man, discovered at Gore Creek, near Kamloops, dates to this period. A radiocarbon estimate revealed that this unfortunate individual died in a mudslide about 8200 years ago. His skeleton indicates a relatively tall and slender physique, a type often associated with inland hunters. Analysis of the bone showed that he ate mostly food from land sources, and only a small amount of marine food, which was almost certainly salmon. Four millennia would pass before salmon fishing began to dominate the Plateau economy.

The **Mobile Period** begins with these few early sites over 8000 years ago and lasts for over four millennia, until the appearance of pit-house villages marks the adoption of more sedentary lifeways. Sites of this period contain a variety of chipped-stone tools. Microblades are common at many sites, but they disappear from the archaeological record sometime before 4000 years ago. Chipped-stone projectile points, like those on the Plains, changed over time. Leaf-shaped and stemmed points used by early Mobile Period hunters were gradually replaced with corner- and basally-notched points. Small side-notched arrowheads mark the subsequent Sedentary Period. Despite the changes, these cultures are assumed to be ancestral to the historic Interior Salish. Since few architectural features have been preserved, however, we know relatively little about village sites of the Mobile Period.

Most archaeological attention in the Plateau has been on the **Sedentary Period**, with its large and highly visible pit-house villages. This style of housing appeared

ABOVE *Excavation at the Keatley Creek site, a pit-house village near Lillooet, British Columbia. Photo by A. McMillan*

LEFT *Detailed reconstruction of a Nlaka'pamux (Thompson) pit-house by the ethnographer James Teit. Archaeological evidence shows that pit-houses had a range of construction styles.*

CMC 22010

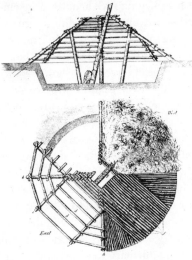

in the Canadian Plateau about 4000 years ago and survived into historic times as the preferred winter home of the Interior Salish and nearby Athapaskans. Pit-houses were circular earth-covered log structures built over excavated depressions. After they were abandoned, the houses decayed and collapsed into the pit, leaving obvious depressions ("house pits") that mark the sites today. The winter villages varied greatly in size, from one or two houses to large concentrations. Over a hundred house pits can still be seen at a few of the larger sites.

Pit-house villages indicate a stable and sedentary way of life, though mobile lifestyles persisted along the eastern edge of the Plateau. Huge surpluses of salmon, taken in the summer and fall and dried for winter use, were stored in bark-lined cache pits, which today crater the ground around the house depressions. Where bone has been well preserved, sites contain harpoon points and other fishing gear, and an abundance of salmon bones. Carbon isotopic analysis on human bone also shows these people obtained much of their protein from salmon.

Although both archaeologists and ethnographers have emphasized fishing and hunting in Plateau life, the gathering of wild plant foods was also important. Even where no trace remains of the plants themselves, there are several indications of their use. Antler handles of digging sticks women used to gather edible roots and bulbs are frequently found. Depressions almost large enough to be confused with house pits provide evidence of earth ovens. Today filled with rock, ash and charcoal, these pits once held quantities of edible roots gathered from upland areas in the spring. Roasting improved both their taste and storage properties, allowing food to be preserved for the winter months when people remained in their pit-house villages.

Permanent village sites in the western Plateau have yielded examples of fine artwork, many pieces resembling those of equivalent age from the adjacent Northwest Coast. Some utilitarian items, such as digging stick handles, were embellished with geometric designs, whereas other artworks included finely carved images in antler and steatite (soapstone). Steatite tobacco pipes, usually trumpet-shaped, were often decoratively carved, and beautifully sculpted steatite bowls took a variety of human and animal forms. One type of carved stone bowl, featuring a seated human figure, was found from Vancouver Island on the coast to Shuswap Lake in the central Plateau. Interior motifs may have inspired some Northwest Coast art. For example, depictions of rattlesnakes, which are endemic to the dry Plateau but not to the coast, have been found on the back or brow of coastal carved stone figures. This imagery, which features humans with frogs or toads and lizards as well as rattlesnakes, suggests levels of meaning unavailable to us but likely associated with shamanism. Whalebone clubs, decorated in a style similar to historic examples from the coast, are occasionally found at Plateau sites and further indicate ties with the coast. Abundant art objects placed with the dead at the Chase "burial mound" (actually a natural ridge used as a cemetery) included steatite carvings, a whalebone club and a unique fragmentary wooden mask, possibly preserved by the numerous copper artifacts also found in the site. The mask has raised peg-like eyes and resembles historic examples used by Salish dancers. A tradition of wooden sculpture, now lost to decay, once linked Plateau art with that of the Northwest Coast. Indeed, we have to question whether there was any sharp distinction between these two areas at that time.

The western Plateau was a strategic trade area. The Fraser Canyon, separating the Plateau from the Northwest Coast, was the major source of the soft steatite used in carving and the hard translucent green nephrite, which was carefully cut

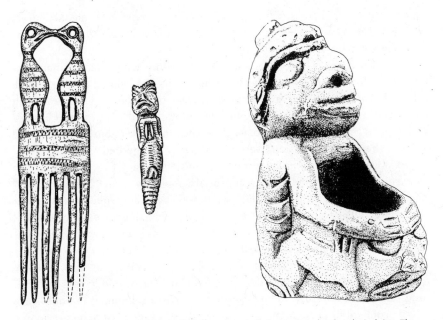

ABOVE LEFT *Small carvings in antler are relatively common in Sedentary Period archaeological sites. The comb adorned with birds and the "rattlesnake-woman" figure were found with an infant burial in a pit-house village site near Lillooet, British Columbia. Drawings courtesy of Arnoud Stryd.* ABOVE RIGHT *A rattlesnake forms the brow of this small (8.7 cm high) steatite seated human figure bowl, found near Lytton at the confluence of the Fraser and Thompson Rivers. Courtesy Simon Fraser University Museum of Archaeology and Ethnology, drawing by Barbara Hodgson*

and polished to form adze blades and chisels for woodworking. Some objects made from nephrite seem far too large and carefully made to have been in everyday use; instead they may have been valuable display items. The canyon also supported one of the major fisheries in British Columbia, and dried salmon was almost certainly widely traded. Such imported goods as obsidian, copper and coastal shell ornaments show long-distance trade. Even pieces of turquoise, which must have originated far to the south, have been found in the Okanagan. Such wealth items presumably conferred prestige and power, hinting that social distinctions characterized these communities.

The most sedentary and culturally complex of the Plateau peoples were in the west, along the Fraser River, where major salmon runs supported dense populations. Evidence can be seen at several very large village sites near the modern town of Lillooet. At Keatley Creek, the most extensively excavated of these sites, over 120 circular depressions mark where houses stood. Archaeologists estimate that at its height 500 to 1000 people lived there in a village considerably larger than any historic example. Several houses exceed twenty metres in diameter, compared to the historic average of six to eight metres. Such huge pit-houses may have been the homes of high-ranking chiefs, or possibly ceremonial structures; in either case they suggest a more complex social organization than was known historically.

Nearby, at another large village site, burials with wealth goods further illustrate social distinctions. One of the larger house pits was a burial plot for a child. Included in the grave were a beautifully carved antler comb and several small sculptures in antler and soft stone, plus several hundred dentalium shell beads, a wealth good traded in from the coast. That such items were buried with a child suggests that social distinctions were at least partially inherited.

Brian Hayden, the archaeologist who excavated Keatley Creek, refers to this period of large villages and evidence for social complexity as the "Classic Lillooet" stage, which reached its height about 2000 to 1000 years ago. Following that time, all the large villages seem to have been abruptly and simultaneously abandoned throughout the region. Hayden and a geographer studying the area have hypothesized that a major landslide blocked the Fraser River about 1000 years ago. This catastrophe would have prevented the salmon from ascending the river, as native traditions document for later slides. A massive landslide would have caused cultural collapse in a society so highly dependent upon salmon, as it would have forced people to disperse into small groups. These societies were just regaining similar levels of complexity at the beginning of the global era, when imported diseases again threatened their culture's survival.

Other archaeological efforts have focussed on the Athapaskan migrations. Members of this linguistic stock pushed south from their homeland in the Subarctic, eventually reaching as far south as the American Southwest. There they became such historic peoples as the Navajo and Apache, who speak languages closely related to those of northern and central British Columbia. In one theory, these people moved southward through the Plateau, and the now-extinct Nicola might have been a remnant of this migration. In the northern Plateau, archaeologists have also attempted to document when the Chilcotin and southern Carrier appeared, but they are generally believed to be late arrivals in their historic homelands. Some writers have seen proof of Athapaskan movements in the distribution of microblades or a particular type of projectile point, yet such tools were not unique to a single ethnic group. Archaeologists generally have been frustrated in their efforts to relate stone tools to known ethnic groups, and evidence for Athapaskan migrations on the Plateau remains elusive.

Among the most dramatic of archaeological remains in the Plateau are the rock art sites. Most are pictographs—painted figures in red ochre (the natural pigment mixed with animal fat or salmon eggs to make a bright and durable paint). Paintings on boulders or cliff faces abound throughout much of Interior Salish territory. They are less common among the Ktunaxa and rare in Chilcotin lands. Depicting humans, animals, supernatural creatures and abstract symbols, they range from single figures to large panels with hundreds of painted images. James Teit's ethnographic work documents the association of these paintings with the guardian spirit

ABOVE *Pictograph sites, such as this one in the Okanagan Valley, are widespread in the Plateau. The rock overhang on the left might once have sheltered an adolescent on his solitary quest for a personal guardian spirit. Under it is painted the image on the right, perhaps depicting his supernatural protector. Photos by A. McMillan*

quest, when adolescents sought secluded locations to fast and wait for an encounter with a supernatural protector. Many of the images on the rocks were painted while praying for supernatural aid or represent guardian spirits. Others record dreams, which were perceived as supernatural messages. Such religious concepts were central to Plateau groups, and the practice of painting these images on rocks is likely ancient, though most still visible would date to later times.

THE INTERIOR SALISH

The international border slices through the centre of the lands occupied by Interior Salish people. Four Salishan languages are spoken on the Canadian Plateau, and others exist to the south.

People speaking the Lillooet language are westernmost. They are divided into the Upper Lillooet (or Stl'atl'imx), on the Fraser River around the modern town of Lillooet, and the Lower or Mt. Currie Lillooet (or Lil'wat) of the Pemberton Valley, which extends into the Coast Mountains. The latter, in particular, were in close contact with coastal groups and brought many coastal customs and trade goods to the Plateau.

The people historically known as the Thompson claim the vital Fraser Canyon and mid-Fraser region, as well as lower reaches of the Thompson River before it joins the Fraser. Named for the explorer who "discovered" the river their ancestors lived along for millennia, these people prefer to call themselves the Nlaka'pamux.

The Okanagan occupy the Okanagan Valley of the southern Canadian Plateau, extending well into the state of Washington. Also speaking a dialect of the Okanagan language were the Lakes people to the east, around the Arrow Lakes. They differed somewhat in culture from the Okanagan proper, being more closely related to the Colville people to the south, who they joined on their reservation in Washington in the late nineteenth century.

The Shuswap, or Secwepemc today, are the northernmost group and inhabit by far the largest territory. Their land stretches from the Fraser River on the west to the Rockies on the east, including the North and South Thompson Rivers and Shuswap Lake.

The Plateau peoples were concentrated along the Fraser and Thompson Rivers, which supported bountiful salmon runs. The Nlaka'pamux and Stl'atl'imx had a particularly high population density, equivalent to anywhere on the Northwest Coast and among the highest in Aboriginal Canada. The major Nlaka'pamux village was at Lytton, at the confluence of the Fraser and Thompson. Here Simon Fraser encountered a community of about 1200 people in 1808. The Okanagan, whose rivers lay near the end of the long Columbia drainage system and had poorer salmon runs, was less densely occupied. In the eastern Plateau, among the Lakes and eastern bands of Secwepemc, population levels were markedly lower.

The Plateau economy was based on a seasonal pattern of movement, in which people lived and worked in small mobile bands from spring to fall. In the winter, several bands formed a larger, relatively permanent village with more substantial housing. There they lived primarily on stored foods and participated in major social and ceremonial activities.

Salmon was the vital Plateau resource, and much of the late summer and fall was spent intercepting the spawning runs. Canyons offered particularly good fishing locations, where masses of large silver fish teemed in the eddies, waiting to fight their way up the next rapids or falls in their journey upriver. There they could be scooped out of the water with large dip-nets, or harpooned or speared or caught in traps. People congregated annually at such fishing locations as the Fraser Canyon, where they built wooden platforms to support themselves along its precipitous walls. The rugged country of the Nlaka'pamux provided numerous excellent fishing spots, and the Stl'atl'imx and many of the Secwepemc had access to smaller canyons. The Lakes moved south to Kettle Falls on the Columbia, where one of their favoured fishing techniques was to place a large basketry trap at the base of the falls so that it interfered with the salmon's leap. Those that failed to clear the falls dropped back into the trap, where the confined space prevented another attempt. The artist Paul Kane described this fishery when he visited the falls in 1847:

> The salmon . . . continue to arrive in almost incredible numbers for nearly two months; in fact, there is one continuous body of them, more resembling a flock of birds than anything else in their extraordinary leap up the falls. . . . The chief

LEFT *Dip-netting for salmon on the Fraser River near Lillooet.* PABC HP68625

told me that he had taken as many as 1700 salmon, weighing on an average 30 lbs. each, in the course of one day. Probably the daily average taken in the chief's basket is about 400. The chief distributes the fish thus taken during the season amongst his people, everyone, even to the smallest child, getting an equal share. *Kane 1968: 218*

Fishing was primarily a male activity, but women were also extremely busy during salmon runs. They had to preserve large quantities of salmon for later use. The fish were cut into fillets and hung on drying racks, to be slowly dried by the warm breezes blowing through the canyons. Roasting preserved salmon well, as it was then dried and pounded into a coarse powder or "salmon pemmican." Dried salmon became a staple food during the winter, allowing large sedentary groups to form. It was also highly valued as a trade commodity to groups lacking a sufficient supply.

Although large numbers of salmon were taken during their annual runs, other species were important throughout the year. Sturgeon, trout, suckers and other fish were caught by a variety of techniques. Some groups even fished with hand lines through the winter ice.

Men also pursued deer, elk, bear, mountain goat and bighorn sheep, as well as smaller prey such as marmot, rabbits and beaver, through much of the year. Hunters favoured the bow and arrow, though they also took animals in snares and deadfall traps. They built long fences to lead deer into snares, or into lakes where they could be hunted from canoes. Hunters frequently used dogs to run down the prey. Some Okanagan even crossed the Rockies to hunt bison on the Plains.

Gathering plant foods also contributed greatly to the diet. In the spring, they enjoyed fresh green shoots of such plants as fireweed and cow parsnip ("Indian rhubarb"). Various edible roots and bulbs, such as balsamroot, bitterroot and wild onion, were dug with sticks of hard wood, then roasted in earth ovens and preserved for winter use. When berries ripened later in the summer, Native People eagerly consumed them fresh and pressed them into dried cakes to be stored for the winter. Groups of women and children, with perhaps a few men, established camps in upland areas abundant in roots or berries, enjoying the opportunity to work together and socialize. Major upland valleys, such as Botanie Valley north of Lytton, attracted people from considerable distances, who came to partake of the harvest but also to trade and visit old friends.

During the coldest winter months people lived in semi-subterranean pit-houses, each of which sheltered several families. They usually chose an area of soft sandy soil near a creek to dig a circular pit. According to James Teit, this task fell to the women, who used their digging sticks and flat-bladed scrapers. Stout rafters were then set in place to support the roof. The log superstructure was covered with bark, then with earth and sod to insulate against the winter cold. Teit's detailed description best documents pit-house construction, but archaeological and ethnographic evidence indicates that a variety of shapes and sizes existed. A notched-log ladder was placed from the inside of the house to an opening at the top, which served as an entrance, smoke hole and skylight. When people slept and during times of danger, the ladder could be set aside and the entrance closed. An elevated platform around the wall was used as sitting and sleeping space. Under the platform and hanging from rafters were baskets and bags containing food and equipment. Although people were warm and secure during the winter months, these houses must also have been dark and smoky, and occupants must have been eager to move again in the early spring, leaving behind only a few old folks content to remain in their insulated homes. Pit-houses could be re-used in following winters, until the timbers began to rot or, as apparently often happened, they became infested with insects, rodents or rattlesnakes. A few groups did not use the pit-house but stayed in mat-covered lodges more typical of the summer months, banking them with earth and snow against the winter cold.

Winter villages ranged from a single large pit-house to a cluster of pit-houses sheltering several hundred people. In the middle of winter they probably would have resembled large mounds of snow, until one noticed well-worn trails leading to the notched-log ladders and smoke escaping from the entranceways on top. On sunny days, people sat outside on the sloping roofs of their homes to work and socialize with their neighbours. Nearby were small huts, constructed for menstruating women and girls entering puberty, who had to be isolated from activities in the main houses. The village might also have had several dome-shaped sweat lodges, where both men and women ritually purified themselves. Bark-lined cache pits, in which food and other goods were stored, might have been lost to sight under dirt and snow, but raised platforms around the houses kept food for more immediate consumption out of the reach of dogs and other animals.

During the mild season, people attended to their fishing, hunting, root-digging or berry-picking camps. Housing was temporary in these satellite camps, as people moved from place to place. The common summer dwelling was a framework of poles covered with mats or bark that could be readily dismantled and moved.

Each winter village (or, in some cases, a small cluster of nearby settlements) was politically autonomous. Village chiefs tended to inherit their positions, and the son of a wealthy and influential chief had a great advantage over other possible candidates. However, he had to prove worthy of the position or his leadership would not be recognized. Each village had several headmen or "chiefs," who were respected for their wealth, oratory, abilities in hunting or fishing, or military affairs. No leader governed groups larger than the winter village or village cluster, and no structure linked the various communities speaking the same language.

Warfare was far from unknown among the Plateau groups. The Secwepemc were embroiled in wars with the Chilcotin, and they occasionally raided the Stl'atl'imx for slaves and dried salmon. The Nlaka'pamux were known as warriors, and they sent out expeditions against the Stl'atl'imx or Secwepemc for plunder, adventure or revenge. A war chief led these parties and a shaman accompanied them, using his supernatural power to weaken the enemy. Most war parties were small, though Teit mentions some Nlaka'pamux expeditions of several hundred warriors. Weapons consisted of spears, bows and arrows, knives and war clubs. According to Teit, the Nlaka'pamux and Stl'atl'imx poisoned arrowpoints with rattlesnake venom or the juice of a small yellow flower. Men wore armour of wooden slats or thick hides and carried shields. In times of danger they would construct a log stockade around the camp; Simon Fraser described a "fortification . . . surrounded with palisades eighteen feet high" among the Stl'atl'imx in 1808. Although the western groups often captured female slaves in war, most of these captives were eventually absorbed into the society and their children were not considered slaves.

The Plateau groups also maintained peaceful trade relationships. Dried salmon, preserved roots and berries, and other foodstuffs were common items of trade. The Stl'atl'imx and Lil'wat were intermediaries in trade with the coast, and it was largely through them that such coastal goods as dentalium and other valuable shells entered the Plateau. In the east, the Lakes traded dried salmon to the Ktunaxa for bison-hide bags and robes. Major fisheries or root-collecting areas drew large numbers of people together, each bringing regional specialties to these large "trade fairs."

Although some groups used dugout canoes of cedar or cottonwood, bark-covered canoes were far more widely distributed. The pointed prow and stern projected under the waterline, leading European observers to refer to them as "sturgeon-nose" canoes. The turbulent rivers of the Plateau, however, largely restricted canoe use to lakes. Most people travelled on foot, transporting personal gear and trade goods on their backs or on the backs of dogs. Snowshoes were widely used for winter travel.

Clothing was prepared from tanned animal hides and generally resembled that of Plains tribes. Male attire was shirts, breechcloths and long leggings, whereas women wore long dresses and short leggings. Both sexes wore deerhide moccasins. Tanned buckskin clothing was a luxury, however, and lower-status individuals had to make do with footgear made of salmon skins. In cold weather they added fur robes and caps. Clothing was often beautifully embellished with porcupine or bird quills, dentalium shells or elk teeth, and in later years with elaborate beadwork. Eagle feathers were also much in vogue, worn either in headbands or attached to clothing.

ABOVE *Nlaka'pamux (Thompson) man and woman in beaded buckskin clothing, 1913.* CMC 20823, 30987

People took considerable care with their appearance. Children of both sexes had their ears pierced, and many also had a hole made in the nasal septum. Inserted in these openings were tubular ornaments of dentalium shell, bird quill or bone, often decorated at each end with pieces of red-headed woodpecker scalp. Necklaces and pendants of dentalium, native copper, grizzly bear claws and other valuables were also worn. Both sexes greased and painted their faces and took care with the hair, oiling it and arranging it in a variety of styles. Simply designed facial tattoos were common, though far from universal, for both men and women.

Artwork in wood was much less developed than on the Northwest Coast, though the Nlaka'pamux and Stl'atl'imx carved powerful images of deceased individuals to set up at cemeteries and occasionally decorated the ends of pit-house ladders. More elaborate was the art of weaving, particularly among western groups. Nlaka'pamux women wove blankets of mountain-goat wool similar to those of their Salish relatives along the lower Fraser, often incorporating complex, brightly coloured geometric patterns. Nlaka'pamux and Stl'atl'imx women also made beautiful coiled cedar-root baskets, carefully working in cherry bark and other materials to form geometric designs. Used for general carrying and storage purposes, some were woven so tightly that they could hold water. Eastern Plateau groups relied more on well-made birchbark containers.

Numerous supernatural beings inhabited the Salish world. Some aided and protected people, some were dangerous, and others were occasionally glimpsed in the woods or waters but took little interest in human affairs. Young people began early in life to prepare themselves to seek supernatural power. At puberty they set out on solitary vigils, fasting and praying while waiting for a guardian spirit to appear in a vision. Although not all who sought such power were successful, those who obtained a vision received supernatural assistance throughout their lives. Some became shamans, gaining power to heal from such spirit encounters. Both men and women could be shamans, healing by extracting the disease-causing object or retrieving the lost soul. Shamans were feared because with their supernatural power they could inflict illness and death as well as cure, and some became malevolent sorcerers.

Some ceremonies reaffirmed religious beliefs, whereas others were purely secular occasions to enliven the long winter months. Throughout the Plateau, Aboriginal People honoured the first roots of the season and the earliest berries to ripen with special ceremonies, and many groups also held a First Salmon rite to welcome the first of the silver masses to ascend the rivers each year. Such ritual observances ensured the continuity of these vital foods. An important winter ceremony, practised on the Canadian Plateau primarily by the Okanagan, was the Guardian Spirit Dance. It was held following instructions received as part of a vision. The dances were performed in winter, when people were assembled in their pit-house villages; failure to do so would result in sickness and death. A more secular event, also carried out during the winter by western groups, was the potlatch, clearly borrowed from the Northwest Coast. To demonstrate his wealth and enhance his prestige, a chief publicly distributed food and goods in a lavish ceremony. The Plateau events, however, were modest compared to the coastal extravaganzas.

Myths and legends of the Plateau Salish featured the exploits of transformers, the greatest being Coyote. Coyote was sent to "put the world in order," transforming the inhabitants into their present human and animal shapes. Coyote brought the salmon up the rivers to the Plateau peoples, after breaking dams on the lower Fraser and Columbia, leaving only rugged canyons where they had stood. Not all of his actions were noble, however, and myths often portray him as greedy, deceitful or obscene. Evidence of Coyote's adventures can be seen throughout the Plateau in various rock landmarks, which are imprints of his passage or are people turned to stone in this mythological age.

THE KTUNAXA

The bountiful but mountainous environment of the easternmost Plateau, up to the high peaks of the Rocky Mountains, was home to the Ktunaxa. These people are generally known in the anthropological literature as the Kutenai (also spelled Kootenay), but that term appears to be derived from a Blackfoot pronunciation of the Ktunaxa word. The drainage of the Kootenay River, including Kootenay Lake, linked the various Ktunaxa bands. With the international border cutting through their territory, they now occupy southeastern British Columbia, northern Idaho and northwestern Montana. Although their land teemed with game, and fish and edible plants were plentiful, the Ktunaxa people were not numerous and population density was low.

The origins of the Ktunaxa are obscure. Their language casts no light on the matter since it has no close relatives (underscoring the unique nature of these mountain-dwelling people), nor do their origin myths clarify this issue, since informants provided Harry Turney-High, the major ethnographer of the Ktunaxa, with conflicting accounts. In one version, the Ktunaxa have always occupied the rich lands of the eastern Plateau, ever since they "woke up" at their "Big Village" of Tobacco Plains, today astride the British Columbia–Montana border. In another version, however, they originated east of the mountains. Certainly this is where they were first encountered by such European explorers as Alexander Henry and David Thompson, the latter providing the clearest statement that the grasslands of southern Alberta were once Ktunaxa territory. Native traditions, historic accounts and the obvious Plains character of Ktunaxa culture have led many researchers to conclude that the Ktunaxa were pushed over the mountains by the Blackfoot, who took control of southern Alberta when they acquired the horse. Others maintain that the Ktunaxa are a Plateau people, who ventured out onto the Plains and borrowed much of Plains culture after the horse arrived in the mid-eighteenth century. The Plains Ktunaxa may have been only a small part of the population, and archaeological evidence suggests that the Ktunaxa have a lengthy history in the Plateau.

ABOVE *A group of Ktunaxa, showing typical Plains traits, ca. 1914.* PABC HP73839

The Upper Ktunaxa, who lived higher on the Kootenay River drainage and closest to the Rockies, strongly resembled the Plains cultures. Although they hunted deer, elk and caribou, they preferred bison. Several times a year the Ktunaxa traversed high mountain passes to hunt on the Plains. Many men, women and children set out on horseback for the summer and fall hunts, whereas smaller groups travelling on snowshoes conducted the mid-winter hunt, which was a much more arduous undertaking owing to deep snow in the passes. Once hunters located the bison herds, they killed the shaggy beasts either from horses, in the fashion of the Plains tribes, during summer and fall, or on snowshoes in winter when hunters could overtake the animals as they floundered in deep snow. Turney-High's informants denied that they ever drove bison over cliffs; however, one myth describes such a technique, which raises the question of whether it reflects an earlier, pre-horse practice of the Ktunaxa or a late diffusion of the story from Plains groups. Although they enjoyed some of the meat fresh, most of it was dried and pounded into pemmican, then stored in Plains-style parfleches (rawhide bags) and taken back over the mountains to be used as a staple food until the next hunt.

Their travels onto the Plains brought the Ktunaxa into conflict with the "enemy people over the mountains," particularly the Blackfoot. As a result, the Ktunaxa organized hunts like military campaigns and preferred to travel in large groups, which made them less vulnerable to attack. Skirmishes took place frequently, and the Ktunaxa displayed all the ferocity of Plains warriors, counting coup on their enemies and taking scalps from the vanquished. Typical of Plains military organizations, members of the Ktunaxa Crazy Dogs Society vowed never to retreat in battle.

The Lower Ktunaxa, farther from the Plains down the Kootenay River and along Kootenay Lake, rarely participated in bison hunts and displayed fewer Plains traits. The animal most important to their economy was the deer, which they hunted in communal drives led by a "deer chief." Long lines of beaters drove the animals to where archers waited, continuing until enough were killed to supply the entire community with dried venison.

The bountiful Ktunaxa environment provided many other resources. Geese, ducks and other birds were abundant. Although the Upper Ktunaxa hunted birds individually, the Lower Ktunaxa banded together, under a skilled "duck chief," to take large numbers of ducks in nets and preserve their flesh as a staple food. All Ktunaxa used hooks, weirs and traps to catch fish of various species, including large sturgeon. The importance of fish in the diet seems out of place in the Plains-oriented culture of the Upper Ktunaxa, but this was a resource no Plateau people could ignore. Similarly, in the use of plant foods the Ktunaxa resembled the Interior Salish. Women used their digging sticks to collect such foods as bitterroot and camas in the spring, and in summer they gathered large quantities of berries, some of which were dried for winter use.

Although they shared a common identity, each band was politically autonomous. Yet when several bands moved together across the mountains, the others would accept the leadership of the Tobacco Plains chief. For the Upper Ktunaxa, military honours conferred prestige and rights to chiefly status, though this position was often hereditary. A council of elders of the Lower Ktunaxa selected as chief the individual with the greatest ability and supernatural strength. Lesser chiefs were skilled men who took charge during such activities as fishing, deer hunting or netting ducks. No class system existed. Among the Upper Ktunaxa high-status positions were held by men who had distinguished themselves by counting coup against the enemy. The Ktunaxa held as slaves any women and children captured in battle, but they were not treated harshly and were usually absorbed into the community through marriage or adoption.

For the Plains-oriented Upper Ktunaxa, the hide-covered tipi was the year-round dwelling, though some informants also recalled use of a mat-

ABOVE *A Ktunaxa chief.* CMC 41202

covered lodge in winter. The Lower Ktunaxa covered their summer tipis with rush mats or covers sewn from dogbane ("Indian hemp"). In winter, they covered elongated lodges, each of which sheltered a number of families, with the same materials. The Ktunaxa did not live in the semi-subterranean pit-houses common to the rest of the Plateau, nor did they adopt sedentary lifeways.

They travelled along lakes and rivers in various watercraft, but most commonly in the "sturgeon-nosed" bark-covered canoe. In this area of mountainous terrain, they went most often on foot, snowshoeing in winter and using the dog as a pack animal. When the horse was introduced in the eighteenth century, the Ktunaxa ranged much farther afield, hunting and trading far out onto the Plains. They packed goods in bags on horses rather than using the Plains-style travois.

The Ktunaxa's tanned-hide clothing conformed to the general Plains-Plateau pattern of shirt, breechcloth, leggings and moccasins for men, and a long dress, leggings and moccasins for women. They added robes, hats and mittens in cold weather. The Ktunaxa rarely decorated their clothing; instead, the whiteness of the hide and lavish use of long fringes supplied aesthetic appeal. Only in recent times, under the influence of such groups as the Plains Cree, has beadwork been added and have Plains-style feather headdresses appeared. Both sexes wore their long hair in braids, which were only cut in mourning. For festive occasions, both sexes painted their faces and adorned their braids with items such as weasel tails.

Ktunaxa religious concepts resembled those of both the Plains and the Plateau. Young people embarked on solitary quests for supernatural guardians, the spirit power they received aiding them in hunting, warfare or other activities throughout their lives. Some guardian spirits gave the power to cure, making human recipients powerful shamans. Objects indicated in a vision were gathered and placed in a sacred medicine bundle, in the fashion of the Plains tribes.

Their ceremonies were almost purely Plains in character. Unlike the Interior Salish, the Ktunaxa did not conduct rituals to welcome the earliest salmon, roots and berries. The major ceremony, which might bring together both Upper and Lower Ktunaxa, was the Sun Dance. Generally held every spring, the dance's exact time and place were revealed to the Sun Dance Chief in a dream. Members of the Crazy Dogs military society were summoned to take charge of proceedings. Although the Ktunaxa had their own distinct version, and lacked such Plains embellishments as the self-torture of young men, the Ktunaxa ritual shared the basic features of the Plains Sun Dance.

Myths of the Ktunaxa reflect influences from several sources. Some have a strong Plains cast, whereas others, particularly those featuring Coyote as transformer, are nearly identical to Interior Salish tales. A few, in which the transformer takes the guise of Raven, closely resemble myths of the Northwest Coast. In mythology, as in much of their culture, the Ktunaxa present an intriguing fusion of ideas from both east and west.

THE PLATEAU ATHAPASKANS

The Athapaskans are one of the great linguistic stocks of Aboriginal North America, occupying the entire western Subarctic from Hudson Bay to the interior of Alaska. At various times in the past, some populations wandered far from their Subarctic homeland and eventually settled in new environments where they took on many of their neighbours' characteristics. This Athapaskan expansion continued in historic times, as groups pushed into the northern Plateau. (Chapter 9 deals more fully with the Athapaskan way of life.)

A small enclave of Athapaskans, the now-extinct Nicola, inhabited the Nicola and Similkameen river valleys of south-central British Columbia when Europeans first entered their homeland. In all but speech they resembled the Interior Salish, living in pit-house villages during the winter and dispersing in summer to their satellite camps of mat-covered shelters. Their economy was the same as other Plateau groups, except that salmon did not ascend their rivers, which forced them to trade for dried salmon with their Salish neighbours. They are believed to be remnants of an early Athapaskan migration southward, or late arrival of a Chilcotin war party, who intermarried with the Interior Salish and settled among them. Disease, intermarriage and Nlaka'pamux, Okanagan and non-Native encroachment on their lands led to the Nicola's disappearance as a distinct people before the end of the nineteenth century.

At the northern edge of the Plateau were the Chilcotin (Tsilhqot'in) and southern bands of the widespread Carrier people. These were the southernmost languages in the huge continuous distribution of northern Athapaskans. Chilcotin country lies between the Coast Mountains and the Fraser River, including most of the Chilcotin River drainage and the headwaters of several rivers flowing west to the Pacific. Both archaeological and ethnographic evidence suggest that the Chilcotin were late arrivals in their modern homeland, perhaps moving in from the north only at the beginning of the global era, attracted by access to European goods through the Nuxalk at Bella Coola and the possibility of establishing themselves as intermediaries in trade to the Plateau. They were still expanding their territory in the late nineteenth century, moving eastward to land along the Fraser formerly held by the Stl'atl'imx, as were several bands of Carrier. Chilcotin traditions recount battles with both the Carrier and Secwepemc.

In the "memory culture" recorded by ethnographers, the Chilcotin reveal many Plateau traits. To supply their diet of country foods, they hunted, fished, dug roots and collected berries through the seasons. Not all Chilcotin had access to salmon, so they traded with the Secwepemc and Nuxalk for additional supplies. In winter, many lived in Plateau-style pit-houses, though these were usually smaller than the Salish ones since they often sheltered only one family. Others retained more typically Subarctic winter houses of logs or poles, roofed with bark. Women made beautiful split-root coiled baskets like the Salish, but Chilcotin examples are distinguished by a strengthening hoop of willow beneath the rim and elaborate decoration, often depicting animals, covering the outer sur-

face. From the Nuxalk over the Coast Mountains they obtained dentalium and abalone shells, eulachon oil and European goods in exchange for cakes of berries, mountain-goat skins and furs. They highly valued the tubular dentalium shells, which they commonly wore as nose and ear ornaments, often embellished with tufts of red-headed woodpecker scalp in the Interior Salish fashion. They also traded these shells to the Salish, whose name for the Chilcotin, according to Teit, means "dentalium people."

Chilcotin society was loosely divided into three classes: nobility, commoners and slaves. They had some knowledge of a clan system, though a child could apparently inherit from either the mother or father. At least some bands developed hereditary chiefs, and such high-ranking men vied for prestige by distributing wealth at potlatches. However, the Chilcotin adopted this complex of traits—perhaps from the Nuxalk—very recently and only weakly grafted them onto an essentially egalitarian society more typical of the Athapaskans.

THE PLATEAU CULTURES IN THE GLOBAL ERA

The Plateau, like other areas in Canada, entered the global era with the trade in furs. This new economy provided many novel technologies but also brought many previously unknown diseases. Native People first encountered the explorers who were agents of the fur trade companies. Alexander Mackenzie passed through the lands of the northern Secwepemc and Chilcotin on his way to the Pacific in 1793. David Thompson was in Ktunaxa country by 1807 and among the

Lakes in 1811. Simon Fraser, on his epic journey in 1808 down the river that now bears his name, came into fleeting contact with the Chilcotin, Secwepemc, Stl'atl'imx and Nlaka'pamux. When these Europeans arrived, horses had already been among the Plateau people for generations. Although the horse was vital to eastern groups such as the Ktunaxa, it played only a minor role as a pack animal in the western Plateau. By the time of Simon Fraser's visit, the Salish had also acquired European goods through trade with the coast. Fraser observed copper kettles and a "gun of large size." More seriously, he also noticed several Native people suffering from smallpox, this dreaded European-introduced disease having reached the Plateau before the Europeans themselves.

In the years following these initial contacts, the fur trade companies established posts in the Plateau. Native people were drawn into the fur trade, which depleted game stocks and created dependence upon new goods, such as firearms and metal tools, brought by the traders.

Intensive contact did not disrupt Native lifeways until 1858, with the gold rush on the Fraser River. An influx of thousands of men seeking quick riches created a mining frontier among the Interior Salish. Although the fur traders saw Native People as essential partners, to the miners they were merely obstacles to be moved or eliminated. Natives were displaced from their traditional village locations and their vital fisheries, and in the lawlessness surrounding this new frontier acts of violence were commonplace.

This population surge led to the proclamation of British Columbia as a Crown colony in 1858, which encouraged permanent settlement. Native People found themselves in continuing conflict with Europeans, who no longer needed their services but wanted their lands. Increasingly these were usurped by new settlers, who rejected Aboriginal claims. In addition, greater contact with the new arrivals subjected Plateau Natives to new outbreaks of diseases such as smallpox and measles. Particularly devastating was the smallpox epidemic of 1862–63 that swept across British Columbia, killing about one-third of the Native population.

Although conditions for Aboriginal People in the 1860s were so appalling that colonists feared an "Indian war," outbreaks of violence were generally minor. The most serious clash came in 1864, as a party of European labourers attempted to construct a wagon road across Chilcotin country. Recognizing how this would affect their land and culture, and blaming the work party for outbreaks of smallpox and harsh treatment of Native employees, a band of Chilcotin attacked their camp, killing fourteen of the seventeen men. Shortly after, the Chilcotin attacked a pack train crossing their country and looted several homesteads, during which several more whites were killed. To quell the uprising, the new colonial government sent out a large military force. After initial failures, the soldiers enticed the Chilcotin into their camp. The Chilcotin, apparently believing they had been promised a truce or pardon, were promptly arrested and taken away for trial. The subsequent hanging of five Chilcotin leaders brought to an end the so-called "Chilcotin War."

Adapting to declining populations and loss of lands, many groups moved. The Lakes joined their relatives on the Colville Reservation in Washington; when the reserve established in British Columbia was abandoned, the Department of Indian Affairs declared the group extinct, a conclusion Lakes descendants now contest. The Nlaka'pamux and Okanagan expanded into the territory of the Nicola, who disappeared as a separate people. Bands of Carrier pushed south into the heart of former Chilcotin country, which was left largely vacant as many of the Chilcotin moved east into former Secwepemc lands along the Fraser River. The Secwepemc had abandoned this land as their numbers dwindled. Considerable differences exist between the modern reserve distribution and ethnographic territories.

The Plateau groups were assigned reserves during the 1870s and 1880s. As each band was a small, separate political unit, these reserves were small and scattered. Each band was given traditional village sites but lost all former hunting and gathering areas. Reserves were allocated out of lands traditionally claimed by Aboriginal groups; they did not sign treaties or otherwise cede any of the remaining land.

When Aboriginal groups were confined to reserves they lost control over important economic resources outside their reserve boundaries. Ranches and settlements soon spread throughout the rest of their traditional lands, driving away game and destroying berry patches and root-digging sites. Many traditional fishing locations at canyons and falls were flooded by dams. Particularly catastrophic was a landslide caused by blasting for railway construction in 1913, which tumbled millions of tons of rock into the Fraser Canyon and blocked the salmon from reaching their spawning grounds. The Fraser's fish stocks plummeted and required decades to recover.

The major ongoing political struggle for Plateau First Nations involves attempts to redress the loss of traditional lands never surrendered through treaty. Early in the twentieth century, Salish chiefs formed an organization termed the Interior Tribes of British Columbia. Ethnographer James Teit assisted this group and joined in a delegation to Ottawa to present their land case. A 1915 meeting led to an alliance of interior and coastal groups known as the Allied Tribes of British Columbia, with the settlement of land claims issues as its major goal. A government amendment to the Indian Act in 1927 raising funds to pursue land claims, and the Allied Tribes association collapsed. More recently, Plateau First Nations have been active in organizations such as the Union of British Columbia Indian Chiefs, which was formed in 1969. George Manuel, a Secwepemc from near Chase, became the first president of this provincial organization; he also served as president of the National Indian Brotherhood and founding president of the World Council of Indigenous Peoples. Saul Terry, a Stl'atl'imx from near Lillooet, headed the union through much of its history. The union is perhaps best known for its uncompromising stand on Aboriginal title and its refusal to participate under the terms of the B.C. Treaty Commission. Accordingly, only a few of the Plateau First Nations are pursuing treaties through that process.

A highly publicized example of conflicts over land issues occurred in the Stein Valley, near Lillooet. Plans to log the valley alarmed the Nlaka'pamux and Stl'atl'imx, who feared damage to their heritage sites in what had been an important hunting and spirit quest area. They sought to block any logging of the valley. Realizing that legal channels would be insufficient, they mobilized public support with large "Save the Stein" summer festivals. The creation of a provincial park on these lands, jointly managed by the province and the Nlaka'pamux, has at least partially resolved the issue.

Plateau First Nations are also taking bold steps in education, to ensure their cultures and languages are preserved, and to provide the skills necessary for modern economic success. Many reserve communities run their own programs, including Aboriginal language instruction, in their schools. The Nicola Valley Institute of Technology near Merritt, founded in 1983, became the first Native-run college in the province. Now a provincially designated institute, it is authorized to grant its own certificates and degrees. The programs focus particularly on business courses and First Nations studies, as well as natural resources and social work classes. In 1989 the Secwepemc Cultural Education Society entered into a collaborative agreement with Simon Fraser University to establish a Native-run post-secondary educational facility on the Kamloops Reserve. Among the programs offered are certificates in First Nations language proficiency and degree-option programs in anthropology and archaeology. The archaeology field school for Aboriginal students has investigated Aboriginal heritage sites on the Kamloops Reserve and trained the personnel who manage their cultural legacy.

Today, as tourists set out for the scenic Fraser Canyon, the beaches of the sunny Okanagan Valley or the mountain splendour of Kootenay National Park, they pay little attention to the small Native communities along the way. Many Interior Salish, Chilcotin and Ktunaxa people still occupy ancestral lands, though they are divided into numerous bands spread across many small reserves. Some, such as the Okanagan, hold valuable real estate as reserve lands, and leasing to non-Natives for residential and recreational use has made them relatively prosperous. Others are not so fortunate. Although little immediately distinguishes these small communities from others around them, many First Nations are attempting to revive traditional customs and ceremonies. When the salmon runs ascend the Fraser River, men can still be seen with their dip-nets poised over the turbulent waters. Casual observers scanning the valley walls around Lillooet or through the Fraser Canyon can still see wooden racks hanging crimson with the flesh of drying salmon, the mainstay of Plateau life for millennia.

CHAPTER 8

The Northwest Coast

· · · · ·

OASTAL RAIN FOREST hugs the Pacific shores from southeastern Alaska to northwestern California, including the entire coastline of British Columbia. Frequently shrouded in clouds, the rainy coast bears a lush green mantle of cedar, fir, hemlock and spruce. Along much of the coast, rugged mountains descend precipitously to the sea, requiring Native cultures to be well adapted to a maritime way of life. Studded with island archipelagos and interposed by bays and fiords, the convoluted coastline offers protected village locations and access to a great variety of resources. Huge dugout cedar canoes once traversed these waterways, transporting people for feasts and ceremonies between large villages of cedar-plank houses. Coastal culture extended far up the major rivers—the Nass, the Skeena and the Fraser—so that even groups lacking direct access to salt water shared the coastal lifestyle. Despite diversity in language and customs, a common cultural pattern existed along the entire Northwest Coast.

Salmon and cedar were the essential resources. Salmon annually ascended the rivers in vast quantities, allowing Native People to accumulate huge food surpluses. The sea supplied fish of many species, seals and sea lions, and almost inexhaustible supplies of clams, mussels and other "beach foods." Compared to the largesse of the sea, foods from the land were less important. Stands of tall, straight-grained cedar, however, provided a near-perfect medium for the talents of Northwest Coast woodworkers. This material was the basis of the elaborate artwork and technology that characterize the Northwest Coast.

This secure economy supported the densest populations and most complex political organizations in northern North America. Social distinctions based on

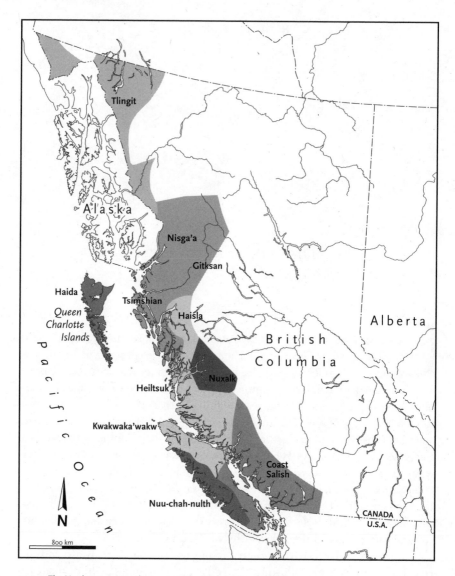

ABOVE *The Northwest Coast culture area with ethnographic groups*

birth, dividing the society into nobles, commoners and slaves, are characteristic of all the coastal First Nations. They also developed a sophisticated art tradition, considered by many to rank among the world's great artistic achievements. Chiefs held elaborate potlatches, at which they validated and enhanced their status by offering huge feasts and publicly distributing wealth. Dancers gave dramatic performances wearing masks and other regalia for which Northwest Coast artists are so justly famed. These complex chiefdoms challenged the assumptions of early anthropologists, who had associated such cultural achievements with agricultural societies, not with people who lived by hunting and fishing.

The Northwest Coast was also the most linguistically diverse area of Aboriginal Canada. At least sixteen languages, from five different language families, were once spoken along the British Columbia coast. In the north are the Haida and Tsimshian (the latter divided into at least two languages, with several major dialects), as well as the Tlingit of the Alaskan Panhandle, whose distribution extends a short distance into Canada. The central groups belong to the Wakashan family, consisting of two major branches. The northern Wakashans are the Haisla, Heiltsuk and Kwakwaka'wakw, who were once erroneously termed the "Kwakiutl," and the southern Wakashan are the Nuu-chah-nulth, speaking two closely related languages. Also on the central coast are the Nuxalk (or Bella Coola), a northern enclave of Salish speakers. On the southern British Columbia coast are the Coast Salish, speaking six related languages. Four of the five language families are found only on the Northwest Coast, and all five are unique in Canada to British Columbia.

HOLOCENE CULTURAL DEVELOPMENTS

By at least 13,000 years ago the glaciers' retreat toward the mountaintops had made large areas of land available for human settlement. The first arrivals would have encountered a landscape markedly different from that of recent times. As glacial meltwater rushed to the ocean, sea levels rose, flooding the coastline and creating such features as a large saltwater arm reaching far up the valley now drained by the Fraser River. Relieved of the great weight of ice, the land also gradually rebounded. Sea levels fluctuated markedly along the entire coast for thousands of years, presenting great obstacles to our search for remains of this period. No trace has been found of the earliest arrivals, whose travels along the now-submerged continental shelf may have been a vital part of the story of how this continent was settled. Even for somewhat later times, much of the evidence has been lost to the ravages of time and the restless movements of the sea.

On the Queen Charlotte Islands (now often called Haida Gwaii) of the northern coast, Parks Canada and Haida archaeologists are making concerted efforts to locate early sites. From the interior of a muddy cave researchers have recently recovered bones of bears that once roamed these shores, along with a portion of a chert spearpoint, possibly carried back to the cave by a wounded animal, in deposits dated at 11,000 years. If this age is confirmed, it will be among the earliest dated traces of human presence in Canada.

These researchers are also examining the sea level history that affects archaeological recovery. From late glacial lows, sea levels at Haida Gwaii rose very rapidly, transgressing the modern shoreline about 9400 years ago. Excavation at Kilgii Gwaay, near the southern end of the island archipelago, revealed artifacts and intact shell deposits from that time in the modern intertidal zone. This site contained not only stone tools, but also bone and even wood utensils, such as wedges and cordage, preserved by waterlogging. Discarded animal bones and shells provide insights into the diet of these early island people. These indicate a fully maritime way of life, involving a range of fish, sea mammals and sea birds, as well as black bears and shellfish. In fact, the faunal pattern generally resembles that from much more recent Haida village sites. Kilgii Gwaay could only have been occupied briefly, perhaps the century between 9500 and 9400 years ago, as the sea continued its relentless rise. It reached its maximum height, about fifteen metres above present levels, by 9000 years ago. Further north in Haida Gwaii, the Richardson Island site, located on a raised beach well above the modern shoreline, provides evidence for this slightly later period. This research shows that sites that predate Kilgii Gwaay are now under water and that later sites should be sought on raised terraces well back in the modern forest. After about 5000 years ago, sea levels on Haida Gwaii gradually dropped toward their modern level, placing Kilgii Gwaay once more along the shoreline.

Soon after the glaciers retreated, the sea level rose so rapidly in Haida Gwaii that individuals would have noticed the change within their lifetimes. Adults who had lived at certain shoreline locations since childhood would have been aware that the sea was constantly encroaching. They would have heard from their parents and grandparents of former villages now well out under the waves. Such geological forces may have inspired oral traditions that have survived this long passage of time. Haida stories prominently feature rapid rises of the sea and tell of land where none exists today.

The **Early Holocene** (about 11,000 to 5500 years ago) encompasses the period before sea levels began to stabilize along the west coast. It has been variously termed the Lithic Stage, the Pebble Tool tradition and the Old Cordilleran culture. At most sites, only stone tools remain of the tool kits once possessed by these early people. Large, leaf-shaped spearpoints and numerous "pebble tools" (smooth cobbles or pebbles picked up from the beach or riverbank and bashed to remove a few flakes, creating a sharp edge) are the trademarks of these early occupants. The pebble tools, though they look crude, could be quickly produced, used for various cutting or chopping tasks, and then discarded. Such tools have been found in deposits dating as far back as 9700 years ago at the Namu site, in Heiltsuk territory on the central coast. They are also abundant at the lowest levels of the 9000-year-old Milliken site in the Fraser Canyon and the deep Glenrose Cannery site on the lower Fraser River. When people first lived at Glenrose over 8000 years ago, this site was near the mouth of the Fraser, now about twenty kilometres downriver. The economy of these early people does not appear to have been as specialized as that of later coast dwellers. They hunted land mammals and they exploited the riches of the sea and rivers. At Milliken the discovery of numerous charred pits of the wild cherry, which ripens during the time of the salmon runs in August and September, suggests that even during this early period Northwest Coast peoples were timing seasonal movements to be at major fishing locations when the salmon appeared.

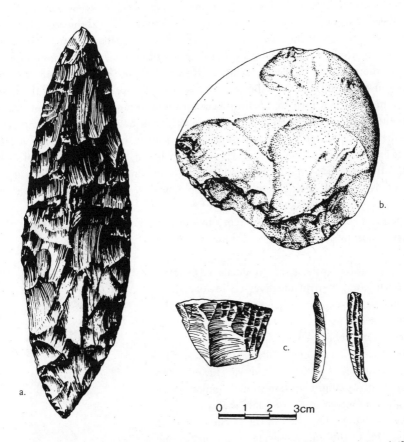

ABOVE *Artifacts from the Early Holocene period on the Northwest Coast: (a) leaf-shaped spearpoint or knife; (b) pebble tool; (c) microblades and microcore. Courtesy Simon Fraser University Museum of Archaeology and Ethnography, drawings by Barbara Hodgson*

Later in this stage small, thin, parallel-sided flakes, like miniature razor blades, struck from specially shaped cores, appeared on the northern and central coast. Known as microblades, these once were hafted as the cutting or piercing edges of composite tools, whose wooden, antler or bone handles have not survived. This was an efficient technology, as it provided the largest cutting surface from small pieces of suitable stone. Microblades originated in northern Eurasia and spread into Alaska by about 11,000 years ago and to the northern Northwest Coast by 9000 years ago. They are found in the early deposits at Richardson Island, on Haida Gwaii, which date to that time. By about 8500 years ago microblades were added to the tool kit at Namu, on the central British Columbian coast. Their discovery on outer coast islands indicates that the people who made the microblades used watercraft and relied heavily on the sea for subsistence.

These relatively small groups grew into large, complex societies in the **Emergent Period** (about 5500 to 1500 years ago). During this period the seas stabilized at close to the levels they are at today, and the land gradually took the shape with which we are familiar. Great stands of cedar covered the land, and more salmon made their way up the rivers each year. New techniques, both for taking salmon and for preserving most of the catch for later consumption, sustained the large communities that formed. Shellfish became an important part of the diet, which resulted in the huge shell middens that mark former habitation sites. Some, such as the famous Marpole midden in southern Vancouver, once spread up to five metres deep over several hectares. Today the layers of crushed clam and mussel shell, with fire-cracked rocks, charcoal and ash, indicate ancient villages where layer after layer of garbage accumulated as people lived seasonally on the sites over thousands of years. All along the coastline and under many modern reserve communities lie vestiges of these ancient village sites.

Excavations at these shell middens have yielded a much more plentiful and diverse array of artifacts than what appears in earlier eras. In part this is because larger populations enjoyed a more secure economic base. Moreover, cultures during this period became increasingly adept at exploiting the rich resources of the rivers and sea. However, earlier cultures might appear more complex if we could see more of their tool kits than just implements of stone. The shell in the middens neutralizes acids in the soil, preserving artifacts of bone, antler and shell that provide a fuller picture of the peoples' technological ingenuity.

Unfortunately, we still do not have objects of raw materials such as wood, bark, root and hide, which were vital to these early artisans but are not preserved in shell middens. Only in deposits that have been continuously waterlogged (termed "wet sites" by archaeologists) do objects of wood or plant fibre survive. Under usual conditions, even the more abundant remains of this period provide only a limited view into the nature of these societies.

Sites from early in the Emergent Period, perhaps covering the first two millennia, are less well known and appear less complex than those from the following two millennia. Stone tools shaped by grinding and polishing have been found at these

ABOVE *This antler sculpture of a man with his hair drawn into a top-knot, from the Glenrose Cannery site on the Fraser River, once served as the handle of a carving tool. Dated at over 4000 years, it is one of the oldest art objects from the Northwest Coast. Laboratory of Archaeology, Department of Anthropology and Sociology, University of British Columbia*

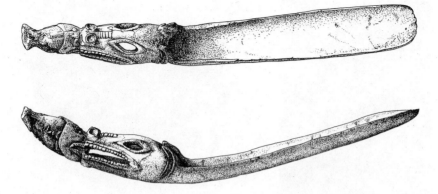

ABOVE *This carved antler spoon, depicting a fish confronting a wolf, was found at the Pender Canal site in a context that suggests ritual use in feeding the dead. The wolf's head is hollow, indicating that it may represent a mask used in rituals. The spoon is radiocarbon dated to about 3600 years ago. Simon Fraser University Museum of Archaeology and Ethnology, courtesy Roy Carlson*

sites, and the earliest known art objects also appear. Particularly impressive is a small antler sculpture from the Glenrose Cannery site on the Fraser River. Depicting a human with what appears to be a beard and an elaborate hairdo drawn into a topknot, it was probably once the handle of a carving tool (the hollow at the back held a beaver tooth as the cutting edge), showing that the practice of decorating functional objects extends far back in time. Labrets (lip plugs worn through a slit in the lower lip) have also been unearthed at these sites. Historically only high-ranking women on the northern coast wore labrets, but Emergent Period sites show both sexes once used them along much of the coast. There is no evidence, however, for the large cedar-plank houses of later times or the social ranking characteristic of ethnographic groups. Emergent Period cultures were clearly becoming more complex but had not yet reached historic forms.

The Pender Island site in the Strait of Georgia, which dates to the end of this initial stage and into the subsequent Locarno Beach phase, provides evidence of emerging social complexity. Labrets found at this site may indicate status distinctions, which are also suggested by different forms of burial treatment. Several individuals were buried with finely carved antler spoons that have handles embellished with zoomorphic images. In several cases, the spoon was placed by the individual's face, leading Roy Carlson, the site excavator, to speculate that they reflect a ritual of feeding the dead, an ancient concept in Salish culture. Carlson argues that the cut-out figures on some of the spoons represent animal masks rather than the animals themselves, and that they are evidence that the potlatch and its attendant masked dances were part of Native life on this coast at least 5000 years ago. From these spoons he also infers that there were shamans and possibly specialized craftspeople in the villages.

ABOVE LEFT *Haida woman wearing a labret, 1884. RBCM PN1053-B.* ABOVE RIGHT *(drawing) A 3000-year-old basket, recovered from waterlogged deposits on the Musqueam First Nation Reserve in Vancouver. Drawing by Kathryn Bernick*

During the final two millennia of this period, the distinctive Northwest Coast cultures emerged. The Locarno Beach phase of the Fraser River/Strait of Georgia region on the south coast dates from roughly 3500 to 2500 years ago. Projectile points chipped of basalt, large points of ground slate and bone, and microblades of quartz crystal are among the more common artifacts from this period. Labrets and earspools (pulley-shaped objects believed to have been worn by perforating and stretching the earlobes) may have indicated status. Although the ethno-graphic cultures did not use earspools, they are found in archaeological sites, and images of humans with such ear ornaments appear on stone sculptures and a carved antler spoon from Pender Island. A small antler carving from the Locarno Beach site depicts a man wearing a conical hat similar in shape to historic bas-ketry examples, and several basketry hats with knobs at the top, historically indi-cating high status, came from waterlogged deposits of this age on the Olympic Peninsula. A site on the Musqueam Reserve in southern Vancouver also yielded 3000-year-old waterlogged basketry, which shows that Locarno Beach people were already masters of the weaver's art.

The culture on the southern coast during the Marpole phase (about 2500 to 1500 years ago) seems to have been even more complex. Particularly common arti-facts are large barbed antler harpoon heads, projectile points chipped from basalt or ground from slate, thin ground-slate knives for filleting salmon, and microblades. Also found were elements of a specialized carpenter's tool kit—antler wedges for splitting straight-grained cedar, carefully polished adze and chisel blades of hard stone for shaping wood, and distinctive hand mauls, laboriously pecked and ground from hard stone, used as hammers to drive wedges and chisels. Although we have no direct evidence for Marpole-phase houses, large circular stains mark

ABOVE *This small seated human figure bowl came from the Marpole site, near the mouth of the Fraser River. Laboratory of Archaeology, Department of Anthropology and Sociology, University of British Columbia.*

where huge posts once stood, suggesting that villages of plank-covered houses similar to those known historically stood along the waterways of the southern coast 2000 years ago.

The Marpole people also produced artworks and objects of personal adornment. They continued to use labrets, and wore long strings of stone and clamshell beads. A few caches containing thousands of beads may have belonged to high-status individuals who displayed this great wealth on special occasions. They also wore necklaces of dentalium shell, an item of affluence traded from western Vancouver Island, as well as a variety of pendants of stone, bone, antler and tooth. Some of these pendants and other small objects are miniature masterpieces of artistic achievement, skillfully depicting images of humans, animals and birds. Such items may have been charms worn by shamans, or they may be representations of guardian spirit powers, or the beginnings of the crest art so well known for many of the historic groups.

Some of the finest surviving Marpole artworks are sculptures in stone, most commonly steatite. Particularly striking examples feature a seated human holding a shallow bowl. Frequently adorning the bowl or merging with some part of the human are snakes, lizards or frogs—presumably powerful shamanic images. Depiction of vertebrae and other skeletal elements on these bowls may represent the shaman's "x-ray vision." Such bowls may have been potent ritual objects. Although they cannot be dated, three such bowls discovered during early excavations at the Marpole midden suggest that most belong to this period. Certainly their style is consistent with other stone and bone carvings found in clearly dated Marpole contexts.

Archaeological evidence indicates that ranked societies, with chiefly classes consolidating their power through lavish displays of wealth, had emerged by Marpole times. Quantities of beads, dentalium shells, native copper and other wealth goods are found in the graves of some individuals. Burials from this period show that infants' heads were bound to artificially flatten their foreheads, perhaps as a mark of noble birth. Flattened foreheads gradually replaced labrets to indicate class distinction. The abundance of wealth items and finely carved artworks suggests that skilled artisans were creating powerful images to enhance the prestige of their wealthy patrons, as was typical of historic Northwest Coast cultures.

Although Marpole is the best known of the late Emergent Period cultures, others were developing in similar fashion elsewhere on the coast. The Paul Mason site, well up the Skeena River on the north coast, has two rows of rectangular house depressions and evidence of two larger separate structures dating to about 3200 years ago. Near the mouth of the Skeena, in Prince Rupert Harbour, the Boardwalk site may also have been a village with two rows of houses about the same time.

Clubs of stone and bone, often elaborately carved, indicate that warfare was becoming important in this area, as do skeletal remains with head and arm injuries produced by such implements. One cache of weapons found at the Boardwalk site included pieces of copper-wrapped wooden rod armour, a beautifully carved whalebone war club, a club made from a killer-whale jaw, a stone club and a large stone dagger. Warfare often accompanied the growing complexity of these societies, as populations increased and chiefs vied for power and prestige. Ambitious leaders plundered their neighbours for slaves and booty, including ceremonial regalia and associated ritual prerogatives. Graves of these warrior-chiefs contain weapons and such exotic wealth goods as copper bracelets and amber beads.

A glimpse into emerging Northwest Coast art and technology in wood comes from the waterlogged Lachane site on the lower Skeena, where remnants of bentwood boxes, bowls, adze and chisel handles, canoe paddles and various styles of basketry have been preserved. A finely carved cedar handle depicts an unidentifiable animal in a fluid style clearly foreshadowing the famous historic art of the northern Northwest Coast cultures. Basketry may provide the most sensitive clues to the ethnic identity of the site's occupants; Dale Croes, an archaeologist who specializes in analyzing waterlogged sites, argues that the Lachane baskets clearly link this earlier population with the historic Tsimshian.

By the end of the Emergent Period the Northwest Coast cultural pattern was firmly in place. Where only eroding shell middens are visible today, villages of large wooden houses once stood. We can imagine these villages bustling with activity, the beaches in front lined with canoes and filled with the comings and goings of fishers and travellers and the welcoming of traders or guests for feasts. Elaborate ceremonies filled the winter months, allowing chiefs to display their wealth and proclaim the glory of their ancestral heritage.

In the **Developed Period** (beginning about 1500 years ago), Northwest Coast cultures took essentially their full historic forms. For the first time, with some caution, equating archaeological remains with specific known ethnic groups is possible. For example, an excavation inside a traditional plank-covered Coast Salish longhouse, still standing on the Musqueam Reserve in Vancouver until the 1960s, revealed a record of Musqueam heritage spanning the last 800 years.

On the south coast, the Developed Period differs considerably from earlier assemblages. Scholars once debated whether arriving Salish speakers replaced Marpole populations or whether there was simply a shift in some aspects of technology and lifestyle. Most now believe the latter. Gone from the archaeological record of this period are barbed harpoons and most other antler tools, as well as the chipped-basalt points so common in Marpole deposits. Instead, sites contain numerous sharpened splinters of bone which served as barbs on a wide range of fishing implements, as well as ground-slate knives used for splitting and scoring fish to prepare them for drying. Barbed harpoons were replaced with three-piece toggling harpoon heads, which held in place by turning inside the body of the salmon or seal. Also almost totally absent are art objects and personal ornaments, such as labrets, beads, pendants and the fine carvings in antler and stone. This lack, however, may mean only a shift to woodcarving and weaving as the major artistic outlets, which preserve poorly in archaeological contexts but were well developed by the historic Coast Salish.

Evidence that considerable cultural complexity continued into the Developed Period comes from the Scowlitz site, located at the mouth of the Harrison River where it joins the Fraser. The Scowlitz First Nation is one of the Fraser River Salish groups in the Stó:lō Tribal Council, with which archaeologists worked closely. The site consists of eighteen rectangular house depressions in a line along the river, with numerous rock cairns and earthen mounds scattered behind and

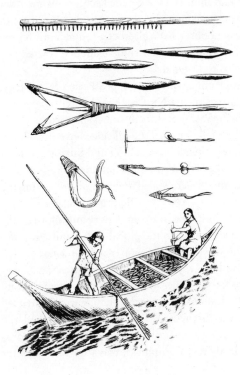

LEFT *The small bone points found in great abundance in Developed Period sites are all that remains of the wide variety of fishing gear employed. They may have served as barbs in fish hooks, as shown in the centre drawings, or as teeth on a herring rake, shown at the top and in use below. Courtesy of the Canadian Museum of Civilization, illustrator Jaclynne Campbell, from* British Columbia Prehistory, *author Knut R. Fladmark, 1986, Ottawa, National Museum of Man, page 107*

among the houses. The largest mound, almost three metres high and in a prominent elevated position at the rear of the site, was excavated in the mid-1990s. At
the base of this mound was a large rock cairn over a burial pit containing the
skeletal remains of an adult male. Around the head of this individual were four
large perforated copper disks and four abalone shell pendants; approximately
7000 dentalium shell beads were also in the grave. Clearly this person held considerable power and status to command such an investment of labour and wealth.

On the west coast of Vancouver Island stone tools of all kinds are relatively
rare, and chipped stone is almost absent. Most of the tools found are of bone, and
small bone points are numerous. Most would once have been parts of composite
fishing gear, whose wooden and bark components have not been preserved. Great
quantities of fish bones, representing many different species, are preserved in the
midden sites and show just how important fishing was. The abundant remains of
seals, sea lions, porpoises and whales of several species also show the extent of the
maritime way of life. Whale bones stacked at the front of the village area, a few
still with embedded portions of the thin mussel-shell harpoon blades, demonstrate archaeologically the vital role of whaling, so evident in the ethnographic
traditions of this area. These cultures are easily recognizable as the direct ancestors of the historic Nuu-chah-nulth people.

On the north coast, artistic traditions continued to develop. Stone sculptures
recovered from the lower Skeena River area include bowls and hafted mauls,
often decorated with human or animal figures. Fine detailed sculptures in antler
show many of the stylized features characteristic of the highly developed art of
the historic cultures. Remains of large houses have also been found, both on the
lower Skeena and Haida Gwaii, which indicates that some leaders attracted numerous followers and that households were ranked.

Waterlogged sites help us to better understand Developed Period technology.
Ozette, a Makah (the southern relatives of the Nuu-chah-nulth) village on the
open coast of the Olympic Peninsula in Washington, is the most spectacular example. About 300 years ago torrential rainfall loosened the hillside above the village,
releasing a mudslide that rushed down the slope, crushing and burying at least
four plank-covered houses. Although the force of the slide flattened dwellings and
broke objects, the houses and their contents were sealed under mud, preserving the
material culture of a society frozen in time—a North American Pompeii.

The Ozette site is unique in providing a nearly complete record of a Northwest Coast society just before its encounter with the global community. It illustrates the variety of implements and the prevalence of artworks and ceremonial
objects, almost entirely of wood and long vanished from other sites. The decorated bowls, boxes, seal or fish clubs, tool handles and other objects demonstrate
that Northwest Coast art was highly developed before the outside world intruded
with the fur trade. After Ozette was discovered, archaeologists searched the
Northwest Coast for additional waterlogged deposits. Although nothing as dramatic as Ozette has come to light in British Columbia, excavations at wet sites

ABOVE LEFT *This beautifully carved bone comb depicting a wolf, dated to about 1200 years ago, was excavated at a shell midden site near the mouth of the Skeena River. The exaggerated eye form, protruding tongue and visible ribs ("x-ray vision") foreshadow historic northern Northwest Coast art.* CMC J19608-5.
ABOVE RIGHT *Many petroglyphs, such as this human figure pecked into the rock near Bella Coola, appear to have been inspired by shamanism. Photo by K. Fladmark*

have yielded such usually perishable items as wooden wedges, bentwood fish hooks, basketry and cordage.

Warfare was common during this time, and it became even more intense after global economic patterns revolutionized competition over important trade routes. On the north coast, warrior-chiefs in armour defended hilltop forts in strategic locations. All along the coast, fortresses or defensive sites—often atop steep-sided headlands or islets—provided refuges to which people could flee during times of danger.

The numerous pictographs and petroglyphs on prominent rock surfaces along the coast display a wide range of styles and, presumably, motivations for their creation. Many appear imbued with spiritual power, and mark where individuals recorded encounters with supernatural beings or shamans communed with the spirit world. Others, particularly on the north coast, appear to be more secular displays of crest art in the historic style. The practice of carving or painting images on rocks may be ancient, but many examples are clearly recent. Images of European sailing ships, for example, are carved into the rock at a site on western Vancouver Island.

THE ETHNOGRAPHIC CULTURES

Villages of large plank-covered houses, monumental wooden sculptures, huge ocean-going dugout canoes and the potlatch ceremony at which chiefs gave away their wealth: these are the images for which ethnographic Northwest Coast cultures are famous. Although all groups carved large sculptures in wood and lived in large wooden houses, each group had its own distinct variations. The art and architecture of the Haida, for example, is readily distinguishable from that of the Kwakwaka'wakw or Salish. The coast is frequently divided into three sub-areas (northern, Wakashan and Coast Salish), but even within these sub-areas major cultural differences are evident.

Except for groups far inland along major rivers, all Northwest Coast people shared a common economy. Trade and ritual exchange helped to balance local differences, as groups with abundant clams and sea urchins, for example, traded with others for seal meat or dried halibut. All along the coast, people relied heavily on the bounty of the sea, beaches and rivers. The three fundamental aspects of the Northwest Coast economy—fishing, sea-mammal hunting and shellfish collecting—all involved the sea. Food from the land played a lesser role in the economy, particularly for such outer-coast people as the Haida and Nuu-chah-nulth. Although the coast provided plentiful foodstuffs, making a living required hard work, skill and intimate knowledge of the local environment.

The fundamental resource was salmon—all five species of Pacific salmon, with annual spawning runs ranging from spring to late fall. Each variety was treated differently. Sockeye, for example, was highly valued for its flavour and was primarily consumed fresh, whereas Chum (or Dog), which spawns late in the year and has a lower fat content, was ideally suited for preservation. Great quantities were dried or smoked to be the staple food for winter months. Open-ocean groups could catch salmon year-round by taking them on a hook and line in salt water. People caught most of their salmon, however, during the annual spawning runs, when they moved to fishing locations near the mouths of rivers and streams. There they harpooned or netted the fish or took them in traps.

Salmon played a vital role in the evolution of Northwest Coast cultures for several reasons. First, salmon was a predictable resource. Native People could count on the salmon to appear at the same locations at roughly the same time year after year, and they could schedule their annual round accordingly. Second, salmon were abundant. Native elders wistfully recall the days when "you could walk across the rivers on their backs," and even the modern, greatly diminished runs are an impressive sight. Also, salmon are quite easy to catch, especially when they are spawning. Finally, salmon can be preserved relatively easily. With such large stores of dried salmon, this food became a year-round staple rather than a seasonal delicacy, and it supported larger populations, a more complex social organization and an elaborate material culture.

Although salmon were the essential resource, many other fish were extremely important in the Northwest Coast economy. The outer-coast Nuu-chah-

ABOVE AND LEFT *Kwakwaka'wakw eulachon fishing at Knight Inlet, 1968. Above: bringing in the catch,* RBCM PN7704-7; *Left: skimming oil from the surface of the cooking tanks,* RBCM PN7722-30

nulth and Haida relied extensively on halibut. Men paddled to offshore halibut banks, often far out to sea, to go after the big fish. Specialized halibut hooks were ingeniously crafted and often decoratively carved. For variety, there were ling cod, flounder and rockfish, also taken on hook and line, and herring, which could be taken during spawning runs—either in nets or with a "herring rake," a long pole studded with sharp bone teeth along the lower portion of one side. While an assistant paddled the canoe, the fisher swept the rake through the water, impaling small fish on the teeth and flipping them into the canoe on the follow-through. Early European observers recorded with astonishment how quickly adept herring fishers could fill their canoes. Native People also sank evergreen boughs attached to floats into the spawning beds, later collecting the thick, sticky herring spawn to be eaten fresh as a delicacy or dried and stored for the winter months. In addition, the eulachon, a small oily smelt that spawns in the spring, could be netted in quantity, allowed to "ripen" for a short period, then cooked in large wooden vats to extract the oil. Eulachon oil was a highly prized condiment, greatly enhancing the flavour of dried salmon and other foods. It was served at feasts, given away at potlatches and traded far into the interior.

Also essential to the coastal diet were the readily available clams, mussels, abalone and other shellfish. In addition, sea urchins, sea cucumbers, octopus, crabs and seaweeds added variety. There is considerable truth to the old adage, "When the tide is out, the table is set"; however, villages of several hundred people could quickly deplete nearby supplies. The task of gathering such food fell largely to the women, who needed only a hard-pointed stick for digging and prying and an open-weave basket for carrying. The huge shell middens all along the coast are ample testimony to their industry.

As well as fishing and collecting intertidal foods, Northwest Coast people hunted both land and sea animals. It was the mammals of the sea, however, that were most prized in the diet and conferred the most prestige on the hunter. Almost all groups hunted seals, sea lions and porpoises, generally by harpooning them from canoes. Agile hunters also clambered over rocky islets to club seals and sea lions. Only the Nuu-chah-nulth of western Vancouver Island paddled their frail craft out onto the open ocean in search of whales, an activity that enhanced the standing of the noble whaler as much as it provided food.

The oil-rich meat and blubber of sea mammals was the most valued, but Aboriginal people hunted many other animals as well. Some groups took waterfowl in nets or with multi-pronged spears. Of the land animals, deer, elk and bear were most important; they were hunted with bows and arrows, or trapped in snares and deadfalls. The mountain goat was difficult to obtain, but it supplied meat and wool for some inland groups and tested a young hunter's abilities.

Although plant foods played a lesser role in the diet, a wide range was gathered. In spring, green shoots of salmonberries and fireweed delighted a palate grown winter-weary of dried foods. So too did clover and fern roots, as well as edible bulbs and tubers that could be extracted easily from the moist soil. The inner bark of the hemlock tree was scraped and pressed into starchy cakes. When the berries ripened—salalberries, salmonberries, huckleberries and others—Aboriginal people ate them fresh and they pressed them into flat cakes and dried them for winter use. Native recipes included mixing fresh berries with salmon eggs and with eulachon oil. In addition, they whipped soapberries into a frothy treat, often known as "Indian ice cream" today, which was eaten with specially carved wooden spoons. Ethnobotanical research continues to document the considerable Native knowledge of plant uses, for medicine, for ritual purposes and in technology, as well as for food.

On top of skill and hard work, finding food required a certain rapport with the supernatural world. In mythic times humans and animals were essentially the same, and animals were believed to be able to transform from one realm to another. The Salmon People, Killer Whale People, Wolf People and others were thought to have their own houses, where they took off their animal cloaks and lived parallel lives to humans. Numerous myths, such as the widespread "woman-who-married-the-bear," discuss how these realms are related and how animals can transfer their powers to human beneficiaries. Because the Salmon People voluntarily left their underwater villages to offer their flesh to humans, they were highly respected. All groups practised a variant of the First Salmon rite, in which the earliest fish of the season were ceremonially welcomed, placed on new mats in the chief's house and sprinkled with white eagle down. After the flesh was consumed the bones were carefully returned to the water to be resurrected for the following year. Aboriginal People also carried out minor rituals to thank a bear or mountain goat for allowing itself to be killed by the hunter. They even offered the cedar tree a prayer of thanks when humans stripped off its cloak of bark to weave their own clothing.

Paramount to Northwest Coast technology was the red cedar. Lightweight, strong and rot-resistant, the aromatic cedar wood could be easily shaped by woodworkers using tools of stone, bone and shell, and later iron. To split large planks from a cedar log, woodworkers inserted wedges of antler or hardwood and gently tapped them with a stone hammer. The long, straight grain split easily. The bark and roots provided raw material for weavers, who crafted beautiful basketry, matting and clothing. The slender, flexible branches or withes were split and twisted to make rope. Although Native People used other trees for specific purposes, red cedar was by far the most important.

Impressive cedar homes lined the beach wherever shelter, food and fresh water could be found. Winter villages were the central places in west coast life. During the mild season the people dispersed to smaller villages and satellite camps to take advantage of seasonally abundant resources. As the stormy season approached, people loaded their canoes with the provisions they had gathered and returned to their sheltered winter villages. There they spent the dark, wet months, comfortable in their large multi-family houses. Although each region of the coast had its own architectural style, all followed a basic pattern. Massive cedar posts supported huge roof beams and a series of rafters, and this framework was covered with split-cedar planks. Patterns of adze marks sometimes embellished beams, and posts were occasionally carved in the form of crest animals. Roof planks were often channelled and overlapped, both to hold them in place and to control rain runoff. Planks were important possessions, and people often transported them to other village sites as they moved with the seasons.

The great artistic achievements of coastal carvers were primarily in wood, particularly cedar. The best-known examples of Northwest Coast art are the so-called "totem poles," the tall, free-standing poles that stood in front of the houses. Artists also carved crests into frontal poles (those against the front of the houses that incorporated the doorway) and on interior house posts. Although regional styles are clearly distinct and not all groups carved free-standing poles, all had a tradition of monumental artwork in wood. Many sculptures were heraldic, as important chiefs hired renowned artists to depict family crests for all to see. Wealthy patrons also commissioned spectacular masks, rattles and feast dishes to use in their winter ceremonials. Everyday items, such as bowls, spoons and storage boxes, were often decorated with finely carved designs. Even such roughly used objects as seal or fish clubs could also be works of art.

ABOVE *Beautifully carved Tsimshian chest with beaver design.* CMC 59642

A good example of the skill of Northwest Coast woodworkers is the bentwood box. The four sides of these containers were formed from a single plank, cut partly through where the corners were to be and then steamed until the fibres could be bent at ninety-degree angles. The fourth corner was pegged or sewn with root, as was the bottom. A fitted lid completed the box. Most were so skillfully constructed that they were watertight and could be used as cooking boxes (adding hot rocks from the fire with tongs to keep the water boiling), water buckets or containers for other liquids. Others stored foods such as dried salmon, halibut, shellfish, roots and cakes of berries. Still others, frequently beautifully decorated with incised and painted designs inlaid with decorative shells, were "boxes of treasures" in which high-ranking people stored their ceremonial regalia. Although the Northwest Coast cultures did not use pottery, it does not mean they lacked suitable clay or the technological ingenuity to make pots—it simply shows that they were able to meet all their needs through their mastery of the woodworkers' craft.

One of the great accomplishments of Northwest Coast woodworkers was the graceful, ocean-going dugout canoe. Constructing these vital craft was a skilled job, and some carvers became specialists. After a huge cedar log had been laboriously hollowed and shaped by adzing, it was filled with water, which was heated by adding red-hot stones, then covered with old cedar-bark matting to hold in the steam. Once the hot water and steam had softened the wood, woodworkers accomplished the crucial task of spreading the canoe's sides to the desired shape. For large ocean-going canoes, separate prow and stern pieces were carved and carefully attached to the hull. The exterior was singed with torches to harden the

ABOVE LEFT *Beautifully crafted dugout canoes, such as these Kwakwaka'wakw examples, made the maritime Northwest Coast lifestyle possible. Photo by E.S. Curtis.* NAC C30189. ABOVE RIGHT *Nuu-chah-nulth women wait for the canoe, with their digging sticks and open-weave baskets used for collecting shellfish, in this posed photograph by E.S. Curtis.* NAC C20845

wood and remove any splinters, then polished with the sandpaper-like skin of the dogfish, so the canoe would glide swiftly and silently through the water. Canoes ranged from small two-person fishing and sealing craft to big vessels for trade or warfare capable of carrying around forty people. The canoes had to be treated with care; men cleared runways on the beach where they could draw them up without damaging them and covered them with mats so they would not crack in the sun. Canoes made the Northwest Coast way of life possible. Almost all travel was by sea as people moved around their rugged homelands, or set out on lengthy voyages to attend feasts, to trade or to raid their enemies. Familiar from early childhood with the vagaries of waves, wind and weather, paddlers skillfully propelled their craft over great distances.

Woodworking was primarily a male task, but the female art was weaving. Basket makers employed a variety of plant fibres, including cedar bark, split cedar and spruce root, and various grasses to produce elegant containers in regionally distinct styles. Baskets were used to carry and store various items, and some were woven so closely that they were watertight and could be used for cooking.

Clothing was also woven from plant fibres, particularly cedar bark that was cut into strips, pounded until it became supple and soft, and then woven on a simple loom. Men wrapped cedar bark blankets around their bodies, whereas women wore skirts of shredded cedar-bark and blankets or cloaks. The blankets were usually fastened at the front with a wooden or bone pin. Wide-brimmed hats protected the wearer from the sun and rain. The drizzle and fog of the rain forest made the tailored-hide clothing so popular elsewhere on the continent useless on the coast. The soft and water-resistant bark provided much better protection from the elements. For colder weather, people added robes of bear fur or sea otter pelts.

Only northern and upriver groups wore footwear since the hide moccasins of the interior were useless to coastal people who were constantly getting in and out of canoes.

All important locations, including house sites, salmon-fishing stations, hunting territories, berry patches and major stands of cedar, were considered private property. Kinship groups sharing a name and a tradition of descent from a common ancestor had ownership, not only of territory but also of important privileges such as names, ritual dances, songs and the right to depict certain crests.

Northwest Coast cultures emphasized inherited rank and privileges. Chiefs and nobles held high-ranking names and controlled access to group-held territories and rights. If they managed the group's resources skillfully, chiefs accumulated wealth, which they could publicly distribute at feasts and potlatches to enhance their status. Commoners, who had not inherited claims to titles or ceremonial privileges, shared in the group's greater prestige and provided the labour necessary to accumulate food and wealth. Slaves, who were usually purchased or captured in war, made up a substantial part of the population. Although they had to perform menial tasks, their lives were not greatly different from commoners. However, they were considered chattel and could be sold, given away at potlatches or killed by a high-ranking chief to demonstrate indifference to his great wealth.

Raiding and warfare were commonplace, even among people who spoke the same language. Raids were frequently to revenge insults or injury, or to take slaves. Less common was full-scale warfare over territory. After a successful raid, warriors burned the houses and turned homeward with their canoes laden—with booty, the severed heads of their vanquished foes, and women and children taken as slaves.

Marriages were contracted with individuals of equivalent rank in other kin groups. High-ranking people often married someone from another village, sometimes a considerable distance away. These marriages forged political alliances and transferred wealth, including names and ceremonial prerogatives.

Central to the whole concept of status and rank was the potlatch. Any change in the status quo required a chief and his kin to invite others to witness their claim. A high-status marriage, the birth of an heir, the assumption of an inherited name, the completion of a new house and the raising of a carved pole were all such occasions. Chiefs might also potlatch to "erase a shame," when they had stumbled during a ceremonial performance or had been taken captive by enemies and ransomed by their people. No individual was recognized to be of a particular status, even if he was clearly the proper heir, until his name was "made good" by public validation at a potlatch.

A prominent feature of the potlatch was the distribution of property (the term "potlatch" actually comes from the word for "gift" in the Chinook jargon, a trade language widely used on the coast in historic times). The largest and most valuable gifts went to high-ranking visitors. Indeed, the potlatch not only validated the status of the giver but also reaffirmed that of the guests. The seating arrangements, order of distribution and size of gift were all carefully planned to reflect each recipient's status. All present listened to speakers for the host group recount their history and their hereditary rights, and all had to be paid as witnesses. Late-nineteenth-century photographs show huge stacks of Hudson's Bay Company blankets, sacks of flour and other items ready for general distribution.

Anthropological descriptions of the potlatch all refer to late time periods, when massive social upheavals were affecting Native life. During this time potlatches became more extravagant and more competitive, as great chiefs fought with wealth to outdo their rivals. Not only were enormous quantities of goods given away, but valuable items were destroyed as gestures of rivalry. Coppers (the shield-shaped copper objects that were the ultimate wealth items in the potlatch system) were broken and canoes were placed on the fire like old logs. Chiefs poured boxes of valuable eulachon oil onto the fire in an attempt to force back high-ranking guests, who would be defeated by this show of wealth. The government banned the potlatch at least partly due to these historic excesses.

Few ethnographic topics have received greater attention than the potlatch. Anthropologists have argued over its interpretations and its functions in Native societies. Certainly it played a pivotal role in social organization. In the absence of a writing system, the potlatch publicly recognized an individual's claim to a particular status or inherited right. It also redistributed food and goods. In fact, far from impoverishing a potlatching chief, it was a system of "banking" or investment, as he would be a recipient at subsequent potlatches.

Performances of masked dancers enlivened the potlatches. Supernatural forces were felt to dwell close to the villages and were most accessible during the winter. Ceremonies kept people occupied and entertained during this time, when there was much less economic activity. More theatre than dance, the performances re-enacted ancestral encounters with supernatural beings, when important rights were transferred to the human world. Skilled artists created dramatic masks and other regalia to enhance the image of supernatural presence.

More secular entertainments occurred year-round, whenever groups of people got together. Racing and feats of strength were common, but nothing was as passionately enjoyed as the gambling games. Particularly popular was *lehal* (the "bones game"), played with pairs of bone cylinders, one of each pair marked, which could be hidden in the hand. While one team guessed at the location of the unmarked bones, their opponents attempted to confuse them with drumming and singing. The game could be long, and both participants and spectators bet heavily over each exchange of the bones.

Any successful endeavour—in hunting and fishing, in gambling, in warfare, in amassing wealth and potlatching—required supernatural aid. To gain this help it was believed that people had to be ritually clean, and this required a "training" period that involved fasting, sexual abstinence, frequent bathing and rubbing the body with hemlock boughs until the skin bled. Some people who acquired particular skill in controlling supernatural forces became shamans, who were blessed

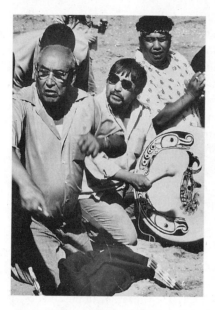

ABOVE *Nuu-chah-nulth men playing "lehal," the "bones game," 1975. The man in the foreground holds the "bones," while the drummers attempt to confuse their opponents. Photo by A. McMillan*

with the ability to cure illnesses. In dramatic firelit performances shamans sang and drummed over their patients, sucking out the disease-causing object or embarking on a perilous psychic journey to restore the lost soul. Both men and women could become shamans, and they were usually attracted to the field by the prospect of greater prestige and payment for successful cures. They were feared as well as respected, since they could also inflict illness or death, and many were suspected of practising witchcraft.

The exploits of supernatural beings and their encounters with human ancestors were the basis for a rich oral tradition. The skies were filled with terrifying supernatural birds, such as the whale-hunting Thunderbird; the woods contained giant human-like monsters; and many powerful beings, some capable of bestowing great wealth, dwelt beneath the waves. Prominent among the myths were those of the trickster/transformer, who put the world and all living things in their present form, a role played by Raven along much of the coast. Raven brought light to the world, releasing the sun from a wooden chest where it had been kept by a mighty chief. Typical of transformer figures, Raven could be foolish, greedy or obscene as well as benevolent, and the stories of his adventures and mishaps kept audiences enthralled. Although myths were instructive, they were also entertaining, and they helped to while away long rainy evenings as people sat around the fires in their large wooden houses.

THE NORTHERN GROUPS

Speakers of three language isolates—Haida, Tlingit and Tsimshian—occupy the northern Northwest Coast. Although their unrelated languages clearly indicate separate origins, these three peoples shared a similar lifestyle, achieving the greatest elaboration of material culture and most sophisticated art style on the coast.

The Haida homeland was the cluster of islands, islets and sheltered waterways making up the Queen Charlotte Islands, known to the Haida as Haida Gwaii. Somewhat before Europeans arrived some groups expanded across Dixon Strait to the north, establishing villages in southernmost Alaska. As a result, the international boundary now divides the Haida, though groups on both sides of

ABOVE *The Haida village of Skidegate, 1878.* CMC 255

the border still interact. The rugged lands of these island dwellers ensured that they were mainly orientated to the sea. Their large dugout canoes took them out after salmon, halibut and sea mammals, and allowed trading expeditions or war parties to reach the mainland. The vast stands of red cedar on Haida Gwaii made possible the Haida achievements as master carvers and canoe builders. Their canoes were eagerly sought in trade; newly carved craft were paddled across to the Tsimshian on the mainland, towing older ones. The new canoes were then exchanged for eulachon oil, and the Haida returned in the older vessels.

To the north were the Tlingit, who inhabited the myriad islands making up the archipelago of southeastern Alaska. The Tlingit were famed seafaring traders, exchanging copper and mountain-goat wool blankets for such goods as slaves and shell ornaments. During the historic fur trade they also travelled far into the interior, taking European goods to the Athapaskans in exchange for the furs demanded by the foreigners. Groups that owned strategic trade routes to the interior, along the valleys of the Chilkat, Taku and Stikine Rivers, prospered in this trade. Some intermarried with Athapaskans and became the Inland Tlingit of extreme northwestern British Columbia and the adjacent Yukon. Although they resembled the Athapaskans in many respects, their language, social organization and ceremonies were Tlingit.

Several languages exist among the largest group, the Tsimshian of British Columbia's northern mainland. The four Nisga'a communities held the Nass River valley, plus adjacent saltwater territory. The seven winter villages (or "tribes") of the Gitksan (literally "People of the Skeena") lay along the Skeena River and its tributaries. Unlike other groups, the Gitksan relied solely on their rivers and mountains, and had no access to coastal resources. Although the Gitksan and Nisga'a are politically and culturally distinct, linguists believe they speak two dialects of one Tsimshian language. A second language, Coast Tsimshian, was spoken by eleven tribes with villages on the lower Skeena and the islands near its mouth. In addition, three winter village groups pushed far to the south, taking over the outer islands formerly held by the northern Wakashans. Most linguists consider their language, the nearly extinct Southern Tsimshian, to be a distinct dialect of Coast Tsimshian.

The territory of the Tsimshian peoples was rich and varied, with salmon in the rivers and the most important eulachon run on the Northwest Coast in the Nass River. Although most groups had access to the whole range of coastal resources, the Gitksan and Nisga'a were riverine people, and they devoted more time to hunting land mammals. Trade helped even out local shortages, and they exchanged such important commodities as eulachon oil and mountain-goat wool far afield.

The social organization of the northern groups distinguished them from other coastal peoples. The Haida and Tlingit divided themselves into two groups (termed "moieties" by anthropologists). Among the Haida these were the Eagles and Ravens, each subdivided into lineages named for their original villages. Tsimshian social organization was similar, except that there were four divisions (termed "phratries") rather than two. Each person had to seek a mate from outside their moiety or phratry; marriage within would have been incestuous. These groups traced descent through the female line, and each child took his or her mother's affiliation. A chief could not transmit his name and property to his own sons since they belonged to a different kin group; instead his sister's sons were his heirs. As high-status marriages were frequently alliances between groups, young men sometimes had to set out for the villages of their maternal uncles to seek their inheritances.

The highly acclaimed northern art primarily depicted crest animals or images from myths. Displaying such figures was a jealously guarded family prerogative. Much of the material culture of these northern people was embellished with crests, from the finely carved miniature figures along the handles of gracefully bent horn spoons to massive wooden sculptures in front of the houses. Among the Haida, men also frequently had their upper bodies tattooed with crest figures. Unique to the Haida was the practice of placing their high-status dead at the top of carved poles, hidden from view behind wooden boards elegantly carved with their main crest figures. The fluid lines and complex, stylized images of northern art, carefully wrapped in shallow carving around the poles and other objects without detracting from their basic shape, contrast sharply with the bolder and more sculptural Wakashan forms to the south.

The northern groups constructed the most substantial architecture on the coast. House walls consisted of carefully fitted cedar planks placed vertically and relatively permanently. Frontal poles were placed against the front wall and had an

ABOVE *Tsimshian chief in ceremonial regalia, including a Chilkat blanket of mountain-goat wool.* NAC c56768

oval entranceway in the body or gaping mouth of the lowest figure. These were most common among the Haida. Inside, house posts were often carved in the shape of the crest animals of the house's occupants. Frequently the central area of the house was excavated to form a lower level in which people sat around the fire. Some important houses had several levels, each covered with planks. The chief and his family slept in cubicles of planks, often painted with crest designs, at the rear of the house. People of lesser rank slept along the side walls, and slaves had the least desirable locations near the door. Boxes and baskets stacked along the walls contained stored food supplies and personal gear. Houses of high rank, like people, had names and histories.

The northern people were noted warriors and slave-raiders, and the Haida in particular were feared by groups as far to the south as the Fraser River. When a Haida canoe suddenly appeared, its paddles flashing rhythmically as the craft bore down on its victims, it could mean sudden death or enslavement for other people. Northern warriors wore wooden slat armour, large wooden helmets surmounted with frightening images and carved wooden visors to protect their faces. In a Gitksan legend, a warrior-chief named Nekt ventured forth from his hilltop fortress to do battle in his armour made from grizzly-bear skin lined with slate tablets. Ambitious chiefs constructed fortifications at strategic locations to control access to major trade routes.

The lives of high-ranking northerners, as befitting people of great wealth, were punctuated with major feasts and potlatches. Although various life crises required such ceremonies, the most important event was the mortuary potlatch. This ceremony both memorialized the greatness of the deceased chief and validated his successor's right to that position. It also allowed the host group to pay debts incurred during the long period of mourning.

At such public occasions chiefs were richly attired in the distinctive northern ceremonial regalia. They wore over their shoulders the Chilkat blanket, a robe of mountain-goat wool finely woven with elaborate designs, and often leggings or a tunic of the same material. The ceremonial headdress included a carved wooden

RIGHT *The abandoned Haida village of Sgaan Gwaii (Ninstints), on the southern Queen Charlotte Islands, has been declared a World Heritage Site. Photo by A. McMillan*

frontlet surmounted with long sea-lion whiskers, with numerous ermine skins hanging down the back. A hollow at the top of the headdress was filled with eagle down, a symbol of peace, which floated through the air and settled on spectators as high-ranking chiefs sedately danced.

Many traditional villages were abandoned because of smallpox and other pressures of the early global era. When Fort Simpson was established in 1834 most of the Coast Tsimshian moved near the post, leaving only large shell middens to mark where their ancestors had lived for millennia. Declining populations forced the Haida to coalesce at two villages, Massett and Skidegate. At the others, the great cedar houses collapsed and the finely carved poles gradually toppled over and were lost to decay. Only at Sgaan Gwaii ("Red Cod Island Town," also known as Ninstints), a remote village at the southern end of Haida Gwaii, has an attempt been made to arrest this gradual destruction. Sgaan Gwaii has been proclaimed a World Heritage Site by the United Nations, a fitting recognition of the genius and talents of the nineteenth-century artists who carved the still-standing poles.

THE WAKASHANS

The Wakashan language family consists of two main branches, whose languages are only distantly related. The term "Wakashan" comes from the observations of Captain James Cook, among the people he called "Nootka," in 1778:

> The word *wakash* . . . was very frequently in their mouths. It seemed to express applause, approbation, and friendship. For when they appeared to be satisfied, or well pleased with any thing they saw, or any incident that happened, they would, with one voice, call out *wakash! wakash! Cook 1784: 337*

Although Wakashan is primarily a linguistic classification, it also designates the central sub-area of the Northwest Coast. In this case it includes the Nuxalk, whose language is Salishan but whose culture most closely fits the Wakashan pattern.

The groups in the Wakashan sub-area have been known historically by inappropriate or erroneous names, which the people to whom they refer largely reject. Today all these groups have adopted names that better reflect their own concepts of their identity. As their languages had no words for such large social units, new terms have had to be created. "Nootka," for example, stems from an error during Cook's visit; the term apparently derives from the word for "come around," as the Native people were trying to direct the famed navigator around the rocks to the cove where their village was located. These people today refer to themselves as the Nuu-chah-nulth (roughly "all along the mountains"). Similarly, "Bella Coola" is an anglicized version of a Heiltsuk word for people who now prefer to be called Nuxalk, from their name for the Bella Coola Valley. "Kwakiutl" is a poor rendering of a Native word ("Kwagiulth" is closer), which in any case refers only to the people at Fort Rupert. Kwakwaka'wakw, meaning "those who speak Kwakwala," is now the collective term for groups sharing this language.

Three languages make up the northern branch of the Wakashan family. The farthest north are the Haisla, today a single community near the town of Kitimat. To the south are the Heiltsuk, a large group with their main centre at Bella Bella, on the central coast. The neighbouring Oweekano speak a distinct dialect of the Heiltsuk language, though they are politically autonomous. Farther south are the many politically separate villages of the Kwakwaka'wakw on northern Vancouver Island and the adjacent mainland coast.

The Nuu-chah-nulth, who occupy the storm-lashed west coast of Vancouver Island and the tip of the Olympic Peninsula in Washington, are also divided into three languages. The northern and central Nuu-chah-nulth groups speak dialects of one language, and the Ditidaht of southern Vancouver Island and the Makah on the Olympic Peninsula have separate but closely related languages. Their rugged environment made the Nuu-chah-nulth among the most maritime of all Northwest Coast peoples. Like the Haida, the Nuu-chah-nulth were famed canoe builders, skillfully carving graceful ocean-going vessels from the huge cedar trees that grow on the outer coast. In such craft they set far out to sea to fish for halibut and hunt sea mammals.

The Nuxalk are a relatively small enclave of Salish speakers on the central coast. Their territory includes the valleys of the Bella Coola and Dean Rivers, plus the long steep-sided inlets that cut through the mountains from the outer coast, giving them access to both inland and saltwater resources. Culturally they more closely resemble their Heiltsuk neighbours, with whom they were in frequent contact, than their distant Salish kin to the south. Their artwork and ceremonial performances, though distinctively Nuxalk, follow the general Wakashan pattern.

The social organization of the Wakashan groups differed considerably from that of northern peoples. Inheritance, including membership in the kin group, could come from either the mother's or father's side, though there was an emphasis on the male line. Members of each kin group (known as *namima* among the Kwakwaka'wakw) traced descent from a common ancestor. Such ancestors were often supernatural beings who became humans early in the history of the world. Kin groups owned fishing sites and other economic resources, as well as such important assets as names, dances, songs and crests, including the rights to depict their supernatural forebears or to re-enact myths in ceremonial performances. Rank came from the closeness of the relationship with these ancestors, based on primogeniture. The rank-conscious Kwakwaka'wakw counted rank not only within the namima but also ranked namima within the "tribe" (the winter village group), and even ranked the tribes. No political authority extended this widely; the highest chief of the first-ranking namima of the first-ranking tribe simply had the greatest prominence on all ceremonial occasions.

Late-eighteenth-century explorers and fur traders described the striking appearance of these people. Cook commented that the Natives of Nootka Sound "rub their bodies constantly over with a red paint of a clayey or coarse ochry substance mixed with oil" and frequently sprinkled mica on the paint to make it glitter. For festive occasions they greased their hair and sprinkled it with bird down. Although young men usually plucked their facial hair, older men often allowed their beards to grow. They pierced their earlobes and the nasal septum for ornaments, including dentalium shells, a wealth item the Nuu-chah-nulth obtained from deep offshore waters and that they also wore as necklaces. Furthermore, to alter the shape of the skull, which was a widespread practice, they bound the foreheads of infants in cradleboards.

Wakashan houses differed considerably from northern styles. The planks that made up the walls were structurally separate from the large permanent framework of posts and beams. A family group might have several house frames at different seasonal villages, and the planks were intended to be easily dismantled and transported. When people moved, planks could be placed across two canoes, providing a convenient platform on which to stack household goods. The planks were then tied horizontally between pairs of upright poles to form walls against the permanent framework. Planks also covered the roof; these were weighed down with poles and rocks against the high winds of winter storms. Although they lacked the plank floors and recessed levels of high-status northern homes, these houses featured benches for sitting and sleeping, and back supports near the fires. Boxes and baskets of preserved foods and personal goods were stacked nearly to the roof, and large quantities of fish hung drying from the rafters. Cook complained of the "stinking of fish, train-oil [whale oil], and smoke," but to the Native residents such odours must have testified to the warmth of their fires, the reassuring winter's supply of food and their success in hunting such mighty quarry as the whale.

ABOVE *The inside of a Nuu-chah-nulth house, 1778. This engraving, from a painting by Cook Expedition artist John Webber, provides a wealth of information on Natives' lives at the beginning of contact with Europeans.* CMC J-2434
LEFT *The Kwakwaka'wakw village of Blunden Harbour, 1901.* RBCM PN256

Of all Northwest Coast peoples, only the Nuu-chah-nulth actively ventured out to sea in pursuit of whales, particularly the California grey and the humpback. The whaling crew had to be well trained to silently propel their canoe alongside their prey, so their leader could thrust his harpoon deep into the animal. Then the crew frantically back-paddled to escape the thrashing of the wounded beast's tail as it dove, taking with it a long line with large floats made from inflated sea-lion skins. Struggling against the floats eventually exhausted the whale, which then could be dispatched with a killing lance. A successful hunt provided a large amount of meat and highly prized blubber to be rendered into oil, and also enhanced the prestige of the whaling chief.

Success at whaling involved far more than rigorous training for the crew. The whaler had to be ritually pure, which required long periods of fasting and sexual abstinence. He retreated to an isolated area for ritual bathing, during which he dove and spouted like a whale, followed by vigorous body scrubbing. Sometimes the whaler's wife shared in the ritual bathing, and while the whaler was on the

RIGHT *The Kwakwaka'wakw village of Alert Bay, 1917.* CMC 41968

hunt she remained motionless in her bed so that the whale would be similarly docile. Some whalers kept shrines in the woods, where they set up human skulls and carved wooden figures representing dead whalers around an image of a whale. The dead were believed to have power over whales and could aid the whaler on the hunt or cause dead whales to drift ashore near the village.

The Wakashan groups shared a distinctive and exuberant art style. Cook noted several large carved wooden figures in the Nuu-chah-nulth house he visited and commented: "Nothing is without a kind of frieze-work or the figure of some animal upon it." Wakashan carving was much more sculptural than the applied northern forms. They extended the basic shape with projecting wings, beaks, legs and other appendages. Thunderbirds soar on outspread wings, and Tsonoqua, a cannibal ogress, reaches with outstretched arms. When commercial paints became available, the Wakashan artists enthusiastically adopted them, adding to the flamboyant nature of their work. Late-nineteenth-century photographs show villages with tall, deeply carved poles and elaborate paintings embellishing the fronts of some houses.

The Wakashans were famed for their large potlatches and elaborate winter ceremonials. The Kwakwaka'wakw forbade economic activities during a sacred winter period, so all their energies could be turned to ceremonies. The ranking of the dances replaced secular ranking during this time. Elaborate regalia, masks that "transformed," and theatrical tricks such as carved figures that "flew" through the darkened houses all enhanced the illusion of supernatural presence.

The Wolf featured most prominently in the Nuu-chah-nulth winter rituals. The sound of whistles from the woods warned people that the Wolf spirits were nearby, ready to abduct their children. Suddenly, men dressed as wolves attacked the villagers and in the confusion made off with the children who were to be initiated. When the children were finally returned they were "wild" and had to be

TOP LEFT *Kwakwaka'wakw mask representing Tsonoqua, the cannibal ogress.* RBCM CPN 9974

TOP RIGHT *The Thunderbird sits atop Tsonoqua on this fine example of a Kwakwaka'wakw totem pole, now standing at Alert Bay, by the master carver Willie Seaweed. Photo by A. McMillan*

LEFT *A Nuu-chah-nulth chief wears a distinctive Thunderbird headdress.* NAC PA140976

"tamed" through ritual dances. Finally the initiates danced in their wolf outfits, demonstrating their return to human state but with new powers received from the Wolves. The flat-sided wooden headdresses dancers wore as part of their wolf costumes are among the best known of Nuu-chah-nulth artworks.

Among the Kwakwaka'wakw, several distinct dance series featured many different supernatural beings. Dances were hereditary and ranked, and dancers often worked their way through a number of lesser positions before being initiated into the most highly ranked dances, such as the *hamatsa* or "cannibal dance." Believed to be living in the home of the fearsome "Cannibal at the North End of the World," the initiate was actually hidden in the woods for a long period of seclusion and instruction. When he returned he was possessed with cannibalistic frenzy, leaping through the smoke hole from the roof onto the fire or rushing into the house to bite members of the audience. Such "victims" were forewarned and were later publicly paid for their role. A small concealed knife could draw a convincing display of blood, and the image could be enhanced by placing small blood-filled bladders in the mouth to be burst at appropriately dramatic moments. Relatives attempted to "tame" the hamatsa with their rattles and songs as he circled the fire. Then the "Cannibal Birds" made their appearance. Dancers, wearing long strips of cedar bark to cover their bodies, performed with the large elaborate masks representing Cannibal Raven, "Crooked-Beak-of-Heaven," with its distinctive hooked beak, and *hokhokw* with its long straight beak that crushed men's skulls. These were among the most dramatic of all performances, as the dancers high-stepped around the fire, swaying the huge masks and loudly clacking their beaks. Finally the hamatsa returned, dressed in ceremonial finery, now "tamed" and restored to his human state.

Many dances relied on theatrical trickery for their effect on the audience. A good example is a woman's dance, the *tokwit*, which involved apparent death and resurrection. In one version, as the woman danced sedately around the fire, she was attacked by a man emerging from the shadows. Knocking her to the ground, the warrior hacked off her head with his whalebone "sword," holding the severed head, streaming with blood, up to the firelight. In actuality, the tokwit had covered her head with her blanket, and the warrior had removed a carved wooden likeness, complete with the tokwit's own hair, that she had been concealing. Bursting the blood-filled bladders attached to the head completed the effect. Attendants rushed in to remove the "body," yet later in the performance the tokwit re-emerged, unharmed, to dance again.

Many masterpieces of Wakashan artistry were created specifically for winter ceremonials. The magnificent masks, which represented a wide range of supernatural beings, were deeply carved to enhance the effect of eerie shadows from the firelight. Early historic headdresses often had mica set into pitch in the eyes, to flash with light as they reflected the fire. Later examples used copper strips or bits of mirror to obtain this theatrical illusion. Many masks, such as those of the Cannibal Birds, were mechanical, allowing the dancers to pull concealed strings to make the beaks open and close with a loud clacking sound. In other cases, the masks could "transform": pulling the concealed strings caused the mask to burst open and reveal an inner being. Skilled artists who could produce novel dramatic effects were eagerly sought by chiefs who wished to amaze their guests. Today when we see these masks displayed in our well-lit museums we should remember that their context has been lost. Try to imagine them in use, in darkened houses lit only by central fires, as skilled dancers conveyed impressions of the supernatural world to their audience.

THE COAST SALISH

The southern coast of British Columbia and south far into Washington State is the homeland of the Coast Salish. Excluding the northern enclave of Nuxalk at Bella Coola, six distinct Salishan languages were spoken by groups on the British Columbia coast. In the north are the Comox, bordering the Kwakwaka'wakw on both Vancouver Island and the mainland and borrowing from them many Wakashan cultural traits. South of the Comox on Vancouver Island were the Pentlatch, who largely succumbed to disease and warfare in the nineteenth century. Below the Comox on the mainland are the Sechelt and Squamish peoples. The largest Salishan language is Halkomelem, which includes such important groups as the Cowichan and Nanaimo on Vancouver Island and all the people along the lower Fraser River, collectively termed the Stó:lō from their name for the river. Finally, the Straits language is spoken on both sides of the Juan de Fuca Strait, with most groups in British Columbia near the city of Victoria.

Most of the Coast Salish had a typical Northwest Coast economy, based primarily on the sea. The Stó:lō, however, were riverine people, and most did not have any access to salt water. The river provided plentiful salmon, eulachon and other fish, and the men hunted waterfowl in the marshes, and deer, bear and mountain goat on the surrounding land. Particularly important was the sturgeon, which they could take year-round in the Fraser and its larger sloughs and tributaries. The Stó:lō devised ingenious techniques to harpoon these large fish while they rested, fat and sluggish, in deep water during the winter, and they used various methods in summer when the sturgeon moved into the sloughs to spawn.

The social organization of the Coast Salish was not as rigid as that of groups to the north: no clear-cut class distinctions were evident. They did not have true "chiefs," the Native term being better translated as "leader." Although people of high birth had a great advantage, the social system was flexible enough for talented individuals of more humble origins to improve their position. Leaders spoke only for their extended families (or households, as they tended to be the group occupying one house). Households were the largest effective political groups, as even winter villages were essentially only clusters of households. There were relatively few slaves, who were purchased or obtained in war, in Salish villages.

The winter village houses consisted of permanent frameworks of posts and beams, covered with split-cedar planks, which were slung horizontally between uprights to form walls. Houses were of the "shed-roof" variety, with a single pitch on the roof sloping gently from front to back. The flat roofs provided convenient platforms for spectators at public events such as potlatches. A number of houses were sometimes joined side by side under a common roof to create one long segmented structure. Simon Fraser observed such dwellings on his famed 1808 journey. One in the Fraser Valley he described as:

ABOVE *Potlatch in progress at a Salish village in Victoria, 1874.* RBCM PN6810

640 feet long ... under one roof. The front is 18 feet high, and the covering is slanting. All the apartments, which are separated in portions, are square ... on the outside, are carved a human figure large as life, and there are other figures in imitation of beasts and birds. *Lamb 1960: 103*

Another, near the mouth of the Fraser, he described as a "fort ... 1500 feet in length." Interior partitions of planks or mats provided privacy for family groups but could be removed to create a large open space for social or ceremonial occasions.

Salish winter dances were very different from the Wakashan masked perform-ances. They emphasized personal acquisition of spirit power rather than theatrical illusions and elaborate regalia. Young people fasted and bathed to ritually purify themselves before embarking on a quest for a guardian spirit. Fortunate individu-als who obtained guardian spirit power could cure sickness, foretell events or be exceptionally successful at hunting or fishing. Guardian spirits also imparted de-tails of songs and dances, through which humans could express their spirit power. During the winter months spirit power became stronger and overwhelmed the human recipients, who danced and sang as directed. Dancing and feasting were al-most continual during these months, and frequently involved reciprocal visits with inhabitants of nearby villages.

With the exception of the *sxwayxwey* mask, a distinctive mask with protrud-ing eyes and bird-like elements that was unique to the Salish, they did not have a strongly developed tradition of ceremonial art. Furthermore, they did not embel-lish their household goods with crest designs. Only the Comox, who were in con-tact with the Kwakwaka'wakw, raised free-standing totem poles. More typical of Salish art were the house posts carved in human or animal form and the grave figures fashioned to represent deceased ancestors. Smaller artworks included carved rattles and engraved designs on spindle whorls and combs. Although the Salish decorated fewer objects, much of their work was of considerable artistic merit. Its personal and religious associations, however, meant that it was less likely to be sold to collectors and museums, and today it is less known to the general public than other variants of Northwest Coast art.

The Salish were accomplished weavers and basket makers. They decorated beautiful coiled baskets of split cedar root with geometric designs in cherry bark and grass, in a style they shared with the Interior Salish. Created in a variety of sizes and shapes, these baskets served many carrying and storage functions. As well as the woven cedar-bark capes and blankets for everyday use, women produced "nobility blankets" of mountain-goat wool mixed with dog hair and other materials, woven on a loom. These ranged from elegantly simple blankets, with only a decorated border, to those covered with complex geometric designs. Recently the women of several Fraser River communities have revived this art and are rediscovering the achievements of their ancestors.

INTO THE GLOBAL ERA

Ships from the outside world finally breached the isolation of what is today British Columbia in the 1770s. Alarmed by the Russian presence in the north, the Spanish attempted to strengthen their claims to western North America with coastal expeditions in 1774 and 1775. They made fleeting contact with Haida and Nuu-chah-nulth groups during these voyages. Far from being overawed by these strange new people in their floating houses, coastal Natives paddled out to the ships, tossing feathers on the water or making other gestures of peace, and initiated trade. Eagerly sought was anything of metal, a wondrous substance that these wealthy foreign traders seemed to possess in abundance.

Only in 1778, when Captain James Cook arrived at Nootka Sound during his third voyage of global exploration, did chronic globalization begin. Cook spent almost a month among the Nuu-chah-nulth, and his journal provides the earliest major account of Northwest Coast Native life. Much of the interaction between the two races centred on trade. In exchange for metal implements, the British obtained furs and various items of Native manufacture. Cook's initial speculation that a profitable fur trade could be established was confirmed when his ships reached China and the thick, soft pelts of the sea otter obtained from the Nuu-chah-nulth commanded high esteem and prices. This was a discovery of momentous consequence for Northwest Coast peoples, because it turned Nootka Sound into a scene of international commerce within only a few years.

By the mid-1780s the rush for fur trade wealth had begun. Initially British, French, Spanish and American vessels vied for pelts collected by Native hunters, but the trade soon dwindled to the British (called "King George men" by the coastal people) and the Americans (known as "Boston men" from their main home port). Ships set out laden with goods for the Native trade; initially the Europeans brought iron tools, but as the market became glutted they shifted to other commodities that might catch the Natives' fancy. After negotiating the best deals possible, traders set sail for China with their valuable cargoes of sea otter pelts. This commerce continued into the second decade of the nineteenth century, until relentless pursuit of the sea otter finally caused its extinction along the British Columbia coast.

Although ship captains stood to make great profits, their counterparts in the Aboriginal communities also gained. Some fortunate and astute Native leaders established themselves as intermediaries in the trade, greatly increasing their own wealth and power. European ship captains and Aboriginal leaders interacted as equals, each controlling access to goods desired by the other. The journals of European observers often grudgingly acknowledge the trading skills of Native chiefs.

In fact, this early maritime commerce bolstered the traditional Native economy. Newly wealthy chiefs invested their gains in traditional ways, holding impressive ceremonies and distributing quantities of goods at potlatches. With iron carving tools and new wealth, they commissioned great works of art on a scale previously unknown. The "forest of totem poles" that greeted later arrivals to the northern villages was possible only because of this trade. Not all of the effects of this early contact period were positive, however; the Europeans brought epidemic diseases that took a dreadful toll in many Native villages. The traders were only interested in making a profit and had no desire to usurp the land or to convert the local inhabitants, though individuals who held such goals were not far behind.

The global era arrived in a two-pronged commercial manoeuvre that merged the maritime and land-based fur trades, the latter arriving on the coast as the former went into decline. Agents of the great fur trade companies had forged routes from the interior to the coast, setting up permanent posts in their wake. The earliest Hudson's Bay Company post on the coast was built in 1827 at Fort Langley, among the Fraser River Salish. Fort Simpson on the northern coast became the centre for nine Tsimshian tribes clustered in a single village around it after 1834. Similarly, Fort Rupert, constructed on northern Vancouver Island in 1849, became the permanent home of four formerly separate Kwakwaka'wakw tribes. Also, the burgeoning town that grew up around Fort Victoria after 1843 attracted many Native People from all along the coast.

This period of permanent fur trade posts had much greater impact on Native life than the fleeting contacts of earlier maritime traders. Wherever forts were established, Native communities grew up around them, and came to rely on European goods rather than on their former economic cycle. Such readily available items as the Hudson's Bay Company blanket replaced laboriously produced traditional crafts. Firearms from traders made intertribal warfare more deadly, and alcohol brought social problems and demoralization to many groups.

In some cases, such as among the Tsimshian at Fort Simpson and the Kwakwaka'wakw at Fort Rupert, the merger of separate tribal units into a single large village created conflicts. A new social order had to be established, and with it mechanisms to resolve the relative ranking of tribal chiefs, each jealous of his power, prestige and social position. Rivalry potlatching became common as chiefs contested for status through competitive gestures and by destroying goods. These aggressive performances and the "whiskey feasts" held around the posts alarmed the growing non-Native communities, which eventually led to the potlatch's legal prohibition.

The most serious of the many problems besetting Native communities at this time was infectious disease. Aboriginal people were not immune to such European-introduced contagions as measles and smallpox, and periodic epidemics had begun as early as the 1780s. As contact with Europeans increased in this more settled period, disease became more widespread. Particularly devastating was the smallpox epidemic that began in Victoria in 1862. As Native groups around the fort became ill, alarmed local authorities put the camps to the torch and forced the Natives out. Many died during their canoe journey home, but others spread the contagion wherever they went so that it soon raged along the entire coast and far into the interior. As many as 20,000 people, or roughly one-third of British Columbia's Native population at the time, died in this catastrophe. Many of the survivors abandoned their villages to coalesce around European trading posts or missions. Weakened and demoralized, these groups were often willing to surrender their traditions for missionaries' promises of assistance and salvation.

Unlike the traders who preceded them, the missionaries intended to radically transform Native lifestyles. They were convinced that the only hope Aboriginal People had for salvation, or even survival, lay in their total assimilation to European beliefs and habits. Filled with the moral virtue of their age, missionaries brought their religious beliefs to the north Pacific coast. They attributed the misery of the Native camps not to the ravages of European diseases but to an inferior lifestyle that had to be changed as rapidly as possible. In their evangelical zeal, they saw themselves as bringing the light of the Gospel to a "dark and revolting picture of human depravity," enveloped in a "dark mantle of degrading superstition" (William Duncan, cited in Fisher 1977: 128).

William Duncan, one of the best-known missionaries from this time, provides a clear example of the link between religious conversion and cultural assimilation. He arrived at Fort Simpson in 1857, sent by the Anglican Church Missionary Society, which had heard disturbing reports about Native conditions around the post. Energetic and hard-working, Duncan soon mastered the Tsimshian language and began preaching. Once he had gained a sizable following, he moved his converts from what he considered the debauched atmosphere of Fort Simpson to Metlakatla, an old abandoned Tsimshian village site, where he established a new Christian community. Duncan moved his flock there in 1862, narrowly missing the smallpox epidemic that ravaged Fort Simpson. Under his strong-willed direction, the community soon grew and prospered. Rows of identical two-storey houses, complete with such Victorian flourishes as picket fences, were built of lumber from the community's sawmill. The schoolhouse and an elaborate church, capable of seating 800 people, dominated village life. As well as

ABOVE *Duncan's model community of Metlakatla, 1881.* PABC HP55793

the sawmill, a trading post, cannery, blacksmith shop and other industries made the village economically self-sufficient. In return, residents had to abide by a list of rules established by Duncan, who forbade most of their traditional practices and stressed a Europeanized Christian lifestyle. As missionary, teacher and magistrate, Duncan held all authority.

Duncan's social experiment at Metlakatla flourished for only a few decades. His stubbornness and inflexibility, however, alienated both government and church authorities, and when the church sent to Metlakatla a bishop whose views on appropriate ritual for Native People were considerably different, Duncan decided to leave. In 1887, after he successfully appealed to the American government for land on which to establish a new settlement, Duncan led his followers out of British Columbia to a location in southern Alaska. With characteristic zeal, he re-created his Christian industrial village at New Metlakatla, and the original settlement became a small, remote fishing community.

The first steps in administering Aboriginal People came after Vancouver Island was declared a Crown colony in 1849. As more and more colonists clamoured for property, they pressured the government to provide small reserves for Native use so the rest of the land would be open for non-Natives to settle. Between 1850 and 1854, Governor James Douglas negotiated fourteen treaties with individual tribes on Vancouver Island, particularly those near Fort Victoria. By the terms of these treaties the land became "the entire property of the white people forever" in exchange for making small compensatory payments and establishing reserves. Although non-Native settlement was expanding, Douglas did not have enough funds to continue his treaty-making policy, and these remained the only treaties signed with Native People of the British Columbian coast until modern times.

Non-Natives continued to pressure the government for lands, which required additional reserve allocations, both on Vancouver Island and in the new colony of British Columbia after 1858. Douglas simply assigned the areas Native leaders requested, based on their traditional use. As a result, a patchwork pattern of reserves evolved, in which each Native community held a number of traditional villages and camp sites. Douglas's successors opposed even these small holdings (which were much smaller than those later established under federal policies), because they felt too much good agricultural land had been given out. The many small, scattered reserves throughout British Columbia today reflect this historic practice.

When British Columbia entered into Confederation in 1871, the province had to transfer responsibility for Aboriginal affairs to the federal government. However the west coast tribes were a long way from Ottawa, the new administrative centre, and the politicians knew little of their particular situation. Moreover, government agents and missionaries saw the new Indian Act as a weapon in their battle against such Native practices as the potlatch, which they felt were hindering their efforts at acculturation. Accordingly, they lobbied the federal government to legislate a ban on such performances. They succeeded in their demands, and in 1884 potlatches became illegal under the Indian Act.

Native People reacted strongly to such a fundamental assault on their customs. Some protested vigorously; others potlatched secretly, evading the agents by holding ceremonies at remote fishing camps rather than in their major villages. Initially, attempts to prosecute offenders were unsuccessful owing to the vague wording of the law; however, by the early 1920s there were several highly publicized trials and convictions. Legal prohibitions against the potlatch remained in effect until the Indian Act was rewritten in 1951.

The economy also was changing during this period. By the early decades of the twentieth century, Native People had become employees of Euro-Canadian enterprises. Some Nuu-chah-nulth and Kwakwaka'wakw men signed aboard sealing schooners as fur seal hunters, setting out on voyages that took them as far afield as Japan or Hawaii until the industry collapsed when a 1911 international treaty halted commercial sealing. Others found work in the logging industry or in the commercial fishery. Fish canneries employed large numbers of Native women, whose families left their villages each summer to camp nearby. When canneries closed all along the B.C. coast in the mid-twentieth century, many Native families lost a major source of income.

Native discontent focussed on the loss of most of their traditional lands. In particular, those groups in more isolated areas did not understand how the government could force them onto small reserves when they had never sold or ceded the rest of their territory. As early as the 1880s the Nisga'a were protesting the appropriation of their lands and demanding compensation. Land claims remain today a contentious issue between Northwest Coast First Nations and the federal and provincial governments.

FIRST NATIONS OF THE NORTHWEST COAST TODAY

Coastal cultures, after enduring decades of neglect and suppression, are enjoying a major resurgence in modern times. Northwest Coast art is recognized as one of the world's great achievements, sparking a commercial demand for the works of talented artists. Newly carved totem poles stand proudly with the few remaining ancient examples in Native villages, and dancers at Native ceremonies perform in beautifully carved masks and headdresses. Potlatches are once again legal, and many modern events are marked by feasting and public distribution of gifts. Some First Nations have established cultural programs and museum displays to interpret their heritage, and many on-reserve schools are teaching Aboriginal languages.

Government attitudes toward Native Peoples are also changing. When pot-latches were banned, the Kwakwaka'wakw defiantly continued the practice, often gathering in secret. In 1922, after a large potlatch, the agent at Alert Bay prose-cuted those involved, striking an infamous bargain in which those who surren-dered their masks, rattles and other potlatch regalia could buy their freedom from jail. Some of these items were sold to an American collector, and the rest were di-vided between what are today the Canadian Museum of Civilization and the Royal Ontario Museum. In recent decades, after the law was revoked and pot-latching could take place publicly, the Kwakwaka'wakw at Alert Bay constructed a large dance house on their reserve and began to press for the return of their lost treasures. Finally, the Canadian government agreed to give back the goods, pro-vided they be put on public display. By 1980 museums had been built in Alert Bay and Cape Mudge, and the newly returned artifacts formed the basis of the collec-tions. These museums do not just display objects, but are dynamic community cultural centres that enhance Kwakwaka'wakw language and traditions.

Northwest Coast Native artists are highly regarded within Canadian art. The living master artists use techniques and concepts that link the anonymous artists of the past with the modern art world. Prominent figures today, to name just a few, include Robert Davidson (Haida), Joe David (Nuu-chah-nulth), Tony Hunt (Kwakwaka'wakw) and Susan Point (Coast Salish); however, other accomplished artists come from virtually all the coastal First Nations. They are innovators who have not only mastered their regional styles but are intent on taking the art in new directions. In addition to the traditional painting and wood carving, Aborigi-nal artists now create gold and silver jewelry, silkscreen prints and sculptures in glass and cast bronze. Although it is strongly rooted in tradition, contemporary Northwest Coast art does not simply reflect nineteenth-century achievements but continues to expand and evolve.

In the coastal communities, fishing continues to be the economic mainstay for many Northwest Coast people, and fleets of fishing boats are a common sight in places such as Old Massett, Bella Bella and Alert Bay. More recently, logging has become important to the Native economy, and a number of First Nations have formed logging co-operatives and companies. Some have developed industries or

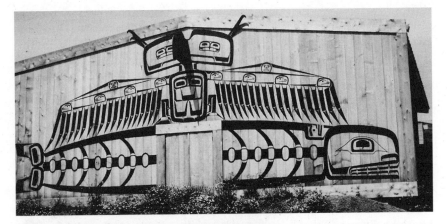

ABOVE *The design of the modern museum and cultural centre at Alert Bay was based on an old-style plank house, with its painted depiction of the Thunderbird over a whale. Photo by A. McMillan.* LEFT *A fine example of recent northern art, this portrait mask is the work of the late Haida carver Freda Diesing. Photo by A. McMillan*

recreational enterprises on their lands, or leased them for such purposes. Tourism, from cultural programs to whale-watching expeditions, provides income for some First Nations. Although many groups have established successful businesses, the small, scattered and isolated nature of the reserves has frustrated other attempts, and lack of employment has forced a large number of people to leave the reserves for the cities. Nearly half of the registered members of B.C. First Nations now live off-reserve, mostly in urban areas.

Land claims based on unsurrendered Aboriginal title continue to be of central concern to coastal First Nations. No federal treaties were signed on the west coast, and the few Douglas treaties of colonial times did not remove the Crown's responsibilities regarding Aboriginal title. First Nations and both levels of government have been embroiled in ongoing negotiations and legal battles.

In a long and costly court case, the Gitksan-Wet'suwet'en Tribal Council, representing seven bands in the Upper Skeena area, took its claim covering a large area of northwestern British Columbia through the Canadian legal system. This is known as the *Delgamuukw* case, after the Gitksan chief who first signed the litigation papers. In a 1991 decision the B.C. Supreme Court ruled against the Gitksan-Wet'suwet'en, greatly angering many Aboriginal leaders by dismissing not only the testimony of the elders who had carefully presented their oral histories to the court but also of anthropologists who gave evidence on their behalf. An appeals court decision in 1993 ruled that Aboriginal rights had not been extinguished, as the original judgement claimed, but it still denied the Gitksan-Wet'suwet'en title to their traditional territories. In the final episode of this legal saga, the Supreme Court of Canada ruled in 1997 that the original trial judge had erred in dismissing the elders' oral histories, and that the outcome might well have been different if this evidence had been fully considered. Accordingly, a new trial was ordered. The Supreme Court justices also declared that Aboriginal title is a right to the land itself, not just a right to use the land for traditional purposes, and that this right is protected under the Canadian constitution. The judgement makes clear that Aboriginal title remains in effect unless specifically removed by legal process such as a treaty. Although the Gitksan-Wet'suwet'en still have not resolved their claims, the *Delgamuukw* decision has reshaped the legal landscape for cases involving Aboriginal title. Its ongoing legacy is that Aboriginal oral traditions must now be given equal weight with other types of legal evidence, and that First Nations must be consulted and their interests taken into account when governments make decisions involving Crown lands.

Only one coastal First Nation to date has reached final settlement on its land claim. For the Nisga'a this has been a long battle tenaciously fought over generations. The people of the four Nass River villages have always rejected outsiders' attempts to control their lands. Government surveyors trying to lay out reserves were ordered out of the valley in 1886. The following year a delegation of Nisga'a chiefs travelled to Victoria to address the government regarding the land issue, but they were rebuffed without a hearing. The Nisga'a Land Committee was subsequently formed and a detailed petition, the first such statement of Aboriginal claim, was sent to the authorities in 1913. Ottawa not only rejected the claim, but the federal government amended the Indian Act in 1927 to prohibit attempts to raise money for land claims.

Eventually, the Nisga'a Tribal Council took their grievance through the Canadian legal system, beginning with the B.C. Supreme Court in 1968. This was the *Calder* case, named for Nisga'a leader and provincial politician Frank Calder. After it was rejected in the lower courts, the Nisga'a finally reached the Supreme Court of Canada, where they received an inconclusive verdict in 1973. Three judges ruled for the Nisga'a, three rejected their claim, and the seventh ruled against the Nisga'a on procedural grounds without commenting on the question of Aboriginal rights. Although it was a technical defeat for the Nisga'a, this case revealed

LEFT *Nisga'a Lisims government building, on the Nass River at New Aiyansh. Photo by A. McMillan*

much legal support for Aboriginal claims and forced a re-evaluation of federal policy across the country. The Nisga'a continued to press for recognition of their rights to their traditional lands, but it took another quarter of a century of negotiation before a final agreement was reached in 1998.

The Nisga'a Final Agreement, which came into effect in 2000 after it was ratified by the three parties, is the final settlement between Canada, British Columbia and the Nisga'a. In it, the Nisga'a receive ownership of about 2000 square kilometres of land in the Nass River valley, encompassing the four villages. These are now Nisga'a lands; they are not reserves under the Indian Act. The final agreement replaces the Indian Act and Nisga'a communities now have their own administrative structure, including a central Nisga'a Lisims government and four village councils. A Nisga'a police service will enforce Nisga'a, provincial and federal laws, including the Criminal Code of Canada. Important cultural places will be protected as designated heritage sites and key geographic locations will be renamed with Nisga'a terms; in addition, an agreement was reached to share Nisga'a cultural items now housed in federal and provincial museums. The Nisga'a will also receive $190 million over time as compensation. In return, the Nisga'a surrender all claims to most of their traditional territory, retaining only about 8 per cent, and they give up certain Indian Act benefits such as tax exemptions. Many critics of the treaty were alarmed that the agreement created what they saw as a separate state, yet Joe Gosnell, the Nisga'a leader who concluded the treaty, repeatedly insisted that the Nisga'a sought to negotiate their way into Canada. In an eloquent and impassioned speech in the B.C. legislature after the province ratified the treaty, Gosnell stated that, "under the treaty the Nisga'a people will join Canada and British Columbia as free citizens—full and equal participants in the social, economic and political life of this province, of this country . . . because under the treaty we will no longer be wards of the state, no longer beggars in our own lands." Gosnell was elected as the first president of the Nisga'a Nation's new government.

Many other First Nations in British Columbia have been pressing for resolution of their claims. In the past the provincial government was reluctant to become involved in such issues, as it maintained that land claims were entirely federal concerns. However, in 1992 it reversed its long-standing position and entered an agreement with Canada and the First Nations of the province to create the B.C. Treaty Commission. The commission facilitates three-way negotiations to resolve disputes over Aboriginal title. The key issues at the negotiating tables include lands, financial compensation, access to resources and self-government measures. At present, fifty-three Aboriginal groups, representing 122 individual First Nations, are taking part in this process. After more than a decade of negotiations, however, not a single treaty has been finalized (the Nisga'a Agreement took place outside the B.C. Treaty Commission). Many agreements-in-principle are now ready to go into the final stage, though this does not guarantee that any treaties will be concluded successfully (several have failed at this point in the past). The negotiations now underway renew hope that new treaties will be finalized in the near future.

Even in the absence of treaties, coastal First Nations have been asserting control over their lands and communities. Well before the Nisga'a signed their treaty, they were directing their educational services, administering their own school district and supplementing the standard provincial curriculum with courses in Nisga'a language and culture. The Sechelt, a Coast Salish group on the mainland coast, negotiated an agreement with Canada and British Columbia in 1986 that established local self-government, transferred title to their reserve lands to the Sechelt and replaced the Indian Act with the Sechelt Indian Self-Government Act. The Haida, following a series of protests, successfully stopped logging companies from felling trees on the southern portion of Haida Gwaii. These lands, now in Gwaii Haanas National Park Reserve, are jointly managed by the Haida Nation and the government of Canada, pending resolution of Aboriginal claims. The present superintendent of the park is Haida.

The grandparents of today's elders paddled their canoes along the rugged coastline, seeking the resources of this bountiful environment. These were the people who suffered through the years when their population declined, their land was appropriated and their culture suppressed. In only a few generations their world was transformed into one of dependence and government control. Today, the situation shows promise of change, as Northwest Coast First Nations are restoring and preserving their cultural traditions, transferring their heritage to a new generation and fighting to ensure that they have the resources to shape their own future.

CHAPTER 9

The Western
Subarctic

. . . . .

THE NORTHERN boreal forest and forest-tundra transition of the Western Subarctic stretches from the interior of Alaska to Hudson Bay. In the north it is bounded by the treeline, though some Subarctic Native groups made seasonal forays after caribou out onto the barrenlands. In the south it grades into the Plains and Plateau. Lakes, rivers and muskeg cover much of its surface. Winters are long and piercingly cold, with deep accumulations of snow, but the forest provides shelter. Summers are short and pleasantly hot, but are plagued by swarms of biting insects. From a southern urban perspective it seems a harsh and demanding environment, yet it was home to many groups of mobile hunters and fishers, whose modern descendants are determined to maintain traditional ties to the land.

Physiographically diverse, the Western Subarctic can be divided into three broad regions. In the east is the rocky Canadian Shield, extending from the Eastern Subarctic across northern Manitoba and Saskatchewan and into Nunavut and the Northwest Territories. To the west, the Northwest Territories, northern Alberta and northeastern British Columbia are in the Mackenzie Lowlands, which slope gradually to the Mackenzie River delta. At the western edge is the Cordillera, the array of mountain ranges and valleys that characterize the Yukon and central British Columbia. In this region many of the rivers flow to the Pacific, which provided Native People with access to bountiful salmon runs, and to trade corridors that linked them with coastal cultures.

For the big-game hunters of the Western Subarctic, caribou and moose were essential resources. Some of the more southerly groups intercepted the bison herds, and in the Cordillera people hunted mountain goat and sheep. Smaller

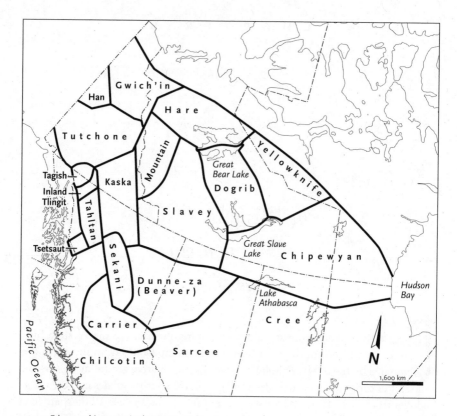

ABOVE *Ethnographic groups in the Western Subarctic*

mammals, especially the snowshoe hare, played an important role in the diet. Great numbers of migratory waterfowl could be taken for brief periods each year, and the lakes and rivers provided whitefish, lake trout, pike, grayling and other fish.

The Athapaskan people, or Dene as many prefer to be called, lived throughout this vast region. More than twenty Athapaskan languages, including those in Alaska, have been defined for the Subarctic. All are closely related, which indicates they differentiated relatively recently. Their classification is somewhat arbitrary since they tend to grade into one another through a series of intermediate dialects, and neighbouring groups usually understood each other's languages.

Athapaskan migrations and cultural adaptations have attracted considerable anthropological interest. From their northern homeland the Athapaskans spread far to the south in a series of separate movements. The Sarcee on the Plains and the Nicola and Chilcotin in the Plateau appear to be relatively recent examples. The Navajo and Apache of the American Southwest, as well as the cluster of Athapaskan language speakers on the Pacific coast around the Oregon-California border, are evidence of earlier, more extensive migrations. When they entered new regions, the Athapaskans adopted patterns of cultural traits that earlier residents had developed. In their northern homeland, for example, the Cordilleran groups borrowed and absorbed many aspects of Northwest Coast cultures. Such diffusion, along with their adaptation to differing local environments, accounts for the considerable cultural diversity among Subarctic Athapaskans.

Speakers of two non-Athapaskan Aboriginal languages also inhabit the Western Subarctic. Tlingit is spoken in extreme northwestern British Columbia and the southern Yukon, which reflects the coastal Tlingit's move inland for furs during the historic fur trade. It has since spread through intermarriage and its widespread use as a ceremonial language, at the expense of Athapaskan languages in the southern Yukon. Cree is spoken more widely, by people in communities throughout northern Manitoba, Saskatchewan and Alberta. (Their culture differs little from the Cree of the Eastern Subarctic, described in chapter 5.)

Cree antiquity in the Western Subarctic has been the subject of debate. Some believe the Cree arrived in the eighteenth century and dramatically expanded their territory at the expense of the Athapaskans during the fur trade. In this view, the Cree had an economic and military advantage over their neighbours because they were in contact with European traders around Hudson Bay and acquired firearms early. Several archaeological studies, however, suggest that the Cree arrived in the Western Subarctic much earlier. Selkirk pottery, which is usually attributed to the Cree, has been found in archaeological sites in northern Manitoba and Saskatchewan. Although Cree speakers, along with other Aboriginal groups, were moving west during the historic fur trade, some earlier writers seem to have exaggerated the dramatic surge from Hudson Bay to the Rockies.

HOLOCENE CULTURAL DEVELOPMENTS

This vast land of northern forests is one of the least-known archaeological areas in Canada and one of the most difficult to interpret. Small groups of hunters moving across the landscape left few traces, and the acidic soils have reduced even these meagre remains to a few simple stone tools. The sites tend to be small and shallow, largely hidden by forest cover, and disturbed or mixed by frost action. Although the pace of archaeological research has recently accelerated, the emerging picture is still far from clear.

Early occupants were the so-called "Paleo-Indians," whose distinctive projectile points are relatively widespread. The earliest styles occur in the west, where fluted points similar to those described in chapter 2 have been found. Most are undated surface discoveries. Only at Charlie Lake Cave in northeastern British Columbia, where hunters took a large form of bison 10,500 years ago, has a fluted point been found in a radiocarbon-dated context. Somewhat later, the appearance of large unfluted spearpoints marked the early complex known as Plano or, in the north, Northern Cordilleran. Most archaeological finds are undated, but at the Canyon site in the southern Yukon, on a bluff today topped by historic Tutchone gravehouses, a small group of ancient hunters left behind a large spearpoint and other stone tools, several bison bones and the remains of a hearth which could be dated to 7200 years ago.

To the east, the huge Laurentide ice sheet blocked human entry until about 8000 years ago. The Plano hunters were the first people to move into this area, leaving behind the large lanceolate spearpoints known on the Plains as Agate Basin, at sites far out onto the barrenlands. The Plano people are assumed to have been big-game hunters, attracted to the north by the large herds of caribou.

At the same time as these early cultures were hunting across the region, a different population was entering from the west. These were people with a Eurasian technology, crossing into North America shortly before Beringia finally disappeared. Small distinctive tools commonly termed microblades—thin, parallel-sided stone flakes with razor-sharp edges that were set as cutting or slicing edges into grooved bone or antler spearpoints or other tools—marked their presence. Stone knives, spearpoints, scrapers and other implements were also part of their tool kits. Microblade technology is evident in Alaska at least 10,700 years ago and somewhat later in the Yukon and adjacent areas of the Northwest Territories and the northern interior of British Columbia. In these regions microblades may indicate that local peoples gradually adopted this technology. At later sites, notched stone projectile points have been found with microblades, which suggests people and ideas mixed throughout a large area.

The microblade technology did not spread east past the Mackenzie River valley, where diversified cultures followed the late Plano hunters. In the rocky Shield country around Hudson Bay, proto-Algonquian cultures became recognizable about 6000 years ago. Termed "Shield Archaic" by archaeologists, these people used notched stone spearpoints, knives and scrapers and occupied an area from the Eastern Subarctic to the eastern portions of the Western Subarctic. The lifeways represented by these archaeological remains would be immediately familiar to the Cree or Innu.

Between about 3500 and 3000 years ago a new group from the north pushed into the lands east of the Mackenzie River and left behind the very small stone tools that were their trademark technology. These were the Tuniit people of Arctic antiquity (see chapter 10). Archaeologists refer to this branch of the Tuniit as Pre-Dorset. Their expansion is associated with colder climatic conditions, which pushed the treeline far to the south. Following the caribou herds, Tuniit hunters moved south as far as what is today northern Saskatchewan and Manitoba. Their occupation of these lands was short-lived, lasting only a few centuries. Traces of their ancient camps consist mostly of scattered stone tools around fire-cracked rocks that once were hearths used to heat their shelters.

The first traces of Athapaskan cultures are still much debated. Some believe the Athapaskans were present during the period when microblades first appeared and spread, which would give them an ancient heritage in the Western Subarctic. Others have traced Athapaskan migrations through later styles of projectile points.

Linguistic and social units, however, cannot be defined through the distribution of stone tools. Furthermore, the ancient Athapaskans were culturally diverse and occupied a wide range of environments, which means they probably left a varied signature in the archaeological record. Nevertheless, the emergence of specific Athapaskan cultures has been charted at archaeological sites in several regions.

In the east, the Taltheilei tradition spans the last 2500 years in the historic homeland of the Chipewyan, Yellowknife and Dogrib Athapaskans. Most of our information comes from around Great Slave Lake and Lake Athabasca, though sites are found more widely in the Northwest Territories, Nunavut, northern Manitoba and Saskatchewan, and parts of Alberta. Evidence of Taltheilei cultures appears far out on the barrenlands, suggesting that these people, like their historic counterparts, ranged between the forests and tundra to intercept migrating caribou herds. The ancient Plano, Algonquian, Tuniit and Athapaskan (Taltheilei) peoples, for example, sequentially occupied the Migod site in southern Nunavut, from which they all hunted the caribou herds out on the barrenlands. Fishing has always been a vital part of the Athapaskan economy as well, as the location of many sites suggests ("Taltheilei" refers to water). Stone-stemmed and lanceolate spearpoints, changing in form over time, as well as knives, endscrapers and stone-slab or boulder-flake hide scrapers (generally known by the Athapaskan term *chithos*) are the characteristic tools. Small notched points that presumably tipped arrows appeared later. Implements of native copper are also relatively common from that time. Finally, beads and other European goods mark the transition to such historic Athapaskans as the Chipewyan.

About 1300 years ago a massive volcanic eruption in the St. Elias Range, at the southern end of the present Yukon-Alaska border, blasted immense quantities of volcanic ash into the air. Winds swept the ash about 1000 kilometres to the east, blanketing the southern Yukon with a thick layer of grit. Visible today along river banks and road cuts, the horizontal white band in the otherwise brown soil is known as White River ash. The eruption and ashfall must have alarmed the local people, darkening the sky, fouling the water and covering the land so that the areas most affected must have been temporarily uninhabitable.

Such conditions would have forced many groups to abandon their country in search of unaffected lands, dispersing to the north and south of the ashfall area. As people moved into regions already occupied by neighbouring people local hostilities likely resulted. Many groups might have been forced to continue their wanderings for considerable distances. Alaskan archaeologist William Workman has pointed out that the time of this environmental disaster corresponds with linguistic estimates of Athapaskan divergence. He suggests that the ashfall was a "triggering mechanism" that stimulated the southward migrations that eventually led to the Navajo and Apache of the American Southwest. However, as these movements are very difficult to demonstrate archaeologically, this hypothesis remains speculative.

As plant and animal life gradually returned to its usual state in the ashfall area, humans reoccupied the land. In the layers overlying the White River ash archaeologists have found implements of the Aishihik culture, dating to just before the advent of the global era. Stone spear and arrow points, knives, chi-thos and wedges for splitting wood are typical artifacts, as are distinctive arrowpoints, awls and other tools of copper. Nuggets of this metal occur locally and were heated and hammered to shape. Such tools continued into the global era and can be linked to the Tutchone people who occupy the southern Yukon today.

High-elevation ice patches in the southern Yukon began to retreat during the warm summers of the late 1990s. Great quantities of caribou dung exposed by the melting ice showed that the animals had congregated long ago on the ice patches to escape the summer heat and biting insects. Human hunters pursued their prey to these locations, leaving behind the spears and arrows they lost during the hunt. As these froze into the ice, they were perfectly preserved and the wooden shafts can now be dated. Short spears or darts, which were hurled by atlatls (spear throwers), have been dated from about 8350 to 1250 years ago. These darts are often found intact, with stone points in place, as well as with preserved sinew, feathers and caribou hair. The bow and arrow appeared about 1300 years ago, after which arrows gradually replaced atlatl darts in the ice patch remains. Stone points disappeared as the intact arrows were tipped with barbed antler points.

The melting ice revealed another remarkable discovery just south of the Yukon border, in northwestern British Columbia. In the summer of 1999, hunters on a glacier came across the almost perfectly preserved remains of a young man who had perished there about 550 years ago. At the time of his death, this individual was wearing a fur garment and a finely woven hat of plant fibres. He was carrying several wooden implements, including an atlatl dart, and food supplies in the form of dried salmon. The hat is of a type characteristic of the coastal Tlingit, and local oral histories tell of frequent travel between the coast and interior over the glacier. The Tutchone people of the Champagne and Aishihik First Nations termed this discovery Kwaday Dan Ts'inchi ("Long Ago Person Found"). They worked with archaeologists and the Tlingit people of Alaska to remove and study these remains, and cremated them and returned the ashes to the glacier following the analysis.

In the northern Yukon, the deeply stratified Klo-kut site, which was occupied from about 1000 years ago into the global era, has shown developments linked to the historic Gwich'in. Excavated stone tools include such distinctive Athapaskan items as tapered-stem projectile points (known as Kavik points) and chi-thos. Well-preserved bone tools such as barbed points, fish-hook components and a carved fish effigy lure, as well as trays and other items of birchbark, have also been recovered and indicate a stable economy of caribou hunting and fishing extending into recent times.

In northern Manitoba and Saskatchewan south of the Taltheilei sites, the archaeological sequence is similar to that of the Eastern Subarctic (see chapter 5).

ABOVE LEFT *Archaeologists examining an arrow with barbed antler point and wooden shaft found preserved in a Yukon ice patch. From left to right are Greg Hare (Government of Yukon), James Baker (Carcross-Tagish First Nation) and Gordon Jarrold (University of Alaska). Government of Yukon photo.* ABOVE RIGHT *Human figure pictograph in northern Saskatchewan. Humans with upraised arms are a common feature of Canadian Shield rock art. Photo by Tim Jones*

About 1800 years ago pottery was introduced from the south, joining side-notched projectile points and other elements of the earlier tool kit. Archaeological remains from after about 1000 years ago consist of the distinctive fabric-impressed Selkirk pottery, small side-notched arrowpoints and other stone tools. These Selkirk sites persist into the global era and are generally associated with such Algonquian people as the Cree.

Closely paralleling the distribution of Selkirk pottery is that of red ochre pictographs. Paintings on prominent rock bluffs along major waterways are common across much of northern Manitoba and adjacent Saskatchewan. Humans, game animals and such mythological beings as Thunderbirds are commonly depicted. Occasional small offerings left near the paintings also suggest the images served a religious function. They are very similar to the numerous pictographs of northern Ontario, and all appear to be the work of Algonquian artists. In the Western Subarctic, these people were the ancestors of the Cree.

THE ATHAPASKANS (DENE)

The broad term "Athapaskan" is simply a linguistic label that indicates a common origin for all the related languages from the interior of Alaska to western Hudson Bay. Its derivation, however, comes not from the people to whom it refers but from the Cree. The Native inhabitants of the Mackenzie basin refer to themselves as Dene ("people"). Athapaskan groups in other areas use similar, though varying, terms. Today the term "Dene Nation" has become the preferred collective self-designation in the Northwest Territories.

The fluid Athapaskan social groups are not the same as political "tribes." Small, highly mobile bands tended to resemble their neighbours in speech and lifestyle, and division into named units is somewhat arbitrary, often reflecting administrative or anthropological convenience rather than Aboriginal reality. Group names indicate linguistic differences, though not all of them spoke entirely separate languages. The now-extinct Yellowknife, for example, were a distinct ethnic entity but they spoke a dialect of Chipewyan. Similarly, some modern linguists classify Slavey, Hare and Mountain as dialects of the same language. Even separate languages, such as Beaver and Sekani, grade into one another through a series of dialects. Modern group names often come from terms applied by European traders or the Cree. As the explorer David Thompson wrote of the Chipewyan, "The country is occupied by a people who call themselves 'Dinnie,' by the Hudson Bay Traders 'Northern Indians,' and by their southern neighbours 'Cheepawyans.'" This Cree term means "pointed skins," referring either to the way they prepared beaver pelts or to the pointed tails on their shirts.

All northern Athapaskans lived by hunting and fishing; gathering plant foods played only a minor role. During the historic fur trade many shifted to hunting and trapping fur-bearing animals. Athapaskan lifeways were flexible, and each group closely adapted to the territory it inhabited. Groups living in the Cordillera on the west, where most rivers drain to the Pacific, differed significantly from those living on the Shield and Mackenzie Lowlands to the east, where the rivers flow north to the Arctic or into Hudson Bay.

THE ATHAPASKANS OF THE SHIELD AND MACKENZIE LOWLANDS

Few environments in Aboriginal North America were as challenging to human survival as the Western Subarctic. Long severe winters and short warm summers characterized the seasons. During the winter, intense cold, deep snow and limited daylight made starvation and death by exposure constant dangers. During the pleasant months of summer, dense swarms of mosquitoes and blackflies meant people had to keep their bodies covered at all times. David Thompson, on western Hudson Bay in 1784, commented: "Summer such as it is, comes at once, and with it myriads of tormenting Musketoes; the air is thick with them, there is no cessation day nor night of suffering from them . . . and [we] were thankful for the cold weather that put an end to our sufferings" (Glover 1962: 17).

Although the land supported huge herds of barren-ground caribou in the northern transitional forest and tundra, woodland caribou and moose in the full boreal forest and numerous fish in the lakes and rivers, these resources were not always predictable. Failure to find animals or poor luck in fishing could mean disaster for the entire group.

ABOVE *Chipewyan caribou-hunting camp on the barrenlands near Fort Churchill, ca. 1880.* CMC 74880

In the east are the Chipewyan, the most numerous and widespread of the northern Athapaskans. They were an "edge-of-the-forest" people, occupying the northern transitional forest west of Hudson Bay and far out onto the tundra or barrenlands. The barren-ground caribou were essential to the Chipewyan, who based their economy on following the herds in their seasonal movements. Both humans and caribou found shelter in the forests during the winter. When the animals began to migrate out onto the barrenlands in the spring, the Chipewyan hunters ambushed them along their major routes. During the summer, humans and the herds ranged far out onto the barrenlands. In the fall, the caribou were again taken in large numbers as they migrated south. Their flesh was cut into thin strips, dried in the sun and pounded into pemmican for winter provisions.

One productive method the Chipewyan used to take caribou was to build large enclosures of brushy trees near caribou migration paths. Samuel Hearne, who travelled with the Chipewyan in the late eighteenth century, claimed to have seen some "that were not less than a mile round." Inside was a maze of fences, with snares placed in every opening. Long lines of brush fences, which Hearne claimed were sometimes "not less than two or three miles," funnelled the animals to the pound's narrow entranceway. Once the caribou had been driven inside, this entrance was blocked with brush. Women and children raced around the fence to prevent animals from escaping, while men speared those entangled in the snares and shot with arrows those that still ran loose. When such techniques succeeded, the hunters captured so many caribou that their group could remain in one place for much of the winter.

Out on the barrenlands during the summer the Chipewyan hunted caribou with bows and arrows or speared them from canoes as they crossed rivers and lakes. Small, light bark canoes were carried from the woods for this purpose.

Hearne also described Chipewyan using lines of sticks to direct the caribou to a narrow pass, where concealed hunters waited.

Caribou were essential for more than food. The Chipewyan relied on caribou hides for clothing and lodge covers, and they cut them into strips for snares, fish nets, snowshoe lacings and many other purposes. Antlers and bones provided raw materials for many of their tools, and the women used sinew to sew clothing. A complete suit of winter clothing, according to Hearne, required eight to eleven hides, which were obtained in August and September when they were thick and unmarred by warble-fly holes. Hearne stated that the Chipewyan killed many animals for their hides at that time, and took only the choicest portions of meat.

Although the caribou were the staff of life to the Chipewyan, much as bison were to the Plains tribes, other animals played a role in the diet. They occasionally hunted musk-oxen while out on the barrenlands, frequently shot or snared arctic hares and took waterfowl seasonally when they were abundant. Fishing was second only to caribou hunting in importance, the Chipewyan using nets or bone hooks to take large quantities. In 1785 David Thompson commented: "When the land is scarce of Deer [caribou] . . . they take to the Lakes to angle Trout or Pike at which they are very expert."

The Chipewyan did not participate in the historic fur trade as enthusiastically as the Cree, but it did cause changes in their culture and distribution. The northern transitional forest provided the caribou that sustained them but it contained few of the fur-bearing animals sought by European traders. Some bands responded to the traders' urgings and pushed into the boreal forests to the south and west, reaching as far as northeastern Alberta in their search for furs. Others, who remained in their former territory and maintained the traditional lifestyle, became known as the "Caribou-Eater" Chipewyan.

To the northwest were the Yellowknife, who spoke a dialect of the Chipewyan language. Their name comes from the copper tools they manufactured from deposits found in their territory along the Coppermine River. Although they were linguistically and culturally Chipewyan, they are mentioned in the historical literature as a separate entity. They were apparently considered as such by Hearne's Chipewyan guides who plundered them, taking young women, furs, and bows and arrows. The Yellowknife, in turn, harassed the Dogrib and other neighbouring groups. In the nineteenth century many perished through disease and the Dogrib's retaliatory attacks. Finally, they disappeared as a distinct group, and the Dogrib and Chipewyan absorbed the survivors and their lands.

The Dogrib occupied the land between Great Bear and Great Slave Lakes. Their culture was similar to the Chipewyan, though they did not venture as far out onto the barrenlands. Caribou were the essential resource, with moose, hare and fish being of secondary importance.

The Hare, between Great Bear Lake and the Mackenzie River, speak a language closely related to Dogrib and differ little from that group. They lived by hunting and fishing, pursuing the barren-ground caribou out onto the tundra in summer. Big game was relatively scarce in their territory, so they relied on fish and hares throughout much of the year. This dependence on hares for food and clothing sufficiently distinguished them from their neighbours to give them their name, but it also led to a precarious existence. Since hares go through a population cycle every seven to ten years, this group suffered periodic food shortages and starvation.

Closely related to the Hare are the Bearlake and Mountain Athapaskans. The Bearlake or Sahtu Dene, today recognized as a distinct group, are a historic fusion of Hare, Dogrib and Slavey people whose ancestors settled around the fur trade posts near Great Bear Lake. The Mountain Athapaskans are the Aboriginal inhabitants of the Mackenzie Mountains, where they hunted moose, woodland caribou and mountain goat. Winter living was challenging as game was scarce and there were few large lakes for ice fishing. Historic records show that starvation was common.

Another closely related language is Slavey. Their territory covers a large area of the Northwest Territories west of Great Bear and Great Slave Lakes, plus northeastern British Columbia and northwestern Alberta. Unlike more northerly Athapaskans, the Slavey were fully a forest people, hunting moose and woodland caribou. Unlike herd animals such as the barren-ground caribou, these species had to be hunted individually with bows and arrows or speared when crossing water. The Slavey also took both large and small game in snares, and they relied heavily on fishing. Although the many small bands speaking dialects of the Slavey language did not constitute any cultural or political unit, they have in recent times used the term "Slavey" to distinguish themselves from other Athapaskans when speaking English. They are also known today as Dene-thah in northern British Columbia and Dene Tha' in northern Alberta.

To the south, along the Peace River of northern British Columbia and Alberta, are the people the traders called the Beaver Indians. They call themselves Dunne-za. The Dunne-za once dwelled farther to the east but, according to Alexander Mackenzie, gun-bearing Cree pushed them westward in the late eighteenth century. The Peace River apparently takes its name from the truce negotiated between these two peoples. The Dunne-za lifestyle was based almost entirely on big-game hunting. Herds of bison came into the open lands along the Peace, and the Dunne-za drove them into pounds in a technique similar to that used by the Plains tribes. Moose were available throughout Dunne-za territory, and Native groups hunted woodland caribou in some areas. Beaver were abundant and were sought for both their meat and fur. Hunters considered fishing to be beneath their dignity and they resorted to it only when they could not find game.

Throughout the Shield and Mackenzie Lowlands, Athapaskan societies were small, simple and highly mobile. The basic unit was the family, composed of a man and his wife or wives, their children and perhaps an aged parent or two. Most groups were polygynous, but only exceptional men could provide for several wives and defend them from other men; Matonabbee, the powerful Chipewyan chief described by Hearne, had seven wives. Several families, bound by ties of kinship and marriage, lived and travelled together throughout much of the year. When fishing was good or more men were needed to communally hunt caribou, much larger groups might gather. Hearne encountered a Chipewyan summer camp of seventy tents, which he estimated "did not contain less than 600 persons."

Leadership was based on ability, and the best hunter or most experienced warrior took charge during that activity. The Chipewyan and Dogrib, with their communal caribou hunts, emphasized leadership more than groups such as the Slavey, in which hunting was an individual activity. Leadership roles were temporary, and all adults felt free to come to their own decisions or join another social group. Flexibility and respect for individual autonomy are at the core of Athapaskan culture.

Although the Athapaskans were not known as ferocious warriors, hostilities were common. Raids between Athapaskan groups were usually to revenge past wrongdoings or to steal women. The Athapaskans also had long-standing enmities with their southern Cree neighbours and with the Inuit in the north. Hearne recounted the savage slaughter of a small Inuit camp by his Chipewyan guides as they travelled to the mouth of the Coppermine River in 1771.

Housing was simple and lightweight so that it could be easily packed up and moved. Throughout the area the conical tipi covered with caribou or moose hide was the most common year-round dwelling. A few groups built more substantial winter structures of poles chinked with moss. In the summer, simple lean-tos were all that was required.

Most groups in the summer travelled primarily by water, in canoes covered with spruce bark or birchbark. In a few areas moosehides were used to cover the canoe frame. Lacking good navigable rivers, the Chipewyan walked out onto the barrenlands carrying small lightweight canoes. In the winter, snowshoes were essential. Goods were carried on toboggans, which were hauled by the women. Dogsleds were unknown until the fur trade period.

Clothing was generally made of tanned caribou or moose hides, and some groups also used hare skins. Both men and women generally wore long pullover shirts or dresses, leggings with attached moccasins and breechcloths. They added mittens, a cap and a robe in the winter. Some northern groups attached hoods to their winter coats, but this is thought to be a late Inuit influence. Fringes and designs in moose hair or porcupine quills were added for decoration. People also tattooed parallel lines on their cheeks or chin and occasionally perforated their nasal septum to insert a quill or other ornament.

The late-eighteenth-century explorers—Hearne, Thompson and Mackenzie—noted a lack of obvious religious practices or ceremonies. These early observers, however, did not delve into the spiritual beliefs held by their Native guides and acquaintances. Later anthropological studies revealed complex religious thought, centring on the relationship between hunters and the animals on which they depended. The Dunne-za sent children into the bush on vision quests,

ABOVE *Slavey shaman at Fort Rae, 1913.*

CMC 26080

to seek supernatural power from the animals. Such experiences were not to be revealed but to be reflected upon and nurtured as private knowledge. Hunters slept near their medicine bundles, which contained images or charms relating to supernatural aid they had received as adolescents. In their dreams they encountered animals and gained assistance and knowledge from their spirit power.

Young men entering puberty had few restrictions, but young women were secluded. They were placed in a small hut, often at some distance from the main camp, where they were attended and instructed by female relatives. They ate only dried meat and had to take liquids through a bone drinking tube; to avoid touching their body they had to use a scratching stick. Throughout most of their lives women were periodically restricted, since men believed that menstruating women were offensive to the animal spirits and thus threatened the hunting success and survival of the entire group. Women saw their "moon sickness" as a sign of potent power, and they used caution to avoid inflicting harm. At such times, women refrained from walking on hunting trails or on ice where men fished or hunted beavers, and they could never touch or step over the personal gear of the hunter. Among the Dunne-za, menstruating women could not even walk behind the lodges for fear of severing the sacred link between the hunter or his medicine bundle and the animals in the bush.

Old age was a difficult time in societies that had to follow game. Individuals who could no longer keep up with the group were left behind. When a person died, the Chipewyan might simply leave the body on the ground; other groups interred their dead or raised them on scaffolds. Some personal possessions of the deceased were burned or left behind and the camp was abandoned.

The supernatural helped many to deal with the uncertainties of everyday life. Dreams provided guidance in making decisions. Shamans could call upon their spirit powers to locate game or to overcome their enemies. Illness was treated by blowing on the afflicted part of the body, or by sucking out a small object believed to have caused the disease. As well as such individual practices, occasional group ceremonies fostered social cohesion. Such gatherings featured feasting, singing, drumming, dancing and gambling.

THE CORDILLERAN ATHAPASKANS

The mountains and plateaus of the Subarctic Cordillera extend from northern Yukon to central British Columbia. Vast stretches of boreal forest cover the rugged landscape, but there are also large areas of meadows, flood plains and muskeg, as well as alpine tundra at higher elevations. Climate varies from among the harshest in the Subarctic in the northern territory of the Gwich'in to more benign among the Carrier in the south. Latitude is not the only consideration; local climatic conditions vary widely according to altitude and proximity to the coast. In the south the Subarctic grades into the open country of the Plateau, and the Chilcotin have been placed in that culture area.

Rivers flowing to the Pacific teemed with salmon during their seasonal spawning cycles. All but the easternmost Cordilleran peoples had access to this reliable food supply. Hence, they could sustain a larger population density and a more settled way of life than the eastern Athapaskans. Other resources, however, played at least as large a role in the economy of most groups. Caribou were essential, particularly to such northerners as the Gwich'in. They also hunted or snared mountain sheep and goats, moose, bear and smaller game. Freshwater fish were important to many groups, and plant foods were more abundant and played a larger role in the diet than among the eastern Athapaskans. Local resources could also be exchanged for exotic foodstuffs, such as eulachon oil, in trade with their coastal neighbours. Many Northwest Coast influences pervaded the lives of the Cordilleran Athapaskans and distinguished them from their kin to the east.

In the north, bordering on the Inuit, are the Gwich'in. Their lands today are in Alaska, Yukon and the Northwest Territories. Salmon ascended the Yukon River system far into Gwich'in territory, though the Mackenzie River groups in the east relied on Arctic char and whitefish instead. Traps were the most productive means of taking fish, and the Gwich'in established summer camps to construct and operate them. Moose, smaller animals and waterfowl were also important, but caribou were paramount to the Gwich'in. They provided the most food, as well as hides for shelter and clothing. Although individual hunters could pursue them, the major technique was the communal surround. Long lines of posts directed caribou to roughly circular enclosures, in which they were snared, speared or shot with arrows.

South of the Gwich'in are the Han, a distinct though little-known society. Their territory is on the Yukon River drainage, straddling the Yukon-Alaska border. They ate mainly fish, particularly salmon, though they also hunted moose and caribou.

The Tutchone occupy the southern Yukon. Some bands depended heavily on annual salmon runs, whereas others primarily hunted. Native copper was found in Tutchone territory and was used extensively to make tools. When the historic fur trade began, the Tutchone were drawn into a trading relationship with the Chilkat Tlingit. Through these ties of trade and intermarriage, the Tlingit heavily influenced Tutchone culture. Tutchone society was divided into two moieties,

LEFT *Gwich'in hunter in the 1840s.* CMC 73453

Wolf and Crow (the latter equivalent to the Tlingit Raven), each of which had several clans in the Tlingit style. Marriage partners had to be of the opposite moiety, and all children took their mother's affiliation.

The spread of Tlingit dominance into the Cordillera is most clearly seen in northwestern British Columbia and the adjacent southern Yukon—the territory of the Inland Tlingit and Tagish peoples. The local Athapaskans traded and intermarried with the Tlingit in the nineteenth century, adopting their language and social organization. They held potlatches, divided their society into Wolves and Crows, and used crests to denote their kin groups. The Tagish language gradually declined and is virtually extinct today.

Also in northwestern British Columbia, along the Stikine River drainage, are the Tahltan. The Stikine provided dependable salmon runs and a major trade route to the Stikine Tlingit on the west. The Tahltan established themselves as intermediaries in the trade between coastal groups and Athapaskans farther inland. They also interacted intensively with the Tlingit, including intermarriage and reciprocal potlatching, and they adopted many elements of Tlingit culture. They had matrilineal moieties (Wolf and Raven) that were divided into clans in the Tlingit fashion.

One group of Athapaskans, the Tsetsaut, breached the mountain barrier and reached the Pacific at the end of several long inlets on the British Columbia–Alaska border. Apparently they were not fully adapted to the coast, as they relied more heavily on inland game hunting than on fishing. Adjacent groups, particularly the Tahltan, harassed and raided them and the survivors were finally absorbed by the Nisga'a. By the early twentieth century the Tsetsaut were extinct.

In the eastern Cordillera of northern British Columbia and southern Yukon are the Kaska and Sekani. The Sekani are virtually indistinguishable from the Dunne-za and appear to have diverged from them only recently. To the north they are mixed with the Kaska, whose speech is closely related to Tahltan. Both lived by hunting moose, woodland caribou and mountain sheep, with fishing being of lesser importance. Since their rivers are in the Mackenzie drainage they did not have direct access to salmon but could take trout and whitefish. Although farther removed from the Northwest Coast than most Cordilleran Athapaskans, they felt some coastal influences. The Kaska divided their society into Wolf and Crow and traced descent through the female line, and several western Sekani bands briefly adopted the matrilineal clans of the Gitksan and western Carrier. Both held modest potlatches. Their cultures are transitional between the Cordillera and the Mackenzie Lowlands.

Occupying a large area of central British Columbia are the many groups known collectively as the Carrier. The name Dakelh is also used today, but it refers more generally to Native People. Variations in culture and language exist between these related groups. Those in the northwest, who today prefer to be known as the Wet'suwet'en, speak a dialect sufficiently distinct that some linguists classify it as a separate language. The upper reaches of both the Fraser and Skeena river basins extend through Carrier territory and provide teeming masses of spawning salmon. Salmon were the staple food for most Carrier groups and supported a relatively settled lifestyle and the highest population density in the Western Subarctic. When the salmon were running, many plant foods were also available and hunting was most productive. In the lean months of late winter, however, supplies of dried foods often ran low, forcing some groups to seek the hospitality of the Gitksan or Nuxalk to the west.

The basic Carrier social group was the extended family, usually consisting of several brothers, their wives and children. When the sons reached adulthood, they brought their wives and children into their family band. Each family held rights to a hunting territory and fishing sites. This typically simple Athapaskan organization began to be elaborated in the fur trade period, as extensive trade and inter-marriage with coastal peoples brought in the potlatch and ranking systems. In the north the Wet'suwet'en, bordering on the Gitksan of the upper Skeena, adopted clan organization with descent traced through the mother. Southern groups, which were in contact with the Nuxalk in the Bella Coola Valley, lacked such clans and traced descent through either the male or female line. In both cases, they painted or carved crests, generally depicting animals, in Northwest Coast style to

ABOVE *Totem pole at the Wet'suwet'en (western Carrier) village of Moricetown. Photo by A. McMillan*

denote particular kin groups. Those closest to the Gitksan adopted much of their ceremonial system. They raised totem poles to display crest privileges, the nobles wore the intricate Chilkat blankets of mountain-goat wool on important occasions, and high-ranking women slit their lower lip to wear a labret as a badge of status.

The Carrier situation was typical of most Cordilleran groups. Contact with the Tlingit, Gitksan and Nuxalk led Athapaskan groups, from the Gwich'in to the northern Carrier, to organize their societies into descent groups, traced matrilineally. "Big men" or "chiefs" amassed power as the rank system spread inland, and they obtained new wealth in trade and transformed it into status through potlatching. Although these "chiefs" had great prestige and were accorded respect, they did not have real political authority; the basic individual autonomy of the Athapaskans was retained.

Potlatches spread to all Cordilleran groups, though they were modest events compared to the extravagances of the Northwest Coast. Each important event—the naming of a child, the assumption of a family crest, a marriage or a funeral—demanded a feast and the distribution of goods. Newly wealthy families could purchase high-ranking titles or crests, or acquire them by sponsoring the funeral potlatch of a former owner. Frequent potlatches, with distributions of wealth, were required to maintain high status.

Trade relations between the coast and interior were of long standing. In exchange for furs and prepared hides, the Athapaskans received wealth goods, such as dentalium shells and woven blankets of mountain-goat wool, and exotic foods, such as eulachon oil, dried clams and seaweed. The "grease trails," so-called for the many boxes of eulachon oil carried far into the interior, were major arteries of trade and travel, along which Native People guided such European explorers as Alexander Mackenzie.

When the Europeans arrived, with their shining array of metal tools and other goods eagerly sought by Native People, trade between coastal and interior groups intensified. Coastal groups denied the Athapaskans direct access to the foreigners but sold them European goods in return for furs. In turn, the Athapaskans with the closest ties to the coast became intermediaries in trade with those farther inland. Although the coastal peoples continued to regard themselves as superior, they found their inland neighbours to be important sources of wealth. Coastal chiefs made excursions far into the interior and sought to consolidate their influence through marriages, offering young women of high rank to Athapaskan leaders. Such kin ties brought many Cordilleran Athapaskans, particularly the Tagish, Tahltan and Carrier, into the Northwest Coast sphere of influence, and they rapidly adopted many elements of coastal social organization.

The requirement of mobility meant that housing was kept simple. The northern Cordilleran peoples—the Gwich'in, Han and Tutchone—made portable dome-shaped winter houses, with moose or caribou hides spread over a framework of bent and tied poles. The Han, like many of the Alaskan Athapaskans, also built rectangular pit-houses, heavily banked with turf to withstand the cold. In the south, the Carrier made winter homes of split poles covered in spruce bark. The Sekani in the east lived in conical lodges wrapped with bark or hide. All of the western groups, from the Gwich'in to the Carrier, constructed rectangular bark-covered structures at summer fish camps, which they used as living quarters as well as for smoking and drying fish. The Carrier borrowed two additional house types: the coastal-style plank house used for potlatches and, among the southern groups, the semi-subterranean pit-house characteristic of the Plateau.

The rugged lands and turbulent rivers of the Cordillera meant most groups travelled on foot. Only in the north was water transport practical for any distance. Most groups lacked birchbark and constructed their canoes of the heavier spruce bark. Many made small dugout canoes, but these were not steamed and spread like coastal dugouts. They also built rafts and other temporary craft to carry people and goods for short distances. In the winter, people snowshoed, dragging their loads on toboggans.

In clothing and appearance, the Cordilleran people differed little from other northern Athapaskans. Robert Campbell, travelling among the Gwich'in and Han in 1851, left a good description of their apparel:

> Their dress which when new is pretty & picturesque, is made of the skin of the moose or the reindeer, principally the latter. The skirt [shirt] or coat is finished in a point, both before & behind, & reaches down to the knees, being frequently ornamented with coloured beads, porcupine quills or long hair. The coat has a hole large enough to admit the head, but does not open in front, & is provided with a hood which can be used, when wanted, as a head-dress. The trowsers or leg covering, & shoes are made of the same material, & the garment made with the hair inside for warmth. *Osgood 1971: 91*

Dentalium shells, which they obtained in trade with the coast, were also used frequently as clothing and hair decorations, and worn as necklaces and as ornaments in perforations through the earlobes and nasal septum. Tattooing, particu-

ABOVE *Carrier woman scraping moosehide with a stone-bladed scraper, 1922.* CMC 56902

larly on the cheeks and chin, was common. The Carrier also donned unique ceremonial regalia, featuring elaborate wigs and breast-plates of dentalium.

In contrast to other Athapaskans, some Cordilleran groups cremated their
dead. The Carrier derive their name from the custom that required a widow to
carry on her back a bag containing the cremated remains of her husband. She had
to transport this bundle throughout the mourning period (a year or more), which
supposedly discouraged early remarriage. At the end of the mourning period,
the remains were placed in a box on top of a post carved with the crest of the
deceased.

In many other traits the Cordilleran people shared the basic Athapaskan lifeways. Shamans interceded with the supernatural world, removing some of the
uncertainty of daily life. Religious concepts centred on the respect for animals
and the hunter's quest to obtain at least one spirit helper. Girls were secluded at
puberty, and menstruating women were isolated and subjected to taboos for fear
of offending the spirits of game animals and fish. Oral traditions told by the elders described how the world came into being and stressed the relationship between humans and animals. Although stories involving Raven clearly originated
on the coast, others reflect pan-Subarctic themes. Under the veneer of Northwest
Coast influences, the simpler egalitarian Athapaskan culture was still evident.

INTO THE GLOBAL ERA

The Chipewyan were the first of the Canadian Athapaskans to come into sustained contact with Europeans. York Factory, a trading post established on southwestern Hudson Bay in 1682, provided trade opportunities primarily for the Cree. Shortly thereafter, the Chipewyan felt the effect of the new economy as the Cree used their newly acquired firearms to plunder them and the Chipewyan suffered severe losses in warfare. The English traders eventually became aware of these "Northern Indians," as they were called, through captives held by the Cree. In an effort to bring them into direct trade, the Hudson's Bay Company organized an expedition to Chipewyan lands and negotiated a peace with the Cree during the winter of 1715–16. This was followed in 1717 by the construction of Fort Churchill, at the mouth of the Churchill River, specifically for the Chipewyan trade.

The Chipewyan, however, failed to wholeheartedly embrace the fur trade lifestyle, as the Cree had done. The caribou herds provided for all their needs, and fur-bearing animals were scarce in the northern transitional forests. As Samuel Hearne noted: "The real wants of these people are few, and easily supplied; a hatchet, an ice-chisel, a file, and a knife, are all that is required to enable them, with a little industry, to procure a comfortable livelihood." He observed that those who went to the fort with furs risked starving on the long trip across the barrenlands and were not better off than those who remained behind with the caribou. Nevertheless, some of the Chipewyan joined their fortunes to the fort, controlling trade with groups farther west. Hoping to break this trade monopoly, Hearne made his famous journey in 1770–71, travelling from Churchill to the Arctic coast at the mouth of the Coppermine River on a mission to bring the "Far Indians" into the post to trade.

When the "free traders" who would form the Montreal-based North West Company arrived, both the Hudson's Bay Company and Chipewyan dominance in the fur trade were threatened. Peter Pond established the first post near Lake Athabasca in 1778. In 1786 a post, later known as Fort Resolution, was built on the southern shore of Great Slave Lake. In 1788 Fort Chipewyan was constructed on Lake Athabasca. Many of the Chipewyan had pushed south into this region for its more abundant fur-bearing animals and preferred to go to the new post rather than undertake the arduous journey to Churchill. The Hudson's Bay Company was forced to abandon its long-standing policy of requiring Natives to bring their furs to the coastal forts and began to establish numerous posts inland. A period of intense rivalry ensued, continuing until the two companies merged in 1821.

Alexander Mackenzie, as an agent of the North West Company, explored to the north and west, reaching the mouth of the mighty river that now bears his name in 1789. Setting out from Fort Chipewyan, he traversed the lands of the Slavey, Hare and eastern Gwich'in. Following this journey, the North West Company constructed several posts in the lower Mackenzie Valley, beginning with Fort Good Hope in 1805. The Gwich'in became intermediaries in trade with the

Inuit, denying the latter access to the posts. They also obtained Russian goods through the Alaskan Athapaskans.

On a second ambitious expedition in 1793, Mackenzie set out to find a route to the Pacific. His travels took him through Dunne-za, Sekani and Carrier territory, and he finally reached salt water at Bella Coola. Although Mackenzie was the first European known to have reached the Carrier homeland, he met people who were already accustomed to European goods through trade with the Nuxalk. He saw iron and brass tools in their possession and he noted one man carrying "a lance that very much resembled a serjeant's halberd." His party fell in with a Carrier group heading to the coast to trade, taking beaver, otter, marten, bear and lynx skins, as well as dressed moosehides obtained from the "Rocky-Mountain Indians" (presumably Sekani). Again, trading posts soon followed exploration. A post existed among the Dunne-za of the upper Peace River by at least 1798. Further west, Fort McLeod was constructed among the Sekani in 1805, and Fort St. James and Fort Fraser among the Carrier in 1806.

Modern scholars have disagreed sharply in their assessment of the impact of the early years of trade had on the Athapaskans. June Helm and other Subarctic ethnographers have championed a model stressing continuity. In this view, the Athapaskans remained essentially in their homelands, adjusting their territorial boundaries only slightly to secure more access to fur-bearing animals or European goods. The new trade items made life easier and were eagerly sought as status goods but they were grafted onto the pre-existing culture without drastically altering it. This stable fur trade era is seen as persisting without major disruptions until the federal government began to administer the Canadian north after 1945.

Some ethnohistorians, such as Shepard Krech III, hold an alternate point of view. They believe that cultures changed radically and populations were dislocated. For example, the Chipewyan, Slavey and Dunne-za lost land and large numbers of people in warfare with the Cree. Such northern peoples as the Dogrib and Hare once lived farther south but were forced into the relatively impoverished northern transitional forest. There they lived a precarious existence and later depended on the trading posts for survival. In this view, the Mackenzie Lowlands Athapaskan practice of tracing kinship bilaterally (through either the mother or the father) was not an ancient trait but a late adaptation to provide greater flexibility in times of decreasing populations.

Certainly one of the major disruptions Europeans brought was epidemic outbreaks of disease. How early such scourges as smallpox wrought their destruction, or how high the toll, cannot be known. By 1781, we have historic records of a devastating smallpox epidemic among the Chipewyan and Cree near Hudson Bay. Hearne estimated that nine-tenths of the Chipewyan around Churchill perished. Influenza, measles, whooping cough and scarlet fever also caused huge losses. Starvation often followed outbreaks of disease, as the survivors were too weakened to provide for themselves. Krech's study of the Gwich'in refers to the "almost constant sickness, disease and mortality" of the nineteenth century and he estimates that approximately 80 per cent of the population died.

Aboriginal People also suffered through the widespread use of liquor as an inducement to trade. As early as 1785, David Thompson lamented that "brandy" was being liberally dispensed to the Native People of western Hudson Bay, commenting: "No matter what service the Indian performs . . . strong grog is given to him, and sometimes for two or three days Men and Women are all drunk, and become the most degraded of human beings" (Glover 1962: 36). The use of alcohol in trade was particularly prevalent during the years of intense rivalry between the two great fur trade companies, after which it was discouraged.

As trading posts continued to be established throughout Athapaskan lands in the nineteenth century, Native People depended increasingly on items from the global economy. Metal tools and European clothing rapidly replaced their Aboriginal counterparts. Firearms and ammunition were among the most important trade goods. Hunting became more of an individual activity, no longer requiring the communal effort to construct corrals or drive the herds to where hunters waited. Steel traps came into use but did not replace Native snares and deadfalls. Commercial twine fishnets supplanted laboriously produced Native examples. Hunters took enough fish and meat that they had a surplus to feed dogs, teams of which were trained to pull sleds or toboggans. Flour, tea and molasses became staples of the Native diet, and tobacco became part of everyday life. To obtain these necessities the Athapaskans spent the winters trapping, bringing to the posts furs valued in the global market.

A state of mutual dependence developed: the posts existed only for the furs brought in by Native trappers, and the Natives altered much of their traditional lifestyle to acquire furs to exchange for outside goods. Global market considerations rather than a sense of reciprocal obligation drove the fur trade companies, however. After the merger of 1821, they closed many posts as a cost-saving measure, despite the effect this had on local First Nations. A group of outraged Dunneza massacred five company employees at a post on the Peace River that was scheduled for closure. In retaliation, the company shut down all posts in the area, subjecting the local Native People to considerable hardship.

Throughout the rest of the nineteenth century most Athapaskans continued to be tied to the fur trade. In isolated northern communities, this way of life persisted well into the twentieth century. This complex of rifles, dog teams, traplines and a global market economy became the "traditional" Athapaskan culture Native informants described to anthropologists.

The latter half of the nineteenth century also saw the arrival of missionaries, predominantly Roman Catholic. Missions were established, generally at the trading posts; however, the priests had to travel extensively to bush camps and isolated communities to keep contact with their converts. Unlike the traders, the missionaries attempted to transform Native cultures to make them conform with Euro-Canadian practices. They introduced schools, which acculturated as much as educated Native children. Although most education was in English, an Anglican missionary among the Gwich'in devised a writing system for their language. By the end of the century, all but the most isolated Athapaskans were at least nominally Christian.

As more Euro-Canadian males moved into the Western Subarctic, a mixed population, now generally known as Métis, grew. In the Mackenzie district, two distinct groups emerged. One was the so-called "Red River Métis," descended from French-Canadian workers in the fur trade and their Aboriginal, usually Cree, wives. They settled in the area as the fur trade spread to the northwest and were later joined by refugees from the Plains after the final defeat of the "Métis Nation" in 1885. The second group was formed in the north from the union of Scottish and English Hudson's Bay Company employees with Athapaskan women. The Métis worked as post employees, interpreters and canoeists, and acted as cultural intermediaries between Natives and Euro-Canadians.

The Cordilleran Athapaskans experienced massive cultural disruption when gold was discovered in their lands. The Cariboo gold rush, which climaxed in 1862, brought a mass of gold seekers into Carrier territory. In the 1870s lesser gold strikes occurred to the north, in the lands of the Sekani, Kaska and Tahltan. Finally, the 1898 Klondike gold rush in the Yukon profoundly affected the Tagish, Tutchone and Gwich'in and almost destroyed the Han, the Native occupants around what became Dawson City. In a matter of months Dawson's population swelled to an estimated 40,000 people, making it the largest Canadian city west of Winnipeg. The few hundred Han were simply swamped by the newcomers. Although Dawson was an ephemeral settlement, it boasted such amenities as saloons, dance halls and brothels. These novel attractions, plus opportunities for wage labour, drew many Athapaskans to Dawson. Some became prospectors or packers, and others worked cutting cordwood or as deckhands on the steamers. Unlike the essential role they played in the fur trade, however, the Athapaskans remained on the margins of the new economy. When the gold rush waned, they found themselves largely abandoned.

As more non-Natives moved into the north, the Canadian government negotiated treaties similar to those signed across the Prairie provinces in the years following Confederation. Treaty 8, signed in 1899, covers northeastern British Columbia, northern Alberta, northwestern Saskatchewan and a small portion of the Northwest Territories (as far north as Great Slave Lake). Increased development in the north and the discovery of oil in the Mackenzie Valley led to Treaty 11 in 1921—the last of the historic federal accords with Canadian First Nations. It covers the lands from Great Slave Lake to the Arctic Ocean, including the entire Mackenzie Valley. No agreements were ever completed in the Yukon or with the Cordilleran peoples of British Columbia. Native leaders saw the treaties essentially as pacts of friendship and assistance, rather than as deeds of sale. However, the terms of the treaties specifically removed Aboriginal title to the land in exchange for small annual payments, reserves and guarantees of continued hunting, fishing and trapping rights. Some promises have yet to be fulfilled, such as establishing reserves for all treaty groups in the Northwest Territories, whereas other rights were continually eroded before being protected in the 1982 constitution.

The "frontier" of Euro-Canadian settlement gradually moved to the north and west. Homesteaders took suitable farming and ranching lands in central British Columbia and along the Peace River of northern British Columbia and Alberta. Farther north, the transportation corridors opened up by the gold rush continued to attract new settlers. Mining camps and permanent towns sprang up throughout much of the Western Subarctic. As new roads were built, the pace of non-Native settlement increased. Construction of the Alaska Highway during World War Two made the formerly remote lands of the Slavey, Kaska and Tutchone accessible to a steady stream of Euro-Canadian arrivals. By the end of the war some Athapaskans, particularly in the south, had long since been displaced from most of their land and had become minorities, while in the north many remote groups were still living a life centred on the trading posts.

THE MODERN DENE

In the post-war years, non-Natives rapidly expanded into Athapaskan lands. Mining, logging and other extractive industries brought in a stream of transient workers from the south, and Aboriginal People progressively became minorities in their homelands. As the population grew, new government services were provided, improving living conditions for the Dene but increasing their dependency.

Particularly important were new government programs in health, education, housing and welfare. Medical facilities were established to combat high rates of tuberculosis and infant mortality. Schools were constructed in many Native communities, and elsewhere children were sent to residential schools in central locations. These schools separated children from their parents and their culture, educated them in a language their parents could not understand and instilled foreign values. Only recently has this trend been reversed. Financial assistance also became available, in the form of family allowances, welfare and old age pensions. All of these programs have encouraged a sedentary life in towns.

The typical Dene village includes a store, school and church. The original trading posts have become stores, which offer a variety of southern goods for cash sale. Wooden-frame housing built under government subsidy is gradually replacing the older log cabin homes. These permanent facilities discourage mobility, though men sometimes leave the villages for short periods to tend traplines or hunt, and whole families occasionally depart to fishing camps during the summer.

Modern transportation has made northern communities less isolated. Snowmobiles and manufactured boats with outboard motors have almost totally replaced snowshoes and canoes. Mining and oil exploration companies are cutting new roads into Athapaskan lands. More small chartered planes are flying people around the north. Hunters and trappers can now quickly travel from their villages to distant locations to find game.

The Dene of the Northwest Territories have been very active politically in recent decades. The Indian Brotherhood of the Northwest Territories was formed in 1970, and later changed its name to the Dene Nation. Although it is dedicated to enhancing education, health and communication among the Dene, it has also focussed on their land claim. To advance their claim, the Dene have had to challenge the government interpretation of Treaties 8 and 11. The Dene position is that these were agreements of mutual friendship and that they surrendered neither their sovereignty nor their rights to their lands through treaties.

In 1973, the Dene filed a legal caveat to halt all further development on their traditional lands. Justice William Morrow of the Supreme Court of the Northwest Territories subsequently conducted a series of hearings in Dene communities. After listening to Native testimony, particularly from individuals who had actually attended the signing of Treaty 11, he concluded that the treaties had been misrepresented or inadequately explained. His ruling favoured the Dene, stating that they should be permitted to advance a claim for title to the land and that "notwithstanding the language of the two treaties . . . there is sufficient doubt on the facts that aboriginal title was extinguished." This judgement was subsequently overturned on technical grounds, but it forced the federal government to recognize that the Dene had a strong negotiating position. That the government has failed to establish reserves promised by treaty also strengthens the Dene argument. Shortly after this decision, the Dene and Métis of the Northwest Territories began their lengthy negotiations with the federal government over land claims and Aboriginal rights.

Meanwhile, oil and gas development threatened Dene lands. Particularly worrisome were plans for a pipeline down the Mackenzie Valley. Strong opposition by Aboriginal People and environmentalists led to a federal inquiry headed by Justice Thomas Berger. Beginning in 1975, Berger travelled to each Dene and Inuit community on the Mackenzie to hold hearings. Native opponents to the pipeline were primarily concerned with the impact on game and fur-bearing animals and the government's failure to settle land claims before any construction began. In his 1977 report, Berger recommended that any such project be postponed to allow time to settle Aboriginal claims. In his words:

> If we build the pipeline, it will seem strange, years from now, that we refused to do justice to the native people merely to continue to provide ourselves with a range of consumer goods and comforts. . . . The pipeline, if it were built now, would do enormous damage to the social fabric in the North, would bring only limited economic benefits, and would stand in the way of a just settlement of native claims. . . . It would leave a legacy of bitterness. *Berger 1977: 200*

The pipeline plans were shelved because of Berger's recommendations and the heavy publicity they received, plus uncertain economic conditions. The Dene were left with a legacy of political organization and articulate leaders that could be mobilized to pursue other agendas, such as land claims.

In the Yukon, where no historic treaties were signed, land claims have been of paramount concern. The Council for Yukon Indians has vigorously pressed its case in negotiations with the federal government. Concern over surrender of Aboriginal title to their lands led individual Yukon First Nations to reject a 1984 agreement-in-principle. Finally, in 1993 an Umbrella Final Agreement was signed between the Government of Canada, the Government of the Yukon and the Council for Yukon Indians. The Yukon First Nations agreed to "cede, release and surrender" their Aboriginal claims to non-settlement land in return for title to over 40,000 square kilometres and financial compensation which will total over $240 million. Yukon First Nations interests will also be protected through membership on various boards and committees dealing with wildlife management, resource development and heritage preservation. Separate agreements with individual First Nations deal with specific issues. This process is still ongoing: by the beginning of 2004 only nine of the fourteen Yukon First Nations had finalized their treaties. The Umbrella Final Agreement also commits the federal government to negotiating separate self-government agreements with Yukon First Nations.

The treaty process in the Northwest Territories remains incomplete. The Dene Nation and the Métis Association of the Northwest Territories negotiated jointly with the federal government, reaching a final agreement in 1990. However, an assembly of the Dene and Métis organizations rejected the agreement later that year, primarily due to concern over extinguishing Aboriginal rights and title to the land.

Not all Dene groups, however, supported that assembly's position. The Gwich'in of the Mackenzie delta withdrew from the broader Dene-Métis claim to negotiate on their own. The Gwich'in Comprehensive Land Claim Agreement was finalized in 1992. Its terms follow the model of the proposed Dene-Métis agreement, providing title to lands (over 20,000 square kilometres, with rights to subsurface minerals for only a portion), financial compensation ($75 million), royalties on resources removed from Gwich'in land and membership on regulatory boards dealing with land and resources. It also called for separate talks on the issue of self-government. The neighbouring Sahtu Dene and Métis of Great Bear Lake also withdrew from the broader claim, striking a similar accord in 1993, which provides financial compensation, title to lands, resource royalties and a commitment from the federal government to negotiate self-government.

Separate self-government agreements have now been completed, both in the Yukon and Northwest Territories. They nullify the Indian bands under the Indian Act and replace them with First Nations governments, and specify local control over social programs as well as clauses to protect language and culture. They typically include, among other things, provisions for Natives to manage their heritage resources, such as archaeological sites. Some also stipulate that Dene place names supersede their non-Native equivalents. Following the Gwich'in Land Claim Agreement, for example, the community of Arctic Red River became

Tsiigehtchic. This is just one of many name changes taking place across Canada's north, as our official maps come closer to Native reality.

Most recently, the Tli Cho Final Agreement of 2003 brought the Dogrib into treaty with Canada. It specified a self-governing Dogrib territory of 39,000 square kilometres, encompassing the four Dogrib communities. They have outright title to these lands, including surface and subsurface resources. A payment of $152 million was compensation for past land use. With this agreement, the Dogrib First Nation Government replaced the four Dogrib bands. This legislative body will have wide-ranging regulatory authority over Dogrib lands, including hunting, fishing and industrial development on the land, and it will be responsible for heritage resources. Although the Dogrib First Nation Government will regulate local issues, it recognizes the primacy of Canadian courts and Parliament.

In British Columbia, where the Cordilleran Athapaskans lack historic treaties, land claims negotiations are proceeding through the B.C. Treaty Commission process. Athapaskan groups in British Columbia presently in talks include the Wet'suwet'en Nation, the Kaska-Dena Council, the Carrier-Sekani Tribal Council, the Cheslatta Carrier Nation and a number of smaller bands. In addition, such Yukon groups as the Carcross/Tagish First Nation and the Champagne and Aishihik First Nations are negotiating through this process for those portions of their traditional territories that fall within British Columbia.

Farther east, historic Treaty 8 encompasses the lands of the Dene and western Woods Cree. In northern Alberta the Lubicon Cree have been involved in a lengthy and bitter land claims dispute. This isolated group was apparently missed during treaty signing and did not apply for lands until much later. A proposed reserve in 1940 was never surveyed due to disputes about the number of band members and consequent reserve size. In subsequent decades oil exploration companies built roads that opened up what had been a remote area but destroyed much of the game upon which the Lubicon depended. Under Chief Bernard Ominayak, the Lubicon organized court challenges, roadblocks and highly publicized protests at the 1988 Winter Olympics in Calgary. The Lubicon maintained that they held Aboriginal title to the land and were entitled to compensation for the destruction of their hunting and trapping way of life. The government insisted, however, that this was simply a specific claim for reserve entitlement. After the bitter collapse of a near-agreement with the Lubicon, the government encouraged some of the Cree to form separate bands. It then negotiated reserve lands and financial compensation with those groups, leaving the remaining Lubicon in a difficult and unresolved position.

Dene leaders have played an active role in political struggles for Aboriginal rights on the national stage. George Erasmus, a Dogrib from the Northwest Territories, served as President of the Dene Nation before becoming National Chief of the Assembly of First Nations for two terms. More recently he was co-chair of the Royal Commission on Aboriginal Peoples. Stephen Kakfwi, a Sahtu Dene, also served as President of the Dene Nation. Most recently, he was the premier of the Northwest Territories.

Wage labour has replaced traditional activities as the economic basis for Native communities in northern Canada. Although transient non-Natives from the south take many jobs in the mining and lumber industries, more Dene are now finding employment through new economic partnerships. These include diamond mines in Dogrib territory, a copper mine in the Yukon, and oil and gas exploration among the Dene Tha' in northern Alberta. Guiding big-game hunters, fighting forest fires and building roads also provide seasonal income. Commercial fisheries exist in a few places, such as around Great Slave Lake, and cattle ranches have been established among the Dunne-za. The global demand for furs has declined, and few individuals still trap as a way of life. Many people, however, hunt and fish for subsistence, to put food on the household's table and to reaffirm Native identity.

Athapaskan languages are still in common use today. Although all are endangered, only Han and Tagish face the immediate threat of extinction. The Dene languages in the Northwest Territories are particularly strong, and some villages communicate primarily in Chipewyan, Dogrib, Slavey or Gwich'in. Six Aboriginal languages, along with English and French, are official languages of the Northwest Territories government. In British Columbia, the Dunne-za, Sekani and Kaska languages are endangered, though Carrier is in a stronger position. Modern school programs that teach Aboriginal languages are helping to ensure their survival, but globalizing forces such as television and the market economy tend to make English all-pervasive and to erode the use of Aboriginal languages.

The later history of the Dene was one of progressive loss of control over their own lives. In recent decades, however, the Dene have managed to reverse this trend. Unlike First Nations in southern Canada, which have lost most of their lands and traditional economy, the Dene still retain much of their heritage. Indeed, many envisage not just survival but an opportunity to flourish: they can follow a Dene lifestyle with the advantages of modern technology but without the traditional fears of winter starvation or the sudden appearance of enemy warriors.

CHAPTER 10

The Arctic

. . . . .

Two northern peoples, the Norse and the Inuit, met in the islands off the Arctic coast of North America just over 1000 years ago. It was the initial encounter between these two distinct groups that meant humanity had encircled the world and had taken the first step toward globalization. The Inuit kayak ultimately proved better adapted to an arctic maritime lifestyle than the Viking warship. When the Norse influence waned after several centuries of trade and confrontation, the ancestors of the Inuit found themselves alone at the top of the world.

The treeline defines the Arctic's southern limit. Around the Mackenzie delta the treeline reaches almost to the Arctic coastline. From there, it drops sharply to the southeast, taking in the eastern Northwest Territories, practically all of Nunavut and a small portion of northern Manitoba where it meets the west coast of Hudson Bay. East of Hudson Bay, the treeline sets off northern Quebec and much of the Labrador coast. Above the treeline is the open tundra, a forbidding vista of glaciated mountains, boulders and gravel, with sparse vegetation. Small patches of stunted trees such as willow occur in sheltered areas, but even such limited growth is rare on the islands of the High Arctic. Physiographically, the land begins at sea level with the flat plain of the Mackenzie delta. From there it rises through landforms as varied as the rocky rolling terrain of the interior barrenlands to the rugged mountains and deeply cut fiords of the eastern High Arctic islands.

Throughout the long winters the Arctic is a windswept, snow-covered, harsh and barren land. Temperatures drop so low even a breeze will sustain a wind chill factor that can freeze exposed flesh in minutes. For nine months or more each year the seas and lakes are frozen solid. Darkness reigns uninterrupted for weeks in mid-winter, yielding only briefly to twilight at midday. Although snow and ice are everywhere, the land is a cold desert that receives very little precipitation.

The brief summer restores life and colour to the landscape. Temperatures, while not hot by southern standards, are pleasant, though freezing conditions and snow flurries can occur at almost any time. The days are long and generally sunny, with a period near midsummer when persistent sunlight dismisses the night, the top layer of ground thaws and colourful plants spring to life across the tundra. The permanently frozen ground just below the surface prevents melt-water from seeping away, and innumerable bogs and ponds cover the land. These are an ideal habitat for mosquitoes and blackflies, which plague humans and animals alike during this otherwise pleasant season.

The extant people of the region are the Inuit, one of the three Aboriginal Peoples recognized in the Canadian Constitution. They speak a language from the Eskimo-Aleut family, which is named for its two major branches. The Aleuts, on the Aleutian Islands of Alaska, are a distinct people who are quite distantly related to the other members of the family. The larger branch, Eskimo, has a major division near Bering Strait. On one side of this division, in eastern Siberia and central and southern Alaska, are the Eskimoan people known as Yup'ik, who speak at least five separate languages. From Bering Strait on the west, the Inuit extend across northern Alaska to Greenland, including all of Arctic Canada. In Canada, the word "Inuit" (meaning "people"; the singular is "Inuk") has now almost totally replaced "Eskimo" (generally, though possibly erroneously, believed to be derived from a derogatory Algonquian term meaning "eaters of raw meat"). Throughout their vast distribution, the Inuit speak a single language (Inuktitut), of which a number of dialects are known. All Eskimos and Aleuts share similar physical features, leading physical anthropologists to classify them with more distantly related Native groups from eastern Siberia in a category known as "Arctic Mongoloids."

Throughout the Arctic the Inuit and their predecessors survived on whatever resources were available. Their economy was based on some combination of hunting land and sea mammals and fishing, with plant foods comprising only a small portion of their diet. They depended most heavily on caribou and seals, which provided a steady, if somewhat monotonous, diet. The hunters did not always succeed in their quests, however, and starvation was an ever-present threat. Resources in Arctic Canada were more limited than either to the west or east, and the population density of this area is lower than in Alaska or Greenland.

ARCTIC CULTURES IN ANCIENT TIMES

The Arctic poses major challenges to southern researchers trying to decipher its ancient heritage. Field seasons are necessarily short, access to many areas is difficult, and the frozen ground only gradually yields its secrets to the archaeologists' patient scraping. Despite such difficulties, the rewards of Arctic archaeology are great. With little or no vegetation or soil to obscure or bury sites, and little disturbance from nature or humans, the surface of the land looks much as it did when ancient people abandoned their camps. Implements lost in the dark and snow of winter hundreds or thousands of years ago remain on the surface to mark the ancient sites. The continually frozen ground has preserved intact materials that are rarely recovered from archaeological sites elsewhere. In addition to objects of bone, antler and ivory, at some locations even such perishable materials as wood and hide have emerged after centuries in the frozen soil.

Near the treeline of the southern Arctic, people of Eskimoan stock were not the first inhabitants. Stone tools, including Plano spearpoints of the Agate Basin form, show that early Holocene hunters moving north pursued the caribou herds far out onto the barrenlands of Keewatin. They likely retreated to the shelter of the forests in winter, just like the historic Chipewyan. The rest of the Canadian Arctic, however, far removed from the treeline, sat empty awaiting sentient life.

People eventually moved into this last uninhabited biome on the continent some time before 4000 years ago. They were already adapted to the Arctic environment. Referred to as "Paleo-Eskimos" by archaeologists, these people were called the Tuniit by the later Inuit. Although not directly ancestral to the historic Inuit, they brought many of the "Eskimo" lifeways into the Arctic.

The **Early Tuniit** stage began as the Tuniit expanded out of Alaska and spread rapidly eastward to Greenland. They brought with them the distinctive assemblage of tiny chipped-stone tools known to archaeologists as the Arctic Small Tool tradition. Their sites are littered with finely crafted miniature implements of stone, such as razor-blade-like microblades, a variety of small scrapers and tiny sharp tools used as tips or side-blades on arrows or harpoons.

The first wave of migration reached the High Arctic about 4000 years ago. Archaeologists use the term Independence, from Independence Fjord on northern Greenland, for the people who left their meagre traces at small, briefly occupied camp sites. The arrivals appear to have dwelled year-round in tents, leaving behind oval rings of boulders that once held down the tents' edges. Two rows of vertically placed stone slabs ran down the centre of each structure, and a box-shaped hearth sat in the middle. Small patches of charcoal indicate fires were used only occasionally in this fuel-impoverished environment. The early Tuniit lacked the soapstone lamps to burn blubber that later Arctic cultures used to heat their enclosed living spaces, and they did not take large numbers of sea mammals to provide blubber for such lamps. Instead, musk-oxen bones dominate the refuse around their encampments. These shaggy ungulates instinctively reacted to such predators as wolves by forming a circle with their horns facing out. This response, however, made them vulnerable to the Tuniit, whose wolf-like dogs triggered the musk-oxen's defensive reflex so the human hunters with lances and bows and arrows could drop a number of animals from a safe distance. Musk-oxen provided a major portion of the Tuniit diet. Despite constant environmental challenges, and

LEFT *Early Tuniit (Independence) artifacts from Devon Island. Clockwise from upper left: two antler harpoon heads, bone needle, two stone points, endscraper, concave sidescraper, knife, endblade, three microblades. Courtesy R. McGhee,* CMC

the absence of dogsleds, blubber lamps and the technology required to build snow houses (igloos), these Arctic pioneers persevered at the northern end of the earth. Huddled in their tents against the cold and dark of an Arctic winter, they braced themselves against the elements to introduce the last chapter in the long history of human colonization of the continent.

Archaeologists know another Early Tuniit culture farther to the south as Pre-Dorset. These people spread throughout the Low Arctic, occupying the interior barrenlands, and continued eastward until they reached the northern Labrador coast. The richer environment supported more caribou and sea mammals and allowed this Early Tuniit population to grow. As a result, they left more traces of their presence than the people of the far north. Only later did their travels take them into the islands of the High Arctic, where they typically settled near polynyas (areas of unfrozen sea water surrounded by ice) that offered access to seals and birds. They also appear to have lived in tents, leaving circular clearings surrounded by rings of boulders to mark their dwelling sites. Any ephemeral homes, such as igloos situated out on the sea ice where seals could be hunted, would have melted and disappeared when the mild season arrived. Occasional discoveries of soapstone lamps for burning blubber suggest that such structures existed, since the close confines of an igloo prohibited other fires. Miniature stone tools of the Arctic Small Tool tradition were used to cut meat, shape wooden and ivory objects, scrape hides and perform various other tasks. Small bone needles were used to sew warm clothing. The Pre-Dorset people hunted land mammals with bows and arrows and sea mammals with harpoons. The harpoon heads (which are almost as important to Arctic archaeologists for classifying cultures as stone projectile points are on the Plains) are of the socketed "toggling" type—that is, they "toggle" or turn to hold fast inside the body of the seal, walrus or small whale.

Evidence that the Pre-Dorset people also hunted inland comes from the Umingmak ("musk-ox" in Inuktitut) site in the interior of Banks Island. The bones of several hundred musk-oxen lie scattered across the surface of this site, and many musk-oxen skulls have been stacked in a line as a windbreak or hunting blind. The large musk-oxen population that inhabits this area must have been a secure food source for small groups of Early Tuniit for centuries.

The climate cooled at the end of the Early Tuniit stage and human populations on the Arctic islands seem to have declined. Some local groups became extinct, and others migrated south, a few following the retreating treeline as far as what is today northern Manitoba and Saskatchewan. In the interior barrenlands these Tuniit became highly specialized caribou hunters. However, depending on a single resource is perilous in the Arctic and often leads to extinction. After about 2800 years ago these Tuniit disappeared from the barrenlands, which reverted to sporadic use by Athapaskan groups from the south. Not until the historic Caribou Inuit arrived did the barrenlands return to Eskimoan peoples.

Archaeologists know the **Late Tuniit** stage as the Dorset culture, which the pioneering Arctic archaeologist Diamond Jenness named after artifact collections from near Cape Dorset on Baffin Island. The Dorset people occupied the Canadian Arctic between 2800 and 1000 years ago. They appear to have developed *in situ*, gradually emerging from the older Pre-Dorset culture. The sites are larger and more numerous, with a greater number and variety of artifacts. Many objects, such as stone tools and harpoon heads, resemble their Pre-Dorset antecedents but have changed in style. Burin-like tools that were ground to shape replaced the small chipped-stone burins the Pre-Dorset used to carve bone and ivory. Similarly, ground-stone knives and other tools became common, supplanting earlier chipped-stone varieties. Large bone knives may have cut snow blocks for constructing igloos. To light and heat their homes the Dorset burned oil from sea mammal blubber in rectangular soapstone lamps. They also introduced ivory sled shoes (which were pegged over the sled runners to protect them on rough ice or gravel) and "ice-creepers" (notched strips of bone or ivory which were tied under the boots to prevent slipping on the ice), suggesting that they hunted seals on the sea ice. In the midst of this technological ingenuity, there are some surprising absences. Gone, for example, are the drill and the bow and arrow, both of which existed in earlier times.

People of this Late Tuniit culture eventually spread throughout the Arctic, including the northernmost islands. Only in the interior barrenlands and the western region around the Mackenzie delta are there no traces of the Dorset where their Pre-Dorset ancestors had lived. In the east, the people of this Tuniit period spread far beyond any previous distribution, eventually colonizing the entire coast of Labrador and the island of Newfoundland. Their occupation of

LEFT *Late Tuniit (Dorset) artifacts. Clockwise from upper left: two harpoon heads, lance head, microblade mounted in a wooden handle, burin-like tool in a wooden handle, two chipped-stone points, ground-slate blade, dart head, needle, ice-creeper. Courtesy R. McGhee,* CMC

Newfoundland, which lasted over a millennium, represents the most southerly extension of any Tuniit or Inuit people.

Like all Arctic inhabitants, the Late Tuniit cultures followed the seasons to wrest a living from their harsh environment. In the spring and summer, they harpooned seals and walrus from the ice edge and perhaps from kayaks in open water. They hunted caribou in the summer, as well as musk-oxen and birds, and they speared Arctic char at favoured fishing locations. In the winter, many bands built snow houses out on the sea ice, where they hunted seals at their breathing holes. Their way of life resembled that of the historic Central Inuit.

Housing also varied with the seasons, as it did for later groups. Their summer dwellings were tents, probably of sealskin. Their winter homes were more substantial, as they were dug slightly into the ground and had walls which were built up of sod and rocks. Flat stone slabs paved the floors, and small sleeping platforms flanked the central working area. A typical village would have been a row of four or five houses sheltering perhaps twenty to thirty people who were closely related. The Tuniit may have built igloos when sealing on the ice as the presence of bone snow-knives and soapstone lamps suggests. Near the end of their lengthy Arctic occupation, the Tuniit also constructed long, rectangular boulder enclosures, known as "longhouses," which some writers have mistaken for Norse ruins. There is no evidence that these structures were ever roofed over or lived in, though they may have had a social or ceremonial function.

A remarkable art form also appeared in the Late Tuniit period. Tiny sculptures, some miniature masterpieces, were fashioned from bone, antler and ivory. Small soapstone carvings have also been found, particularly in northern Labrador. Where wood has been preserved, it was also an important medium for the carvers' skill. Images of humans, animals and birds provide insight into the Tuniit world. Wooden and soapstone carvings of people give details of clothing, including parkas, which had high collars rather than hoods. Clusters of human faces peer out from segments of caribou antler. Polar bears, major Arctic predators capable of stalking humans for food, were a popular motif among the many animals depicted. Despite the danger, the Tuniit apparently hunted the bears, at least occasionally, and their images in art may be related to the hunt. Some of the carvings seem simply playful: for example, several small soapstone figures of seated bears and some small ivory sculptures of people playing or adults carrying children on their shoulders.

Much of the art gives the overwhelming impression of supernatural matters and shamanic activity. Masks range from full-size wooden ones, possibly worn by

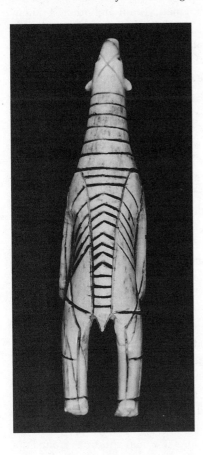

ABOVE *Dorset life-sized wooden mask from Bylot Island, possibly used by a shaman. Traces of red paint still survive. Wooden pins along the side may have been used to fasten the mask to clothing.* CMC K75-493. LEFT *Dorset ivory carving of a polar bear (16 cm long). Typical of such figures, it shows skeletal elements and joints. A slit on the throat contains a sliver of ivory. It may represent the spirit helper of a shaman. Photo by Diane Lyons*

shamans, to small bone and soapstone maskettes. Dorset-style faces also gaze down from the rock outcrops on which they were carved on several small islands off the Arctic coast of Quebec. Their commanding presence on the stark landscape suggests that these were places of ritual importance. Small ivory polar bears appear as if they are flying through the air. They are covered with designs of skeletal elements and joints, which may represent the animal being butchered, or may reveal the shaman's "x-ray vision." Powerful shamans among the historic Inuit were supposed to be able to divest themselves of flesh and blood, and to fly through the air as skeletons. The polar bear's power, along with its human-like qualities, would make it an ideal spirit helper. The Dorset carvings range from detailed naturalism to highly abstracted forms, and from complete figures to only parts of an animal's body, such as a head or a hoof. Several human-animal carvings hint at the link between the shaman and his spirit helper. Some of the bears have slits in the throat, into which have been placed red ochre and slivers of wood or ivory, suggesting a hunting ritual. More intriguing are similar slivers in the chests of human figures, a practice that resembles witchcraft rituals in many cultures.

Determining the kinship between the enigmatic Tuniit and other "Eskimo" people raises numerous questions. Skeletal remains are rare in the Arctic, but burial sites from Newfoundland indicate that the Tuniit were Arctic Mongoloids who were distinct from Indian populations of the area. Yet the Tuniit were not directly related to the historic occupants of the Arctic, and therefore they cannot be termed "Inuit." In their legends the Inuit refer to an earlier race that they called the Tuniit. Oral narratives describe the Tuniit as strong and peaceful people who were great seal hunters. These legends likely reflect ancient traditions from when the ancestors of the Inuit met their predecessors, the Tuniit, in Arctic latitudes.

Around 1000 years ago the people of the last Tuniit culture, the Dorset, were beset with new challenges, new conditions and new arrivals. A warming trend in the Arctic affected the distribution of animals on which they depended and encouraged foreign peoples to enter their lands. To the east, the Norse established colonies in Greenland and made occasional forays to Baffin Island or Labrador, where Arctic Natives would have had their first contact with Europeans. Far more significant, however, was the flood of new arrivals from the west. These people were the Thule, the direct ancestors of the modern Inuit, who came from Alaska and rapidly spread across the Arctic to Greenland and northern Labrador.

Extinctions are common in the Arctic archaeological record, and we cannot be certain that the Tuniit survived to meet the Inuit. If they did coexist briefly, no one is sure what fate befell the Tuniit. Inuit legends describe a period of peaceful coexistence before the two groups quarrelled and the Tuniit were driven away. The Thule's elaborate technology must have given them a competitive advantage over the more conservative Dorset, who were either killed, displaced or absorbed. Only a few tantalizing hints of cultural contact and borrowing exist in the archaeological record. Although the Dorset had disappeared from the central Arctic by about 1000 years ago, they appear to have hung on for a few more centuries around the eastern shores of Hudson Bay and in northern Quebec. Some archaeologists have even pointed to the now-extinct Sadlermiut of Southampton Island, whose dialect was distinct and who relied on chipped-stone tools, as early twentieth-century descendants of the Dorset. Most authorities, however, reject such a notion.

The **Inuit** stage began with the arrival of the Thule culture (which lasted from about 1000 to 400 years ago) in the Canadian Arctic. Named for a site in Greenland, the Thule appeared from the west as a general warming trend reduced the amount of sea ice and created more open water for bowhead whales and other large sea mammals. Climatic changes alone could not have caused this migration; population pressure in Alaska or the invention of a more efficient whaling technology may have initiated the exodus. Thule whale hunters, travelling in skin boats in the summer and dogsleds in the winter, moved rapidly eastward, bringing with them a rich and varied material culture. Almost certainly speaking Inuktitut, they were the direct ancestors of the Arctic's historic inhabitants.

Thule people introduced many new items of technology for sea-mammal hunting. They had both the *kayak* (a small, single-person hunting boat, completely enclosed except for an opening at the top to admit the hunter) and the *umiak* (a larger, open, hide-covered boat for transporting goods and people and for hunting whales). New forms of large harpoon heads, along with floats, allowed hunting of sea mammals, including large whales, on open water. A number of specialized tools show that the Thule hunted seals on the ice in the winter. Long bone probes detected the shape of the seals' breathing holes, small stools provided comfort for the sealer in his long wait, plugs prevented blood loss from the wound, and snow goggles reduced the glare off the ice to prevent snow-blindness. Travel over the ice became easier with dog traction, which the Thule seem to have introduced. Although the Dorset had small sleds, there is no evidence that dogs pulled them. Thule sites yield various toggles and buckles to harness the dogs, as well as physical remains of the dogs themselves.

From their Alaskan homeland they brought numerous other ingenious innovations. To cut meat or prepare hides they had *ulus*, the semicircular "women's knives," with ground-slate blades and wooden or bone handles. They kept fine bone needles in decorated bone needle cases, and small bone thimbles on anchor-shaped thimble holders. The bow drill, where the drill shaft was rapidly turned by looping the bowstring around it and moving the bow back and forth, was widely used to work bone and ivory. For land hunting, they reintroduced the bow and arrow and used small weights of antler and bone in bolas to capture low-flying ducks and geese.

The Thule also brought the Alaskan practice of manufacturing pottery lamps and other vessels. Pottery is common at Thule sites in the western Arctic and it is found at early levels in sites farther east. Thule pottery is thick, poorly fired, coarse and crumbly, and Arctic archaeologists have aptly termed it "Thule crudware." Pottery making was abandoned throughout most of the Canadian Arctic because clay was difficult to obtain, as was the wood to fire it. Instead, the Thule

ABOVE LEFT *Thule artifacts. Top row: whaling harpoon head, two sealing harpoon heads, arrowhead, fish-spear prong; second row: ulu with native copper blade, adze head, knife with iron blade, bird-spear sideprong; third row: dog harness buckle, thimble holder, needle case, comb, snow-knife; bottom: snow goggles. Courtesy R. McGhee,* CMC. ABOVE RIGHT *Copper Inuit man using a bow drill.* NAC PA117148

carved much more durable lamps and cooking pots of soapstone, a trait they may have learned from their Tuniit predecessors.

Thule art is much less dramatic than that of the Dorset. Often adorning functional objects, it appears to be decorative rather than supernaturally powerful like Dorset art. Incised designs on bone and ivory surfaces depict tents, hunters with bows and arrows, and whalers in umiaks. Patterns of circles and dots, produced with the bow drill, decorate a variety of objects. Small sculptures include humans (usually female) in wood, bone and ivory, and flat-bottomed ivory figures of swimming birds, often with a woman's head and torso. The latter were likely tossed in a game but they may reflect the Inuit belief in an association between the mythical sea goddess Sedna and sea animals.

The Thule built substantial winter houses, which were probably more comfortable than Tuniit homes. They brought the basic style from Alaska but in the wood-scarce Canadian Arctic they substituted whale ribs and jaws for driftwood logs as construction materials. The entrance tunnel sloped downwards, trapping cold air below the level of the house. Inside, the floor was paved with flat stones. These were also used to construct a sleeping platform, which was elevated to take

ABOVE *A Thule winter house, after removal of the collapsed roof. A raised sleeping area is in the foreground,* *and a sunken entrance tunnel can be seen at the rear of the house. Courtesy R. McGhee,* CMC

advantage of the warmer air and create a storage space below. Baleen (the tough, fibrous material from the mouths of bowhead whales) was placed on the platform to form a springy mattress, then covered with caribou hides. The walls were made of stone, and whalebone rafters supported the roof, which was formed of hides topped with a thick layer of turf. Heated and lit with oil-burning lamps, these houses must have been warm and secure refuges against the Arctic winter. The ruins of such structures, today visible as small circular mounds of rock, whale-bone and baleen, are found across the Arctic, including the northernmost islands. Specialized tools such as snow-probes (for judging the snow's depth and consistency) and snow-knives (for cutting blocks suitable for building) show that the Thule also built snow houses, though probably only at temporary camps. In the summer, the Thule were much more mobile, and camped in hide-covered tents.

Whaling played a major role in Thule life. As the large bowhead whales moved into their summer feeding waters along the gulfs and straits of the Arctic islands, swimming slowly and near the surface, men in umiaks hunted them with large harpoons. Even if a successful hunt was relatively rare, a whale would have provided several tonnes of meat and blubber, which was enough to feed a Thule village for many months. Nowhere, however, did the Thule exclusively depend upon whales. Some moved into areas where whaling would not have been feasible, and relied instead on seals and walrus. Caribou, musk-oxen and waterfowl, as well as fish, were also important sources of food.

The Thule used the readily available boulders of the Arctic landscape to construct a variety of things. Circles of rocks mark where tents stood, and jumbles of rock and whalebone identify the winter villages. They built boulder cairns over their dead and over caches of meat. Piled boulders also kept umiaks and kayaks off the ground and away from dogs. At favoured fishing locations, the Thule constructed stone dams or weirs to intercept the annual runs of Arctic char. *Inuksuit* (*inukshuk* is the singular), rocks stacked to resemble humans, funnelled caribou to where the hunters waited, and some also may have been landmarks on flat and featureless snow-covered terrain. As great "movers-of-boulders," the Thule altered the landscape, leaving numerous traces of their presence for modern archaeologists.

In the east the Thule were in contact with the Norse, who had established colonies in Greenland. Although the Norse sagas tell only of hostility with the Thule (whom they termed *skraelings*, or "savages"), archaeological discoveries of smelted iron, bronze and copper at a number of Canadian Thule sites suggest that trade also took place. Particularly dramatic was the discovery on Ellesmere Island of fragments of chain mail, the typical armour of medieval Europe, along with woollen cloth, iron boat rivets and sections of wooden barrels dating to the mid-thirteenth century. These objects may have been traded with the Greenlandic Inuit; however, the discovery of part of a folding bronze balance, of the type Norse traders used to weigh small objects, suggests that the Norse might have travelled to Ellesmere. A small wooden figure excavated from a thirteenth-century Thule house on Baffin Island appears to show a European dressed in the long robes of his time, with a cross on his chest. This little Thule figure may record an encounter with strangers of another race. Trade could have been profitable on both sides, with the Thule anxious to acquire metal for their tools and the Norse seeking wealth in the form of polar bear skins, walrus hides and ivory.

Iron-bladed tools seem to have become an important part of Inuit technology by the thirteenth century. Despite the common misconception that they were remote until very recently, the Inuit of the central Arctic were using iron tools hundreds of years before direct contact with Europeans. Analysis of the metal shows they had access to both meteoric iron from Greenland and smelted iron of Norse origins. Indeed, Arctic archaeologist Robert McGhee has suggested that we should consider the Thule an "Iron Age" people and that demand for this important material may have been one of the motivations behind the Thule migration into the eastern Arctic.

At the end of the Thule period they again came briefly into contact with outsiders. The European "Age of Discovery" brought ships into eastern Arctic waters in search of the fabled Northwest Passage. Martin Frobisher led the first voyage, which arrived in AD 1576. One of his officers described the Native People they encountered, stating: "they be like to Tartars, with long blacke haire, broad faces, and flatte noses, and tawnie in colour, wearing Seale skinnes. . . . The women are marked in the faces with blewe streakes downe the cheekes, and round about the eies." An artist who accompanied the expedition in the following year left paintings that show people essentially identical to the nineteenth-century Inuit.

Many Inuit cultures described by later explorers, however, seem less complex than their Thule ancestors. Their technology appears simpler and the way of life less secure. These changes began as the climate cooled after about AD 1200 and continued through the "Little Ice Age," which lasted from about AD 1600 to 1850. As sea ice blocked the large whales from returning to their former feeding locations, the Thule whale hunt collapsed. Groups turned to whatever food was available locally, usually a combination of seal, caribou and fish. As a result of these local adaptations, the Thule from various areas became increasingly distinct. In the central Arctic such basic Thule traits as the umiak were lost and permanent winter houses were replaced with temporary shelters such as skin tents and domed snow houses. On the northern islands of the High Arctic, the cooler conditions meant starvation or migration for the local inhabitants, leaving the land unoccupied. Some families may have joined relatives around the open water and bird cliffs of northwestern Greenland. There an isolated remnant population known as the Polar Eskimo survived, believing themselves to be the only people in the world until they entered the global era in the nineteenth century. The historic Inuit clearly inherited the rich Thule tradition, though not all of this legacy survived the colder climate.

TRADITIONAL INUIT CULTURE

Although eastern groups had sporadically encountered Europeans for centuries, prolonged contact came late to the Canadian Arctic. The more isolated Central Inuit met few outsiders until late in the nineteenth century, and even then they maintained their traditional hunting and fishing lifestyle, with the addition of a few imported material items, into the twentieth century. They welcomed anthropologists such as Diamond Jenness, who was part of the Canadian Arctic Expedition (1913–18), and the Danish researchers Knud Rasmussen, Therkel Mathiassen and Kaj Birket-Smith, who were part of the Fifth Thule Expedition (1921–24), into their camps. Unlike anthropologists in more southerly parts of Canada, who had to reconstruct earlier ways of life from the memories of informants, these researchers were able to observe functioning traditional societies by living with them and recording their activities. The volumes of information on the Central Inuit, who are among the best-known of Arctic peoples, tend to overshadow the regional diversity which characterized the Canadian Arctic.

For all but a few inland-dwelling groups, the sea provided the most important resources. Throughout the Arctic the Inuit could take small ringed seals, which live under the sea ice in winter, as well as larger but less numerous bearded seals. The Greenland (or harp) seals, which inhabit open water, were only available to the eastern Inuit. Seals supplied food for humans and their dogs, oil to heat their homes and cook their food, and hides that could be made into boots, summer clothing, tents, harpoon lines and dog harnesses. Groups from Igloolik and Baffin

ABOVE *Inuksuit ("like men") channel caribou to where the hunters wait.* NAC PA129873

Island to Labrador hunted walruses, which also live in open water. Walrus provided meat and blubber, ivory from their tusks and tough hides that could be used for various purposes, including covering boats. Although some groups in the east and west hunted large whales, most Canadian Inuit pursued the smaller narwhals and belugas.

The harpoon was essential for hunting sea mammals, and the Inuit developed many ingenious forms for various hunting techniques. Hunters in kayaks or, in some places, umiaks often pursued their prey in open water. They also took seals along the edge of the ice, or where the animals hauled themselves out of the water to bask in the sun. Most ingenious was the technique the Central Inuit developed to hunt seals at their breathing holes in the winter ice. After his dogs had sniffed out the breathing hole under the snow, the hunter used a long probe to determine its shape, so he would know where to thrust the harpoon. He might carefully set a small piece of down over the hole, so that its movement would indicate when the seal arrived. Perhaps sheltering himself from the winter wind with a low wall of snow blocks, and with his harpoon at the ready, the hunter patiently settled down for what might be a long wait. If the seal finally returned to the hole and the harpoon thrust hit its target, the hunter enlarged the hole to draw out his kill, plugged the wound to preserve the blood, and dragged the seal to his sled.

On land, caribou was by far the most important prey. As well as meat, the caribou provided hides for warm winter clothing, sinew for thread and antler as an important raw material for tools. The Inuit hunted caribou with bows and arrows or speared the animals from kayaks as they swam across lakes or rivers. One

ABOVE *Central Inuit spearing fish at a stone weir, ca. 1915.* CMC 37080

common technique, which the Thule had used earlier, was to drive the caribou between converging lines of inuksuit, which directed the caribou to where archers were concealed in shallow pits or to a water crossing where the hunters waited by their kayaks.

Other land mammals played a lesser role. Musk-oxen were easy to hunt because of their habit of standing in a defensive circle when attacked, which made them vulnerable to hunters with bows and arrows. Even polar bears, despite being fearsome predators, were hunted for their meat and hides. Hunters also took various birds, from waterfowl to ptarmigan.

Fishing was the other major part of the economy for most Inuit groups. They speared fish from the ice edge or from rocks over the water. Occasionally men fished from their kayaks. In the winter, people laboriously chipped holes through the thick ice to jig for fish with hook and line. Many of the central groups moved inland late in the summer to intercept the runs of Arctic char at their stone weirs. After repairing the damage to the rock walls caused by the winter ice, the people waited for the fish to arrive. As the Arctic char swam upstream, they were channelled into an enclosed central basin. When enough fish had amassed, men and women waded into the frigid water with their leister spears. These were wooden shafts, at the ends of which were two flexible prongs of antler or horn with sharp bone barbs to slip over and grasp the fish while a sharp central point impaled it. Staying in the water as long as their numbed limbs would allow, people quickly speared large numbers of fish with this ingenious implement, stringing them on a long line which was then hauled to shore. They ate some of the catch fresh, then dried and cached the rest under rocks for later use.

The Inuit lived almost totally on the flesh of animals and fish, and differed from most non-agricultural societies by relying little on gathered foods. Wherever birds nested, people could collect eggs to provide a welcome change of diet. Except in more southerly regions, such as Labrador, a few berries were the only plant foods available. Yet some plant food was obtained indirectly; for example, after a fresh caribou kill the Inuit eagerly consumed the partially digested contents of the animal's stomach.

Although eating meat alone is not a nutritionally balanced diet, the Inuit stayed healthy because they ate nearly every part of the animals they killed. They valued sea mammals for their thick layer of blubber as much as their meat. *Muktuk*, the skin and attached blubber of the beluga and other whales, was highly prized. The Inuit extracted the marrow of broken caribou bones, and consumed the brains, heart and other organs. After a seal kill, hunters gathered for a ritual snack of raw liver. During the task of butchering, hunters also ate fish and animal eyeballs as tasty morsels. They saved seal intestines, which they braided, dried and stored for later consumption.

The Inuit enjoyed most of their food raw, particularly in the central area where fuel for cooking was scarce. However, even there some meat was cooked in soapstone pots over small fires of moss or willow twigs, or over the blubber lamp. It was frequently boiled, with blubber and blood added to make a thick broth. In the winter, the Inuit chipped off and chewed small pieces of frozen caribou meat. Although the Arctic was a natural deep-freeze and food could be stored for a considerable period of time, some of it did putrefy. This decay, however, only enhanced the taste, and some traditional recipes required it. For example, to prepare one particular savoury meal a whole sealskin, complete with the blubber layer, was stuffed with small sea birds and left under rocks until the contents had turned to the consistency of cheese.

Food sharing was essential for small groups of people living together harmoniously; distributing the results of all hunters' successes compensated for the vagaries of individual luck and reduced jealous hostilities. This practice reached its most formal level among the central groups at their winter sealing camps, where each hunter was bound to the others by precise rules. When a man killed a seal it was taken to his igloo, where his wife butchered it, giving different portions to the wives of the other hunters according to their specific relationship. The hunter kept little for himself but would share in all his partners' future kills.

The successful food quest also required that taboos be strictly observed. Most pervasive throughout the Arctic was the belief that the products of land and sea should not be mixed. Seal and caribou meat could never be cooked together, for fear that supernatural retribution would bring storms, starvation or sickness. For the same reason, all sewing of caribou skins for winter clothing had to be completed before people moved to their sealing camps on the sea ice. In addition, as among most hunting people, menstruating women had to obey numerous restrictions to avoid offending the animals.

There were times, however, when the hunters' skills and strict observation of taboos failed, and the community faced starvation. This threat meant that population size had to be kept low. The Inuit occasionally practised infanticide, particularly for females, as most families preferred raising boys who would become hunters. Elderly people who could no longer keep up with the group had to be abandoned. When food ran out in late winter, the elderly and the very young usually perished first, and starvation might stalk a whole village. Under such extreme conditions, some people resorted to cannibalism to survive, but this was considered an abhorrent act.

Dogs were the only domestic beasts of burden among the Inuit. In the summer they were pack animals and in the winter they pulled sleds. They played an important role in hunting, sniffing out the seals' breathing holes under the snow and holding musk-oxen and polar bears at bay. However, their drain on food supplies meant that each family owned only a few. During those distressing hungry periods, the dog itself might become a meal.

The snow and frozen seas made possible winter travel by dogsled over long distances. The sled (*komatik*) consisted of crossbars lashed with sealskin thongs to the runners, making it very flexible. The runners were covered with mud or moss and water, which froze into a hard, slick coating that allowed the sled to glide easily over the snow. Wood was used to build sleds wherever it was available, but elsewhere Inuit ingenuity found substitutes. Crossbars could be made of caribou bones or antlers, and runners could be made of rolled-up and frozen musk-oxen skins or even of frozen fish wrapped in sealskin. In the summer, the Central Inuit walked inland, which was difficult on the marshy tundra, packing their goods on their backs and on dogs. Only the Mackenzie Delta Inuit and the eastern groups travelled by water to any extent, transporting their goods in umiaks.

Caribou hides, which the Inuit took in the fall when they were in the best condition, were essential for winter clothing because caribou hair is hollow and traps air as insulation. In the winter, the Inuit wore two layers of coats, trousers, stockings and boots; the outer layer was sewn with the hair on the outside, the inner with the hair next to the body. Summer clothing was a single layer, often of sealskin. Sealskin boots were also indispensable for these wetter months, so Inuit women perfected a technique for sewing boots without puncturing the pelt at the seam. Women's clothing was often more elaborate and patterned differently than men's, with baggy trousers, large hoods and extra space at the back where babies were carried against the mother's skin. Strips of white hide from the underside of the caribou provided decoration. Although the basic design was the same, regional differences distinguished local groups.

The women's skill in preparing warm winter clothing was as crucial to the group's survival as the men's ability to bring in food. Women spent much of their time making and mending clothing, particularly boots, which wore out quickly. Boots also became stiff and hard after use and had to be thoroughly chewed to restore them to their former soft and supple condition.

Women also cared for the soapstone lamp (*kudlik*), which was used to heat and light the home, cook food, melt water and dry clothing. Seal blubber stored in

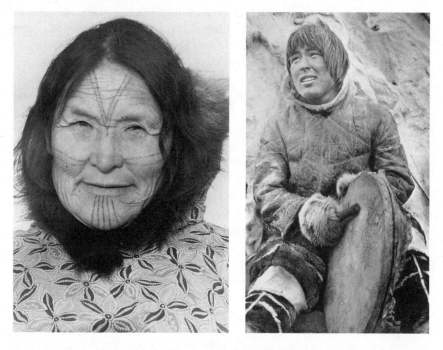

ABOVE LEFT *Tattooed lines in traditional fashion adorn the face of this Copper Inuit woman, ca. 1949–50. Photo by Richard Harrington.* NAC PA145007. ABOVE RIGHT *Central Inuit drummer, ca. 1915.* CMC 50918

bags gradually produced oil that could be burned, but fresh blubber had to be pounded. The moss wick also required constant tending.

Although personal adornment was limited, women customarily emblazoned tattoos on their faces. Straight lines radiated from the nose and mouth across the forehead, cheeks and chin. The operation was performed by older women, who drew a needle threaded with soot-darkened sinew under the skin. Some women also had their hands and arms tattooed.

The Inuit married at an early age, and girls in particular were often betrothed at birth. As survival would be difficult without a spouse, virtually all adults married, males as soon as they developed the necessary hunting skills and girls at puberty. The practice of female infanticide, however, led to a marked shortage of women among such Central Inuit as the Netsilik. Despite this, polygyny was relatively common, though only the most skilled hunters could support more than one wife and almost never were there more than two. Polyandry was less common, but occasionally women had several husbands, particularly in areas where the demographic imbalance favoured women. A female shaman, for example, might have had more than one husband. This imbalance also led to such practices as spouse exchange and "sexual hospitality." Men might lend or exchange wives on a short-term basis or as part of a longer semi-ritualized bond of friendship and mutual aid. In the latter case the men usually were song-fellows during drum dance festivals and wife-exchange was part of a broader pattern of sharing.

Social groups varied with the seasons. Several families, generally related through the males (brothers or father and sons), remained together throughout most of the year. Larger social groups formed when food was abundant or more people were needed. For example, the winter sealing camps of the Central Inuit required many hunters to watch the breathing holes, and often brought together a community of about a hundred people. Task-specific activities, such as the caribou hunt among the Caribou Inuit or whaling among the Labrador and Mackenzie Delta Inuit, could easily bring together large numbers of people. Leadership was improvised for these task forces; the most experienced and respected elder's opinion carried the greatest weight.

Hostilities occasionally arose over competition for women and the jealousies engendered by living in close quarters throughout the long winters. Without any strong leadership positions, methods of social control were limited. Some conflicts were resolved through the song duel, in which two opponents publicly ridiculed each other's behaviour through carefully composed songs. Each was expected to accept this rebuke with good grace. Another way of dealing with unacceptable behaviour was for the band simply to move, leaving the offender behind. Anger sometimes led to murder, which some accounts indicate was not uncommon. Retaliation in kind, being the justice of the land, compelled the murderer and his family to flee to avoid retribution from the victim's kin. Sometimes a blood feud ensued between the two families, resulting in additional deaths. In rare cases, an individual's actions might sufficiently threaten the group that they collectively decided to execute the offender.

The Inuit quarrelled sporadically with their Dene, Cree or Innu neighbours, though more often they avoided each other. The Mackenzie Delta Inuit came into contact with the Gwich'in and Hare, the Caribou Inuit shared some of their territory with the Chipewyan, and the Inuit of northern Quebec and Labrador frequently encountered the Cree and Innu. Suspicion and hostility were deep-seated, and traditions of violence and murder existed. However, trade and occasional intermarriage also occurred.

Some control over an uncertain world came from the *angakok* (shaman). Both men and women could obtain spirit power, which allowed them to communicate with the supernatural realm. In public performances the angakok went into a trance, speaking in the voice of a spirit helper. These shamanic powers enabled angakoks to cure the sick, divine the future and summon supernatural aid when the animals could not be found or when storms kept hunters trapped in their homes.

Inuit myths and legends helped explain the physical world and the parallel spirit world. Supernatural beings, often malevolent, were everywhere, howling in the winter storms or lurking under the surface of the water. One widespread myth is the story of the sea goddess, who is known by many names among the various Inuit groups but is commonly called Sedna. The myth is long and has many versions but it tells of a young woman who married a dog and a bird (a petrel or fulmar), which appeared in human form. When Sedna's father came in his skin boat to rescue her from the rocky island where her bird husband had taken her, a great storm came up and threatened to capsize the boat. To lighten his load, the father tossed his daughter overboard. When she tried to climb back in, he cut off the joints of her fingers, which fell into the sea and became seals. Still she clung to the side of the boat, so her father cut off the rest of her fingers, which became walruses. Still failing to dislodge her, the heartless father cut off her hands, which became whales. The young woman sank to the bottom of the sea, where she lives today as the mother and protector of all sea mammals. She demands respect, and if her taboos are not strictly observed, she will withhold her bounty by entangling sea mammals in her hair, thus bringing starvation to the people.

In the fall, before winter sealing, the Inuit held an important ceremony to appease the wrath of Sedna for any taboo violations. The angakok went into a trance, during which he visited Sedna in her underwater home to discover the cause of her displeasure. He would soothe her temper by using his special ivory comb on her hair, and in so doing would release the entangled sea mammals. Wearing strange clothing and a leather mask, the angakok also performed a trick in which he appeared to be harpooned like a seal but recovered from the ordeal without harm. Those born in summer and those born in winter held a tug-of-war to ritually enact the constant struggle of the seasons. If the winter side won there would be enough food that season. Then the angakok paired off the men and women to reinforce the custom of spousal exchange, which was done to placate the sea goddess.

Members of the community often came together to enjoy each other's company and recreate (often in specially constructed buildings), particularly during the relatively inactive winter period. The Inuit held festivals, at which people played drums, danced and sang. In some communities women entertained by "throat singing," making resonant sounds from deep in the throat. One of the more popular of the many games was cup and pin, in which a player held a bone pin attached with sinew to a bone drilled with holes, which he swung into the air and attempted to skewer with the pin. A favourite pastime of the women was "cat's cradle," or string figures, in which players created a variety of patterns from a length of sinew stretched between the hands. The Inuit were also great story-tellers, captivating their audience with tales that ranged from recent adventures to ancient legends. As the winter storms raged and the long dark days lingered outside their homes, they amused themselves with games, songs and stories.

THE MACKENZIE DELTA INUIT

The Inuit of the western Canadian Arctic, around the Mackenzie delta and the Yukon coast, today call themselves Inuvialuit (singular is Inuvialuk), which means "real people." Their closest cultural ties are with their kin in northern Alaska. Their territory was rich in sea mammals and fish, which supported the largest villages and densest population in Arctic Canada. Estimates of the mid-nineteenth-century population range from 2000 to 4000 people. They were divided into five subgroups, each with its own territory, known collectively as the Chiglit.

Large bowhead whales came into the Beaufort Sea, and people living along the coast hunted them from umiaks. In the Mackenzie delta the major prey was the beluga, which came into the shallow waters in large numbers to feed during summer. The estuary provided a natural trap, as men in kayaks could form a line across the river and drive the beluga upstream onto the shoals, where they were easily killed. Inuit hunters could take several hundred of these small whales in a single drive, providing plenty of meat and blubber for winter use. Fishing, sealing and caribou hunting were also part of their economy.

During the summer beluga hunt, the delta people clustered at their village of Kittigazuit. With a population of up to 1000 people, it was among the largest Inuit communities. The houses were large, permanent, semi-subterranean structures, constructed of driftwood logs covered with earth for insulation. Long sunken entrance tunnels, which acted as cold traps, led to trapdoors into the living area. Several families occupied each dwelling. With the forest nearby and many drift logs in the river, wood was always at hand for construction and for fuel. Snow houses were built only as temporary shelters, such as when jigging for fish out on the ice during late winter.

Many traits link the Mackenzie Delta Inuit with those in northern Alaska. They shared a similar house style, and they both constructed separate "men's houses" in the villages. Pottery was used for lamps and cooking pots, though these were less important than farther east as there was an abundance of wood for open fires. Trays, ladles and many other objects were also made from wood. Like their Alaskan relatives, the Mackenzie Delta Inuit men wore labrets of polished stone or ivory through perforations on each side of the mouth. Village "headmen," chiefs who inherited their office through the male line, were another Alaskan influence.

Epidemics nearly exterminated the Chiglit, the original inhabitants of the Mackenzie delta area, in the late nineteenth and early twentieth centuries. As the Chiglit population decreased, Alaskan Inuit moved eastward, first attracted by trade with American whalers on the coast and later by the rich trapping potential of the delta. The few remaining Chiglit have been largely assimilated by those with a more recent Alaskan heritage. The inhabitants of the western Canadian Arctic today consider themselves separate from other Canadian Inuit, preferring to be known as Inuvialuit.

THE CENTRAL INUIT (COPPER-NETSILIK-IGLULIK-BAFFINLAND)

The "Eskimo" stereotype, with its image of fur-clad, igloo-dwelling seal hunters, comes from the Central Inuit. These groups occupy much of the Canadian Arctic, from Victoria Island and the Coppermine River on the west to Baffin Island in the east. Often included in this category are the Caribou Inuit, though they live

ABOVE *Iglulik hunter pulling in two captured seals, ca. 1952–53. The small umiak at right is for retrieving seals shot from the floe edge. Photo by Richard Harrington.* NAC PA129874

inland and rely nearly completely on caribou. The Central and Caribou Inuit lost more of their Thule heritage than other Canadian Inuit when individual groups adapted to their local environments during the Little Ice Age.

In the west, the Netsilik ("people of the seal") and the Copper Inuit (named for the native copper found in their area) lived an annual round attuned to the rhythm of winter and summer, sea and land. When the shallow coastal waters froze each winter into an unbroken expanse of ice between the islands and peninsulas, these people depended almost entirely on hunting seals at their breathing holes in the ice. In the summer they moved inland to hunt caribou and to fish. They also pursued musk-oxen and polar bears, though these accounted for relatively little of the diet. The umiak was unknown, and the kayak was used only to kill caribou on inland lakes and rivers.

The groups farther east, the Iglulik on the Melville Peninsula and northern Baffin Island and the Baffinland Inuit who occupied the rest of the island, lived near large areas of water that remained open during the winter and supported such sea mammals as bearded seals, walrus, belugas and narwhals. Occasionally they even took large Greenland whales, as bowheads are known in the east. In the winter, hunters harpooned sea mammals from the floe edge, as well as seals at their breathing holes. In the summer, some hunters remained on the coast to pursue sea mammals from kayaks, and others went inland to hunt caribou.

Because of their mobile lifestyle, the Central Inuit built no permanent structures. In the winter, they lived in the domed snow house, or igloo, a dwelling they could construct quickly from material that was available everywhere. It was built with a long entrance passageway that provided cold storage and prevented colder air from reaching the living space. Inside they sculpted raised sleeping platforms

ABOVE *Inside a Central
Inuit igloo, 1903. The
women are sitting on
a platform covered with
furs. At left is the cooking area, with pots
suspended over an
oil-burning lamp.*
CMC 2883. LEFT *Seal-
skin tent on Baffin Is-
land, 1924.* CMC 68941

of snow, which they covered with musk-oxen or polar bear skins and caribou-
hide sleeping robes. A block of clear ice acted as a window. Some groups lined the
interior walls with skins suspended from the roof to trap a layer of colder air
against the walls. This way they could heat the room to a higher temperature
without melting the snow blocks. Two or three houses were sometimes built close
together so they could share an entrance passageway. For festivals a large dance
house was often constructed by incorporating several houses whose interior walls
were then removed. Soapstone lamps burning blubber supplied heat and light. In
the spring, when the igloos began to drip, the Inuit lived briefly in structures with
snow walls and entranceways and caribou-hide roofs. Such dwellings were also
built in autumn, when the snow was not sufficiently firm to construct igloos. In
summer, people carried only light tents of caribou hide or sealskin to their inland
homes.

ABOVE *Copper Inuit igloos, ca. 1915. Harpoons and other gear are stuck in the walls and sleds are raised on snow blocks to protect their rawide lashings from the dogs.* CMC 37018

Raw materials were scarce in this central region. The Copper Inuit were the most fortunate as they had good sources of native copper and soapstone and some driftwood. Elsewhere, people relied on trade or on their ingenuity in finding available substitutes. They met their material needs mainly with ice and snow, bone and antler, and hide and fur, with only a few tools of wood, copper and stone.

One other group, the now-extinct Sadlermiut (or Sallirmiut) of Southampton Island in Hudson Bay, should be included among the Central Inuit. They were apparently distinct, speaking a separate dialect and manufacturing tools of chipped stone rather than the more common ground stone. They were maritime hunters, primarily of walrus and polar bear. Some writers have claimed Dorset ancestry for the Sadlermiut; however, most of their technology indicates that they shared the same Thule heritage as their neighbours. An epidemic disease introduced by a whaling ship led to their extinction in the winter of 1902–03.

THE CARIBOU INUIT

The barren interior west of Hudson Bay was home to the Caribou Inuit, whose origins have long fascinated anthropologists. After members of the Fifth Thule Expedition extensively described the Caribou Inuit culture in the 1920s, Kaj Birket-Smith proposed his model of interior origins for the Inuit. The Caribou Inuit, with their simple way of life and rudimentary material culture, were regarded as "Proto-Eskimos," the last vestiges of a way of life that existed before most Inuit became coastally adapted sea-mammal hunters.

Later research disproved Birket-Smith's theory and indicated that Caribou Inuit culture, far from being the remnant of a more ancient stage, developed recently. When Samuel Hearne travelled through the barrenlands with his Chipewyan companions in the 1770s, the only occupants were other Athapaskans. Over a century later, when the Tyrell brothers crossed the southern barrens in the 1890s, they met only Inuit. Disastrous epidemics killed many Chipewyan and broke their hold on the barrenlands, as did the construction of inland trading posts that made unnecessary the long trek across the barrens to Hudson Bay. The Inuit, descendants of the Thule people who had settled along the coast of Hudson Bay, began to spread inland sometime in the late eighteenth or early nineteenth century, largely because of the European presence on the coast. Firearms made caribou hunting more efficient, and the fur trade provided the incentive for inland trapping. The simple life and meagre material culture documented in the ethnographic literature were the result of cultural disintegration and more than a century of dependence on Euro-Canadian technology.

The Caribou Inuit became highly specialized to an interior way of life, and they relied almost totally on the caribou herds. They hunted using the same techniques as other Inuit, including stalking with bows and arrows, spearing from kayaks at water crossings and using inuksuit to direct the caribou to convenient ambush spots. During the autumn migrations, they had to take enough animals to make warm clothing from their hides and cache much of the meat. In the winter, when most of the caribou had retreated south to the forest, people relied on their stores of caribou meat, which they supplemented by fishing through the ice and hunting musk-oxen. This specialized economy was precarious; if the caribou failed to appear in sufficient numbers, people went hungry or even starved.

In most aspects of their culture the Caribou Inuit resembled other Central Inuit. Their technology was simpler, however, because they abandoned most of their Thule heritage when they adapted to life in the barrenlands. They lacked blubber for their lamps, which were often merely flat stones with natural depressions, so occasionally they burned caribou fat, which provided light but little heat. In the winter, people lived largely in unlit igloos, warmed only by the occupants' body heat. Inside the igloo, temperatures were bearable but not comfortable, and it was not warm enough to dry clothing. The only method they had to accomplish this was to take their wet apparel into their beds, sleeping with it next to their skin. Cooking had to be done over a small fire built in a separate alcove off the entrance tunnel, so they ate most of their food frozen and raw. Even the eastern bands, which had access to seals and beluga along the coast of Hudson Bay, preferred to follow the herds of caribou inland.

Periodic shortages and starvation continued into the twentieth century as hunting with rifles took a heavy toll on caribou and musk-oxen numbers. In the few years just before 1920, the caribou became scarce and hundreds of Caribou Inuit starved. The people described in the ethnographies, known primarily through the writings of Birket-Smith and Rasmussen, were the weakened survivors of these disastrous years. Epidemic diseases and periodic famines continued into the mid-century, leading the Caribou Inuit to the verge of extinction. Farley Mowat brought their plight to public attention in his popular books, *The People of the Deer* (1952) and *The Desperate People* (1959). Mowat's stinging

ABOVE *Inuit hunter with kayak and two freshly killed belugas. The harpoon line with inflated floats is still attached to the whale in the foreground. Photograph taken at Little Whale River, northern Quebec, in 1865.* NAC C8160

accounts of administrative incompetence added to a growing awareness of the appalling conditions under which Inuit across the Arctic were living. In response the government encouraged Inuit people to move into permanent settlements where services could be provided. With the exception of Baker Lake, Caribou Inuit villages are now on the coast, leaving their former homeland, the barrens, largely abandoned.

THE INUIT OF NORTHERN QUEBEC AND LABRADOR

The Thule expanded east of Hudson Bay within the last millennium, leaving the first trace of their presence in the Ungava region of Nunavik (Quebec beyond 55°N latitude) about AD 1350. A century later they were setting up their camps along the coast of Labrador. This area seems to have been spared the worst effects of the Little Ice Age, and much of the Thule heritage persisted well into the global era.

The waters of this eastern region are richly stocked with sea mammals, and Inuit hunters pursued walrus, ringed seal, bearded seal, harp seal, narwhal, beluga and even the large Greenland, or bowhead, whale. In the summer, they harpooned their prey from kayaks, or umiaks in the case of the large whales, and in the winter, from the ice edge. In most areas, they also hunted seals at their breathing holes in the ice. Whaling required ritual preparation that involved observing taboos, magically treating implements and consulting with a shaman's spirit helpers for information to plan the hunt. Such rituals strongly resemble those Alaskan Inuit whalers performed, and suggest the former presence of a widespread Thule whale cult that was relinquished in the central area.

Almost all groups hunted caribou in the interior, particularly in the fall when they needed hides for winter clothing. A few small bands in northern Quebec remained inland for much or all of the year, drawing nearly all of their needs from the caribou herds in the same fashion as the Caribou Inuit. Other bands lived year-round on the islands of eastern Hudson Bay, subsisting on sea mammals, polar bears and birds. Lacking sufficient caribou skins for clothing, they developed local alternatives, such as eider-duck-skin parkas and polar-bear pants and winter boots.

Fishing was also important, both in the sea and inland, where the Inuit took Arctic char during their annual runs. Birds and bird eggs were a major source of food in some areas. Although only a small part of the diet, berries and other plant foods were more plentiful along the Labrador coast than elsewhere in the Arctic. In addition, the tidewaters of northern Quebec yielded mussels and sea urchins, which the Inuit ate only occasionally but resorted to in times of famine.

The igloo was the standard winter home in Nunavik, but it was only a temporary shelter in Labrador. Labrador Inuit lived for up to six months of the year in large, permanent, semi-subterranean structures, similar to those of the Thule period. The walls were of sod or stone, with a sod-covered roof supported on rafters of whale bones or timber. A long covered entrance passage led to the house, and a skylight of translucent seal intestine was set into the roof over the entrance. In Nunavik, the Inuit used stone and turf houses with hide roofs in the transitional periods, when the igloos began to drip in the spring and again when the autumn snow was not yet sufficiently firm. As elsewhere in the Arctic, skin tents were the summer dwellings.

Although much of the Thule heritage had survived the colder climate, it could not long withstand the impact of sustained globalism after the first Europeans appeared. A long string of explorers, whalers, traders and missionaries wrought dramatic changes on their culture. The eastern groups were the first to feel the impact, but a wave of change was about to engulf the entire Arctic region.

THE INUIT IN THE GLOBAL ERA

Globalization first came to the Arctic when the Inuit encountered the Norse who had settled in Greenland. Whether through hostilities (according to Norse sagas and Inuit legends) or through trade (as revealed by archaeology), the spark of contact ignited the fuse of globalism. This pattern continued for centuries. Fishers and whalers from several European nations followed in the Viking wake as each exploited the rich waters off the Labrador coast. Sporadic encounters soon shifted to more sustained contact. The search for the Northwest Passage, the fabled shortcut to the riches of the Orient, was a major incentive for European exploration. The Inuit coveted the iron tools and exotic goods the foreign visitors brought, yet through mutual misunderstanding and suspicion the encounters often ended in bloodshed. Martin Frobisher, during the first of his three voyages in 1576, sailed into what is now Frobisher Bay on Baffin Island and encountered "men in small boates made of leather." Frobisher initially established friendly relations through trade, but those ended when five of his men disappeared with a party of Inuit. Hostile encounters marked his return visit in 1577, and Frobisher himself received an Inuit arrow in the buttocks. Suspicion and hostility continued to characterize contact between Inuit and outsiders. Trading vessels followed the explorers' ships, particularly after the Hudson's Bay Company was established in 1670. However, most trade from Hudson Bay was with the Natives of the fur-rich forest, which gave them the advantage of firearms long before their Inuit rivals.

Inuit contact with the trading vessels was fleeting, but when the next wave of Europeans arrived they were motivated by religious fervour and they intended to stay. The earliest encounters were in Labrador, where Moravian missionaries, familiar with the Inuit language from Greenland, helped the English governor of Newfoundland negotiate peace with the Inuit in 1765. Shortly after, the Moravians began establishing missions along the Labrador coast, beginning with Nain in 1771. As well as a church, each mission contained a trading post to supply the goods upon which the Inuit had become dependent. The Inuit settled in permanent wooden houses at these self-contained, self-supporting communities. Although many elements of their culture were lost under Moravian influence, they enjoyed a lengthy period of near isolation from other outside influences.

Globalism was inflicted last on the Central Inuit. Early in the nineteenth century European explorers broke through the barriers of ice and cold that had kept the world at bay. These early contacts were fleeting, peaceful, and had little impact on Inuit culture except for the introduction of some items of European manufacture. The romantic search for the elusive Northwest Passage still lured adventurers. Some wintered with their ships in the Arctic ice so they could continue to search over several years. Beginning in 1821 William Parry and George Lyon explored western Hudson Bay and the Melville Peninsula, spending two winters in the territory of the Iglulik. The Natives received them peacefully and entertained them with dancing in their snow-house village. Descriptions from these contacts provide the most important ethnographic data until the comprehensive study of the Fifth Thule Expedition a century later. Sir John Franklin also surveyed parts of the Arctic coast but he is best known for the tragic expedition of 1846. Attempting to thread his way through an ice-choked passage in the central Arctic, Franklin and his ships became trapped in the ice as winter closed around them. His entire crew of 129 men perished. In the following years many ships searched unsuccessfully for survivors, and in the process they explored much new coastline and brought most Inuit groups into contact with Europeans.

The nineteenth century also brought commercial whalers into the Arctic. At first the whalers pursued their prey along Davis Strait and Baffin Bay, off the coast of Baffin Island, but by 1860 much of the hunt took place in northern Hudson Bay, where the whalers typically wintered over. There they interacted with the Inuit, who clustered around the whaling bases where they could find work as crew on the whaleboats or as provisioners of fresh meat for the whalers. In return they received such typical trade goods as firearms, iron tools, metal pots and kettles, woollen clothing, beads and tobacco. Even such items as kerosene lamps and canvas tents became common among the Inuit, and whaleboats largely replaced the umiak.

Although the whalers hastened the erosion of traditional Inuit culture in the eastern Arctic, their impact was far less damaging than in the west. There American whalers, after depleting Alaskan stocks, moved into Canadian waters by 1890. Herschel Island, off the Yukon coast, became their wintering base, attracting Inuit from both Alaska and the Mackenzie delta. There the whalers liberally dispensed alcohol, debauched Inuit women and brought diseases that nearly destroyed the Inuit communities. The whaling period came to a rapid end after 1910, when overhunting reduced whale populations and the market for baleen collapsed.

Fur traders soon arrived to fill the vacuum left in the Inuit economy by the departure of the whalers. In the nineteenth century the Inuit had few opportunities to participate in the fur trade. Some took their furs far to the east, to the Moravian missions in Labrador or, after 1830, to Fort Chimo on Ungava Bay, and others made the long trek south to Fort Churchill. In the west, trade began when Fort McPherson was constructed in the Mackenzie delta region in 1840. However, only in the early decades of the twentieth century, with a steady rise in fur prices, did the Hudson's Bay Company build many posts across the north. To satisfy their need for imported goods, the Inuit had to supply the traders with furs. Those of white fox were most valued, along with muskrat in the Mackenzie delta region. Firearms and steel traps became essential as the Inuit tied their economy to the trade in fox pelts, trapping inland in winter rather than hunting on the coast as they had in former years. Booming fur prices in the 1920s meant relative wealth for many, but a market collapse in the 1930s put an end to this period of affluence.

After fur trade posts were established, the missionaries, both Roman Catholic and Anglican, arrived. New communities formed around the missions and the posts as Inuit came in from the land. These settlements were often the catalysts that set in motion major cultural changes. The missionaries attacked such traditional practices as polygamy, spouse exchange and shamanism, but also introduced education and medical assistance.

The whaling era in particular had taken a toll on the Inuit. Smallpox, measles and influenza epidemics devastated many groups. Syphilis and other venereal diseases became rampant among those near the whaling bases. Alcohol abuse, particularly in the western Arctic, led to murders and demoralization. Famine frequently followed outbreaks of disease, as there were too few able-bodied hunters to provide food. The Sadlermiut became extinct, and the Chiglit of the Mackenzie delta almost succumbed. Neither the shamans' curing techniques nor the newcomers' medical knowledge could halt the drastic population decline across the Arctic.

The Canadian government did not make its presence felt in the north until its sovereignty in the High Arctic was threatened. For several decades the North West Mounted Police (later the Royal Canadian Mounted Police) were the major government representatives in the Arctic. In 1903 the police established a post at Fullerton Harbour, a wintering station for whalers in Hudson Bay. In the same year, they created two posts in the western Arctic, at the Herschel Island whaling station and at the Fort McPherson fur trade post. Although they were not there to administer the Inuit, the police brought new concepts of law and justice and forcefully suppressed such practices as infanticide and blood feuds. Aside from the police presence, the government provided no services, leaving the missionaries to supply rudimentary education and health care.

Major changes and new economic opportunities came with World War Two, as Canadian and American military personnel moved into strategic Arctic locations. The construction of roads, airfields, hangars, barracks and other facilities created an employment boom for the Inuit. In the Cold War era of the 1950s, there was another surge of job opportunities building the DEW (Distant Early Warning) line of radar installations, which stretched from Alaska to Baffin Island. An instant town grew up around Inuvik when its strategic location was chosen as the administrative centre of the western Arctic. The newly focussed attention on the north exposed the neglect of the Inuit occupants and forced the government to get more involved in their welfare.

THE MODERN INUIT

By the 1950s the Canadian government's policy of passive sovereignty could not withstand the geopolitical evolution of the post-war years and it was forced to assume a more active role in Inuit affairs. The remnants of the old North-West Territories were governed from Yellowknife on the Mackenzie River and services formerly provided by missionaries, fur traders or police were transferred to federal administrators, who became a permanent feature of northern communities. Tuberculosis was rampant, and many Inuit were uprooted from their families and culture for lengthy hospital treatment in southern Canada. Northern nursing stations and health programs were finally established to deal with continued high rates of infant mortality and other health problems. Schools were built at many Inuit settlements. The government also extended family allowances, old age pensions and other benefits of the welfare state to the Inuit on the same basis as other Canadians.

To administer their Inuit wards, the federal government encouraged them to settle in permanent communities and adopt a sedentary lifestyle. Many Inuit abandoned their hunting camps in favour of government-subsidized housing, education for their children, health care and other services. The church and the trading post were also features of the settlements, though Inuit-run co-operative stores shortly challenged the latter. Several administrative centres, such as Inuvik

ABOVE *Inuit family at a hunting camp near Pond Inlet, Baffin Island, 1975. Photo by Jeff Hunston*

in the west and Iqaluit in the east, became larger towns, with shopping malls, hotels, hospitals, regular air service and other amenities of southern Canadian life.

Inuit from many smaller settlements were relocated to larger centres for administrative convenience and economy. Some Inuit were induced to settle in remote areas, presumably with promises of access to seals and other game. Such schemes, however, were also designed to bolster Canadian sovereignty over the northern islands. In the mid-1950s Inuit families from northern Quebec and from Baffin Island were moved to areas of the High Arctic that had been unoccupied since Thule times. They established the small communities of Resolute, on southern Cornwallis Island, and Grise Fjord, on southern Ellesmere Island. The Inuit of Grise Fjord became Canada's most northerly permanent residents. These moves were not without government coercion, however, and some Inuit are now demanding an apology and compensation for suffering. Testimony to the Royal Commission on Aboriginal Peoples in 1993 referred to the "cruel and inhumane" policy of forced relocations and charged that the Inuit were used as "human flagpoles" to ensure Canada's sovereignty in the High Arctic.

A caste-like social system quickly developed between the Inuit and the *Qallunaat*, the Inuktitut term for the non-Native, generally temporary, residents of the north. The latter held the positions of authority as government administrators, teachers, missionaries, shopkeepers or police, while the Inuit were left with the menial jobs. Status differences were clearly evident in the communities and often the Qallunaat occupied a separate part of town. Failing to understand the new institutions and the language in which business was conducted, the Inuit were excluded from decision making. Only later in the twentieth century did the Inuit begin to assert effective control over their own lives.

Although the benefits of life in the settlements are evident, there was also a price to pay. For many, unemployment and idleness replaced the hard work and self-sufficiency of the camps. Readily available alcohol led to social and health problems and brought many Inuit into conflict with the law. Depression and anxiety encouraged alcohol abuse and contributed to high levels of violence and suicide. The Inuit became increasingly dependent on food purchased from the stores, despite its high cost and inferior nutritional value compared with a traditional diet. A constant barrage of cultural stimuli from the south—through television, radio and the Internet—continues to erode values and beliefs that have survived for millennia. In just a few decades the transplanted suburban life from southern Canada has proved more destructive to Inuit culture than the previous centuries of contact.

The introduction of new technology links the Inuit of the settlements with mainstream modern life. Boats with outboard motors have replaced kayaks and snowmobiles have largely supplanted dogsleds. Three-wheeled all-terrain vehicles are also common. Air travel links the scattered Arctic communities and provides access to cities in the south. Satellite communication systems bring southern television programs to northern homes. Modern and traditional elements of Inuit life are merged, as Inuit children in their prefabricated homes watch television beside grandmothers cutting seal meat with ulus.

Since most Arctic communities lack any real economic base, unemployment levels tend to be high. Many of the few available jobs are part-time or seasonal. Most families require government assistance payments. Trapping could no longer sustain a livelihood, and though hunting continues to put meat on the table for most families, the high cost of fuel and ammunition is an inhibiting factor. Hunting and trapping expeditions help reaffirm traditional values and maintain ancestral ties to the land.

Various government programs have attempted to modernize the territorial economic base. One such experiment early in the twentieth century assumed that the Inuit could herd reindeer, a form of Arctic pastoralism practised in northern Scandinavia. The reindeer were transplanted to Labrador and the western Arctic but herding them did not meet with any lasting success in either area. Inuit-run co-operatives, which were introduced during the 1960s, have proven more profitable. These originally manufactured northern goods for sale, and later expanded to provide stores and other services in the north. Along with government, co-operatives became the major employers of Inuit.

Most successful of the federal programs has been the investment in commercial art forms. Although the Inuit sold small carvings in early contact times, modern Inuit art had its beginning just before 1950, when the Canadian artist James Houston visited several communities in northern Quebec. Impressed with some small sculptures he collected, he encouraged local Inuit carvers to produce more

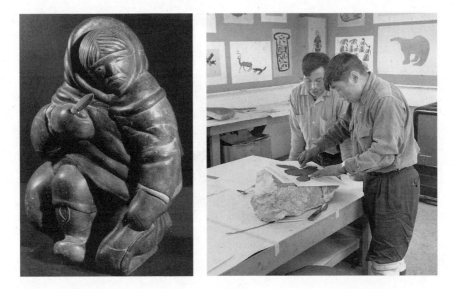

ABOVE LEFT *A fine example of modern Inuit soapstone carving.* CMC J 8609. ABOVE RIGHT *Two Inuit artists working on a stone block print at the art centre in Cape Dorset, 1961. Photo by B. Korda.* NAC PA145607

work, particularly in soapstone, as a much-needed source of new income. Backed by the federal government and the Hudson's Bay Company, Houston's experiment in marketing Inuit art to southerners achieved rapid success. The newly produced sculptures were in great demand, and carvers quickly became active in many northern communities.

Inuit soapstone sculptures have a raw power and vitality that make them attractive to southern art collectors, though they differ considerably from more traditional Inuit artworks. The earlier sculptures were made primarily in ivory, and were small, portable and often functional. In contrast, contemporary Inuit art features large, elaborate figures that mix soapstone, bone, antler and ivory to create sculptures destined for art galleries and mantelpieces. Whereas traditional motifs often mediated between the human and spirit worlds, market demands largely determine the form of the modern art. Contemporary works commonly depict Arctic animals or hunting and domestic scenes, though spirit beings from the legends are also carved in stone. Over the last half century, Inuit artists have transformed their aesthetic traditions into a distinctive art style that is among the most significant of their cultural exports. Inuit carvers are known nationally and internationally for the quality and originality of their work, and art production provides a stable income for many northerners.

The success of soapstone carving quickly led to experiments with other media, such as printmaking. James Houston brought printmaking techniques he had learned in Japan to Cape Dorset on Baffin Island, where he taught local artists to blend their aesthetic culture with a new medium. That community has remained

ABOVE *Kenojuak Ashevak with two of her prints, Cape Dorset, 1980. Photo by Judith Eglington.* NAC
PA140297

the dominant Inuit print centre, though several others now also produce prints. Most important is the stone-block print: a relief design is carved onto a flat slab of soapstone, which is then inked and the paper pressed onto it. Stencilled prints and copperplate engravings are also produced. From Cape Dorset have come such renowned artists as Kenojuak, Kananginak and Pitseolak. Kenojuak Ashevak's flamboyant depictions of fantasy birds are among the most famous Inuit works of art. One of her creations, *Enchanted Owl*, has been frequently illustrated, including on a Canadian stamp. Over the course of her lengthy printmaking career she has been awarded numerous honours, including the Order of Canada and a National Aboriginal Lifetime Achievement Award.

Until recently, many Inuit supplemented their income by selling sealskins. However, animal rights activists led a successful public relations campaign against commercial sealing. In 1982, public outrage against the bloody clubbing of infant ("whitecoat") harp and hooded seals along Canada's east coast led to a European boycott of all seal products. This protest destroyed the market for the adult ringed-seal skins the Inuit took traditionally, and caused considerable hardship in areas with few other sources of income. Although the boycott eventually ended, the sealskin trade never recovered, and today remains a marginal enterprise.

Since persistent global forces have entrenched themselves in the Arctic, the Inuit have learned to harness the potential of foreign institutions to improve the quality of life. The political evolution of the Inuit in the second half of the twentieth century was remarkable. Two or three generations ago they lived in the manner of their ancestors, but during the second half of the twentieth century they adapted their society and culture to take control of the apparatus necessary to run a modern political state. There have been both successes and setbacks, and these have yielded a civil authority with the skills and knowledge to promote the political aspirations of Arctic people in the global era. The Inuit Tapiriit Kanatami (formerly Inuit Tapirisat of Canada), which means "Inuit united within Canada," was founded in 1971 and was an early expression of Inuit political aspirations. The association represents Inuit people across four political jurisdictions of Arctic Canada: the Inuvialuit in the Northwest Territories and the Inuit of Nunavut, the Nunavik region of Quebec and Labrador. Its mandate is to promote Inuit culture and identity, and to present a common front on political, economic and environmental issues concerning the Inuit. Settlement of Aboriginal claims to the land was one early focus of political activity, but that task is now nearing completion.

Another example of Inuit political mobilization is the development of a "pan-Inuit" movement across the top of the world that allows Inuit of different countries to compare experiences and strengthen their common identity. The first Inuit Circumpolar Conference was held at Barrow, Alaska, in 1977, and brought together Inuit from Alaska, Canada and Greenland. Although several thousand Inuit live in Siberia, they were only able to participate after 1989 when the former Soviet Union released its grip. The conference officially adopted the term "Inuit" for all people formerly known as "Eskimo," despite major linguistic differences among them. The Greenlandic Inuit experience with "home rule" (Greenland is a self-governing province of Denmark) encouraged Canadian Inuit to seek greater political autonomy. Similarly, the settlement of Aboriginal land claims in Alaska in 1971 spurred Canadian Inuit in their negotiations.

The first land claim settlement to affect the Inuit in Canada was the James Bay and Northern Quebec Agreement, signed in 1975. In return for surrendering their Aboriginal title to the land so the Quebec government could proceed with hydroelectric development, the Cree and Inuit of northern Quebec received a cash settlement (the Inuit share was about $90 million), ownership of certain lands (nearly 9000 square kilometres for the Inuit), and exclusive hunting, fishing and trapping rights over a much larger area. The Inuit founded the Makivik Corporation to administer their share of the compensation money, part of which was used to establish regional businesses. Air Inuit, which was originally set up to transport the teams that were negotiating the agreement, provides commercial service to the scattered communities in northern Quebec. The Makivik Corporation created the Avataq Cultural Institute, with its headquarters near Montreal, to operate its various cultural programs. It organizes Inuit Elders' conferences, conducts research and prepares protection plans at archaeological sites, helps to develop community cultural centres and promotes official recognition of Inuit place names. It also initiated an Inuit Topographic System to map the cultural geography of Nunavik. Settlement money has financed publications in Inuktitut to promote the language. The Kativik School Board oversees education in the Inuit villages and ensures that one of the languages of instruction is Inuktitut. Unlike the Cree, the

Quebec Inuit chose a municipal government model, in which each village controls its own local matters. Local self-government, however, remains in Inuit control only as long as they maintain a population majority.

Not all Quebec Inuit communities accepted the agreement, and many Inuit feel that neither the federal nor the provincial government has fully honoured its commitments. Dissatisfaction also exists with what many see as Quebec's excessive interference with local self-government. In recent years, Quebec's Inuit organizations have been evolving toward a more politically autonomous regional government, with its own assembly and constitution and use of Inuktitut as an official language. The Quebec Inuit are also split over the province's plans to proceed with the next phase of the James Bay hydroelectric project. Like the Cree, many Inuit oppose any further development on their lands. The Makivik Corporation, however, signed an agreement-in-principle with the Quebec government in 1994, accepting significant financial compensation for environmental damage from the massive project. Relations with the province were strained, however, when the Inuit communities held their own referendum a week before the 1995 referendum on Quebec independence. Like their Cree neighbours, the Inuit voted 95 per cent in favour of remaining in the Canadian federation. Although the Inuit population is small in relation to the province as a whole, their vote was symbolically valuable to a federal campaign that was floundering.

The second land claims settlement with the Inuit was in the western Arctic, where the Committee for Original Peoples' Entitlement (COPE) negotiated on behalf of the six Inuvialuit communities. The result was the Inuvialuit Final Agreement, which was completed in 1984. This agreement adopts a corporate model as its basic framework and articulates the mechanisms for village government and self-management within the Northwest Territories. By surrendering Aboriginal title to the land, COPE negotiated a $45 million compensation package and title to about 91,000 square kilometres of land. The deal includes subsurface rights for some of the land, which is an important consideration in the potentially oil-rich area of the Beaufort Sea. Inuvialuit corporations own the land and initiate business ventures and investments with the money. The agreement also provides hunting and fishing rights, measures to protect Arctic wildlife and Inuvialuit membership on various management boards.

The Tungavik Federation of Nunavut (TFN) represented the Inuit of the rest of the Northwest Territories. This organization pressed forward on two related issues: settling their land claim and establishing a political accord to create an Inuit homeland in a separate territory to be known as Nunavut ("our land" in Inuktitut). After an agreement-in-principle was reached in Igloolik in 1990, the final land claim settlement was ratified and signed in 1993. The Inuit of the Nunavut Settlement Area agreed to "cede, release and surrender" all Aboriginal claims to the land in exchange for title to about 350,000 square kilometres, with mineral rights included for just over 10 per cent. For all other lands the Inuit have joint control with the federal government over land-use planning, wildlife management and environmental issues. They retain the right to hunt, fish and trap throughout Nunavut. The settlement also provides about $1.15 billion in financial compensation and resource royalty sharing. To administer the fund the Inuit created the Nunavut Trust, which uses the interest to support Inuit businesses and education and to provide an income-support program for Inuit hunters. The Inuit Heritage Trust manages all heritage sites within Nunavut, and issues permits to researchers. The Government of Canada also agreed to establish the separate territory of Nunavut with a legislative assembly of its own.

The Inuit viewed the territorial government in Yellowknife as both distant and culturally alien, and their long-standing political goal had been to establish their own territory. In 1982, a government plebiscite on whether to divide the Northwest Territories to create Nunavut passed with a narrow majority: people of the eastern Arctic were solidly in favour and those in the western regions were generally opposed. Also contentious was where to draw the boundary that would distinguish Nunavut, with its Inuit majority, from what would remain of the Northwest Territories, where the Dene, Métis and most non-Natives resided. The initial proposal placed the boundary along the treeline, from the Mackenzie delta to the NWT-Manitoba border near Hudson Bay. The Inuvialuit, however, opted not to join Nunavut. Dene claims to hunting territories out on the barrenlands further confused the discussion. After considerable debate, a 1992 referendum approved an essentially east-west division by a narrow margin.

Nunavut came into being on 1 April 1999, culminating a remarkable political history that began in the isolated hunting camps. It marked the first major change to the map of Canada since Newfoundland joined Confederation in 1949. Stretching from the Manitoba border to the northern tip of Ellesmere Island, Nunavut encompasses one-fifth of Canada's total land mass, or 1,900,000 square kilometres. At the time it was created, Nunavut had a population of about 27,500 people, of whom about 22,000 were Inuit. Although Iqaluit is the capital, government operations are necessarily highly decentralized, and air travel has been invaluable in this vast land of scattered settlements without connecting roads. Inuktitut is the language of government in a legislative assembly dominated by Inuit. As the Inuit comprise about 80 per cent of the population, Inuit self-government is assured.

With the signing of the Nunavut agreement, Inuit land claims were completed across Arctic Canada except for Labrador. Settlement in this remaining jurisdiction is now nearly complete. The Labrador Inuit Association reached an agreement-in-principle with the Government of Canada and the province of Newfoundland and Labrador in 2001. Through this agreement the Inuit of Labrador will own and govern 15,800 square kilometres of land, comprising about 6 per cent of Labrador, and will co-manage a much larger area with the provincial government. In addition to financial compensation for extinguishing Aboriginal title, the Inuit will receive a share of the mining tax earned through the massive nickel-mining operation at Voisey's Bay. Negotiations on the final Labrador Inuit Land Claims Agreement have now been concluded, though the three parties involved must finally ratify the agreement before it comes into effect.

The Inuit population in Canada has grown rapidly over the past few decades. Even today the great majority of Inuit live in their homeland, though the number in urban centres, such as Montreal and Ottawa, is also growing. Inuktitut is among the healthiest of Aboriginal languages. A large majority of the Nunavik population speaks it, and it is the primary language of Nunavut, though fewer people speak the language in the western Arctic and Labrador. Many school programs in Arctic settlements promote the use of Inuktitut. According to Statistics Canada's 2001 survey of Aboriginal People, Inuit children are the most likely to receive instruction in their own language. The missionaries introduced two written forms of Inuktitut, one based on syllabics and the other using the Roman alphabet, and both are still widely used. Now there are Inuktitut dictionaries, which define new words for objects and concepts that did not exist in the traditional language. As the Inuit reclaim their traditional lands, community names are restored to Inuktitut from English or French. Community newspapers and radio programs in Inuktitut reach many Inuit homes, and a television network, the Inuit Broadcasting Corporation, produces programs in both Inuktitut and English.

Within only a generation the Inuit have been catapulted into the modern world, and they continue to make an impression on their fellow Canadians. In 2001 Zacharias Kunuk won the prestigious Camera d'Or award for Best First Feature Film at the Cannes Film Festival for his film *Atanarjuak* (*The Fast Runner*). He was the first Inuk and Canadian to be awarded that honour. Joining the pantheon of Inuit artists to receive wide acclaim is singer Susan Aglukark, whose songs regularly receive radio play across Canada and internationally. When the 2003 National Hockey League season began, Jordin Tootoo started with the Nashville Predators as the first Inuk hockey player to reach the NHL. Also in 2003, Paul Okalik, the premier of Nunavut, addressed the French National Assembly, the first Canadian Aboriginal leader to do so.

Many older people now resident in Arctic towns lived as nomadic hunters only a few decades ago, and some individuals still obtain part of their food from the land. Most of the amenities of southern life are available, but the Inuit have had to adapt their lifestyle considerably to participate in the modern economy. Although energy-starved southerners still demand natural resources, land claims agreements and the creation of Nunavut ensure that the Inuit will remain in control of their own destinies.

CHAPTER 11

The Métis

. . . . .

W HEN OUR ANCIENT ancestors left Africa to claim the world, their separate paths led them to opposite ends of the earth and caused them to become strangers to each other. When humanity finally circled the globe and two branches met in North America, their apparent differences did not preclude close social interaction. From the union of European men and Aboriginal women emerged a distinct people, the Métis (from a French word meaning "mixed"). This was one more milestone in the long march toward an integrated global community.

No records suggest that Native People mixed with the Norse when they first breached the icy chasm that separated them. If the Norse sagas are any indication, their encounters were usually hostile. Although the later arrival of other Europeans occasionally led to bloodshed, the all-male crews of the fishing, trading or exploring vessels frequently sought the casual company of Aboriginal women. Thus, French fishermen from the Brittany coast left many descendants among the Mi'kmaq and Maliseet. However, these children were never a significant minority and they were raised as Mi'kmaq and Maliseet. No separate social group emerged.

In New France, racial mixing was initially encouraged to bolster the population and strengthen French claims to the land. Samuel de Champlain told his Native allies: "Our young men will marry your daughters, and we shall be one people." Many Acadian communities grew through extensive admixture with local Native People. Frequently the process worked in reverse, as young men opted for the freer country life of their trading partners. A French official complained in 1685 that "those people with whom we mingle do not become French, our people become Indian" (Peterson 1978: 47). In either case, the children were raised as Indian or European, and no distinct Métis identity emerged.

The fur trade lured many French *coureurs de bois* westward, where they established stable unions, particularly with Cree and Ojibwa women. Marriages were *à la façon du pays* ("in the custom of the country"). Lacking any formal ceremony, they were often as much about trade as they were about romance. Kinship ties from such marriages forged alliances that facilitated trade. Native wives were valued as interpreters during trade negotiations and for their domestic skills, such as making moccasins and snowshoes, or drying meat and dressing furs. As male children often followed their fathers into the fur trade, the voyageurs became increasingly of mixed heritage.

Somewhat different relations were forming to the north, around Hudson Bay. There the English and Scottish employees of the Hudson's Bay Company remained in their coastal forts, surrounded by the Cree who provided furs and provisions. Initially, company policy discouraged any mixing of the races. Indians were barred from the forts except during trading forays, and employees were banned from visiting Native camps. Some officers imposed a near-military abstinence on their men, whereas others themselves took "country" wives. Some, such as Henry Kelsey, temporarily deserted the company to follow their Aboriginal wives. Later, as competition with the North West Company forced the company inland, it relaxed its policies and such unions became commonplace. Unlike the coureurs de bois and voyageurs who often spent their lives among their Aboriginal kin, Hudson's Bay Company men in the early years of the trade usually returned to Britain. Most of their progeny were absorbed into the mothers' families. Only a few high-ranking officers sent their sons to be educated in England or Scotland, or later in Montreal. Other country-born sons of officers found work at the posts, as traders, interpreters or labourers.

By the mid-eighteenth century, a large "mixed-blood" population had congregated around the Great Lakes. Increasingly, the French coureurs de bois settled with their Native families in permanent communities. Later the Scottish employees of the North West Company joined them. Substantial communities of log cabins sprang up at such strategic locations as Sault Ste. Marie. Some inhabitants were farmers, while others worked as voyageurs and clerks in the fur trade. As the population grew, marriages within the mixed-blood group became common. The Great Lakes Métis were beginning to merge the separate elements of their heritage into a common culture. However, depleted fur stocks and the escalating traffic of non-Native settlers from the east early in the nineteenth century brought new pressures to Métis life. Many sought the refuge of the eastern Plains, where they coalesced to form a distinctive Métis culture and proclaimed a "new nation."

THE RED RIVER MÉTIS

Emergent Métis culture blended attributes from the two parent races to create a distinct society. Not only was this group physically distinguishable, it also had a unique aesthetic, intellectual and material culture. These traits appeared early in the nineteenth century on the Plains, particularly near the confluence of the Red and Assiniboine Rivers (today in the heart of Winnipeg). There the Métis established themselves as buffalo hunters and provisioners for the North West Company, and served as an essential link in the long trade chain from Montreal to the far-flung fur posts that extended to the Athabasca region. Geographic and social isolation, as well as a shared lifestyle, created a sense of solidarity and fomented a group identity. Years of bitter confrontation between the two great fur trade companies also helped to forge the concept of a new nation on the eastern Plains.

The Métis lifestyle and freedom were threatened when the Hudson's Bay Company, which controlled the vast expanse called Rupert's Land, granted Lord Selkirk land along the Red River for an agricultural colony. The first Scottish settlers arrived in 1812, the year that war broke out between British and American forces along the Great Lakes frontier. The North West Company, incensed that the new community lay directly on its main trade route from Montreal, did everything possible to subvert the colonists' plans. Its agents warned Métis leaders that the settlers would usurp Métis land and put an end to their livelihood. Leaders of the new settlement confirmed these fears by prohibiting the running of buffalo on horseback and by forbidding the sale of pemmican to the North West Company. These actions struck at the very heart of Métis culture.

Cuthbert Grant, a charismatic and popular leader, responded to this threat by awakening the nascent nationalism of his Métis community. Like many of his peers, he was the son of a Scottish Nor'wester and an Aboriginal woman, but unlike his peers he had been formally educated in Montreal. Taking the title "Captain General of all half-breeds," he led his troops to the inevitable clash, known as the Battle of Seven Oaks. When the smoke cleared, the colony's governor and twenty settlers lay dead, while the Métis lost one man. Although they did not permanently drive out the colonists, the Métis had firmly established their rights in the area. Métis nationalism flourished in the years following Seven Oaks and eventually coalesced around such emotional symbols as a flag and the commemorative songs of their beloved bard, Pierre Falçon. Cuthbert Grant also founded the first Métis settlement west of the Red River colony. His new community, Grantown, buffered the Red River colony from marauding Dakota war parties.

The winds of change grew stronger in the years following 1821, when the North West Company merged with the Hudson's Bay Company under the latter's charter. When posts closed after the merger, unemployment soon followed. Former employees were encouraged to settle with their Aboriginal wives and country-born offspring along the Red River. The Métis tended to have large families and their population swelled so they were soon a majority in the region.

Most marriages took place within the mixed-blood group, which strengthened their common ties, but Métis women were often courted by white settlers as well. No new outside attempt at colonization disrupted the Métis, and the new nation flourished in virtual isolation for half a century.

Despite their new political consciousness as a single people, the diverse parental cultures were still strong when the Red River settlement was founded. Their fathers' Christian heritage sustained them spiritually, and though their Aboriginal beliefs were suppressed they did not disappear. The French Métis, who formed the largest part of the population, were devout Roman Catholics, whereas the English were Anglicans and the Scots were Presbyterians. In the early historic accounts of the settlement, the term Métis described the French-speaking, Catholic branch, and "half-breed" was more commonly applied to English-speaking Protestants. Many of the anglophone families maintained small farms, while the French Métis tended to live a more mobile lifestyle. Social, racial and economic distinctions between the various groups led to tension and strife. Many ties of intermarriage, however, helped to bind members of the community, as did participating in such activities as the communal bison hunt. Many spoke both European languages, plus Cree or Ojibwa from their mother's side. In time an emergent language, known as *Michif,* grew from the combination of French nouns and Cree verbs and syntax. Ojibwa words were also incorporated in the eastern portion of its distribution.

Like their Aboriginal kin of the Plains, the Métis' identity was inspired by the bison, though this was more economic than spiritual. The annual bison hunt was conducted on a large scale as a commercial endeavour and was one of the defining Métis practices. Meat from the hunt was processed into pemmican, which was then traded to the Hudson's Bay Company. Pembina, on the Red River just south of the American border, was a favourite rendezvous for Métis travelling in their distinctive two-wheeled Red River carts pulled by horses or oxen. The carts, which were used to transport equipment and haul meat, were made entirely of wood bound with rawhide. The axles could not be greased, since the dirt that then collected soon cut through the wood. Like a symphony of discordant instruments, these cart brigades filled the prairie air with cacophonous groans as the wooden wheels strained against their wooden axles. Compared to the quiet Aboriginal caravans of travois, the wooden cart brigades produced such disturbing noise that they were blamed for driving away the bison. The hunts quickly grew to major proportions; in 1840 over 1600 people and 1200 carts met at Pembina. Cart trails rutted the prairies as hunting parties set out after the herds.

From their Aboriginal kin the Métis adopted the strict code of the hunt, which was typically associated with the Plains Indian military societies. Anyone who threatened the general hunt by disturbing the herds could be punished. The Métis chose officers and imposed strict discipline, both to ensure success on the hunt and to ward off raids by hostile Dakota.

ABOVE *"Half-breeds Running Buffalo," by the Canadian artist Paul Kane, captures the excitement and the dangers of the Métis bison hunt. Kane participated in this hunt near Fort Garry in 1846.* ROM

Like the Aboriginal hunters around them, they favoured the technique of "running the buffalo." Mounted on swift "buffalo horses," Métis hunters raced into the stampeding herd. Riding at full gallop alongside a selected target, the hunter poured gunpowder into the barrel of his gun, spat in a lead ball from a supply carried in his mouth, pounded it down by abruptly striking the butt on his saddle, and lowered the barrel to fire. Quickly dropping a glove or some other personal object to mark his kill, the hunter raced on to select another animal and repeat the process. An experienced hunter on a good horse could kill as many as ten or twelve animals on a run.

The obvious dangers that regularly brought death and serious injury enhanced the excitement of the hunt. Men might be gored, thrown from their horses and trampled, or accidentally shot in the dust, noise and confusion. One nineteenth-century observer, zoologist William Hornaday, related the dangers:

> It often happened that the hunter found himself surrounded by the flying herd, and in a cloud of dust, so that neither man nor horse could see the ground before them. Under such circumstances fatal accidents to both men and horses were numerous. It was not an uncommon thing for half-breeds to shoot each other in the excitement of the chase; and, while now and then a wounded bull suddenly turned upon his pursuer and overthrew him, the greatest number of casualties were from falls. *Verbicky-Todd 1984: 145*

As the dust of the hunt settled, men sought the animals they had killed and immediately began to skin and butcher them. The bulk of the labour, however, fell to the women. They cut the meat into strips, dried it in the sun and over fires, pounded it into coarse powder, mixed it with melted fat and crushed berries, and stored it in hide bags. Creaking brigades of Red River carts hauled back huge loads of pemmican, destined as provisions for the distant posts of the fur trade.

As the bison hunts spread far out onto the Plains, the Métis came into bitter conflict with the Dakota. Not only were they depleting the herds in Dakota hunting grounds, but the Métis were closely associated by blood and marriage with the Cree and Ojibwa, the traditional enemies of the Dakota. The Métis adopted their military discipline and large group size while on the hunt to counter the ever-present threat of Dakota attacks. Numerous skirmishes led to a decisive battle in 1851. Although they faced a larger armed force, the Métis circled their carts and dug shallow rifle pits. Their improvised fort stood fast against their attackers' charges while Métis marksmen with their buffalo guns directed one withering volley after another toward them. After suffering terrible losses, the Dakota withdrew, leaving the Métis in undisputed control of the eastern Plains.

The unsustainable hunting practices of the commercial trade soon depleted the bison herds. By the 1850s, the Métis had to move farther and farther afield in search of game. With such distances to travel, many families began to "winter over" on the Plains, at such wooded oases as Moose Mountain, Wood Mountain and the Cypress Hills. Known as *hivernants* ("winterers"), these hunters relied less on manufactured goods and embraced a lifestyle similar to the Plains Natives. A member of the Palliser Expedition, visiting an hivernant camp near Fort Edmonton in 1858, described the inhabitants:

> A motley troop with loaded horses and dogs, travelling in a style hardly different from Indians. There were about 200 men, women, and children in the band, with forty tents, which were merely Indian wigwams of buffalo skins sewn together and stretched over poles. . . . They wore clothes of European manufacture, but even those of the men who could speak French preferred to speak Cree. *Spry 1963: 109–10*

More permanent hivernant settlements of log cabins soon began to spring up across the Plains.

The Métis expressed their distinct identity in a variety of clothing styles that mixed elements of their European and Aboriginal heritage. Men commonly wore capotes (long hooded coats), with brightly coloured sashes or belts, trousers and moccasins. Women wore European dresses, with dark shawls or blankets covering the head and shoulders, and moccasins. Alexander Ross, a prominent member of the Red River colony, described one individual:

> . . . we met a stout, well-made, good-looking man, dressed in a common blue capote, red belt, and corduroy trousers; he spoke French, and was a Canadian. That, said I, pointing to his dress, is the universal costume of both Canadians and half-breeds. *Ross 1856: 190*

ABOVE *Métis traders, ca. 1872–75.* NAC C4164

The red sash, a tradition adopted from the French voyageurs, is a particularly important emblem of Métis identity. In addition, Métis women were skilled beadworkers who produced elaborate floral designs to decorate moccasins, pouches and other items. So distinctive a trait was this that the Dakota knew them as "the flower beadwork people."

Social gatherings and festivities, drawn from the various aspects of their heritage, strengthened Métis identity. Festive occasions were an excuse to clear furniture from the house to make room for dancing. Vernacular music reverberated in the cabin once the fiddle, a legacy of their French and Scottish background, was pulled from its case. With this beloved musical instrument tucked in his neck, a fiddler would defy revellers to keep step with his vigorous, rowdy tunes. Dances of the Plains Indians, French jigs and Scottish reels were combined in frenetic, energetic footwork. The "Red River jig" became synonymous with Métis celebrations. Men, in particular, prided themselves on their energy, often dancing until they wore through their moccasins.

By the 1860s, a half-century after they had secured the eastern Plains as their cultural epicentre, economic forces put new pressures on the Métis way of life. The fur trade, once the economic powerhouse of North America, was in decline, and a new economy was dawning around the globe. Any endeavour that relied too heavily on human labour, or an outdated trade network and a barter economy, was no match for the steamships that had appeared on the Red River and the industrial economy they represented. The creaking Red River carts no longer followed the meagre herds of bison that remained on the eastern Plains. Métis bison hunters were forced to either abandon the hunt or move west in search of the remaining herds. Crop failures resulted in hardship in the colony. Even more distressing for Métis nationhood was the national dream of Sir John A. Macdonald.

The new nation of Canada was anxious to assert control over the British claim in Rupert's Land. Macdonald, as the first prime minister, was determined to preside over the construction of a country that would stretch from sea to sea.

By 1869 the Hudson's Bay Company, despite never having cleared the Aboriginal title to the land, yielded to pressure and transferred the vast extent of Rupert's Land to the new Canadian government. Even before this non-existent title was finally transferred, a stream of settlers from Ontario began claiming lands along the Red River. Surveyors started to lay out square lots, emulating the Ontario township system, and disregarded the long, narrow Métis river lots. The federal government continued to deny the existence of Métis title to the lands they occupied and did nothing to ease their fears or hostility. Instead the bureaucrats processed the transfer as a simple real estate transaction with little concern for the area's occupants.

A leader with the charisma and prominence of Cuthbert Grant was needed to champion Métis aspirations, and a young Louis Riel heeded the call. Like Grant, he had been educated in Montreal, where he studied law. Riel could unite the various factions around Red River because of his fluent command of French, English and Cree. The French Métis initiated the resistance, and the anglophone half-breeds either reluctantly supported them or remained neutral. However, other factions in the community welcomed the Protestant settlers from the east. Backed by a force of armed men experienced in bison hunts and skirmishes with the Dakota, Riel seized Fort Garry, the centre of the Red River settlement, and proclaimed a provisional government. His supporters elected representatives to draft the conditions under which they would enter Confederation. Their demands included rights to their own elected legislature, representation in the Parliament of Canada, and official status for both the French and English languages.

Riel soon faced a crisis for his government in the Thomas Scott case. Scott was a recently arrived Protestant settler from Upper Canada who sought to overthrow the provisional government and bring the area quickly into Confederation. He was vehemently anti-Catholic and thoroughly disdainful of the Métis. Scott's attempts to incite an uprising resulted in his capture by angry Métis, after which he was court-martialled and shot. Riel's failure to intervene and stop the execution earned him the bitter enmity of Protestant Ontario, forcing his exile and contributing eventually to his own execution.

The demands of Riel's provisional government led directly to the Manitoba Act of 1870, which created the new province of Manitoba (though at a mere one hundred square miles it comprised only a small portion of the modern province). Several provisions of the Manitoba Act dealt with Métis concerns over lands. The Métis were assured title to their river-lot holdings and an additional 1.4 million acres was promised to Métis families. These land allocations were amended several times, however, and the entire process was delayed and mismanaged. Eventually Métis families received scrip certificates for land, but these ended up largely in the hands of speculators. This flawed process, plus pressures from the flood of new settlers into Manitoba, meant that few Métis experienced any long-term benefit.

The negotiations preceding Manitoba's entry into Confederation called for a general amnesty for those involved in the "resistance." Unfortunately the amnesty meant little, and Riel and other leaders were forced into exile south of the border when British and Canadian troops arrived. Despite his absence, Métis people never forgot Louis Riel's efforts on their behalf. He was elected three times to the federal Parliament in Ottawa, though he was never able to take his seat. Many still consider him the Father of Manitoba.

Although many Métis demands were met, it was an ephemeral victory. Before long, Protestant farmers from Ontario had claimed most of the land. Where the Métis were once the dominant population along the Red River, they suddenly found themselves reduced to a small minority. Moreover, the new arrivals were openly contemptuous of the Métis and hostile to anyone who had taken part in the "rebellion." Several prominent Métis members of the provisional government were killed and others were beaten. Many Anglo-Protestant half-breeds continued living on their farms north of Fort Garry and gradually blended in with the new settlers. The French-speaking, Catholic Métis, however, bore the brunt of discrimination, and many of them moved west, following the migrations begun by the hivernants decades earlier. In what are today Saskatchewan and Alberta, the Métis established substantial log-cabin communities, and attempted to continue a lifestyle as hunters, freighters and farmers. In little more than a decade, however, the expanding Canadian frontier overtook them.

THE MÉTIS AND THE NORTHWEST REBELLION OF 1885

By the mid-1880s, the old economy of hunting bison to provision the fur trade was becoming a wistful memory. Like the bison herds, the fur trade had all but disappeared, replaced by agriculture and fledgling industrial capitalism. Such economic forces conspired to cause great unrest in the Canadian west. The Cree and Assiniboine were starving on their reserves. Métis communities relied increasingly on farming, which forced an end to their mobile lifestyle. Few owned title to their land, and they felt threatened by the increasing tide of settlers brought in by rail and steamships. When the government sent surveyors west to divide the land into square lots the Métis could only recall their bitter experience along the Red River. Once again the traditional Métis practice of establishing narrow lots extending back from the rivers was ignored. Fearing that they were to be dispossessed again, the Métis petitioned for recognition of their land rights. The government responded, but far too slowly to allay Métis fears, and without firmly committing to grant their requests.

The centre of Métis discontent was around the fork of the Saskatchewan River, where a number of communities had formed. One of the most prominent leaders was Gabriel Dumont, a former sharpshooter and buffalo hunter. When the buffalo hunts ended he turned to homesteading, operating a ferry that

RIGHT *Gabriel Dumont, the famed Métis buffalo hunter and military leader of the Northwest Rebellion, after his flight from Batoche. Glenbow Archives NA-1063-1*

crossed the Saskatchewan River and running a small store near a town called Batoche. Dumont did not have the formal education in Montreal that had propelled his predecessors into their leadership roles; his schooling was based on his horse and rifle and his faith. He felt ill-prepared for the approaching discussions with the federal government and he decided to recruit a more learned voice to articulate Métis aspirations. At a meeting attended by white settlers and anglophone half-breeds as well as Métis, he convinced the assembly that Louis Riel, who had defended their interests so vigorously at Red River, was needed again. Dumont, the emissary, set out with three others to find Riel.

The Riel they located in Montana was considerably different from the man who had been the focus of the resistance at Red River. Forced into exile and pursued by bounty hunters, he had suffered a nervous breakdown and been placed in mental asylums in Quebec. He had become obsessed with the idea that he had a divine mission to fulfill: to create a new French-Catholic state in the Canadian northwest. The invitation to return to the Métis people was his route toward achieving God's will.

A politician and religious zealot rather than a soldier, Riel attempted to replicate his strategy of 1869. He prepared petitions outlining Métis grievances to the government, but his followers were anxious for more direct action. Riel and his men seized the parish church at Batoche and once again proclaimed a provisional government. They elected a slate of officers, though most of the power was held by Riel and by Gabriel Dumont, who became "head of the army."

Riel's personal drama, as it played out along the Saskatchewan River in 1885, was quite different from what had happened at Red River in 1869. Rupert's Land was a dim memory, and Canada held effective control of the North-West Territories. Moreover, Canada had an army in the east, the North West Mounted Police in the west and a transportation network capable of deploying military resources to any region of the Dominion. Where it had taken several months for British troops to reach Red River in 1870, a new transcontinental railway had opened up the west. Despite gaps in the rail link with the east, troops quickly moved to the scene of the uprising. From the initial proclamation that formed the provisional government to the fall of Batoche, the Northwest Rebellion lasted scarcely two months.

The first skirmish took place near Duck Lake, where the North West Mounted Police arrived to assert the authority of the Dominion of Canada. Dumont's Métis, with a few Cree and Assiniboine from nearby reserves, controlled the surrounding woods. Twelve police soon lay dead and the rest were forced to flee. Métis forces could have pursued them and inflicted greater casualties, but Riel admonished his followers. After this defeat, the police abandoned Fort Carlton and regrouped at the larger settlement of Prince Albert.

News of the Métis victory at Duck Lake spread quickly among the surrounding Native communities. Riel's messengers urged them to join in common cause with their Métis kin. Disillusioned with the treaties, chafing under the drudgery of life on their reserves and starving due to a misguided government restraint policy, many Cree and Assiniboine joined the rebellion. Several hundred Cree besieged the fort at Battleford, looting and burning surrounding homes and stores. There they were joined by Assiniboine who had left their reserve after killing their farm instructor and a settler. Farther to the northwest, the Cree warriors of Big Bear's band killed the Indian agent, two priests and six others at Frog Lake and forced the residents to abandon Fort Pitt, which they pillaged and burned.

The deaths at Frog Lake sent shock waves through the halls of Parliament and forced the government to act decisively. Although Métis insurrection by itself had not caused a great deal of government concern, the spectre of a general Native uprising across the west certainly did. The government hastily dispatched forces to quell the Métis rebellion before it could spread. The troops were divided into three columns to launch a three-pronged assault on the insurgents. One column headed after Big Bear's Cree, and another proceeded to relieve Battleford. The main column, under General Middleton, prepared to confront the Métis forces at Batoche.

Riel opposed Dumont's tactics of guerrilla warfare and still hoped to negotiate peacefully with the Canadian government. The advance of the army, however, required action, and Dumont hastened with his men to meet the troops before they could reach Batoche. At the Battle of Fish Creek, Métis sharpshooters, though greatly outnumbered, temporarily halted the army's advance. Meanwhile, a second army column had moved against the Cree on Poundmaker's reserve. Poundmaker, a reluctant participant in the hostilities, took action to defend his community. His successful counterattack at Cut Knife Hill forced the Canadian troops to retreat. Poundmaker and his warriors headed toward Batoche but were too late to join the fight.

The final outcome of the Battle of Batoche could never have been in doubt. A few hundred Métis with smooth-bore muzzle-loaders were no match for nearly a thousand soldiers with rifles, cannons and the rapid-fire Gatling gun. Métis supplies of ammunition were low, and by the end of the conflict many were reduced to firing nails and pebbles. Nevertheless, deeply dug into rifle pits and trenches, the Métis held off the military onslaught for four days. Finally, the rifle pits were overrun, and the Métis defenders fled to the woods.

As fugitives, Riel and Dumont acted in characteristically different fashion. Riel agreed to surrender, to "fulfill God's will" and to continue to plead the cause of the Métis to the Government of Canada. Dumont, the man of action, reacted to Middleton's demand for his surrender with the terse response: "I have still ninety cartridges to use on his men." He soon fled to the United States, where, for a brief period, this colourful frontiersman entertained audiences with his shooting and riding skills in Buffalo Bill Cody's Wild West Show. Later, he quietly returned to his homeland and lived out his life around Batoche. Poundmaker surrendered shortly after Riel, but Big Bear eluded the troops for several months. A number of Cree and Métis fled to Montana, where today their descendants live on the Rocky Boy Reservation.

The trials that followed sent a number of Métis, Cree and Assiniboine to prison. Big Bear and Poundmaker each received a three-year sentence. Their spirits and health broken by imprisonment, both men died shortly after their release. Eight Cree and Assiniboine men were hanged at Battleford for the murders at Frog Lake and elsewhere. Most attention, however, focussed on the trial of Louis Riel.

A central issue in the trial was Riel's mental stability. A plea of insanity would almost certainly have saved him from the gallows. Riel, however, strongly believing in his divine mission, refused to weaken his impassioned speeches by allowing a claim of insanity. Despite a recommendation for mercy from the jury that convicted him, Riel was sentenced to hang.

This verdict embroiled much of the country in controversy. English Canada, having never forgiven Riel for the death of Thomas Scott fifteen years earlier, saw him as a traitor and demanded his execution. French Canada saw him as the defender of its language and religion in the west and demanded a pardon. Appeals to commute the death sentence came from around the world. The infuriated Macdonald declared: "He shall hang though every dog in Quebec bark in his favour." French Canadians saw the death sentence as the wedge driving apart the two solitudes. Disapproval was so strong in Quebec that Macdonald's Conservative party went into a century of political decline there. In Regina, on 16 November 1885, Riel's sentence was carried out. The Métis dreams of a new nation, which began with Cuthbert Grant in 1817, died on the gallows with Louis Riel.

ABOVE *Métis prisoners at the courthouse in Regina, August 1885. Photo by O.B. Buell.* NAC PA118760.

LEFT *Big Bear (seated at left, with youngest son Horse Child) and Pound-maker (seated at right) in custody at Regina after the rebellion.* NAC C187211-5.

THE MÉTIS IN THE LAST CENTURY

The Métis defeat marked the end of the "Old West." Hunters, trappers and traders gave way to immigrant farmers who were eager to fence and plow the land for their farms. Once again, the Métis were dispersed. Some sought the open spaces of Montana, while others retreated northward into the boreal forest, reaching as far as the Mackenzie River, where they continued to hunt and trap. Those who remained were left on the fringes of the new economic order.

The events following the battle at Batoche had shattered Métis self-identity. They had become "non-people" when government policy refused to recognize separate status. As Macdonald stated: "If they are Indians, they go with the tribe; if they are half-breeds they are whites." Some Métis emphasized the French and Catholic aspects of their heritage, whereas others, particularly in the north, merged with Indian groups and later took treaty. Nearly a century passed before the Métis received any accommodation in Canada. Not until 1982, when the Constitution Act defined Aboriginal People as the Indians, Inuit and Métis, did they finally regain widespread recognition as a distinct people.

Before that time, it was rarely acknowledged that the Métis held Aboriginal rights. However, they were issued the "half-breed scrip," a certificate for a certain number of acres of Dominion land or cash value redeemable in purchase of such lands (commonly $240 or 240 acres). When Indian treaties were signed, individuals of mixed heritage were offered the option of scrip rather than treaty. This provided an immediate financial inducement to surrender their Aboriginal status, but few Métis obtained any long-term benefit, since poverty forced most to sell the certificates to speculators who followed the scrip commissions. Federal practice concerning the Métis differed from that applied to their Indian kin, since Aboriginal rights were extinguished individually rather than collectively. Such a policy denied the Métis a land base and other benefits of treaty, and many Métis today insist that their Aboriginal rights could not have been extinguished by such an inadequate process.

Well into the twentieth century, many Métis lived in deplorable economic conditions, shut out from mainstream Canadian life yet excluded from the reserves and federal programs for Indians. Where hunting and trapping were no longer possible, people earned a bare existence cutting wood and doing other odd jobs. Métis shantytowns grew up on the outskirts of villages and alongside reserves; other Métis built cabins on Crown land such as road allowances. The Great Depression between the two world wars pushed many Métis even further into poverty and despair.

By the 1930s political action finally brought the Métis' desperate situation to government attention, particularly in northern Alberta, where transfer to provincial jurisdiction affected many Métis squatters on Crown land. The Métis Association (now the Métis Nation) of Alberta was formed to create awareness of their situation and promote their interests. Leaders such as Malcolm Norris and Jim Brady forcefully articulated Métis grievances and helped revive Métis nationalism. As a result, the Alberta government formed the Ewing Commission to investigate the health, education and general welfare of Métis people, and their recommendations led to passage of the Métis Betterment Act in 1938. Twelve Métis colonies, similar in nature to Indian reserves, were established in north-central Alberta. Although four were later rescinded, the remaining eight settlements are home to about 6000 Métis today. The western settlements are largely agricultural, whereas ranching has been more important for those to the east. For over half a century this was the only formally recognized communal Métis land base in the country.

Differences in perception, however, set the stage for continuing conflict. The commissioners and government agents viewed the settlements as "colonies," run by the government to help destitute Métis become successful farmers. The Métis aspirations, articulated by such leaders as Norris and Brady, were for a self-governing Métis entity with a defined land base. From the start they resented what they saw as excessive government control, and their lack of land security was reinforced in 1960 when the Alberta government unilaterally terminated one of the occupied settlements in spite of Métis objections. Another major source of friction, which developed into a prolonged legal battle, was a dispute over control of subsurface rights to oil and gas resources.

This continuing conflict led Peter Lougheed's Conservative government to establish a committee, chaired by former lieutenant-governor Grant MacEwan, to review the Métis Betterment Act. The committee's 1984 report recommended that the Métis be awarded a greater degree of self-government and that land ownership be transferred to the settlements. These recommendations, plus a desire to end the lengthy court proceedings over oil and gas revenues, led to a 1989 agreement. In exchange for dropping their legal suit the Métis communities received $310 million, to be paid over seventeen years. Legislation enacted in 1990 allowed for limited self-government, granted full title to the lands that make up the settlements and amended the Alberta Act to constitutionally entrench the legal title.

The Métis have taken an active role in political and cultural issues over the last few decades. The Métis National Council provides a strong national voice for Métis aspirations. It represents the provincial Métis organizations in Ontario, the three Prairie provinces and British Columbia. The Gabriel Dumont Institute of Métis Studies and Applied Research, with branches in Regina, Saskatoon and smaller centres, is the educational wing of the Métis Nation of Saskatchewan. Although it is affiliated with the Universities of Regina and Saskatchewan, it is an independent Métis-operated institution. It offers a variety of educational services, including courses in Métis Studies, and it promotes Métis identity. The annual "Back to Batoche" event in Saskatchewan is a social occasion that reaffirms and celebrates the various facets of Métis culture. Fiddling contests, square dances and jigs, Red River carts and red sashes feature prominently at all such events that promote Métis identity. Smaller, regional Métis festivals serve a similar function.

Although Canada's Constitution Act of 1982 recognizes the Métis as Aboriginal People, their constitutionally protected Aboriginal rights have never been defined. Moreover, determining who is entitled to recognition as Métis remains unclear. Unlike other Aboriginal Peoples, the Métis are not enumerated and are not administered directly by the federal government. A negotiated agreement, the Métis Nation Accord, attempted to deal with these problems. The Métis National Council, along with provincial and territorial Métis groups, and the federal and corresponding provincial governments signed the accord, which defined a Métis as an Aboriginal Person who self-identifies as Métis and is a descendant of those Métis who were entitled to land grants or scrip under the provisions of the Manitoba Act of 1870 or the Dominion Lands Acts. It called for the federal government to take responsibility for Métis and to enumerate them to determine their eligibility for Métis rights. It also committed the federal and provincial governments to negotiating with the Métis regarding self-government and a land base. That agreement, however, was part of the broader constitutional reform package known as the Charlottetown Accord, which the Canadian public soundly defeated in 1992. Whether any part of this agreement will yet be implemented remains uncertain.

As Aboriginal People, the Métis are entitled to pursue land claims issues. Recent treaty negotiations in the Northwest Territories have included both Dene and Métis. In addition, some Métis have land claims which grew out of their own unique history. The Manitoba Métis Federation has launched legal action against the governments of Manitoba and Canada over lands reserved for the Métis in the Manitoba Act of 1870. They maintain that amendments to the Manitoba Act, which deprived many Métis of their land entitlements, were unconstitutional. They also claim that the government mismanaged the grant program and did not fulfill the conditions agreed upon when Métis leaders at Red River negotiated their place within Canada. As descendants of the Métis at Red River in 1870, the Manitoba Métis argue that they are entitled to compensation in money and land. A 1990 Supreme Court of Canada decision cleared the way for the Métis to proceed with their legal action, though little progress has yet been made. The stakes are considerable as large areas of modern Winnipeg and the surrounding communities sit on lands of the former Red River settlement, much of which the Métis maintain was set aside for them under the terms of the Manitoba Act.

The Métis won a significant legal victory on 19 September 2003, when the justices on the Supreme Court of Canada unanimously dismissed the charges against Steve and Roddy Powley of Sault Ste. Marie, Ontario, for hunting out of season without a licence. Although the case began in the province of Ontario, the *Powley* decision in the Supreme Court will reverberate across the country. This legal recognition that the Métis hold Aboriginal hunting rights clearly implies they possess other Aboriginal rights. For example, the Kelly Lake Métis in northeastern British Columbia are involved in an ongoing legal dispute with British Columbia over resource development on their lands. In delivering its decision, the Supreme Court stressed that a mechanism will have to be established to formally identify Métis rights-holders. This would be akin to Indian status as the court insisted on a degree of continuity and stability to support an Aboriginal rights claim. Self-definition and acceptance as a member of a Métis community, with demonstrated ancestral ties to that community, form the new basis for Métis identity.

From the "forgotten people" of a few decades ago, the Métis have once again registered on public consciousness. The events at Fort Garry and Batoche, so crucial to the history of western Canada, have inspired renewed interest in Métis issues. Batoche is now a National Historic Park, and statues of Louis Riel stand outside the provincial legislative buildings in both Regina and Winnipeg. Riel's execution remains a subject of debate, and many groups have presented demands for a retroactive pardon. The controversial Métis leader continues to symbolize the tensions in Canadian society, between east and west, French and English, Natives and non-Natives. Globalization has increasingly brought geographically isolated people together to produce mixed-heritage populations, and the Métis historical narrative provides a unique example of this broader phenomenon.

CHAPTER 12

Aboriginal People and Canada:
Emerging Relations

. . . . .

ACH OF THE PRECEDING chapters described the long tenure of Aboriginal
People in their respective homelands since the last Ice Age. Those early
millennia form a mute history that can be discerned primarily from the
archaeological record. When the first people arrived near the end of the Pleistocene, North America truly was *terra nullius,* an empty land. Thereafter, they
explored and colonized intensely as they expanded throughout North and South
America. During the long era of land-claiming they created their cultural traditions as they met the challenges of their environments. No region of the Americas was left vacant, and the concept of an empty land grew moot.

Aboriginal People did not just leave their ancient signature in the archaeological record; they also passed on technological innovations such as the kayak that
remain popular in the modern world. Some Aboriginal cultural innovations, including foods, amusements and aesthetics, also are embedded in modern daily
life. When Native People began experimenting with plant domestication, for example, they set in motion events that introduced new modes of life unattainable
by their hunting and gathering kin. The corn, beans and squash they harvested
from their fields and gardens are still vital ingredients in meals prepared in the
kitchens of the world. Aboriginal People have made many positive contributions
to the modern world, but embracing modern ways has come at a steep cost.

Like globalization, modernity was not a uniform event. Wherever this new
world extended, Aboriginal languages and traditions grew weaker. The traditional cultures described in the previous chapters once seemed secure, yet they
are gradually eroding. Many customary vocations have all but disappeared,

creating economic and social turmoil in isolated communities. Whether the case is a poor diet resulting in poor health, alcohol-induced despair robbing children of parental care or gas-sniffing youth burning out their lives, modernity seems only to destroy traditional cultures without providing adequate positive options.

Aboriginal People collided with modernity with little to buffer, filter or mitigate the experience. They lost traditions, languages and lifeways. Yet they were expected to embrace modernity and thrive in its various forms without vocations, skills or, worst of all, hope. This contest between modern times and traditional cultures has sparked a crisis of identity about Aboriginal People's place in this milieu of change, and has fuelled a conflict that is played out in cultures, communities, families and individuals.

Modern times also have introduced the nation state. Aboriginal People now have a symbiotic relationship with Canada. Their origin and autonomy does not depend on Canada, yet Canada dominates their reality. Neither side will disappear anytime soon, but no resolution to their disputes is evident yet. Making sense of this confusion is much like watching two teams locked in struggle in an unfamiliar game and seeing only an organized riot. Without knowing the history of the struggle and the rules of engagement, the play seems chaotic, whereas understanding the context makes the action coherent. In the negotiations between Aboriginal People and Canada, like in a game, both sides have a strategy to achieve their goals. However, as in any contest, there can be only one victor and the objective is to be on the winning side. The two sides in this contest, though, have reached a stalemate. Neither side can withdraw, win or lose, so the only option is to play on, devising a strategy for the game ahead. Colonization is offered as an alternative paradigm for imagining an activist agenda for the future of Aboriginal People. They have already colonized urban Canada, and the experience of the ancient hunters who first discovered and colonized America may be the inspiration for the project ahead.

BECOMING MODERN

Globalization, the trend toward an integrated world system, is the common experience of Aboriginal People everywhere. The first encounters between Inuit and Europeans in the Canadian Arctic ushered in this new era, but different parts of the continent have felt its effects at varying times. Even isolated regions, such as Hudson Bay during the fur trade and whaling eras, were sometimes its epicentre because Aboriginal People were essential to the nascent capitalist system. Since then they have struggled to understand the modern world and to control their encounter with it. They have not participated in the diaspora that is symptomatic of persistent globalism, and the role they will play in such a world is still unknown.

This notion of an integrated world system, or globalism, gave rise to the gloomy tale told in First Nations communities of the hegemonic powers that invaded and seized their Aboriginal homelands. In this story the descendants of the people who discovered a *terra nullius* at the end of the Ice Age and who colonized it successfully thrived in the lifeways they practised. Some farther south even created remarkable civilizations that counted their citizens in the millions. When this narrative is told, antiquity is always the golden age because later, when foreign powers are introduced, the story tells of a dark age. Aboriginal People still struggle to understand the logic that came to govern their lives after the "invasion." They resist because they know their history will end when every Aboriginal Person is assimilated into the larger society. Canada will then use Aboriginal distinctiveness to enhance and legitimate its rule. In fact this is already happening, as numerous Aboriginal images are used to represent Canada to the world. Resistance is a natural reaction to domination; indeed, generations of warriors have defended the frontiers of their homelands. Even when they were outnumbered or outgunned, they stood their ground because their choice to avoid assimilation at all costs was so clear. In the early years of the struggle, Aboriginal People took up arms to defend their interests. However, as they lost more lands and resources, that mode of resistance weakened.

To be sure, Aboriginal nations did not willingly join the game of global domination. Outside forces threw them into the contest. Native People were not clear on the rules of engagement and by the time they realized all that was at stake they were out of time and too depleted in numbers and resources to mount a counterattack. By 1885, when the final Métis rebellion was crushed, the contest for control of the continent was already over. Thereafter Canada continued to grow in population and prosper as a modern nation, whereas Aboriginal People went into population decline and were quietly placed at the edges of modern society. This became a time of recovery. As most of Canada's overt aggression had dwindled to benign neglect, the only item on Aboriginal People's agenda was survival. They became the vanishing race, and their near-absence from public discourse during much of the twentieth century seemed to confirm that notion.

The darkest days of declining population did not end until the 1920s, when the introduced diseases that had devastated Native communities finally abated. As late as 1932 Diamond Jenness was gloomily predicting the inevitable demise of Aboriginal People in his major compendium *The Indians of Canada*. When the "vanishing race" doctrine was translated into public policy it became the basis for the surrender of reserve lands. According to this logic, since fewer Indians occupied those "lands reserved for Indians" there was no need to set aside so much land.

Fortunately Aboriginal People outlived those sad expectations. The national census of 1931 confirmed what bureaucrats in the Department of Indian Affairs had suspected. As Indian agents assigned to the various reserves dutifully submitted accounts listing how many people were eligible for assistance, growing the number of status Indians became obvious. This unexpected turn even caused the federal government to rethink and abandon its land surrender policy. However, the "lands reserved for Indians" did not expand when the population rebounded beyond the original enrollments. Instead, they remained static in size, and the odious land surrenders later became the basis for many disputes. Where federal politicians had interpreted these events as their victory, history has revealed the onset of a century-long stalemate.

ABORIGINAL PEOPLE IN CANADA'S FIRST CENTURY

Since Canada's beginning in 1867, successive federal governments, like reluctant guardians of uninterested wards, have treated Aboriginal People with varying degrees of indifference, malice and support. Aboriginal People continue to be ambivalent about their identity as Canadians while Canadians seem genuinely hurt when Aboriginal People denounce them. When Matthew Coon Come, former Grand Chief of the northern Quebec Crees, successfully campaigned for the leadership of the Assembly of First Nations in 2000, he proclaimed: "I am not a Canadian!" For rejecting his citizenship, he was heaped with scorn in editorial columns across the nation. Others have taken a more conciliatory tack and are willing to work within the system to improve the quality of life in their communities. Elijah Harper, for example, a Cree from northern Manitoba, used his position as a member the Manitoba legislature to defeat the Meech Lake Accord during the summer of 1990.

Although Aboriginal People are compelled to deal with Canada, they have never developed strong emotional attachments to it. They find themselves unenthusiastic citizens of a nation that was created at their expense. They are more likely to announce their loyalty and emotional attachment to their First Nation than they are to Canada. When they express nationalistic sentiments, their imagined communities are the customary homelands that exist parallel to, but separate from, Canada. Aboriginal People have had difficulty accepting the epic narrative Canada fosters as the country's "official" history because they remember that their homelands were erased so Canada could be possible.

Canada's common culture is built on the idea of two founding nations (English and French), and government support for two official languages entrenches that idea. It does not mention the country's original inhabitants except in such commonly used phrases as "Canada's Aboriginal People" or "Canada's First Nations," which describe this relationship in possessive terms. Apparently Canada views its Aboriginal People in much the same manner that it regards its Crown lands and other resources, and this has led to the uneasy stalemate between them. However, the mutual interests acquired over centuries have created a symbiosis that is now integral to both parties. This is an artifact of Canada's national identity.

At Canada's birth, only the federal and provincial governments were given any role to exercise authority in the new country. When the powers of government were divided, Aboriginal People were conspicuously absent. They were mentioned in the British North America Act (now known as the Constitution Act, 1867) only when they were assigned their status as wards of the federal government, which was allotted responsibility for "Indians, and Lands reserved for Indians." For Indians, this decree came to mean a marginal existence lived within the impoverished borders of the paltry lands reserved for them. It also led to strong social, political and economic bonds with the federal state, but not with the provinces in which they resided.

As wards of the federal government, Aboriginal People were subject to separate legislation (the Indian Act, 1876) that defined them as legally different from all other Canadians. When the Indian Act was imposed, legislators were motivated by evolutionary theories of the time, which suggested that human cultures began in savagery, proceeded through barbarism and culminated with European civilization. With that scenario in mind, the legislators held that Aboriginal People were less developed than people of European descent, and had to be taught the ways of civilized society and be watched over by a benign guardian. The colonial-era Gradual Civilization Act of 1857 was the type of public policy that flowed from that world view, which the Indian Act of 1876 perpetuated. Although this evolutionary world view gradually fell out of fashion, government policy did not change. Anyone who balked at this outmoded cultural superiority complex only encountered the state's ability to impose its will.

Although the BNA Act made Aboriginal People wards of the state, the federal government entered into treaties with its domestic charges. The treaties followed a long tradition of such agreements by British colonial governments. The earliest were the "peace and friendship treaties," signed during the late seventeenth to late eighteenth centuries between the British and Aboriginal People of what is today Atlantic Canada. The British sought these agreements to forge political alliances with Native groups and gain their assistance in wars with the French. These early treaties did not involve purchase or surrender of the land, nor did they promise reserves or annuities. Once European settlement began in earnest, treaties shifted from "peace and friendship" to land surrenders. Between about 1780 and 1850 British authorities negotiated small land conveyance treaties with the First Nations of what was to become southern Ontario. These treaties varied greatly but often involved small, one-time payments. Only occasionally did they allocate reserves or guarantee hunting and fishing rights. Some were imprecise, such as the so-called "Gunshot Treaty" of 1787, which covered lands along the shores of Lake Ontario as far inland as a gunshot could be heard on a clear day.

In 1850 Commissioner W.B. Robinson was dispatched to Sault Ste. Marie to negotiate treaties with the Natives of the upper Great Lakes. Known as the Robinson-Superior and Robinson-Huron Treaties, they involved the surrender of large areas of land in exchange for reserves, lump-sum cash payments, annual payments to each member of the band and promises of hunting and fishing rights over unoccupied Crown lands. These large-scale treaties set the stage for the later federal treaties, which took similar form.

On the Pacific coast, the colony of Vancouver Island also began to purchase Aboriginal title to the land to make way for European settlement. James Douglas, as chief factor of the Hudson's Bay Company and governor of the colony, negotiated agreements with individual bands, extinguishing Aboriginal title to the lands around Victoria, Nanaimo and Fort Rupert between 1850 and 1854. In return for surrendering their land, which became "the Entire property of the White people for ever," the Natives were confirmed in possession of their village sites and fields, assured that they would be "at liberty to hunt over the unoccupied lands, and to carry on fisheries as formerly," and given small payments. The amounts were trifling: the entire Victoria area was obtained for 371 blankets. A shortage of funds kept Douglas from conducting further agreements, and most of British Columbia remained non-treaty.

After Confederation, the new Dominion of Canada began to assert its authority in the west. To construct a railway to the west coast and encourage agricultural settlement on the Prairies, the government sought to extinguish any Aboriginal claims to the land. The "numbered treaties" began with Treaty 1, affecting the Ojibwa and Cree of southern Manitoba, in 1871. By the time Treaty 7 was signed with the Blackfoot, Sarcee and Stoney of southern Alberta only six years later, the lands from western Lake Superior to the Rockies had been covered. Except for a northward addition to Treaty 6, treaty making came to a halt for twenty-two years, until gold and oil discoveries in the north brought about a new spate of negotiations. Treaty 8 in 1899 to Treaty 11 in 1921 removed Aboriginal title in northern Ontario, the rest of the Prairie provinces, northeastern British Columbia and the western half of the Northwest Territories. Finally, the Williams treaties of 1923, which extinguished Aboriginal title to the last unsurrendered lands in southern Ontario, brought the historic treaties to a close.

Although there were minor differences, all federal treaties were similar. Aboriginal People agreed to "cede, release, surrender, and yield up" their rights to the land in exchange for reserves, small cash payments, ammunition and fishing twine, uniforms and medals for the chiefs, annual payments to each band member and promises of continued hunting and fishing rights. For decades annual "treaty days" featured a government official flanked by uniformed Mounties dispensing payments. Members of treaty bands still receive an annual payment, amounting to only $5 per person under most treaties.

Aboriginal People received very little for surrendering nearly half of Canada's land surface to the federal government. Furthermore, there appear to be great differences between what Native People were told they were signing and the actual written words of the treaties. Gifts such as flags and medals enhanced the illusion that these were pacts of friendship and mutual assistance between nations, but the written provisions more closely resembled deeds of sale. First Nations today want the treaties interpreted in a broad perspective, reflecting the spirit in which they were signed. They maintain that treaties should be considered living documents that evolve and change in response to the shifting conditions of modern Canada, and that their treaty rights include the recognition of Aboriginal self-government.

That Aboriginal People did not enter Confederation on equal terms with other Canadians fuels their estrangement from Canadian society. Major policy initiatives consistently emanated from the view that Aboriginal People were incom-

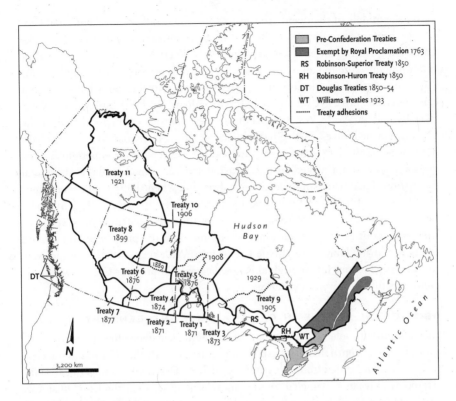

Pre-Confederation Treaties
Exempt by Royal Proclamation 1763
RS   Robinson-Superior Treaty 1850
RH   Robinson-Huron Treaty 1850
DT   Douglas Treaties 1850–54
WT   Williams Treaties 1923
······   Treaty adhesions

Treaty 11 1921
Treaty 10 1906
Treaty 8 1899
Hudson Bay
1908
DT
Treaty 6 1876
Treaty 5 1876
1929
1889
Treaty 9 1905
Treaty 7 1877
Treaty 4 1874
Treaty 2 1871
Treaty 1 1871
Treaty 3 1873
RS
RH
WT
Atlantic Ocean
N
3,200 km

ABOVE *Treaty areas in Canada*

petent to make decisions that would affect their communities, and unilateral government action in alienating and disposing of their lands and resources became symptomatic of Canada's policies. The first time Aboriginal rights became an issue at law was in the *St. Catherine's Milling and Lumber Company* case of 1888. Aboriginal People were not directly involved in this case, which was a boundary dispute between Ontario and the federal government. In attempting to assign the disputed lands to Manitoba, Canada argued that Aboriginal title had existed until Treaty 3 in 1873 transferred such rights to Canada. Once the court issued a ruling favouring Ontario, the federal government ignored First Nations, such as the Nisga'a in British Columbia, that were pressing their Aboriginal title claims.

As part of the terms of its union with Canada, British Columbia had relinquished control over Indian affairs to the federal government. The Aboriginal land question in that province clung tenaciously to the public agenda despite repeated attempts to brush it off. An Indian reserve commissioner was initially assigned the task of settling the issue in 1892, and a second commission with that task followed in 1912. When the commission's work was completed to the satisfaction of the federal and provincial governments, the Indian Act was amended to disallow use of the courts to pursue land claims.

By the middle of the twentieth century the quality of life for Aboriginal People was beginning to improve, albeit in minor ways. Before World War Two, the Canadian government easily legislated away all acts of protest. Indeed, it routinely amended the Indian Act to control even trivial aspects of daily life: legislating a prohibition on alcohol or a restriction on entering pool halls was not considered too intrusive on the daily life of Indians. With the outbreak of World War Two, as in World War One, thousands of Aboriginal men enlisted in the Canadian armed forces. Aboriginal soldiers returning to civilian life brought back new ideas about their relationship with their country: their experiences convinced them that unfinished business existed between Canada and the Aboriginal population. Their activism yielded one concession when the federal government committed itself to overhauling and modernizing the Indian Act. It delivered a revised statute in 1951 that removed some of the more discriminatory sections, such as the outlawing of traditional ceremonies and the prohibition on raising funds and hiring lawyers to pursue land claims. With such initiatives underway, the quality of justice for Aboriginal People began to improve as Canada was completing its first century of existence.

ABORIGINAL PEOPLE IN CANADA'S SECOND CENTURY

As Aboriginal People began to modernize they looked about for places to invest their dreams. Eventually their aspirations collided with the traditional government policies inherited from an earlier colonial era. Disoriented and perplexed Native political leaders struggled to offer something other than the usual business, and impatient youth in the young population refused to be the passive Indians of popular imagination. The spark of unrest brought on by the civil rights movement in the 1960s rekindled the urge for resistance. Inspired by the gains made by other oppressed people in modern North America, Aboriginal People in Canada were increasingly willing to challenge the *status quo*. They would no longer sit quietly by and allow the federal government to treat them as possessions.

While Canadians were celebrating the centennial of their country, Aboriginal People were becoming aware that Canada had systematically suppressed their rights to practice their natural autonomy. Within the first decade of its second century, Canada had to contend with Aboriginal People clamouring for self-determination. They organized protest marches, sit-ins, occupations, delegations to Ottawa and London, petitions to the Queen and blockades to oppose the federal government's injurious policies. Suddenly the angry activism of young Natives espousing "Red Power" replaced the common image of the stoic Indian. After the centennial celebrations wore off, Canadians woke up to Aboriginal People speaking out about unfinished business and trampled rights. These Aboriginal rights were not confined to those involving Aboriginal title. They also included the rights of individuals who were affected by official statutes, especially several clauses in the Indian Act that were the source of much discontent, particularly among Indian women.

ABORIGINAL RIGHTS AS HUMAN RIGHTS

The defining moment in the shift toward recognizing the rights of Aboriginal People took place during Canada's centennial year. On the evening of 8 April 1967, Joseph Drybones, a middle-aged Dene man, got drunk at the Old Stope Hotel in Yellowknife. After he was ejected from the hotel, he was picked up by the police and charged under section 94(b) of the Indian Act for being an Indian intoxicated off a reserve. Unlike other citizens of the Northwest Territories, who would have been charged under the Liquor Ordinance of the Northwest Territories, Joseph Drybones was prosecuted for being Indian. After World War Two, when the federal government had amended and ostensibly modernized the Indian Act, it retained the section that banned Indians from entering bars; possessing, drinking or making alcohol; or being drunk in public. Joseph Drybones was charged under this provision. Since he spoke no English, he pleaded guilty and was duly fined. Whether he understood the proceedings became a cause for appeal.

The procedural stages of justice brought his case before the territorial appeals courts where it was accepted that section 94(b) of the Indian Act was inconsistent with the Canadian Bill of Rights. The Crown then appealed that decision before the Supreme Court of Canada. The case rested upon the defendant being the target of two contradictory laws and being denied justice because of unequal treatment under the law.

The Canadian Bill of Rights was born on the election trail in 1957, as John Diefenbaker, then leader of the Progressive Conservative Party, campaigned for Prime Minister. After his election, on 1 July 1960, it was passed into law during a special session of Parliament. The Bill of Rights, however, lay in abeyance for almost a decade because of its implications concerning judicial activism until counsel for Joseph Drybones invoked it to support his case. Specifically, section 1 of the Bill of Rights guaranteed equality of all persons before the law and section 2 stated that laws would not infringe on personal freedoms based on race. Had Drybones been charged under the Liquor Ordinance of the Northwest Territories instead of the Indian Act, the sanction would have been less severe.

On 20 November 1969, the Supreme Court of Canada, in a six to three decision, struck down section 94(b) of the Indian Act as inconsistent with the Canadian Bill of Rights. The minority expressed the opinion that the entire Indian Act could be construed as discriminatory, and the Bill of Rights would then make the entire act inoperative. Their concerns were guided by the principle that the courts had no mandate to repeal legislation. The majority expressed the opinion that the Bill of Rights was merely a guide for interpreting a law of Canada and that rendering one clause inoperative would not completely demolish the Indian Act. The decision had an immediate effect on the lives of Aboriginal People. No longer could they be denied rights that other Canadians enjoyed, including the rights of mobility and the freedom to make their own choices.

The *Drybones* decision signalled the end of direct government control. Its influence, however, has not generally been fully appreciated, in part because it was overshadowed by a major public policy debate in the same year. Prime Minister Pierre Trudeau had come to power in 1968 and among his first acts as prime minister was a review of Canada's policy toward Aboriginal People. His Minister of Indian Affairs, Jean Chrétien, drafted the federal government's 1969 White Paper on Indian Policy, which proposed the abolition of special status for Indian People, the repeal of the Indian Act and the phasing out of federal administration over Indians. Stinging critiques, such as Cree politician Harold Cardinal's diatribe in his 1970 book *The Unjust Society*, branded this policy paper as a betrayal. Trudeau had opposed any special rights for one segment of society as anathema to a modern democracy. His "just society" was built on equality for all its members, and Aboriginal rights were seen as an encumbrance that denied full membership in society. The sharp debate jostled loose a century of pent-up Native resentments, and lack of recognition of Aboriginal and treaty rights led to the emergence of new and effective Aboriginal leaders who opposed the White Paper and forced its withdrawal. Shock waves from this failed policy were still being felt when the *Drybones* decision altered the state's fundamental relationship with Indians.

After nearly a century of learned dependency, Aboriginal People could finally enjoy the right to make their own choices. Christmas was the first holiday that many could legally celebrate with alcohol, and on New Year's Eve of 1969 they could openly toast the festivities. For many families, however, the 1970s ushered in a long decline into dysfunction. Alcohol abuse, violent crimes, broken families and fragmented communities became normal conditions on many reserves straining under years of economic neglect.

The changes began almost immediately. On the reserves, Native People were accustomed to taking orders from the Indian agents and often the local priest. When they suddenly had the option to decide for themselves where to live, many voted with their feet and left their reserves. There was little anyone could do to stop them. Women, long subjected to gender discrimination under the paternalistic Indian Act, challenged the definition of Indian. Under the act, a woman who married outside her band was required to enroll in the band of her husband. If she married a non-Indian, her Indian status was taken away by law. Ironically, a non-Native woman who married an Indian man became a status Indian in her husband's band. "Indian" was thus a legal category, which only partially corresponded to biological or cultural reality.

Jeannette Lavell, an Ojibwa from Manitoulin Island, and Sandra Lovelace, a Maliseet from the Tobique First Nation in New Brunswick, are among a number of First Nations women known for their courageous struggles to obtain gender equality. Shortly before the centennial of the Indian Act, Lavell challenged the legality of a statute that openly supported gender discrimination. After a successful appeal based on the Bill of Rights in a lower court, Lavell's case reached the Supreme Court of Canada in 1974. The court rejected her argument, ruling that the federal government had the authority to determine Indian status notwithstanding the Bill of Rights. This case was divisive for First Nations People; as most major Indian organizations opposed Lavell. With the White Paper of 1969 still fresh in the memories of those involved, they feared that a successful challenge to the Indian Act would give the federal government the excuse to revise or even repeal the act without the consent of Indian People. Blocked from further court challenge, Lovelace proceeded to take her case to the United Nations human rights tribunal. In 1981, Canada was found to be in violation of the international covenant on human rights. Although this was an embarrassment to Canada, the ruling could not force the federal government to alter its legislation.

Achieving justice for First Nations women had to wait until after 1982, when Canada's Constitution Act replaced the former British North America Act. Pierre Trudeau had secured the backing of Aboriginal leaders by promising to enshrine Aboriginal rights in the new constitution. However, when he found the provincial leaders would support his initiative if Aboriginal rights were not included, Trudeau backed out of his original promise. Aboriginal People quickly mobilized their energies to protest yet another betrayal by this prime minister. Through angry protest marches on Parliament Hill and on provincial capitals, they forced Canadian politicians to grudgingly agree to a compromise. As a result, section 35, "Rights of the Aboriginal Peoples of Canada," was inserted in the constitution. This brief section recognizes and affirms "existing Aboriginal and treaty rights." It further specifies that the Aboriginal Peoples of Canada are the Indians, Inuit and Métis. The Charter of Rights and Freedoms, which guaranteed equality for men and women, was an integral part of the constitutional package. This document became the supreme law of the land, and it was far different from the earlier Bill of Rights that had proved so impotent when confronted with gender discrimination in the Indian Act.

The Indian Act clearly conflicted with the Charter and had to be amended to conform. In April 1985 the federal government passed Bill C-31, which finally removed the discriminatory clauses that had so easily severed Indian status from Indian women. As a result, gaining or losing status through marriage is no longer possible. Bill C-31 also reinstated Indian status to all those who had lost it, plus their first generation offspring. The resultant surge in enrollment greatly swelled the status Indian population and placed considerable pressures on the lands and resources of First Nations across Canada.

ABORIGINAL RIGHTS AS LAND CLAIMS

Aboriginal People across the country pressed for their rights to hunt and fish and to receive some recognition and just settlement for their traditional lands that were never surrendered through treaty. Among the most persistent claimants were the Nisga'a of the Nass River valley in northwestern British Columbia. After the Indian Act was revised in 1951, Nisga'a Chief Frank Calder hired a young lawyer, Thomas Berger, to help represent the First Nation in a land claim case against the federal government. Calder and Berger's persistence through the next two decades culminated in an ambiguous judgement from a deeply divided

Supreme Court in the 1973 case known as *Calder v. the Attorney General of British Columbia.* Although the case was dismissed, the court's obvious division influenced the federal government to reverse its earlier reluctance to accept the concept of Aboriginal title. In 1974 the government released the Native claims policy paper entitled "In All Fairness," in which it articulated its new position. In the same year, the Office of Native Claims was opened in Ottawa with a mandate to deal with Aboriginal claims outside the courts. In 1980, the Supreme Court issued a ruling in the *Baker Lake* case, among the Inuit of what is now Nunavut, that established a test for determining if an Aboriginal title claim was valid. That legal test required Aboriginal groups to demonstrate that they were part of an organized society that had occupied the land and held it to the exclusion of all other people before English sovereignty was established over the area. In addition to comprehensive land claims based on unsurrendered Aboriginal title, the government also developed a mechanism for negotiating specific claims, which are based on breach of lawful obligation, such as unfulfilled treaty promises or improper alienation of reserve lands.

One significant outcome of the *Calder* decision and subsequent government policy shifts has been community evolution away from the Indian Act model of Aboriginal governance, which was more about control than responsible government. "Reserves are for Indians" used to be one of those slogans that neatly summed up the position of First Nations people in Canadian society. After the Northwest Rebellion of 1885, the federal government instituted a pass system that forced all Indians to obtain permission if they wished to leave their reserve. Controlling their movements and isolating them on reserves, especially in the west, reduced government concerns of unrest for the poor treatment that Indians received in Canada. This situation changed little throughout the first half of the twentieth century, when Aboriginal populations reached their nadir. Impeding out-migration from reserves and implementing effete policies and initiatives that tended to generate poverty became the legacy of the Indian Act. For example, the restrictive farming policy Indian Affairs applied on the Prairies emphasized horse power and hand tools long after neighbouring non-Native farmers became mechanized and industrial farming became common.

Once Aboriginal communities started to assume some control over their own governance, they began to experiment with different formulae in their relations with their federal administrator. After enjoying a century-long monologue the federal government has found it difficult to engage in dialogue, and it has been slow to surrender power to local communities. Nevertheless, Aboriginal People have persisted, and legal decisions such as in *Calder* and *Baker Lake* have amplified their aspirations. They have honed their political skills to reach final agreements that provide local control to replace such government institutions as the Indian Agent. Over time Indian reserves and their band governments have evolved into First Nations.

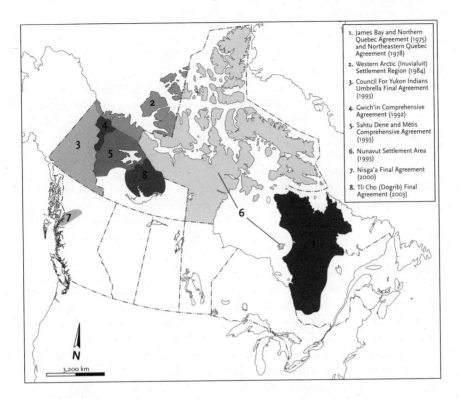

1. James Bay and Northern Quebec Agreement (1975) and Northeastern Quebec Agreement (1978)
2. Western Arctic (Inuvialuit) Settlement Region (1984)
3. Council For Yukon Indians Umbrella Final Agreement (1993)
4. Gwich'in Comprehensive Agreement (1992)
5. Sahtu Dene and Métis Comprehensive Agreement (1993)
6. Nunavut Settlement Area (1993)
7. Nisga'a Final Agreement (2000)
8. Tli Cho (Dogrib) Final Agreement (2003)

N

3,200 km

ABOVE *Comprehensive land claim settlement areas*

Implementing powers of responsible government began for the Cree and Inuit in Quebec with the 1975 James Bay and Northern Quebec Agreement. It was extended in 1978 to one group of Innu (the Naskapi of Schefferville). The principle of local self-government was consolidated in the Cree-Naskapi (of Quebec) Act in 1984. This model of village government and self-management introduced new modes of life among people who were accustomed to country foods and the bush economy. Village life came with a wage economy, white-collar and service jobs, and tourism, factors which led most people from their traditional lifeways. Within a decade hydroelectric development, industrial forestry and global economics dominated their communities. Their rapid adaptation to modern life was clearly demonstrated in their battle to stop further development projects. Their media campaign eventually caused the Quebec government to shelve its plans, at least temporarily, for massive hydroelectric projects across the north. From the start, the Cree, Inuit and Innu knew they could not keep the modern world at bay, but they pursued a land claim agreement to adopt this changing environment on their own terms.

Nearly a decade passed before another such agreement materialized. In 1984 the Inuvialuit of the Mackenzie delta and Beaufort Sea reached a settlement agreement with the federal government. It was the harbinger of the accelerating rate of political change in the north. The next decade ushered in final settlements with the Gwich'in (1992) and Sahtu Dene and Métis (1993) in the Northwest Territories, as well as the Umbrella Final Agreement with the Council for Yukon Indians (1993), which provided the framework under which individual Yukon First Nations reached final settlements. It also saw the Nunavut Final Agreement of 1993 that brought the territory of Nunavut into existence in 1999. The Tli Cho (Dogrib) Final Agreement of 2003 in the Northwest Territories is the most recent of the northern land claims settlements. With these agreements, settlement of Aboriginal claims across Canada's north nears completion.

For the Nisga'a, whose determined effort to assert their land claim had forced change upon the Canadian government, their century-long struggle ended favourably. After failing in the Supreme Court and being stonewalled by a hostile provincial government for decades, they finally achieved agreement with both levels of government. The "Nisga'a Treaty" became a reality only after the New Democratic Party, led by Premier Michael Harcourt, swept to power in 1992. His brand of social democracy was more sympathetic to Aboriginal People and their aspirations than the previous regime. He reversed the politically embedded policy of denial that successive governments had espoused since colonial times. The claim started by Frank Calder eventually fell to the younger shoulders of Joe Gosnell, who finally brought negotiations to a successful resolution in 1998. After all parties ratified it, the Nisga'a Final Agreement became law in 2000, and a new Nisga'a government came into being.

After reversing its policy, the provincial government proceeded with an ambitious agenda to settle Aboriginal land claims. As few historic treaties have been signed in British Columbia, this remains one of the largest areas of "unfinished business" between Aboriginal People and Canada. An accord between the federal and provincial governments and First Nations in the province in 1992 created the B.C. Treaty Commission to facilitate land claims negotiations. Although no treaties have yet been finalized under the treaty commission, many First Nations are in negotiations and several agreements-in-principle have been reached. Completed treaties will likely emerge from this process in the near future. The Sekani of McLeod Lake, in the northern interior of the province, pursued a different course that began with Treaty 8 encompassing their homeland. Although that treaty had ostensibly covered all of northeastern British Columbia in 1899, the Sekani had never signed it. A new agreement in 2000 compensated them for entitlements arising out of the historic treaty.

One important policy change is the type of land tenure arising from land claim settlements. Indian reserves, as defined in the Indian Act, are not the objective of Aboriginal groups pursuing land claims. Reserves were eighteenth- and nineteenth-century attempts to place Aboriginal lands under Crown title. The trend today is for settlement lands, owned and governed by Aboriginal communities. In some treaties different types of settlement lands are specified, with a lower category that may not confer ownership or provide subsurface rights. Another trend is for Aboriginal People to co-manage traditional lands, even outside the settlement area, so they can control issues of use and development, or to be members of various decision-making bodies concerning lands and resources.

JUMPING OFF THE BAND WAGON

Native People living on reserves have long pressed for some alternative to the restrictions of the Indian Act. Indian reserves ("reservation" is the American term) are lands set aside, according to the Indian Act, for the "use and benefit" of specific Indian bands. Title to the land, however, is held by the Crown, which makes the reserves pockets of federal jurisdiction within the provinces. Under the terms of the Indian Act, an Indian band cannot sell or otherwise dispose of reserve lands because the Crown holds the land title and only allows the Indians to use and occupy them. In some places Aboriginal People have come to own their lands through modern treaties, which transferred reserves into owned settlement lands. At present, the archaic concept of "Indians, and lands reserved for Indians," which stems from the British North America Act of 1867, is rapidly being transformed into a community of First Nations.

One of the earliest experiments to replace the Indian Act with community government and self-management was on the Sechelt Reserve, which lies beside the town of Sechelt in British Columbia. The Sechelt Indian Self-Government Act (1986) was unique in that it was not a land claim. It did not challenge provincial jurisdiction in a province that at that time did not recognize Aboriginal claims, but the bill did require companion legislation. The intent of the bill was to replace one act with another to facilitate local administration of Sechelt lands. The Sechelt received title to their reserve lands, the right to draft their own constitution and laws, and are no longer bound by the Indian Act. This successful experiment with self-government has allowed the Sechelt to prosper economically and culturally. The agreement applied only to Sechelt Reserve lands, however, and the Sechelt continue to pursue settlement for their broader traditional lands through the B.C. Treaty Commission process.

When Canadian governments agreed to include the statement on Aboriginal rights in the 1982 constitution, the federal government also agreed to host three constitutional conferences dedicated to defining them. Little progress resulted from the first and second conferences, and by the third one Trudeau had retired and a Progressive Conservative government led by Brian Mulroney had taken the reins of power. Provincial premiers refused to accept pleas to validate the Aboriginal right to self-government, claiming that it was too vague to implement as public policy. With provincial leaders demanding a precise definition, and revealing the extent of their opposition to Aboriginal rights, the last meeting disintegrated into acrimony and distrust. Aboriginal leaders took this rejection particularly hard as the constitutional option to enshrine self-government had been exhausted without achieving anything.

After the constitutional conferences on Aboriginal rights failed, the first ministers met once again in 1987 at the prime minister's country retreat at Meech Lake in the Gatineau hills. This time the objective was to clarify Quebec's status within the Canadian federation. Although the Aboriginal right to self-government had seemed too vague to be reconciled in the earlier meetings, Quebec's demand to be recognized as a distinct society, even without a precise definition, became the centrepiece of the Meech Lake Accord. It spelled out the minimum demands necessary to get Quebec's signature on the constitution. Prime Minister Brian Mulroney gambled that creating an atmosphere of crisis would force Quebecers and other Canadians to set aside their misgivings about the accord and agree to its conditions. He called the first ministers meeting mere weeks before its three-year deadline for ratification, hoping that the tight schedule would guarantee limited public debate and minimal opposition in the provincial legislatures. That strategy almost succeeded, except for two hold-out provinces: Newfoundland and Manitoba.

Manitoba's minority government meant that for the accord to pass it had to receive the legislature's unanimous consent before proceeding to committee and public hearings. One lone Cree MLA, Elijah Harper, from the Manitoba riding of Rupert's Land, adroitly manipulated the legislature's procedural rules to frustrate the federal government's plans. Desperate politicians shuttled between Ottawa and Winnipeg vainly seeking some last-minute deal with Aboriginal leaders in an effort to save the accord. Quebecers were simply stunned by its approaching failure. By refusing to pass the bill, Harper managed to delay it long enough to reach the deadline that effectively killed the Meech Lake Accord. This action impressed the concerns of Aboriginal People upon the Canadian public.

Canada still struggles to come to terms with Aboriginal People. The country has laudable stature on the world stage as a peacekeeper nation and champion of human rights. Yet Canadian politicians could only bristle when Glenn Babb, the South African ambassador to Canada, visited the Peguis Indian Reserve in southern Manitoba in 1987. Canada, which had consistently denounced South Africa's apartheid regime, suddenly found itself in a debate over who had the more abusive policy toward Aboriginal People within its borders. After telling themselves for generations that what they were doing for Aboriginal People was right, Canadians were genuinely surprised to be singled out for criticism by the international community. The constitutional conference debacle was just one more example of Canada's refusal to accommodate the aspirations of Aboriginal People.

Aboriginal rights, however, have never been defined and uncertainty remains about which rights enjoy the protection of the constitution. The first case involving Aboriginal rights under section 35 reached the Supreme Court of Canada in 1990. Ronald Sparrow of the Musqueam First Nation in British Columbia was charged with fishing illegally for salmon on the Fraser River. He was acquitted by the court, which ruled that his Aboriginal right to fish had priority over restrictive fishing laws. Since then several lawsuits, including the important *Delgamuukw* case, have reached the Supreme Court to test the limits of Aboriginal law. Such cases have added clarity to the phrase "existing Aboriginal rights," and broadened the scope of traditional land claims.

Today Canada contains approximately 2300 reserves, though the number varies according to historical circumstances and government policy. Of these, over 1600 are in British Columbia. This reflects a different history of reserve allocation, rather than any huge Aboriginal land base. In British Columbia each band received various small seasonal village and camp locations as reserves, on a per capita formula far below that used for the federal treaties across the rest of western Canada. As a result, each First Nation today holds several reserves, which tend to be small, scattered and in many cases economically useless. Some, however, such as the Musqueam and Kamloops First Nations, are situated near large urban areas, where they can pursue a range of economic enterprises. Similar circumstances across the country have stimulated First Nations economic development. Urban sprawl has reached and encircled many formerly isolated communities, transforming them by default into urban reserves.

Many First Nations must contend with urbanization. Typically, existing reserve lands were set aside when Aboriginal populations were at their smallest, so any increase in number would initiate a land crisis. As their populations have grown, many Native People have moved from their reserves to urban Canada, but in many cases those remaining on-reserve also have to adjust to higher-density living. The Kahnawake First Nation outside Montreal, for example, has more than 7000 people living on-reserve. Given the reserve's proximity to the city, and the network of bridges, highways, railways and seaways that now crisscross its land, Kahnawake resembles many of the surrounding bedroom communities that discharge commuters into Montreal daily. On other reserves in or close to urban centres, such as that of the Kamloops First Nation, bands are actively developing their land to encourage leasehold sales in residential subdivisions. The target market for the Kamloops band's upscale houses is not its own members, but rather well-off buyers from the general population. The band expects to build on its previous success leasing parcels of land as an industrial park and business district servicing the city of Kamloops.

New urban reserves have been created in the late twentieth century as compensation for unfulfilled treaty land entitlements or as a result of the old reserve land surrender policy. This innovative experiment with urban reserves has taken place primarily in Saskatchewan. For example, a new urban reserve was established in Prince Albert in 1982, when the Peter Ballentyne Cree Nation chose forty-one acres in compensation for an earlier surrender. Generally commercial in nature rather than residential, these urban reserves allow bands to develop economically and to benefit from opportunities in neighbouring municipal economies. Tax exemptions under the Indian Act for income earned on the reserve provide further incentives. Such an environment nurtures an entrepreneurial culture that professionally qualified band members can use to good advantage. Aboriginal People are becoming an invigorating force in the municipal economy, as business owners and as employers of both band members and other local citizens.

THE STALEMATE WITH CANADA

Changes wrought by the *Drybones* and *Calder* decisions still reverberate across Aboriginal communities more than three decades later. The traditional relationship between the federal guardian and the Aboriginal ward has been fundamentally altered. As Aboriginal People and government officials continue to struggle over control, the nature of the game continually changes.

Although a game is an imperfect analogy for historical relations between Aboriginal People and Canada—and considering Aboriginal history in terms of a contest between rival powers is not meant to trivialize that experience—it is a useful analytical tool. As players in the grand game of history, Aboriginal People have reached a stalemate with their opponents. When they consider their options, cultural survival is too defeatist and narrow in focus, whereas struggle and resistance have exhausted their potential. The objective this time is not about liberation or declaring victory, it is about finding a new way to live with Canada. To move toward this new goal, Aboriginal People need a new strategy.

Several paradoxes orbit this stalemate, adding to its complexity. First, the federal and provincial governments have already wrested effective control of Canada, but the dispossessed Aboriginal People continue to influence the development plans slated for their traditional lands. Second, Aboriginal People constitute an ultraminority within the general population, yet they legitimately command a disproportionately large share of public discourse. Third, Aboriginal issues are near the top of the public policy agenda at the same time as Aboriginal People are marginalized. Finally, there are too few Aboriginal People to direct change to their advantage, but at the same time they are too robust to be dismissed.

Glimpses of this stalemate can be instructive by what they reveal of the bigger picture. The remnants of armed resistance that began many generations ago flared once again during the standoff at Oka, Quebec. The events during the summer of 1990 encapsulated the stalemate between Canada and Aboriginal People. They also revealed the ultimate futility of armed resistance today. When the Mohawk community of Kanesatake was forced to take up arms to defend land they considered theirs, they had no plan beyond stopping developers from turning the contested land with their community's cemetery into a golf course. When hostilities escalated into an armed standoff, the Mohawk had no strategy for getting out of the game. Their defensive situation provided few options, which ensured that the game would inevitably dissolve into chaos and arrest. Therein lies the modern conundrum for Aboriginal People. They find themselves in a stalemate with their opponent: they are not willing to admit defeat and assimilate, but there is no point to fantasies about the end of non-Native rule.

When the Canadian army finally got involved at Oka, it had all the advantages and its field commanders had an explicit order: end the standoff, if possible without casualties. Their strategy was to surround and isolate the warriors and continually shrink the perimeter. In the waning days of summer, the end of the game arrived when the Canadian army claimed its checkmate. The warriors had to content themselves with a moral victory and all the benefits that flow from that.

A subsequent documentary film deftly captured the spirit of that time. Alanis Obomsawin, a noted First Nations (Abenaki) filmmaker and activist, wrote and directed this documentary. Its title, *Kanehsatake: 270 Years of Resistance!*, spoke to the sentiments that have fuelled the Aboriginal struggle since economic interests collided with political hegemony. After the game, when the warriors were arrested and led away, yet again to face the victor's justice, the resistance became a struggle against the hopelessness and ennui that follow capitulation. Struggle and resistance have consumed the energies of generations of freedom fighters, but events such as at Oka, or the confrontations at Gustafson Lake, British Columbia, and Ipperwash, Ontario, in 1995, suggest that this option is no longer viable.

Aboriginal People have inherited a culture of resistance and a legacy of heroes and martyrs, so to speak of surrender now would be to betray those ancestors who gave their lives to the resistance. To abandon the struggle now is to admit defeat, and no one is prepared to do that. Surrender is undesirable because it is the first step toward assimilation, which is as unpalatable as ever. Even integration into the larger society with recognition of a distinct Aboriginal identity, which has been offered as a gesture of accommodation, is rejected as little more than soft-core assimilation. Therefore, identifying a common vision that can absorb the energies of future generations is the greater challenge in the present. It means asking questions such as: Is assimilation the only option? What lies beyond struggle and resistance? One possible answer is colonization, a process leading to Aboriginal People becoming significant political and economic participants in Canada's urban centres. The term "colonization" conjures negative images of the European model, which was so disastrous for Aboriginal People. However, Aboriginal People can consider the manner in which their ancient ancestors first colonized *terra nullius*. The slow deliberate expansion of people at the end of the Ice Age stands in contrast to the intrusive, hegemonic colonialism of recent history.

COLONIZING CANADA

Colonization is not a future objective, it is already occurring. Aboriginal People began colonizing urban Canada shortly after the centennial celebrations abated. The trajectory away from wardship began with the *Drybones* decision, and each decade since then has contributed to a new and markedly different relationship with Canada than in its first century. The original decision allowed Aboriginal People to make personal choices about alcohol, which had been banned by law. The results were mixed. Many Aboriginal People exercised this new right to make decisions, yet the immediate effect was chaos as communities adjusted to the devastating effects of chronic alcohol abuse. Suddenly "drunk Indians" were all too common on skid row. They may have been disoriented, but they were the first generation to think outside of the reserve and to colonize urban Canada. Although the freedom to choose all too often led to the familiar themes of family dysfunction and systemic violence, street people and broken lives, it really did change the thinking of the second generation.

The idea of choice also spread to education. Before 1969, First Nations education was still largely coupled with religious denominations in church-run residential schools. These institutions reflected the assimilationist goals of earlier times: Children were punished for speaking their own languages or for practising Aboriginal customs, and discouraged from having contact with their families or home communities. The residential school experience has left a bitter legacy of lost traditions and broken families for First Nations People. Secular education in public schools soon replaced these obsolete halls of learning, and the improved educational opportunities allowed many Aboriginal students to overcome the barriers that had kept them from post-secondary education. By the 1980s Aboriginal People increasingly ventured onto university and college campuses in Canada, where they earned diplomas and degrees that enhanced their personal economic security. A better education meant better career choices, and an actual Aboriginal middle class began to emerge. Not only did these Aboriginal People develop middle class values, they broke the poverty cycle and encouraged others to do the same.

At present, the Aboriginal middle class still comprises a modest slice of the demographic pie. However, like the Aboriginal population as a whole, it is growing. With wealth comes more economic clout, and as this group matures it will demand greater attention as a political constituency. Its members will direct the Aboriginal population's urban agenda, and form a professional bloc on reserves and in remote communities. Motivated by relative economic security, the Aboriginal middle class has tended to abandon the rhetoric of struggle and resistance and reject such protests as roadblocks, which pose considerable risk to the participants. Typically these actions have involved disaffected youths who were defying the patience of their elders and leaders to press their cause. However, such actions also invite the state to demonstrate its power to impose its will, and participants risk arrest and costly legal actions.

Colonization is a subversive, middle-class ideology. It does not depend on direct actions that could jeopardize economic security; it succeeds by infiltrating the extant infrastructure of urban life. In fact colonization is already well underway. Approximately 43 per cent of the status Indian population in Canada lives off-reserve, and the number increases each year. Although this demographic shift is evident in all major Canadian cities, it is particularly noticeable in such Prairie centres as Winnipeg, Regina and Edmonton. Saskatchewan has established urban reserves, and that province has had a long history of exporting its public policy initiatives to other jurisdictions in Canada.

Another type of urban colony results from comprehensive land claims, such as the Nisga'a Final Agreement in British Columbia. That agreement provides one model for constituting an urban colony and imbuing it with real political power. Nisga'a self-governance recognizes members who live away from the Nass River valley homeland but who are entitled to its benefits. Many Nisga'a living in urban areas can participate in the governance structure through urban locals established in Prince Rupert, Terrace and Vancouver. These urban locals are like chapters in a union; they each have an executive that is analogous to the union's stewards.

From experiments in democracy such as these, Aboriginal politicians will move into civic and provincial politics. As Aboriginal voters in larger cities begin to coalesce around common concerns, they will begin to influence mainstream politics. The Aboriginal middle class will lay the groundwork for the next phase of colonization: taking control of the reins of power.

EPILOGUE

Three and a half decades after the *Drybones* decision, the third generation of Aboriginal People to inherit the legacy is already active. When they come of age after 2009, many of them will make up a political class that participates actively in civic and provincial politics. Early indications are evident already at places such as Simon Fraser University in British Columbia, where the student body elected Wade Dorvault, a member of the Gitksan First Nation, as president of the student society in 2003. He is among the leading edge of emerging Aboriginal politicians who will exemplify the strengths of traditional cultures transplanted into urban Canada. As the urban Aboriginal population grows, it will eventually reach a critical mass, which will organize politically to effect change in their urban communities.

Although Frank Calder, the Nisga'a chief, held a seat in the British Columbia legislature, with only a brief interruption, from 1949 to 1979, his experience can only be described as anomalous. Elijah Harper in Manitoba is another example of a prominent Aboriginal politician elected to a provincial legislature. In general, however, few Aboriginal candidates appear on the ballot when provincial elections are called. That situation is about to change. Urban Aboriginal People are presently dispersed throughout the general population so they do not typically constitute a bloc of voters. However, as more and more Aboriginal People move into cities, they will mobilize and they will nominate candidates who appeal to the general electorate for civic and provincial politics. Then, Canadians will be surprised to hear that a major Canadian city, perhaps Winnipeg or Regina, has elected an Aboriginal mayor. Before 2029, at the end of the third generation, an Aboriginal premier may well be elected in one of the provinces.

Perhaps the most serious challenge ahead lies not in the political sphere, but in the personal health of average citizens. Aboriginal People carry a disproportionately large burden of poor health for their population size. Many of the illnesses that afflict them come from lifestyles associated with poverty and substance abuse. Unfortunately, Aboriginal People have become all too familiar with the damage that alcohol can inflict on a developing foetus. Chronic poverty still characterizes too many Aboriginal communities.

The switch from country foods to fast foods in one or two generations has led to an epidemic of metabolic disorders, such as obesity, diabetes, gall-bladder diseases and cancers of the digestive system. Some claim this "New World Syndrome" of metabolic disease is genetic in origin. Through cycles of famine and plenty, the hypothesis goes, nature selected for Aboriginal People the so-called "thrifty" gene, which adapted the body's metabolism for extended periods of hunger. Now that there are no cyclical famines, the "thrifty" gene is detrimental. Although such genetic explanations have merit, metabolic disease is also an affliction of poverty. A healthy lifestyle and proper diet can go a long way toward preventing it. Some disturbing trends related to viral diseases are also starting to appear. Just as smallpox weakened Aboriginal populations in centuries past, HIV/AIDS and emergent pathogens such as SARS threaten to do the same in the twenty-first century.

What's next? Perhaps the upcoming generation will finally witness the demise of the Indian Act, though that document has been remarkably tenacious despite various attempts to replace it. Most recently, the failure of the unpopular First Nations Governance Act initiative, endorsed by Jean Chrétien during his final term as prime minister but rejected by his successor, Paul Martin, suggests that the Indian Act will be around for another generation. Nevertheless, the momentum of change almost assures that the Indian Act will eventually be removed. In the meantime, First Nations will continue to negotiate their way out from under the constraints of the Indian Act, as the Sechelt did in 1986 and as other First Nations have accomplished through land claim settlements. Those First Nations with historic treaties may succeed in negotiating updated and modernized treaties that reflect their new relationship with Canada. Perhaps this is the generation that will witness the election of an Aboriginal premier. They might even see the day when the governor general is Aboriginal or when an Aboriginal judge is appointed to the Supreme Court. They may even witness the Assembly of First Nations evolve into some form of governmental entity.

The fifth generation after *Drybones* will appear in 2049. Although we can only speculate, theirs will be the group that establishes its own distinct institutions within the fabric of Canadian society. It will be the generation to witness the completion of Canada's second century. Beyond that lies the future.

. . . . .

CHAPTER ONE *Anthropological Research and Aboriginal People*
The classic ethnographic study of Canadian First Nations, though now badly out of
date, is that of Jenness (1977, originally published in 1932). Miller (2000) and Dickason (2002) provide historical overviews. Brizinski (1993) has developed an introduc-
tory text for Native Studies. Articles on Aboriginal groups across Canada appear in
books of readings edited by Magocsi (2002), Morrison and Wilson (2004), Fisher and
Coates (1996), and Cox (1988).

A popular account of early Native life as seen through archaeology is given in
McGhee (1989). Wright (1995, 1999) provides a detailed synthesis of Canada's archaeological past to AD 500.

Swayze (1960) reviews the lives of three prominent Canadian anthropologists: Diamond Jenness, Marius Barbeau and W.J. Wintemberg. Nowry (1995) provides a detailed study of Marius Barbeau, as does Cole (1999) for Franz Boas. Dyck and Waldram
(1993) and Hedican (1995) examine the applied role of the anthropologist in public
policy involving Aboriginal Peoples.

Brizinski, Peggy. 1993. *Knots in a String: An Introduction to Native Studies in Canada.*
2nd ed. Saskatoon: University Extension Press, University of Saskatchewan.
Campbell, Lyle, and Marianne Mithun, eds. 1979. *The Languages of Native America:
Historical and Comparative Assessment.* Austin: University of Texas Press.
Cole, Douglas. 1999. *Franz Boas: The Early Years, 1859–1906.* Vancouver: Douglas &
McIntyre.
Cox, Bruce A., ed. 1988. *Native People, Native Lands: Canadian Indians, Inuit and Metis.*
Ottawa: Carleton University Press.
Dewdney, Selwyn, and Franklin Arbuckle. 1975. *They Shared to Survive: The Native
Peoples of Canada.* Toronto: Macmillan.

Dickason, Olive P. 2002. *Canada's First Nations: A History of Founding Peoples from Earliest Years.* 3rd ed. Toronto: McClelland & Stewart.

Dyck, Noel, and James B. Waldram, eds. 1993. *Anthropology, Public Policy and Native Peoples in Canada.* Montreal and Kingston: McGill-Queen's University Press.

Fisher, Robin, and Kenneth Coates, eds. 1996. *Out of the Background: Readings on Canadian Native History.* 2nd ed. Toronto: Copp Clark Pitman.

Foster, Michael K. 1982. "Canada's first languages." *Language and Society* 7: 7–16.

Hedican, Edward J. 1995. *Applied Anthropology in Canada: Understanding Aboriginal Issues.* Toronto: University of Toronto Press.

Jenness, Diamond. 1977. *The Indians of Canada.* 7th ed. Toronto: University of Toronto Press.

Kehoe, Alice B. 1992. *North American Indians: A Comprehensive Account.* 2nd ed. Englewood Cliffs, NJ: Prentice-Hall.

McGhee, Robert. 1989. *Ancient Canada.* Ottawa: Canadian Museum of Civilization.

Magocsi, Paul Robert, ed. 2002. *Aboriginal Peoples of Canada: A Short Introduction.* Toronto: University of Toronto Press.

Miller, J.R. 2000. *Skyscrapers Hide the Heavens: A History of Indian-White Relations in Canada.* 3rd ed. Toronto: University of Toronto Press.

Morrison, David A. 1992. *Arctic Hunters: The Inuit and Diamond Jenness.* Hull, QC: Canadian Museum of Civilization.

Morrison, R. Bruce, and C. Roderick Wilson, eds. 2004. *Native Peoples: The Canadian Experience.* 3rd ed. Don Mills, ON: Oxford University Press.

Nowry, Laurence. 1995. *Marius Barbeau: Man of Mana.* Toronto: NC Press.

Price, John. 1979. *Indians of Canada: Cultural Dynamics.* Scarborough, ON: Prentice-Hall.

Rohner, Ronald P., ed. 1969. *The Ethnography of Franz Boas.* Chicago: University of Chicago Press.

Swayze, Nansi. 1960. *The Man Hunters: Famous Canadian Anthropologists.* Toronto: Clarke, Irwin.

Wright, J.V. 1995. *A History of the Native People of Canada: Volume 1 (10,000–1,000 BC).* Hull, QC: Canadian Museum of Civilization.

———. 1999. *A History of the Native People of Canada: Volume 2 (1,000 BC–AD 500).* Hull, QC: Canadian Museum of Civilization.

CHAPTER TWO *Terra Nullius: The Land That Was Empty*

A considerable body of literature exists for this topic. Recent overviews include those by Dillehay (2000), Dixon (1999) and Meltzer (1993). A detailed study of Beringia is given in West (1996). Fagan (1987) provides a popular volume on the peopling of the Americas, and Koppel (2003) gives a journalist's perspective on recent evidence for the coastal route.

Bonnichsen, Robson, and K.L. Turnmire, eds. 1991. *Clovis: Origins and Adaptations.* Corvallis, OR: Center for the Study of the First Americans, Oregon State University.

———, eds. 1999. *Ice Age People of North America: Environments, Origins and Adaptations.* Corvallis, OR: Center for the Study of the First Americans, Oregon State University Press.

Bryan, Alan L., ed. 1978. *Early Man in America from a Circum-Pacific Perspective.* Occasional Papers No. 1 of the Department of Anthropology, University of Alberta, Edmonton.

Buchner, A.P. 1981. *Sinnock: a Paleolithic Camp and Kill Site in Manitoba.* Papers in Manitoba Archaeology, Department of Cultural Affairs and Historical Resources, Historic Resources Branch, Winnipeg.

Carlisle, R.C., ed. 1988. *Americans Before Columbus: Ice-Age Origins.* University of Pittsburgh Ethnology Monographs 12, Pittsburgh.

Chapdelaine, Claude, ed. 1994. *Il y a 8000 Ans à Rimouski: Paléoécologie et Archéologie d'un Site de la Culture Plano.* Paléo-Québec No. 22, Recherches Amérindiennes au Québec, Montreal.

Cinq-Mars, J. 1979. "Bluefish Cave I: a late Pleistocene eastern Beringian cave deposit in the northern Yukon." *Canadian Journal of Archaeology* 3: 1–32.

Crawford, Michael H. 1998. *The Origins of Native Americans: Evidence from Anthropological Genetics.* Cambridge: Cambridge University Press.

Dillehay, Thomas D. 2000. *The Settlement of the Americas: A New Prehistory.* New York: Basic Books.

Dixon, E. James. 1999. *Bones, Boats & Bison: Archeology and the First Colonization of Western North America.* Albuquerque: University of New Mexico Press.

Driver, Jonathan C. 1998. "Human adaptations at the Pleistocene/Holocene boundary in western Canada, 11,000 to 9000 BP." *Quaternary International* 49/50: 141–50.

———. 1999. "Raven skeletons from Paleoindian contexts, Charlie Lake Cave, British Columbia." *American Antiquity* 64(2): 289–98.

Ellis, Christopher, and D. Brian Deller. 2000. *An Early Paleo-Indian Site Near Parkhill, Ontario.* Mercury Series, Archaeological Survey of Canada Paper 159, Canadian Museum of Civilization, Hull, QC.

———. 2002. *Excavations at the Caradoc Site (AfHj-104): A Late Paleo-Indian Ritual Artifact Deposit.* Occasional Papers of the London Chapter, Ontario Archaeological Society, London, ON.

Fagan, Brian M. 1987. *The Great Journey: The Peopling of Ancient America.* London: Thames and Hudson.

Fedje, D., J.M. White, M.C. Wilson, D.E. Nelson, J.S. Vogel, and J.R. Southon. 1995. "Vermilion Lakes site: adaptations and environments in the Canadian Rockies during the latest Pleistocene and early Holocene." *American Antiquity* 60(1): 81–108.

Fladmark, Knut R. 1979. "Routes: alternate migration corridors for early man in North America." *American Antiquity* 44(1): 55–69.

———. 1981. "Paleo-Indian artifacts from the Peace River district." In *Fragments of the Past: British Columbia Archaeology in the 1970s,* ed. K.R. Fladmark, 124–35. *B.C. Studies* 48.

Fladmark, Knut R., Jonathan C. Driver, and Diana Alexander. 1988. "The Paleoindian component at Charlie Lake Cave (HbRf 39), British Columbia." *American Antiquity* 53(2): 371–84.

Forbis, Richard G. 1968. "Fletcher: a Paleo-Indian site in Alberta." *American Antiquity* 33(1): 1–10.

Fox, W.A. 1980. "The Lakehead Complex: new insights." In *Collected Archaeological Papers*, ed. D.S. Melvin, 117–51. Archaeological Research Report 13, Ontario Ministry of Culture and Recreation, Historical Planning and Research Branch, Toronto.

Gramly, Richard M. 1982. *The Vail Site: a Paleo-Indian Encampment in Maine.* Buffalo, NY: Bulletin of the Buffalo Society of Natural Sciences.

Greenberg, Joseph H. 1987. *Language in the Americas.* Palo Alto, CA: Stanford University Press.

Greenberg, Joseph H., and Merritt Ruhlen. 1992. "Linguistic origin of Native Americans." *Scientific American* (Nov.) 94–99.

Greenberg, Joseph H., Christy G. Turner II, and Stephen L. Zegura. 1986. "The settlement of the Americas: a comparison of the linguistic, dental, and genetic evidence." *Current Anthropology* 27: 477–97.

Gryba, Eugene M. 1983. *Sibbald Creek: 11,000 Years of Human Use of the Alberta Foothills.* Archaeological Survey of Alberta, Occasional Paper No. 22, Edmonton.

———.1985. "Evidence of the fluted point tradition in Alberta." In *Contributions to Plains Prehistory*, ed. D. Burley, 22–38. Archaeological Survey of Alberta, Occasional Paper No. 26, Edmonton.

Haynes, C. Vance Jr. 1966. "Elephant hunting in North America." *Scientific American* 214(6): 104–12.

Haynes, Gary. 2002, *The Early Settlement of North America: The Clovis Era.* Cambridge: Cambridge University Press.

Hoffecker, J.F., W.R. Powers, and T. Goebel. 1993. "The colonization of Beringia and the peopling of the New World." *Science* 259: 46–53.

Hopkins, David M., John V. Matthews Jr., Charles E. Schweger, and Steven B. Young, eds. 1982. *Paleoecology of Beringia.* New York: Academic Press.

Jablonski, Nina G., ed. 2002. *The First Americans: The Pleistocene Colonization of the New World.* Memoirs of the California Academy of Sciences No. 27, San Francisco.

Julig, P.J. 1984. "Cummins Paleo-Indian site and its paleoenvironment, Thunder Bay, Canada." *Archaeology of Eastern North America* 12: 192–209.

Kehoe, Thomas F. 1966. "The distribution and implications of fluted points in Saskatchewan." *American Antiquity* 31(4): 530–39.

Kooyman, B., M.E. Newman, C. Cluney, M. Lobb, S. Tolman, P. McNeil, and L.V. Hills. 2001. "Identification of horse exploitation by Clovis hunters based on protein analysis." *American Antiquity* 66(4): 686–91.

Koppel, Tom. 2003. *Lost World: Rewriting Prehistory—How New Science is Tracing America's Ice Age Mariners.* New York: Atria Books.

MacDonald, George F. 1968. *Debert: A Paleo-Indian Site in Central Nova Scotia.* Anthropological Papers No. 16, National Museums of Canada, Ottawa.

McGhee, Robert. 1989. "Who owns prehistory? The Bering Land Bridge Dilemma." *Canadian Journal of Archaeology* 13: 13–20.

Mandyk, Carole A.S., Heiner Josenhans, Daryl W. Fedje, and Rolf W. Mathewes. 2001. "Late Quaternary Paleoenvironments of Northwestern North America: Implications for Inland versus Coastal Migration Routes." *Quaternary Science Reviews* 20: 301–14.

Martin, P.S., and H.E. Wright Jr., eds. 1967. *Pleistocene Extinctions: The Search for a Cause.* New Haven, CT: Yale University Press.

Meltzer, David R. 1993. "Pleistocene peopling of the Americas." *Evolutionary Anthropology* 1(5): 157–69.

Morlan, Richard E. 1977. "Fluted point makers and the extinction of the arctic-steppe biome in eastern Beringia." *Canadian Journal of Archaeology* 1: 95–108.

Pettipas, Leo 1985. "Recent developments in Paleo-Indian archaeology in Manitoba." In *Contributions to Plains Prehistory*, ed. D. Burley, 39–63. Archaeological Survey of Alberta Occasional Paper No. 26, Edmonton.

Roberts, Arthur. 1985. *Preceramic Occupations along the North Shore of Lake Ontario.* National Museum of Man Mercury Series, Archaeological Survey of Canada Paper No. 132, Ottawa.

Shutler, Richard Jr., ed. 1983. *Early Man in the New World.* Beverly Hills and London: Sage Publications.

Stork, P.L. 1979. *A Report on the Banting and Hussey Sites: Two Paleo-Indian Campsites in Simcoe County, Southern Ontario.* National Museum of Man Mercury Series, Archaeological Survey of Canada Paper No. 93, Ottawa.

———. 1982. "Paleo-Indian settlement patterns associated with the strandline of Glacial Lake Algonquin in southcentral Ontario." *Canadian Journal of Archaeology* 6: 1–31.

———. 1984. "Glacial Lake Algonquin and early Paleo-Indian settlement patterns in southcentral Ontario." *Archaeology of Eastern North America* 12: 286–98.

Szathmary, Emöke J.E. 1993a. "Genetics of aboriginal North Americans." *Evolutionary Anthropology* 1: 202–20.

———. 1993b. "MtDNA and the peopling of the Americas." *American Journal of Human Genetics* 53: 793–99.

West, Frederick Hadleigh, ed. 1996. *American Beginnings: The Prehistory and Paleoecology of Beringia.* Chicago: University of Chicago Press.

CHAPTER THREE *The Atlantic Provinces*

The archaeology of Atlantic Canada is discussed in two books by Tuck: *Newfoundland and Labrador Prehistory* (1976a) and *Maritime Provinces Prehistory* (1984). In addition, Tuck (1976b) provides a detailed account of the Port au Choix cemetery.

Most of our information on traditional Mi'kmaq life comes from the seventeenth-century accounts. Particularly important are those of Biard in the *Jesuit Relations* (Thwaites 1896–1901), Lescarbot (1907–14; originally published 1609), Denys (1908; originally published 1672) and LeClercq (1910; originally published 1691). An early published ethnography on the Mi'kmaq is by Wallis and Wallis (1955). For the Beothuk, the major sources are Howley (1915) and Marshall (1996). Summary articles on the Beothuk, Mi'kmaq and Maliseet in the Northeast volume of *Handbook of North American Indians* (Trigger 1978) are also useful. A Mi'kmaq perspective on the clash of cultures is given by Paul (2000).

Bailey, Alfred G. 1969. *The Conflict of European and Eastern Algonkian Cultures, 1504–1700.* 2nd ed. Toronto: University of Toronto Press.

Bartels, Dennis. 1991. "Newfoundland Micmac claims to land and 'status.'" *Native Studies Review* 7(2): 43–51.

Bock, Philip K. 1966. *The Micmac Indians of Restigouche: History and Contemporary Description.* National Museum of Canada, Bulletin No. 213, Ottawa.

Carignan, Paul. 1975. *The Beaches: A Multi-Component Habitation Site in Bonavista Bay.* National Museum of Man Mercury Series, Archaeological Survey of Canada Paper No. 39, Ottawa.

———. 1977. *Beothuck Archaeology in Bonavista Bay.* National Museum of Man Mercury Series, Archaeological Survey of Canada Paper No. 69, Ottawa.

Coates, Ken S. 2000. *The Marshall Decision and Native Rights.* Montreal and Kingston: McGill-Queens University Press.

Davis, Stephen. 1978. *Teacher's Cove: A Prehistoric Site on Passamaquoddy Bay.* New Brunswick Archaeology Series 1, No. 1, Fredericton.

———. 1991. *Micmac.* Tantallon, NS: Four East Publications.

Denys, Nicolas. 1908. *The Description and Natural History of the Coasts of North America (Acadia).* Toronto: Champlain Society.

Dickason, Olive P. 1976. *Louisbourg and the Indians: A Study in Imperial Race Relations, 1713–1760.* History and Archaeology No. 6, Parks Canada, Ottawa.

Fitzhugh, William W. 1972. *Environmental Archaeology and Cultural Systems in Hamilton Inlet, Labrador.* Smithsonian Contributions to Anthropology No. 16, Smithsonian Institution Press, Washington.

———. 1975. "A Maritime Archaic sequence from Hamilton Inlet, Labrador." *Arctic Anthropology* XII(2): 117–38.

———. 1978a. "Maritime Archaic cultures of the central and northern Labrador coast." *Arctic Anthropology* XV(2): 61–95.

———. 1978b. "Winter Cove 4 and the Point Revenge occupation of the central Labrador coast." *Arctic Anthropology* XV(2): 146–74.

Gonzalez, Ellice B. 1981. *Changing Economic Roles for Micmac Men and Women: An Ethnohistoric Analysis.* National Museum of Man Mercury Series, Canadian Ethnology Service Paper No. 72, Ottawa.

Gould, G.P., and A.J. Semple, eds. 1980. *Our Land: The Maritimes.* Fredericton: Saint Anne's Point Press.

Howley, James P. 1974. *The Beothucks or Red Indians: The Aboriginal Inhabitants of Newfoundland.* Toronto: Coles. (Originally published 1915.)

Isaac, Thomas. 2001. *Aboriginal and Treaty Rights in the Maritimes.* Saskatoon: Purich Publishing.

Jackson, Doug. 1993. *"On the Country": The Micmac of Newfoundland.* St. John's: Harry Cuff Publications.

LeClercq, Father Chrétien. 1910. *New Relation of Gaspesia, With the Customs and Religion of the Gaspesian Indians.* Toronto: Champlain Society.

Lescarbot, Marc. 1907–14. *The History of New France* (3 vols.). Toronto: Champlain Society.

McGee, H.F., ed. 1974. *The Native Peoples of Atlantic Canada: A Reader in Regional Ethnic Relations.* Carleton Library No. 72. Toronto: McClelland and Stewart.

McGhee, Robert, and James A. Tuck 1975. *An Archaic Sequence from the Strait of Belle Isle, Labrador.* National Museum of Man Mercury Series, Archaeological Survey of Canada Paper No. 34, Ottawa.

Marshall, Ingeborg C.L. 1985. *Beothuk Bark Canoes: An Analysis and Comparative Study.* National Museum of Man Mercury Series, Canadian Ethnology Service Paper No. 102, Ottawa.

————. 1996. *A History and Ethnography of the Beothuk*. Montreal and Kingston: McGill-Queens University Press.

Martijn, Charles A., ed. 1986. *Les Micmacs et La Mer*. Montreal: Recherches Amérindiennes au Québec.

Miller, Virginia P. 2004. "The Micmac: a maritime Woodland group." In *Native Peoples: The Canadian Experience*, 3rd ed. R.B. Morrison and C.R. Wilson, 248–67. Don Mills, ON: Oxford University Press.

Paul, Daniel N. 2000. *We Were Not the Savages: A Mi'kmaq Perspective on the Collision between European and Native American Civilizations*. Halifax: Fernwood.

Pastore, Ralph T. 1992. *Shanawdithit's People: The Archaeology of the Beothuks*. St. John's: Atlantic Archaeology Ltd.

Prins, Harald E.L. 1996. *The Mi'kmaq: Resistance, Accommodation, and Cultural Survival*. Fort Worth, TX: Holt, Rinehart and Winston.

Rowe, Frederick W. 1977. *Extinction: the Beothuks of Newfoundland*. Toronto: McGraw-Hill Ryerson.

Sanger, David. 1973. *Cow Point: An Archaic Cemetery in New Brunswick*. National Museum of Man Mercury Series, Archaeological Survey of Canada Paper No. 12, Ottawa.

Speck, Frank G. 1915. "The Eastern Algonkian Wabanaki Confederacy." *American Anthropologist* 17: 492–508.

————. 1922. *Beothuk and Micmac*. Indian Notes and Monographs, Museum of the American Indian, Heye Foundation, New York.

Such, Peter. 1978. *Vanished Peoples: The Archaic, Dorset and Beothuk People of Newfoundland*. Toronto: NC Press.

Thwaites, Reuben G., ed. 1896–1901. *The Jesuit Relations and Allied Documents* (73 vols.). Cleveland: Barrows Brothers.

Trigger, Bruce, ed. 1978. *Handbook of North American Indians*, Vol. 15: Northeast. Washington: Smithsonian Institution Press.

Tuck, James A. 1970. "An archaic Indian cemetery in Newfoundland." *Scientific American* 222(6): 112–21.

————. 1975. "The northeastern maritime continuum: 8000 years of cultural development in the far northeast." *Arctic Anthropology* XII(2): 139–47.

————. 1976a. *Newfoundland and Labrador Prehistory*. Ottawa: National Museum of Man.

————. 1976b. *Ancient People of Port au Choix*. Institute of Social and Economic Research, Memorial University of Newfoundland, St. John's.

————. 1976c. "An archaic Indian burial mound in Labrador." *Scientific American* 235(5): 122–29.

————. 1984. *Maritime Provinces Prehistory*. Ottawa: National Museum of Man.

Turnbull, Christopher J. 1976. "The Augustine site: a mound from the Maritimes." *Archaeology of Eastern North America* 4: 50–62.

Upton, L.F.S. 1979. *Micmacs and Colonists*. Vancouver: University of British Columbia Press.

Wallis, Wilson D., and Ruth S. Wallis. 1955. *The Micmac Indians of Eastern Canada*. Minneapolis: University of Minnesota Press.

————. 1957. *The Malecite Indians of New Brunswick*. National Museum of Canada, Bulletin No. 148, Anthropological Series No. 40, Ottawa.

Whitehead, Ruth Holmes. 1980. *Elitekey: Micmac Material Culture from 1600 AD to the Present.* Halifax: Nova Scotia Museum.

———. 1982. *Micmac Quillwork.* Halifax: Nova Scotia Museum.

———. 1991. *The Old Man Told Us: Excerpts from Micmac History 1500–1950.* Halifax: Nimbus Publishing.

Wicken, William C. 2002. *Mi'kmaq Treaties on Trial: History, Land, and Donald Marshall Junior.* Toronto: University of Toronto Press.

Wien, Fred. 1986. *Rebuilding the Economic Base of Indian Communities: the Micmac in Nova Scotia.* Montreal: Institute for Research on Public Policy.

CHAPTER FOUR *The Iroquoians of the Eastern Woodlands*

A useful source, providing summary articles on all the Iroquoian groups, is the Northeast volume of the *Handbook of North American Indians* (Trigger 1978).

Archaeological overviews are given in two popular books by J.V. Wright: *Ontario Prehistory* (1972) and *Quebec Prehistory* (1979). Warrick (2000) provides a detailed summary.

The major primary sources for the seventeenth-century Iroquoians are the *Jesuit Relations* (Thwaites 1896–1901), Champlain (Biggar 1922–36) and Sagard (1939). Particularly important studies of Huron life are those by Trigger (1976, 1990), Tooker (1964) and Heidenreich (1971). Sioui (1999) provides the perspective of a Huron-Wendat scholar. A major ethnographic source for the Neutral is G.K. Wright (1963). Useful studies of the Iroquois are Snow (1994) and Fenton (1998).

General accounts of the Mohawk confrontations of 1990 are given in York and Pindera (1991), Hornung (1991), Johansen (1993), Pertusati (1997) and Ciaccia (2000). Goodleaf (1995) provides a Mohawk perspective.

Alfred, Gerald R. 1995. *Heeding the Voices of Our Ancestors: Kahnawake Mohawk Politics and the Rise of Native Nationalism.* Don Mills, ON: Oxford University Press.

Bechard, Henri. 1976. *The Original Caughnawaga Indians.* Montreal: International.

Becker, Mary Druke. 2004. "Iroquois and Iroquoian in Canada." In *Native Peoples: The Canadian Experience,* 3rd ed., ed. R.B. Morrison and C.R. Wilson, 229–47. Don Mills, ON: Oxford University Press.

Biggar, H.P., ed. 1924. *The Voyages of Jacques Cartier.* Publications of the Public Archives of Canada No. 11, Ottawa.

———, ed. 1922–36. *The Works of Samuel de Champlain* (6 vols.). Toronto: Champlain Society.

Chapdelaine, Claude. 1989. *Le Site Mandeville à Tracy: Variabilité Culturelle des Iroquoiens du Saint-Laurent.* Montreal: Recherches Amérindiennes au Québec.

Ciaccia, John. 2000. *The Oka Crisis: A Mirror of the Soul.* Dorval, QC: Maren Publications.

Clermont, N., C. Chapdelaine, and G. Barré. 1983. *Le Site Iroquoien de Lanoraie: Témoignage d'une Maison-Longue.* Montreal: Recherches Amérindiennes au Québec.

Dodd, Christine. 1984. *Ontario Iroquois Tradition Longhouses.* National Museum of Man Mercury Series, Archaeological Survey of Canada Paper No. 124, Ottawa.

Ellis, Chris J., and Neal Ferris, eds. 1990. *The Archaeology of Southern Ontario to AD 1650.* London, ON: Ontario Archaeological Society.

Engelbrecht, William. 2003. *Iroquoia: The Development of a Native World*. Syracuse, NY: Syracuse University Press.

Fenton, William N. 1971. "The Iroquois in history." In *North American Indians in Historical Perspective*, ed. E.B. Leacock and N.O. Lurie, 129–68. New York: Random House.

———. 1998. *The Great Law and the Longhouse: A Political History of the Iroquois Confederacy*. Norman, OK: University of Oklahoma Press.

Finlayson, William D. 1977. *The Saugeen Culture: A Middle Woodland Manifestation in Southwestern Ontario* (2 vols.). National Museum of Man Mercury Series, Archaeological Survey of Canada Paper No. 61, Ottawa.

———. 1985. *The 1975 and 1978 Rescue Excavations at the Draper Site: Introduction and Settlement Patterns*. National Museum of Man Mercury Series, Archaeological Survey of Canada Paper No. 130, Ottawa.

Foley, Denis P. 1977. "Six Nations traditionalist social structure." *Man in the Northeast* 13: 107–12.

Fox, William A., and J. Eldon Molto. 1994. "The Shaman of Long Point." *Ontario Archaeology* 57: 23–44.

Frisch, Jack A. 1976. "Some ethnological and ethnohistorical notes on the Iroquois in Alberta." *Man in the Northeast* 12: 51–64.

Goodleaf, Donna. 1995. *Entering the War Zone: A Mohawk Perspective on Resisting Invasions*. Penticton, BC: Theytus Books.

Heidenreich, Conrad. 1971. *Huronia: A History and Geography of the Huron Indians 1600–1615*. Toronto: McClelland and Stewart.

Hoover, Michael L., and the Kanien'kehaka Raotitiohkwa Cultural Center. 1992. "The revival of the Mohawk language in Kahnawake." *Canadian Journal of Native Studies* 12(2): 269–87.

Hornung, Rick. 1991. *One Nation Under the Gun: Inside the Mohawk Civil War*. Toronto: Stoddart Publishing.

Hunt, George T. 1940. *The Wars of the Iroquois*. Madison: University of Wisconsin Press.

Jamieson, James B. 1983. "An examination of prisoner-sacrifice and cannibalism at the St. Lawrence Iroquoian Roebuck site." *Canadian Journal of Archaeology* 7(2): 159–75.

Jamieson, Susan M. 1981. "Economics and Ontario Iroquoian social organization." *Canadian Journal of Archaeology* 5: 19–30.

Johansen, Bruce E. 1993. *Life and Death in Mohawk Country*. Golden, CO: North American Press.

Johnston, Charles M., ed. 1964. *The Valley of the Six Nations*. Toronto: Champlain Society.

Johnston, Richard B. 1968. *The Archaeology of the Serpent Mounds Site*. Occasional Paper No. 10, Art and Archaeology, Royal Ontario Museum, Toronto.

———. 1979. "Notes on ossuary burial among the Ontario Iroquois." *Canadian Journal of Archaeology* 3: 91–104.

Kenyon, Walter A. 1968. *The Miller Site*. Occasional Paper No. 14, Art and Archaeology, Royal Ontario Museum, Toronto.

———. 1982. *The Grimsby Site: A Historic Neutral Cemetery*. Toronto: Royal Ontario Museum.

Kidd, Kenneth E. 1953. "The excavation and historical identification of a Huron ossuary." *American Antiquity* 18(4): 359–79.

Kurath, Gertrude P. 1968. *Dance and Song Rituals of Six Nations Reserve, Ontario.* National Museum of Canada, Bulletin No. 220, Ottawa.

Lennox, Paul A. 1981. *The Hamilton Site: A Late Historic Neutral Town.* National Museum of Man Mercury Series, Archaeological Survey of Canada Paper No. 103, Ottawa.

Miller, J.R. 1992. "The Oka controversy and the federal land-claims process." In *Aboriginal Land Claims in Canada: A Regional Perspective,* ed. Ken Coates, 215–41. Toronto: Copp Clark Pitman.

Mitchell, Grand Chief Michael. 1989. "Akwesasne: an unbroken assertion of sovereignty." In *Drum Beat: Anger and Renewal in Indian Country,* ed. Boyce Richardson, 105–36. Toronto: Assembly of First Nations and Summerhill Press.

Morgan, Lewis H. 1962. *League of the Iroquois.* New Jersey: Citadel Press.

Noble, William C. 1978. "The Neutral Indians." In *Essays in Northeastern Anthropology in Memory of Mariam E. White,* ed. W.E. Engelbrecht and D.K. Grayson, 152–64. Occasional Publications in Northeastern Anthropology No. 5, Department of Anthropology, Franklin Pierce College, Rindge, NH.

———. 1984. "Historic Neutral Iroquois settlement patterns." *Canadian Journal of Archaeology* 8(1): 3–27.

———. 1985. "Tsouharissen's chiefdom: an early historic 17th century Neutral Iroquoian ranked society." *Canadian Journal of Archaeology* 9(2): 131–46.

Noon, John A. 1949. *Law and Government of the Grand River Iroquois.* Viking Fund Publications in Anthropology No. 12, New York.

Pendergast, James F., and Bruce G. Trigger. 1972. *Cartier's Hochelaga and the Dawson Site.* Montreal: McGill-Queen's University Press.

Pertusati, Linda. 1997. *In Defense of Mohawk Land: Ethnopolitical Conflict in Native North America.* Albany: State University of New York Press.

Richter, Daniel K. 1992. *The Ordeal of the Longhouse: The Peoples of the Iroquois League in the Era of European Colonization.* Chapel Hill, NC: University of North Carolina Press.

Rogers, Edward S., and Donald B. Smith, eds. 1994. *Aboriginal Ontario: Historical Perspectives on the First Nations.* Toronto: Dundurn Press.

Sagard, Father Gabriel. 1939. *The Long Journey to the Country of the Hurons,* ed. G.M. Wrong. Toronto: Champlain Society.

Schlesier, Karl H. 1976. "Epidemics and Indian middlemen: rethinking the Wars of the Iroquois." *Ethnohistory* 23(2): 129–45.

Schoolcraft, Henry R. 1975. *Notes on the Iroquois.* New York: Bartlett & Welford. (Originally published 1846.)

Shimony, Annemarie A. 1961. *Conservatism among the Iroquois at the Six Nations Reserve.* Yale University Publications in Anthropology No. 65, New Haven.

Sioui, Georges E. 1999. *Huron-Wendat: The Heritage of the Circle.* Vancouver: UBC Press.

Snow, Dean R. 1994. *The Iroquois.* Cambridge, MA: Blackwell.

———. 1995. "Migration in prehistory: the northern Iroquoian case." *American Antiquity* 60(1): 59–79.

Stothers, David M. 1977. *The Princess Point Complex.* National Museum of Man Mercury Series, Archaeological Survey of Canada Paper No. 58, Ottawa.

Thwaites, Reuben G., ed. 1896–1901. *The Jesuit Relations and Allied Documents* (73 vols.). Cleveland: Barrows Brothers.

Tooker, Elisabeth. 1964. *An Ethnography of the Huron Indians, 1615–1649.* Bureau of American Ethnology Bulletin 190, Smithsonian Institution, Washington.

Trigger, Bruce G. 1976. *The Children of Aataentsic: A History of the Huron People to 1660* (2 vols.). Montreal and London: McGill-Queen's University Press.

———. 1985. *Natives and Newcomers: Canada's "Heroic Age" Reconsidered.* Montreal and London: McGill-Queens University Press.

———. 1990. *The Huron: Farmers of the North.* 2nd ed. Fort Worth, TX: Holt, Rinehart and Winston.

———, ed. 1978. *Handbook of North American Indians,* Vol. 15: Northeast. Smithsonian Institution, Washington.

Vincent Tehariolina, Marguerite. 1984. *La Nation Huronne: Son Histoire, Sa Culture, Son Esprit.* Quebec City: Éditions du Pélican.

Wallace, Anthony F.C. 1969. *The Death and Rebirth of the Seneca.* New York: Random House.

Warrick, Gary A. 1984. *Reconstructing Ontario Iroquoian Village Organization.* National Museum of Man Mercury Series, Archaeological Survey of Canada Paper No. 124, Ottawa.

———. 2000. "The precontact Iroquoian occupation of southern Ontario." *Journal of World Prehistory* 14: 415–66.

Weaver, Sally M. 1972. *Medicine and Politics among the Grand River Iroquois.* National Museums of Canada, Publications in Ethnology No. 4, Ottawa.

Wright, Gordon K. 1963. *The Neutral Indians: A Source Book.* Occasional Papers of the New York State Archaeological Association No. 4, Rochester, NY.

Wright, J.V. 1966. *The Ontario Iroquois Tradition.* National Museum of Canada, Bulletin No. 210, Ottawa.

———. 1972. *Ontario Prehistory.* Ottawa: National Museum of Man.

———. 1974. *The Nodwell Site.* National Museum of Man Mercury Series, Archaeological Survey of Canada Paper No. 22, Ottawa.

———. 1979. *Quebec Prehistory.* Ottawa: National Museum of Man.

Wright, J.V., and J.E. Anderson. 1963. *The Donaldson Site.* National Museum of Canada, Bulletin No. 184, Ottawa.

———. 1969. *The Bennet Site.* National Museum of Canada, Bulletin No. 229, Ottawa.

York, Geoffrey, and Loreen Pindera. 1991. *People of the Pines: The Warriors and the Legacy of Oka.* Toronto: Little, Brown & Co.

CHAPTER FIVE *The Algonquians of the Eastern Woodlands and Subarctic*

Particularly important ethnographic sources are the works of Densmore (1929) and Landes (1937, 1938, 1968) on the Ojibwa. Speck's (1935) study of the Naskapi, dealing primarily with religious beliefs, is an ethnographic classic. Field studies from more recent periods include Rogers's descriptions of the Round Lake Ojibwa (1962, 1983) and the Mistassini Cree (1963, 1967, 1972, 1973), Dunning's (1959) of the Pekangekum Ojibwa, Hallowell's (1992) of the Berens River Ojibwa and Cummins's

(2004) of the Attawapiskat Cree. Mailhot (1997) and Samson (2003) provide detailed studies of the Labrador Innu. Shkilnyk's (1985) disturbing book documents recent social disintegration on the Grassy Narrows Reserve near Kenora. Bishop (1974) and Ray (1974) provide excellent historical analyses.

In addition, particularly useful are the relevant summary articles in the Subarctic (Helm 1981) and Northeast (Trigger 1978) volumes of the *Handbook of North American Indians*.

Angel, Michael. 2002. *Preserving the Sacred: Historical Perspectives on the Ojibwa Midewiwin*. Winnipeg: University of Manitoba Press.

Ashini, Daniel. 1989. "David confronts Goliath: The Innu of Ungava versus the NATO Alliance." In *Drum Beat: Anger and Renewal in Indian Country*, ed. Boyce Richardson, 45–70. Toronto: Assembly of First Nations and Summerhill Press.

Bishop, Charles A. 1970. "The emergence of hunting territories among the northern Ojibwa." *Ethnology* 9: 1–15.

———. 1974. *The Northern Ojibwa and the Fur Trade*. Toronto: Holt, Rinehart and Winston.

———. 1994. "Northern Algonquians, 1550–1760" and "Northern Algonquians 1760–1821." In *Aboriginal Ontario: Historical Perspectives on the First Nations*, ed. Edward S. Rogers and Donald B. Smith, 275–306. Toronto: Dundurn Press.

Bishop, Charles A., and M. Estellie Smith. 1975. "Early historic populations in northwestern Ontario: archaeological and ethnohistoric interpretations." *American Antiquity* 40: 54–63.

Brightman, Robert A. 1993. *Grateful Prey: Rock Cree Human-Animal Relationships*. Los Angeles: University of California Press.

Brown, Jennifer S.H. 1986. "Northern Algonquians from Lake Superior and Hudson Bay to Manitoba in the historical period." In *Native Peoples: the Canadian Experience*, ed. R.B. Morrison and C.R. Wilson, 208–36. Toronto: McClelland and Stewart.

Clément, Daniel, ed. 1996. *The Algonquins*. Hull, QC: Canadian Museum of Civilization.

Cooper, John M. 1936. *Notes on the Ethnology of the Otchipwe of the Lake of the Woods and Rainy Lake*. Washington, DC: Catholic University of America.

Cummins, Bryan D. 2004. *"Only God Can Own the Land": The Attawapiskat Cree*. Toronto: Pearson.

Danziger, Edmund J., Jr. 1978. *The Chippewas of Lake Superior*. Norman, OK: University of Oklahoma Press.

Dawson, K.C.A. 1977. "An application of the direct historic approach to the Algonkians of northern Ontario." *Canadian Journal of Archaeology* 1: 151–81.

———. 1982. "The Northern Ojibwa of Ontario." In *Approaches to Algonquian Archaeology*, ed. M.G. Hanna and B. Kooyman, 81–96. Department of Archaeology, University of Calgary.

———. 1983. "Prehistory of the interior forest of northern Ontario." In *Boreal Forest Adaptations: The Northern Algonkians*, ed. A.T. Steegman Jr., 55–84. New York and London: Plenum Press.

Densmore, Frances. 1929. *Chippewa Customs*. Smithsonian Institution, Bureau of American Ethnology, Bulletin 86, Washington.

Dewdney, Selwyn. 1975. *The Sacred Scrolls of the Southern Ojibway*. Toronto: University of Toronto Press.

————. 1978. "Birth of a Cree-Ojibway style of contemporary art." In *One Century Later*, ed. I.A.L. Getty and D.B. Smith, 117–25. Vancouver: University of British Columbia Press.

Dewdney, Selwyn, and Kenneth E. Kidd. 1967. *Indian Rock Paintings of the Great Lakes.* 2nd ed. Toronto: University of Toronto Press.

Dunning, R.W. 1959. *Social and Economic Change among the Northern Ojibwa.* Toronto: University of Toronto Press.

Feit, Harvey A. 2004. "Hunting and the quest for power: the James Bay Cree and whiteman development." In *Native Peoples: The Canadian Experience*, 3rd ed., ed. R.B. Morrison and C.R. Wilson, 101–28. Don Mills, ON: Oxford University Press.

Francis, Daniel, and Toby Morantz. 1983. *Partners in Furs: A History of the Fur Trade in Eastern James Bay 1600–1870.* Montreal and Kingston: McGill-Queen's University Press.

Grim, John A. 1983. *The Shaman: Patterns of Religious Healing Among the Ojibway Indians.* Norman, OK: University of Oklahoma Press.

Hallowell, A. Irving. 1955. *Culture and Experience.* Philadelphia: University of Pennsylvania Press.

————. 1992. *The Ojibwa of Berens River, Manitoba: Ethnography into History*, ed. Jennifer S.H. Brown. Fort Worth, TX: Holt, Rinehart and Winston.

Helm, June, ed. 1981. *Handbook of the North American Indians, Vol. 6: Subarctic.* Washington: Smithsonian Institution Press.

Henriksen, Georg. 1982. *Hunters in the Barrens: The Naskapi on the Edge of the White Man's World.* Institute of Social and Economic Research, Memorial University of Newfoundland, St. John's.

Hessel, Peter. 1993. *The Algonkin Nation: The Algonkins of the Ottawa Valley.* Arnprior, ON: Kichesippi Books.

Hickerson, Harold. 1960. "The Feast of the Dead among the seventeenth century Algonkians of the Upper Great Lakes." *American Anthropologist* 62: 81–107.

————. 1970. *The Chippewa and Their Neighbors: A Study in Ethnohistory.* New York: Holt, Rinehart and Winston.

Hind, Henry Y. 1973. *Explorations in the Interior of the Labrador Peninsula: The Country of the Montagnais and Nasquapee Indians.* New York: Krause Reprint. (Originally published 1863.)

Hoffman, W.J. 1891. "The Mide'wiwin or Grand Medicine Society." In *Seventh Annual Report of the Bureau of Ethnology, 1885–86*, 143–300. Washington: Smithsonian Institution.

Honigmann, John J. 1956. "The Attawapiskat Swampy Cree: An Ethnographic Reconstruction." *Anthropological Papers of the University of Alaska* 5(1): 23–82.

Jenness, Diamond. 1935. *The Ojibwa Indians of Parry Island, Their Social and Religious Life.* National Museum of Canada, Bulletin No. 78, Anthropological Series No. 17, Ottawa.

Johnson, Basil. 1976. *Ojibway Heritage.* Toronto: McClelland and Stewart.

————. 1982. *Ojibway Ceremonies.* Toronto: McClelland and Stewart.

Kenyon, Walter A. 1970. "The Armstrong Mound on Rainy River, Ontario." *Canadian Historic Sites, Occasional Papers in Archaeology and History* 3: 66–84.

————. 1986. *Mounds of Sacred Earth: Burial Mounds of Ontario.* Toronto: Royal Ontario Museum.

Knight, Rolf. 1968. *Ecological Factors in Changing Economy and Social Organization among the Rupert House Cree.* Anthropology Papers No. 15, National Museum of Canada, Ottawa.

Landes, Ruth. 1937a. *Ojibwa Sociology.* New York: Columbia University Contributions to Anthropology. (AMS Press reprint 1969.)

———. 1937b. "The Ojibwa of Canada." In *Cooperation and Competition Among Primitive Peoples,* ed. Margaret Mead, 87–127. New York: McGraw-Hill.

———. 1971. *The Ojibwa Woman.* New York: Columbia University Contributions to Anthropology. (Originally published 1938.)

———. 1968. *Ojibwa Religion and the Midewiwin.* Madison: University of Wisconsin Press.

Leacock, Eleanor. 1954. *The Montagnais "Hunting Territory" and the Fur Trade.* American Anthropological Association Memoir No. 78.

Leacock, Eleanor. 1986. "The Montagnais-Naskapi of the Labrador Puninsula." In *Native Peoples: the Canadian Experience,* ed. R.B. Morrison and C.R. Wilson, 140–71. Toronto: McClelland and Stewart.

MacGregor, Roy. 1989. *Chief: the Fearless Vision of Billy Diamond.* Markham, ON: Penguin Books.

McLuhan, Elizabeth, and Tom Hill. 1984. *Norval Morrisseau and the Emergence of the Image Makers.* Toronto: Art Gallery of Ontario and Methuen Publications.

Mailhot, José. 1997. *The People of Sheshatshit.* Institute of Social and Economic Research, Memorial University, St. John's.

Martijn, Charles A., and Edward S. Rogers. 1969. *Mistassini-Albanel: Contributions to the Prehistory of Quebec.* Centre D'Etudes Nordiques 25, Université de Laval, Quebec.

Mason, Leonard. 1967. *The Swampy Cree: A Study in Acculturation.* Anthropology Papers No. 13, National Museum of Canada, Ottawa.

Morantz, Toby. 1983. *An Ethnohistoric Study of Eastern James Bay Cree Social Organization, 1700–1850.* National Museum of Man Mercury Series, Canadian Ethnology Service Paper No. 88, Ottawa.

———. 2002. *The White Man's Gonna Getcha: The Colonial Challenge to the Crees in Quebec.* Montreal and Kingston: McGill-Queen's University Press.

Morrisseau, Norval. 1965. *Legends of My People, The Great Ojibway.* Toronto: Ryerson Press.

Preston, Richard J. 2002. *Cree Narrative: Expressing the Personal Meanings of Events.* 2nd ed. Montreal and Kingston: McGill-Queen's University Press.

Rajnovich, Grace. 1994. *Reading Rock Art: Interpreting the Indian Rock Paintings of the Canadian Shield.* Toronto: Natural Heritage/Natural History.

Ray, Arthur J. 1974. *Indians in the Fur Trade.* Toronto: University of Toronto Press.

Reid, C.S. "Paddy," and Grace Rajnovich. 1991. "Laurel: a re-evaluation of the spatial, social and temporal paradigms." *Canadian Journal of Archaeology* 15: 193–234.

Richardson, Boyce. 1991. *Strangers Devour the Land.* Vancouver: Douglas & McIntyre.

Rogers, Edward S. 1962. *The Round Lake Ojibwa.* Toronto: Royal Ontario Museum.

———. 1963a. *The Hunting Group—Hunting Territory Complex among the Mistassini Indians.* National Museum of Canada, Bulletin No. 195, Ottawa.

———. 1963b. "Changing settlement patterns of the Cree-Ojibwa of northern Ontario." *Southwestern Journal of Anthropology* 19: 64–88.

———. 1967. *The Material Culture of the Mistassini.* National Museum of Canada, Bulletin No. 218, Ottawa.

———. 1972. "The Mistassini Cree." In *Hunters and Gatherers Today,* ed. M.G. Bicchieri, 90–137. New York: Holt, Rinehart and Winston.

———. 1973. *The Quest for Food and Furs: The Mistassini Cree, 1953–1954.* National Museum of Man, Publications in Ethnology No. 5, Ottawa.

———. 1983. "Cultural adaptations: the Northern Ojibwa of the boreal forest 1670–1980." In *Boreal Forest Adaptations: The Northern Algonkians,* ed. A.T. Steegmann, Jr., 85–141. New York and London: Plenum Press.

Salisbury, Richard F. 1986. *A Homeland For the Cree: Regional Development in James Bay 1971–1981.* Montreal and Kingston: McGill-Queen's University Press.

Samson, Colin. 2003. *A Way of Life That Does Not Exist: Canada and the Extinguishment of the Innu.* Institute of Social and Economic Research, Memorial University, St. John's.

Schmalz, Peter S. 1991. *The Ojibwa of Southern Ontario.* Toronto: University of Toronto Press.

Shkilnyk, Anastasia M. 1985. *A Poison Stronger Than Love: The Destruction of an Ojibwa Community.* New Haven, CT: Yale University Press.

Sinclair, Lister, and Jack Pollock. 1979. *The Art of Norval Morrisseau.* Toronto: Methuen.

Speck, Frank G. 1915. "The family hunting band as the basis of Algonkian social organization." *American Anthropologist* 17: 289–305.

———. 1935. *Naskapi: the Savage Hunters of the Labrador Peninsula.* Norman, OK: University of Oklahoma Press.

Southcott, Mary E. 1984. *The Sound of the Drum: The Sacred Art of the Anishnabec.* Erin, ON: Boston Mills Press.

Tanner, Adrian. 1979. *Bringing Home Animals: Religious Ideology and Mode of Production of the Mistassini Cree Hunters.* Institute of Social and Economic Research, Memorial University, St. John's.

Teicher, Morton I. 1960. *Windigo Psychosis: A Study of a Relationship between Belief and Behavior among the Indians of Northeastern Canada.* American Ethnological Society, distributed by the University of Washington Press, Seattle.

Thwaites, Reuben G., ed. 1896–1901. *The Jesuit Relations and Allied Documents* (73 vols.). Cleveland: Barrows Brothers.

Trigger, Bruce G., ed. 1978. *Handbook of North American Indians, Vol. 15: Northeast.* Washington: Smithsonian Institution Press.

Turner, Lucien M. 1894. *Ethnology of the Ungava District, Hudson Bay Territory.* Eleventh Report of the Bureau of Ethnology, Smithsonian Institution, Washington.

Tyrell, J.B., ed. 1916. *David Thompson's Narrative of His Explorations in Western America, 1784–1812.* Toronto: Champlain Society.

Vecsey, C. 1983. *Traditional Ojibwa Religion and its Historical Changes.* Philadelphia: American Philosophical Society.

Wadden, Marie. 1991. *Nitassinan: The Innu Struggle to Reclaim Their Homeland.* Vancouver: Douglas & McIntyre.

Warren, William W. 1984. *History of the Ojibway People.* St. Paul: Minnesota Historical Society Press. (Originally published 1885.)

Wright, J.V. 1967. *The Laurel Tradition and the Middle Woodland Period.* National Museum of Canada, Bulletin No. 217, Ottawa.

————. 1972a. *The Shield Archaic*. National Museums of Canada, Publications in Archaeology No. 3, Ottawa.

————. 1972b. *Ontario Prehistory*. Ottawa: National Museum of Man.

————. 1979. *Quebec Prehistory*. Ottawa: National Museum of Man.

CHAPTER SIX *The Plains*

Bryan (1991) provides a general overview of archaeology on the Canadian Plains; Brink and Dormaar (2003) present articles dealing with Alberta; provincial summaries are given in Vickers (1986), Dyck (1983) and Pettipas (1983). Summary articles on Plains archaeology and ethnography are available in the Plains volume of the *Handbook of North American Indians* (DeMallie 2001).

Among the ethnographic groups, the Blackfoot are the best documented. Important ethnographic sources are Wissler (1910, 1912, 1913), Ewers (1958), McClintock (1910) and Grinnell (1962). Dempsey (2004) gives a useful summary. Other major ethnographic works include Lowie (1909) and Denig (2000) on the Assiniboine, Mandelbaum (1979) on the Plains Cree and Jenness (1938) on the Sarcee. The Canadian Dakota are well covered in books by LaViolette (1944), Wallis (1947) and Howard (1984), and in articles by Kehoe (1970) and Stanley (1978).

Adams, Gary. 1977. *The Estuary Pound Site in Southwestern Saskatchewan*. National Museum of Man Mercury Series, Archaeological Survey of Canada Paper No. 68, Ottawa.

Ahenakew, Edward. 1973. *Voices of the Plains Cree*. Toronto: McClelland and Stewart.

Arthur, George W. 1975. *An Introduction to the Ecology of Early Historic Communal Bison Hunting Among the Northern Plains Indians*. National Museum of Man Mercury Series, Archaeological Survey of Canada Paper No. 37, Ottawa.

Barron, F. Laurie, and Joseph Garcea. 1999. *Urban Indian Reserves: Forging New Relationships in Saskatchewan*. Saskatoon: Purich.

Barry, P.S. 1991. *Mystical Themes in Milk River Rock Art*. Edmonton: University of Alberta Press.

Brink, Jack. 1979. *Excavations at Writing-On-Stone*. Occasional Paper No. 12, Archaeological Survey of Alberta, Edmonton.

————. 1986. *Dog Days in Southern Alberta*. Occasional Paper No. 28, Archaeological Survey of Alberta, Edmonton.

Brink, Jack, and John F. Dormaar. 2003. *Archaeology in Alberta: A View from the New Millennium*. Calgary: Archaeological Society of Alberta.

Brumley, John H. 1975. *The Cactus Flower Site in Southeastern Alberta: 1972–1974 Excavations*. National Museum of Man Mercury Series, Archaeological Survey of Canada Paper No. 46, Ottawa.

————. 1976. *Ramillies: A Late Prehistoric Bison Kill and Campsite Located in Southeastern Alberta, Canada*. National Museum of Man Mercury Series, Archaeological Survey of Canada Paper No. 55, Ottawa.

————. 1988. *Medicine Wheels on the Northern Plains: A Summary and Appraisal*. Archaeological Survey of Alberta, Manuscript Series No. 12, Edmonton.

Bryan, Liz 1991. *The Buffalo People: Prehistoric Archaeology on the Canadian Plains*. Edmonton: University of Alberta Press.

Buckley, Helen. 1992. *From Wooden Ploughs to Welfare: Why Indian Policy Failed in the Prairie Provinces*. Montreal and Kingston: McGill-Queen's University Press.

Byrne, William J. 1973. *The Archaeology and Prehistory of Southern Alberta as Reflected by Ceramics*. National Museum of Man Mercury Series, Archaeological Survey of Canada Paper No. 14, Ottawa.

Calder, James M. 1977. *The Majorville Cairn and Medicine Wheel Site, Alberta*. National Museum of Man Mercury Series, Archaeological Survey of Canada Paper No. 62, Ottawa.

Capes, Katherine H. 1963. *The W.B. Nickerson Survey and Excavations, 1912–15, of the Southern Manitoba Mounds Region*. Anthropology Papers No. 4, National Museum of Canada, Ottawa.

Carter, Sarah. 1990. *Lost Harvests: Prairie Indian Reserve Farmers and Government Policy*. Montreal and Kingston: McGill-Queen's University Press.

Corrigan, Samuel W. 1970. "The Plains Indian powwow: cultural integration in Manitoba and Saskatchewan." *Anthropologica* 12: 253–77.

Curtis, Edward S. 1970. *The North American Indian, Vol. 6*. New York: Johnson. (Originally published 1911.)

DeMallie, Raymond J., ed. 2001. *Handbook of North American Indians, Vol. 13: Plains*. Washington: Smithsonian Institution.

Dempsey, Hugh A. 1972. *Crowfoot: Chief of the Blackfoot*. Edmonton: Hurtig.

———. 2004. "The Blackfoot Nation." In *Native Peoples: The Canadian Experience*. 3rd ed., ed. R.B. Morrison and C.R. Wilson, 275–96. Don Mills, ON: Oxford University Press.

Denig, Edwin Thompson. 1961. *Five Indian Tribes of the Upper Missouri*. Norman, OK: University of Oklahoma Press.

———. 2000. *The Assiniboine*. Regina: Canadian Plains Research Center.

Dyck, Ian G. 1977. *The Harder Site: A Middle Period Bison Hunter's Campsite in the Northern Great Plains*. National Museum of Man Mercury Series, Archaeological Survey of Canada Paper No. 67, Ottawa.

———. 1983. "The prehistory of southern Saskatchewan." In *Tracking Ancient Hunters*, ed. H.T. Epp and Ian Dyck, 63–139. Regina: Saskatchewan Archaeological Society.

Eddy, John A. 1977. "Medicine wheels and Plains Indian astronomy." In *Native American Astronomy*, ed. A.F. Aveni, 147–69. Austin: University of Texas Press.

Elias, Peter Douglas. 1988. *The Dakota of the Canadian Northwest: Lessons for Survival*. Winnipeg: University of Manitoba Press.

Ewers, John C. 1958. *The Blackfoot: Raiders on the Northwestern Plains*. Norman, OK: University of Oklahoma Press.

———. 1980. *The Horse in Blackfoot Indian Culture*. Washington: Smithsonian Institution Press.

Finnigan, James T. 1982. *Tipi Rings and Plains Prehistory: A Reassessment of their Archaeological Potential*. National Museum of Man Mercury Series, Archaeological Survey of Canada Paper No. 108, Ottawa.

Forbis, Richard G. 1962. "The Old Women's Buffalo Jump, Alberta." In *Contributions to Anthropology 1960, Part I*, 56–123. National Museum of Canada Bulletin No. 180, Ottawa.

———. 1977. *Cluny: An Ancient Fortified Village in Alberta*. Occasional Papers No. 4, Department of Archaeology, University of Calgary.

Frison, George C. 1978. *Prehistoric Hunters of the High Plains*. New York: Academic Press.

Gordon, Bryan H.C. 1979. *Of Men and Herds in Canadian Plains Prehistory*. National Museum of Man Mercury Series, Archaeological Survey of Canada Paper No. 84, Ottawa.

Grinnell, George Bird. 1962. *Blackfoot Lodge Tales*. Lincoln: University of Nebraska Press.

Hanks, Lucien M., and J.R. Hanks. 1950. *Tribe Under Trust: A Study of the Blackfoot Reserve of Alberta*. Toronto: University of Toronto Press.

Hanna, Margaret G. 1976. *The Moose Bay Burial Mound*. Anthropological Series No. 3, Saskatchewan Museum of Natural History, Regina.

Hind, Henry Youle. 1971. *Narrative of the Canadian Red River Exploring Expedition of 1857 and of the Assiniboine and Saskatchewan Exploring Expedition of 1858*. Edmonton: Hurtig.

Hlady, Walter M., ed. 1970. *Ten Thousand Years: Archaeology in Manitoba*. Winnipeg: Manitoba Archaeological Society.

Howard, James H. 1961. "The identity and demography of the Plains-Ojibwa." *Plains Anthropologist* 6: 171–78.

———. 1984. *The Canadian Sioux*. Lincoln: University of Nebraska Press.

Hungry Wolf, Adolf. 1977. *The Blood People*. New York: Harper & Row.

Jenness, Diamond. 1938. *The Sarcee Indians of Alberta*. National Museum of Canada Bulletin No. 90, Anthropological Series No. 23, Ottawa.

Kehoe, Alice B. 1968. "The Ghost Dance religion in Saskatchewan, Canada." *Plains Anthropologist* 13: 296–304.

———. 1970. "The Dakota in Saskatchewan." In *The Modern Sioux*, ed. Ethel Nurge, 148–72. Lincoln: University of Nebraska Press.

———. 1989. *The Ghost Dance: Ethnohistory and Revitalization*. New York: Holt, Rinehart and Winston.

Kehoe, Alice B., and Thomas F. Kehoe 1979. *Solstice-Aligned Boulder Configurations in Saskatchewan*. National Museum of Man Mercury Series, Canadian Ethnology Service Paper No. 48, Ottawa.

Kehoe, Thomas F. 1973. *The Gull Lake Site: A Prehistoric Bison Drive Site in Southwestern Saskatchewan*. Publications in Anthropology and History No. 1, Milwaukee Public Museum.

Kennedy, Dan (Ochankugahe). 1972. *Recollections of an Assiniboine Chief*. Toronto: McClelland and Stewart.

Keyser, James D. 1977. "Writing-On-Stone: rock art on the northwestern Plains." *Canadian Journal of Archaeology* 1: 15–80.

Keyser, James D., and Michael A. Klassen. 2001. *Plains Indian Rock Art*. Seattle: University of Washington Press and Vancouver: UBC Press.

Kidd, Kenneth E. 1986. *Blackfoot Ethnography*. Manuscript Series No. 8, Archaeological Survey of Alberta, Edmonton.

Kroeber, A.L. 1908. "Ethnology of the Gros Ventre." *Anthropological Papers of the American Museum of Natural History*, Vol. 1, Pt. 4, 145–281.

LaViolette, Gontran. 1944. *The Sioux Indians in Canada*. Regina: Marion Press.

Lewis, Oscar. 1942. *The Effects of White Contact Upon Blackfoot Culture With Special Reference to the Role of the Fur Trade*. Seattle: University of Washington Press.

Lowie, Robert H. 1909. "The Assiniboine." *Anthropological Papers of the American Museum of Natural History,* Vol. 4, Pt. 1, 1–270.

MacEwen, Grant. 1973. *Sitting Bull: The Years in Canada.* Edmonton: Hurtig.

McClintock, Walter. 1910. *The Old North Trail.* London: Macmillan.

Mandelbaum, David G. 1979. *The Plains Cree: An Ethnographic, Historical, and Comparative Study.* Saskatoon: Canadian Plains Research Center, University of Regina.

Millar, J.F.V. 1981. "Mortuary practices of the Oxbow complex." *Canadian Journal of Archaeology* 5: 103–17.

Milloy, John S. 1988. *The Plains Cree: Trade, Diplomacy and War, 1790 to 1870.* Winnipeg: University of Manitoba Press.

Moore, T.A., ed. 1981. *Alberta Archaeology: Prospect and Retrospect.* Lethbridge, AB: Archaeological Society of Alberta.

Mountain Horse, Mike. 1979. *My People The Bloods.* Calgary: Glenbow-Alberta Institute and the Blood Tribal Council.

Nicholson, B.A. 1990. "Ceramic affiliations and the case for incipient horticulture in southwestern Manitoba." *Canadian Journal of Archaeology* 14: 33–59.

Peers, Laura. 1994. *The Ojibwa of Western Canada, 1780 to 1870.* Winnipeg: University of Manitoba Press.

Pettipas, Leo F., ed. 1983. *Introducing Manitoba Prehistory.* Papers in Manitoba Archaeology, Department of Culture, Heritage and Recreation, Winnipeg.

Ray, Arthur J. 1974. *Indians in the Fur Trade.* Toronto: University of Toronto Press.

Reeves, Brian O.K. 1978. "Head-Smashed-In: 5500 years of bison jumping in the Alberta Plains." *Plains Anthropologist,* Memoir 14, Pt. 2, 151–74.

Reeves, Brian O.K. 1983. *Culture Change in the Northern Plains: 1000 BC–AD 1000.* Occasional Paper No. 20, Archaeological Survey of Alberta, Edmonton.

———. 1990. "Communal bison hunters of the Northern Plains." In *Hunters of the Recent Past,* ed. L.B. Davis and B.O.K. Reeves, 168–94. London: Unwin Hyman.

Sharrock, Susan R. 1974. "Crees, Cree-Assiniboines, and Assiniboines: interethnic social organization on the far northern Plains." *Ethnohistory* 21(2): 95–122.

Skinner, Alanson. 1914a. "Notes on the Plains Cree." *American Anthropologist* 16: 68–87.

———. 1914b. "The cultural position of the Plains Ojibwa." *American Anthropologist* 16: 314–18.

———. 1914c. "Political organization, cults, and ceremonies of the Plains-Ojibwa and Plains-Cree Indians." *Anthropological Papers of the American Museum of Natural History,* Vol. 11, Pt. 6, 474–542.

Snow, Chief John. 1977. *These Mountains are our Sacred Places.* Toronto: Samuel Stevens.

Stanley, George F.G. 1978. "Displaced Red Men: the Sioux in Canada." In *One Century Later,* ed. I.A.L. Getty and D.B. Smith, 55–81. Vancouver: University of British Columbia Press.

Syms, E. Leigh. 1977. "Cultural ecology and ecological dynamics of the ceramic period in southwestern Manitoba." *Plains Anthropologist,* Memoir 12, Pt. 2.

———. 1979. "The Devils Lake–Sourisford Burial Complex on the Northeastern Plains." *Plains Anthropologist* 24(86): 283–308.

Tarasoff, Koozma J. 1980. *Persistent Ceremonialism: the Plains Cree and Saulteaux.* National Museum of Man Mercury Series, Canadian Ethnology Service Paper No. 69, Ottawa.

Verbicky-Todd, Eleanor. 1984. *Communal Buffalo Hunting Among the Plains Indians.* Occasional Paper No. 24, Archaeological Survey of Alberta, Edmonton.

Vickers, J. Roderick. 1986. *Alberta Plains Prehistory: A Review.* Occasional Paper No. 27, Archaeological Survey of Alberta, Edmonton.

Wallis, Wilson D. 1919. "The sun dance of the Canadian Dakota." *Anthropological Papers of the American Museum of Natural History,* Vol. 16, 317–80.

———. 1947. "The Canadian Dakota." *Anthropological Papers of the American Museum of Natural History,* Vol. 41, Pt. 1.

Wissler, Clark. 1910. "Material culture of the Blackfoot Indians." *Anthropological Papers of the American Museum of Natural History,* Vol. 5, Pt. 1.

———. 1912. "Social organization and ritualistic ceremonies of the Blackfoot Indians." *Anthropological Papers of the American Museum of Natural History,* Vol. 7.

———. 1913. "Societies and dance associations of the Blackfoot Indians." *Anthropological Papers of the American Museum of Natural History,* Vol. 11, Pt. 4.

———. 1914. "The influence of the horse in the development of Plains culture." *American Anthropologist* 16: 1–25.

Wissler, Clark, and D.C. Duvall. 1909. "Mythology of the Blackfoot Indians." *Anthropological Papers of the American Museum of Natural History,* Vol. 2, Pt. 1.

CHAPTER SEVEN *The Plateau*

By far the most important ethnographic sources for the Canadian Plateau are the works of James Teit (1900, 1906, 1909, 1930), particularly his detailed study of the Nlaka'pamux (Thompson) (1900). The Ktunaxa (Kutenai) are not well documented; Turney-High's (1941) rather late ethnography is the standard source. Ray (1939) provides a useful overview of the entire Plateau. Detailed overview articles are provided in the Plateau volume of the *Handbook of North American Indians* (Walker 1998).

The archaeology of the Canadian Plateau is summarized in two works by Fladmark (1982, 1986), which deal with all of British Columbia. An overview of the late period is given by Richards and Rousseau (1987). Hayden (1997) gives a good account of archaeology at a major Plateau village.

Boas, Franz. 1918. *Kutenai Tales.* Smithsonian Institution, Bureau of American Ethnology, Bulletin 59, Washington.

Carstens, Peter. 1991. *The Queen's People: a Study of Hegemony, Coercion and Accommodation among the Okanagan of Canada.* Toronto: University of Toronto Press.

Curtis, Edward S. 1911. *The North American Indian, Vol. 7.* New York: Johnson Reprint.

Drake-Terry, Joanne. 1989. *The Same as Yesterday: The Lillooet Chronicle the Theft of Their Lands and Resources.* Lillooet, BC: Lillooet Tribal Council.

Fisher, Robin. 1977. *Contact and Conflict: Indian-European Relations in British Columbia, 1774–1890.* Vancouver: University of British Columbia Press.

Fladmark, K.R. 1982. "An introduction to the prehistory of British Columbia." *Canadian Journal of Archaeology* 6: 95–156.

———. 1986. *British Columbia Prehistory.* Ottawa: National Museums of Canada.

Hayden, Brian, ed. 1992. *A Complex Culture of the British Columbia Plateau: Traditional Stl'atl'imx Resource Use.* Vancouver: University of British Columbia Press.

———. 1997. *The Pithouses of Keatley Creek: Complex Hunter-Gatherers of the Northwest Plateau.* Case Studies in Archaeology, Fort Worth, TX: Harcourt Brace.

Hayden, Brian, and June M. Ryder. 1991. "Prehistoric cultural collapse in the Lillooet area." *American Antiquity* 56: 50–65.

Hayden, Brian, and Rick Schulting. 1997. "The Plateau interaction sphere and late prehistoric cultural complexity." *American Antiquity* 62(1): 51–85.

Hewlett, Edward S. 1973. "The Chilcotin uprising of 1864." *BC Studies* 19: 50–72.

Hudson, Douglas. 2004. "The Okanagan." In *Native Peoples: The Canadian Experience.* 3rd ed., ed. R.B. Morrison and C.R. Wilson, 353–76. Don Mills, ON: Oxford University Press.

Ignace, Marianne, and Ron Ignace. 2004. "The Secwepemc: traditional resource use and right to land." In *Native Peoples: The Canadian Experience.* 3rd ed., ed. R.B. Morrison and C.R. Wilson, 377–98. Don Mills, ON: Oxford University Press.

Kane, Paul. 1968. *Wanderings of an Artist.* Edmonton: Hurtig.

Kennedy, Dorothy I.D., and Randy Bouchard. 1978. "Fraser River Lillooet: an ethnographic summary." In *Reports of the Lillooet Archaeological Project,* ed. A.H. Stryd and S. Lawhead, 22–55. National Museum of Man Mercury Series, Archaeological Survey of Canada Paper No. 73, Ottawa.

Keyser, James D. 1992. *Indian Rock Art of the Columbia Plateau.* Seattle: University of Washington Press.

Lamb, W. Kaye, ed. 1960. *The Letters and Journals of Simon Fraser, 1806–1808.* Toronto: Macmillan.

Maud, Ralph, ed. 1978. *The Salish People: The Local Contributions of Charles Hill-Tout, Vols. 1 and 2.* Vancouver: Talonbooks.

Ray, Verne F. 1939. *Cultural Relations in the Plateau of Northwestern America.* Los Angeles: Southwest Museum.

Richards, Thomas H., and Michael K. Rousseau. 1987. *Late Prehistoric Cultural Horizons on the Canadian Plateau.* Publication No. 16, Department of Archaeology, Simon Fraser University, Burnaby, BC.

Rousseau, Mike K. 1993. "Early prehistoric occupation of south-central British Columbia: a review of the evidence and recommendations for future research." *BC Studies* 99: 140–83.

Sanger, David. 1968. "The Chase Burial Site EeQw: 1, British Columbia." *Contributions to Anthropology VI: Archaeology,* 86–185. National Museums of Canada, Bulletin 224, Ottawa.

———. 1970. "The archaeology of the Lochnore-Nesikep locality, British Columbia." *Syesis 3,* supplement 1.

Schulting, Rick J. 1995. *Mortuary Variability and Status Differentiation on the Columbia-Fraser Plateau.* Burnaby, BC: Archaeology Press, Simon Fraser University.

Stryd, Arnoud. 1983. "Prehistoric mobile art from the mid-Fraser and Thompson River areas." In *Indian Art Traditions of the Northwest Coast,* ed. R.L. Carlson, 167–81. Burnaby, BC: Archaeology Press, Simon Fraser University.

Teit, James A. 1900. *The Thompson Indians of British Columbia.* American Museum of Natural History Memoir, Vol. 1, Pt. 4, 163–392. (AMS Press reprint 1975.)

———. 1906. *The Lillooet Indians.* American Museum of Natural History Memoir, Vol. 2, Pt. 5, 193–300. (AMS Press reprint 1975.)

———. 1909. *The Shuswap.* American Museum of Natural History Memoir, Vol. 2, Pt. 7, 443–758. (AMS Press reprint 1975.)

———. 1912. *Mythology of the Thompson Indians.* American Museum of Natural History Memoir, Vol. 8, 199–416. (AMS Press reprint 1975.)

————. 1930. *The Salishan Tribes of the Western Plateaus.* Bureau of American Ethnology, Annual Report 45, Washington.

Turney-High, Harry H. 1941. *Ethnography of the Kutenai.* Memoir No. 56, American Anthropological Association, Menasha, WI.

Walker, Deward E, Jr., ed. 1998. *Handbook of North American Indians, Vol. 12: Plateau.* Washington: Smithsonian Institution.

Wilmeth, Roscoe. 1978. *Anahim Lake Archaeology and the Early Historic Chilcotin Indians.* National Museum of Man Mercury Series, Archaeological Survey of Canada Paper No. 82, Ottawa.

Wilson, Robert L., and Catherine Carlson. 1980. *The Archaeology of Kamloops.* Publication No. 7, Department of Archaeology, Simon Fraser University, Burnaby, BC.

York, Annie, Richard Daly, and Chris Arnett. 1993. *They Write Their Dreams on the Rock Forever: Rock Writings in the Stein River Valley of British Columbia.* Vancouver: Talonbooks.

CHAPTER EIGHT *The Northwest Coast*

An invaluable source, providing summary articles on all Northwest Coast groups, is the *Handbook of North American Indians: Northwest Coast* (Suttles 1990).

The major ethnographic sources are Swanton (1909) for the Haida; Emmons (1991), Krause (1956) and Oberg (1973) for the Tlingit; Boas (1897,1909) for the Kwakwaka'wakw; Drucker (1951) and Arima (1983) for the Nuu-chah-nulth; McIlwraith (1948) for the Nuxalk and Barnett (1955) and Duff (1952) for the Coast Salish. Drucker (1965) provides a good general treatment.

Ames and Maschner (1999) and Matson and Coupland (1995) examine Northwest Coast archaeology. Fladmark (1986) gives an excellent account of British Columbia archaeology. Historic overviews are provided by Duff (1964), Fisher (1977) and Gunther (1972).

Adams, John W. 1973. *The Gitksan Potlatch.* Toronto: Holt, Rinehart and Winston.

Ames, Kenneth M. 1981. "The evolution of social ranking on the Northwest Coast of North America." *American Antiquity* 46: 789–805.

Ames, Kenneth M., and Herbert D.G. Maschner. 1999. *Peoples of the Northwest Coast: Their Archaeology and Prehistory.* London: Thames and Hudson.

Amoss, Pamela. 1978. *Coast Salish Spirit Dancing.* Seattle: University of Washington Press.

Arima, E.Y. 1983. *The West Coast (Nootka) People.* Victoria: British Columbia Provincial Museum.

Assu, Harry, with Joy Inglis. 1989. *Assu of Cape Mudge: Recollections of a Coastal Indian Chief.* Vancouver: University of British Columbia Press.

Barbeau, Marius. 1928. *The Downfall of Temlaham.* Edmonton: Hurtig.

————.1950. *Totem Poles* (2 vols.). National Museum of Canada, Bulletin No. 119, Ottawa.

————. 1958. *Medicine Men on the North Pacific Coast.* National Museum of Canada, Bulletin No. 152, Ottawa.

Barnett, H.G. 1938. "The nature of the potlatch." *American Anthropologist* 40: 349–58.

————. 1955. *The Coast Salish of British Columbia.* Eugene: University of Oregon Press.

Boas, Franz. 1897. *The Social Organization and the Secret Societies of the Kwakiutl Indians*. New York: Johnson. (Reprinted in 1970.)

———. 1909. *The Kwakiutl of Vancouver Island*. Memoir of the American Museum of Natural History, Vol. 5.

———. 1916. *Tsimshian Mythology*. Washington: U.S. Bureau of Ethnology. (Reprinted in 1970.)

———. 1935. *Kwakiutl Culture as Reflected in Mythology*. New York: American Folklore Society. (Reprinted in 1976).

———. 1966. *Kwakiutl Ethnography*, ed. Helen Codere. Chicago: University of Chicago Press.

Boelscher, Marianne. 1988. *The Curtain Within: Haida Social and Mythical Discourse*. Vancouver: University of British Columbia Press.

Borden, Charles E. 1975. *Origins and Development of Early Northwest Coast Culture to About 3000 BC*. National Museum of Man Mercury Series, Archaeological Survey of Canada Paper No. 45, Ottawa.

Boyd, Robert. 1999. *The Coming of the Spirit of Pestilence: Introduced Diseases and Population Decline Among Northwest Coast Indians, 1774–1874*. Vancouver: University of British Columbia Press.

Burley, David V. 1980. *Marpole: Anthropological Reconstructions of a Prehistoric Northwest Coast Culture Type*. Publication No. 8, Department of Archaeology, Simon Fraser University, Burnaby, BC.

Canada, British Columbia, Nisga'a Nation. 1998. *Nisga'a Final Agreement*. Queen's Printer.

Carlson, Roy L., ed. 1983. *Indian Art Traditions of the Northwest Coast*. Burnaby, BC: Archaeology Press, Simon Fraser University.

Carlson, Roy L., and Luke Dalla Bona, eds. 1996. *Early Human Occupation in British Columbia*. Vancouver: UBC Press.

Clutesi, George. 1969. *Potlatch*. Sidney, BC: Gray's.

Codere, Helen. 1950. *Fighting With Property*. Seattle: University of Washington Press.

Cole, Douglas, and Ira Chaikin. 1990. *An Iron Hand Upon the People: The Law Against the Potlatch on the Northwest Coast*. Vancouver: Douglas & McIntyre.

Cook, Captain James. 1784. *A Voyage to the Pacific Ocean*. London: W. and A. Strahan.

Croes, Dale R., ed. 1976. *The Excavation of Water-Saturated Archaeological Sites (Wet Sites) on the Northwest Coast of North America*. National Museum of Man Mercury Series, Archaeological Survey of Canada Paper No. 50, Ottawa.

Culhane, Dara. 1998. *The Pleasure of the Crown: Anthropology, Law and First Nations*. Burnaby, BC: Talonbooks.

Curtis, Edward S. 1915. *The North American Indian, Vol. 10: Kwakiutl*. New York: Johnson. (Reprinted in 1970.)

———. 1916. *The North American Indian, Vol. 11: Nootka and Haida*. New York: Johnson. (Reprinted in 1970.)

Dewhirst, John. 1980. *The Yuquot Project, Volume 1: The Indigenous Archaeology of Yuquot, a Nootkan Outside Village*. History and Archaeology 39, Parks Canada, Ottawa.

Drucker, Philip. 1951. *The Northern and Central Nootkan Tribes*. Smithsonian Institution, Bureau of American Ethnology Bulletin 144, Washington.

———. 1965. *Cultures of the North Pacific Coast*. San Francisco: Chandler.

Drucker, Philip, and Robert F. Heizer. 1967. *To Make My Name Good*. Berkeley and Los Angeles: University of California Press.

Duff, Wilson. 1952. *The Upper Stalo Indians of the Fraser River of B.C.* Anthropology in British Columbia Memoir No. 1, British Columbia Provincial Museum, Victoria.

———. 1964. *The Indian History of British Columbia, Volume 1: The Impact of the White Man*. Anthropology in British Columbia Memoir No. 5, British Columbia Provincial Museum, Victoria.

———.1969. "The Fort Victoria treaties." *BC Studies* 3: 3–57.

———1975. *Images: Stone: B.C.* Surrey, BC: Hancock House.

Ellis, David W., and Luke Swan. 1981. *Teachings of the Tides*. Nanaimo, BC: Theytus Books.

Emmons, George Thornton. 1991. *The Tlingit Indians*, ed. Frederica de Laguna. Vancouver: Douglas & McIntyre and New York: American Museum of Natural History.

Fedje, Daryl W., and Tina Christensen. 1999. "Modelling paleoshorelines and locating early Holocene coastal sites in Haida Gwaii." *American Antiquity* 64(4): 635–52.

Fedje, Daryl W., Rebecca Wigen, Quentin Mackie, Cynthia Lake, and Ian Sumpter. 2001. "Preliminary results from investigations at Kilgii Gwaay: an early Holocene archaeological site on Ellen Island, Haida Gwaii, British Columbia." *Canadian Journal of Archaeology* 25: 98–120.

Fisher, Robin. 1977. *Contact and Conflict: Indian-European Relations in British Columbia, 1774–1890*. Vancouver: University of British Columbia Press.

Fladmark, Knut R. 1982. "An introduction to the prehistory of British Columbia." *Canadian Journal of Archaeology* 6: 95–156.

———. 1986. *British Columbia Prehistory*. Ottawa: National Museum of Man.

Garfield, Viola E., and Paul S. Wingert. 1966. *The Tsimshian Indians and Their Arts*. Seattle: University of Washington Press.

Gibson, James R. 1992. *Otter Skins, Boston Ships, and China Goods: The Maritime Fur Trade of the Northwest Coast, 1785–1841*. Montreal and Kingston: McGill-Queen's University Press.

Goldman, Irving. 1975. *The Mouth of Heaven: An Introduction to Kwakiutl Religious Thought*. New York: Wiley.

Gunther, Erna. 1966. *Art in the Life of the Northwest Coast Indians*. Portland, OR: Portland Art Museum.

———. 1972. *Indian Life on the Northwest Coast of North America as Seen by the Early Explorers and Fur Traders during the Last Decades of the Eighteenth Century*. Chicago: University of Chicago Press.

Harkin, Michael E. 1997. *The Heiltsuks: Dialogues of Culture and History on the Northwest Coast*. Lincoln: University of Nebraska Press.

Hawthorn, Audrey. 1979. *Kwakiutl Art*. Vancouver: Douglas & McIntyre.

Hill, Beth, and Ray Hill. 1974. *Indian Petroglyphs of the Pacific Northwest*. Surrey, BC: Hancock House Publishers.

Holm, Bill. 1965. *Northwest Coast Indian Art: An Analysis of Form*. Seattle: University of Washington Press.

———. 1983. *Smoky-Top: The Art and Times of Willie Seaweed*. Seattle: University of Washington Press and Vancouver: Douglas & McIntyre.

Hoover, Alan L., ed. 2000. *Nuu-chah-nulth Voices, Histories, Objects and Journeys*. Victoria: Royal British Columbia Museum.

Jenness, Diamond. 1955. *The Faith of a Coast Salish Indian*. Anthropology in British Columbia Memoir No. 3, British Columbia Provincial Museum, Victoria.

Jilek, Wolfgang G. 1982. *Indian Healing: Shamanic Ceremonialism in the Pacific Northwest Today*. Surrey, BC: Hancock House.

Jonaitis, Aldona, ed. 1991. *Chiefly Feasts: The Enduring Kwakiutl Potlatch*. New York: American Museum of Natural History and Vancouver: Douglas & McIntyre.

Kenyon, Susan M. 1980. *The Kyuquot Way: A Study of a West Coast (Nootkan) Community*. National Museum of Man Mercury Series, Canadian Ethnology Service Paper No. 61, Ottawa.

Kirk, Ruth. 1986. *Wisdom of the Elders: Native Traditions on the Northwest Coast*. Vancouver: Douglas & McIntyre.

Krause, Aurel. 1956. *The Tlingit Indians*. Seattle: University of Washington Press.

Lamb, W. Kaye, ed. 1960. *The Letters and Journals of Simon Fraser, 1806–1808*. Toronto: Macmillan.

LaViolette, F.E. 1973. *The Struggle for Survival: Indian Cultures and the Protestant Ethic in British Columbia*. Toronto: University of Toronto Press.

MacDonald, George F. 1983. *Haida Monumental Art*. Vancouver: University of British Columbia Press.

———. 1996. *Haida Art*. Vancouver: Canadian Museum of Civilization and Douglas & McIntyre.

MacDonald, George F., and Richard Inglis. 1975. *The Dig: An Archaeological Reconstruction of a West Coast Village*. Ottawa: National Museum of Man.

Macnair, Peter. 2004. "From Kwakiutl to Kwakwaka'wakw." In *Native Peoples: The Canadian Experience*, 3rd ed., ed. R.B. Morrison and C.R. Wilson, 431–46. Don Mills, ON: Oxford University Press.

Macnair, Peter L., Alan Hoover, and Kevin Neary. 1980. *The Legacy*. Victoria: British Columbia Provincial Museum.

McIlwraith, T.F. 1948. *The Bella Coola Indians* (2 vols.). Toronto: University of Toronto Press.

McKee, Christopher. 2000. *Treaty Talks in British Columbia: Negotiating a Mutually Beneficial Future*. 2nd ed. Vancouver: UBC Press.

McMillan, Alan D. 1999. *Since the Time of the Transformers: The Ancient Heritage of the Nuu-chah-nulth, Ditidaht, and Makah*. Vancouver: UBC Press.

Matson, R.G., and Gary Coupland. 1995. *The Prehistory of the Northwest Coast*. San Diego, CA: Academic Press.

Maud, Ralph, ed. 1978. *The Salish People: The Local Contributions of Charles Hill-Tout* (Vols. 2–4). Vancouver: Talonbooks.

Miller, Jay. 1997. *Tsimshian Culture: A Light Through the Ages*. Lincoln: University of Nebraska Press.

Mitchell, Donald H. 1971. "Archaeology of the Gulf of Georgia Area, a Natural Region and its Culture Types." *Syesis*, Vol. 4, supplement 1, British Columbia Provincial Museum, Victoria.

Molloy, Tom. 2000. *The World is Our Witness: The Historic Journey of the Nisga'a into Canada*. Calgary: Fifth House.

Murray, Peter. 1985. *The Devil and Mr. Duncan*. Victoria: Sono Nis Press.

Niblack, Albert P. 1890. *The Coast Indians of Southern Alaska and Northern British Columbia*. New York: Johnson. (Reprinted in 1970.)

Oberg, Kalervo. 1973. *The Social Organization of the Tlingit Indians*. Seattle: University of Washington Press.

Persky, Stan (commentator). 1998. *Delgamuukw: The Supreme Court of Canada Decision on Aboriginal Title*. Vancouver: Douglas & McIntyre.

Raunet, Daniel. 1984. *Without Surrender, Without Consent: A History of the Nishga Land Claims*. Vancouver: Douglas & McIntyre.

Rohner, Ronald P. 1967. *The People of Gilford: A Contemporary Kwakiutl Village*. National Museum of Canada, Bulletin No. 225, Ottawa.

Rohner, Ronald P., and Evelyn C. Rohner. 1970. *The Kwakiutl: Indians of British Columbia*. New York: Holt, Rinehart and Winston.

Rose, Alex. 2000. *Spirit Dance at Meziadin: Chief Joseph Gosnell and the Nisga'a Treaty*. Madeira Park, BC: Harbour Publishing.

Rosman, Abraham, and Paula Rubel. 1971. *Feasting With Mine Enemy*. New York: Columbia University Press.

Seguin, Margaret, ed. 1984. *The Tsimshian: Images of the Past, Views for the Present*. Vancouver: UBC Press.

Spradley, James P., ed. 1969. *Guests Never Leave Hungry: The Autobiography of James Sewid, a Kwakiutl Indian*. New Haven, CT: Yale University Press.

Sproat, Gilbert Malcolm. 1987. *The Nootka: Scenes and Studies of Savage Life*. Victoria: Sono Nis Press.

Stearns, Mary Lee. 1981. *Haida Culture in Custody*. Seattle: University of Washington Press.

Stewart, Hilary. 1977. *Indian Fishing: Early Methods on the Northwest Coast*. Vancouver: Douglas & McIntyre.

———. 1984. *Cedar*. Vancouver: Douglas & McIntyre.

———. 1990. *Totem Poles*. Vancouver: Douglas & McIntyre.

Stott, Margaret A. 1975. *Bella Coola Ceremony and Art*. National Museum of Man Mercury Series, Canadian Ethnology Service Paper No. 21, Ottawa.

Suttles, Wayne. 1955. *Katzie Ethnographic Notes*. Anthropology in British Columbia Memoir No. 2, British Columbia Provincial Museum, Victoria.

———. 1974. *The Economic Life of the Coast Salish of Haro and Rosario Straits*. New York: Garland.

———. 1987. *Coast Salish Essays*. Vancouver: Talonbooks.

———, ed. 1990. *Handbook of North American Indians, Vol. 7: Northwest Coast*. Washington: Smithsonian Institution.

Swanton, John R. 1909. *Contributions to the Ethnology of the Haida*. Memoir of the American Museum of Natural History Vol. 5.

Tennant, Paul. 1990. *Aboriginal Peoples and Politics: The Indian Land Question in British Columbia, 1849–1989*. Vancouver: UBC Press.

Usher, Jean. 1974. *William Duncan of Metlakatla*. National Museums of Canada, Publications in History No. 5, Ottawa.

Van Den Brink, J.H. 1974. *The Haida Indians*. Leiden: E.J. Brill.

Wolcott, Harry F. 1967. *A Kwakiutl Village and School*. New York: Holt, Rinehart and Winston.

Woodcock, George. 1977. *Peoples of the Coast*. Edmonton: Hurtig.

CHAPTER NINE *The Western Subarctic*

An important source on all aspects of Subarctic Athapaskan life is the Subarctic volume of the *Handbook of North American Indians* (Helm 1981). Standard ethnographic sources on traditional Athapaskan cultures are Birket-Smith (1930), Emmons (1911), Goddard (1916), Honigmann (1946, 1954), Jenness (1937, 1943), McClellan (1975), McKennan (1965), Morice (1893) and Osgood (1936, 1971). VanStone (1974) provides a general anthropological overview, while Abel (1993) provides a historic overview of the NWT Dene. Clark (1991) summarizes the archaeology of the Western Subarctic.

The late-eighteenth century journals of Hearne (1971), Thompson (Glover 1962) and Mackenzie (1971) give early historic glimpses into Athapaskan life. A good summary of fur trade changes on Athapaskan cultures is given by Yerbury (1986).

For descriptions of recent and modern Athapaskan cultures see Hara (1980), Helm (1961, 2000), Savishinsky (1974), Slobodin (1962), Smith (1982) and VanStone (1965). In addition, both Brody (1981) and Ridington (1988) provide sensitive accounts of modern life among the Dunne-za.

Abel, Kerry. 1993. *Drum Song: Glimpses of Dene History.* Montreal and Kingston: McGill-Queen's University Press.

Albright, Sylvia. 1984. *Tahltan Ethnoarchaeology.* Publication No. 15, Department of Archaeology, Simon Fraser University, Burnaby, BC.

Asch, Michael with Robert Wishart. 2004. "The Slavey Indians: the relevance of ethnohistory to development." In *Native Peoples: The Canadian Experience.* 3rd ed., ed. R.B. Morrison and C.R. Wilson, 178–97. Don Mills, ON: Oxford University Press.

Balikci, Asen. 1963. *Vunta Kutchin Social Change.* Northern Co-ordination and Research Centre, Department of Northern Affairs and National Resources, Ottawa.

Berger, Thomas R. 1977. *Northern Frontier, Northern Homeland: The Report of the Mackenzie Valley Pipeline Inquiry* (2 vols.). Ministry of Supply and Services Canada, Ottawa.

Birket-Smith, Kaj. 1930. *Contributions to Chipewyan Ethnology.* New York: AMS Press. (Reprinted in 1976.)

Bone, Robert, Earl Shannon, and Stewart Raby. 1973. *The Chipewyan of the Stony Rapids Region.* Saskatoon: Institute for Northern Studies, University of Saskatchewan.

Brody, Hugh. 1981. *Maps and Dreams.* Vancouver: Douglas & McIntyre.

Canada, Indian and Northern Affairs. 1992. *Gwich'in Comprehensive Land Claim Agreement.* Ottawa.

———. 1993a. *Sahtu Dene and Metis Comprehensive Land Claim Agreement.* Ottawa.

———. 1993b. *Umbrella Final Agreement: Council For Yukon Indians.* Ottawa.

Christian, Jane, and P.M. Gardner. 1977. *The Individual in Northern Dene Thought and Communication: A Study in Sharing and Diversity.* National Museum of Man Mercury Series, Canadian Ethnology Service Paper No. 35, Ottawa.

Clark, A. McFadyen. 1974. *The Athapaskans: Strangers of the North.* Ottawa: National Museum of Man.

Clark, Donald W. 1991. *Western Subarctic Prehistory.* Hull, QC: Canadian Museum of Civilization.

Coates, Ken S. 1991. *Best Left as Indians: Native-White Relations in the Yukon Territory, 1840–1973.* Montreal and Kingston: McGill-Queen's University Press.

Cruikshank, Julie. 1979. *Athapaskan Women: Lives and Legends*. National Museum of Man Mercury Series, Canadian Ethnology Service Paper No. 57, Ottawa.

———. 1990. *Life Lived Like a Story: Life Stories of Three Yukon Elders*. Vancouver: UBC Press.

———. 1991. *Reading Voices: Oral and Written Interpretations of the Yukon's Past*. Vancouver: Douglas & McIntyre.

Dene Nation. 1984. *Denendeh: A Dene Celebration*. Yellowknife: Dene Nation.

Duncan, Kate C. 1989. *Northern Athapaskan Art: A Beadwork Tradition*. Vancouver: Douglas & McIntyre.

Emmons, G.T. 1911. *The Tahltan Indians*. Anthropological Publications of the University of Pennsylvania Museum, Vol. 4, No. 1.

Fiske, Jo-Anne. 2000. *Cis Dadeen Kat/When the Plumes Rise: The Way of the Lake Babine Nation*. Vancouver: UBC Press.

Fumoleau, Rene. 1973. *As Long as This Land Shall Last: A History of Treaty 8 and Treaty 11*. Toronto: McClelland and Stewart.

Furniss, Elizabeth. 2004. "The Carrier and the politics of history." In *Native Peoples: The Canadian Experience*. 3rd ed., ed. R.B. Morrison and C.R. Wilson, 198–222. Don Mills, ON: Oxford University Press.

Gillespie, Beryl C. 1975. "Territorial expansion of the Chipewyan in the 18th century." In *Proceedings: Northern Athapaskan Conference, 1971*, ed. A. McFadyen Clark, 350–88. National Museum of Man Mercury Series, Canadian Ethnology Service Paper No. 27, Ottawa.

Glover, Richard, ed. 1962. *David Thompson's Narrative 1784–1812*. Toronto: Champlain Society.

Goddard, John. 1991. *Last Stand of the Lubicon Cree*. Vancouver: Douglas & McIntyre.

Goddard, Pliny Earle. 1916. *The Beaver Indians*. Anthropological Papers of the American Museum of Natural History, Vol. 10, Pt. 4, 203–93.

Goldman, Irving. 1940. "The Alkatcho Carrier of British Columbia." In *Acculturation in Seven American Indian Tribes*, ed. Ralph Linton, 333–86. Gloucester, MA: Peter Smith.

———. 1941. "The Alkatcho Carrier: historical background of crest prerogatives." *American Anthropologist* 43: 396–418.

Gordon, Bryan H.C. 1976. *Migod—8,000 Years of Barrenland Prehistory*. National Museum of Man Mercury Series, Archaeological Survey of Canada Paper No. 56, Ottawa.

Goulet, Jean-Guy A. 1998. *Ways of Knowing: Experience, Knowledge, and Power Among the Dene Tha*. Vancouver: University of British Columbia Press.

Hara, Sue Hiroko. 1980. *The Hare Indians and Their World*. National Museum of Man Mercury Series, Canadian Ethnology Service Paper No. 63, Ottawa.

Hearne, Samuel. 1971. *A Journey From Prince of Wales's Fort in Hudson's Bay to the Northern Ocean*. Edmonton: Hurtig.

Helm, June. 1961. *The Lynx Point People: The Dynamics of a Northern Athapaskan Band*. National Museum of Canada, Bulletin No. 176, Ottawa.

———. 1972. "The Dogrib Indians." In *Hunters and Gatherers Today*, ed. M.G. Bicchieri, 51–89. New York: Holt, Rinehart and Winston.

———, et al. 1975. "The contact history of the Subarctic Athapaskans: an overview." In *Proceedings: Northern Athapaskan Conference, 1971*, ed. A. McFadyen Clark,

302–49. National Museum of Man Mercury Series, Canadian Ethnology Service Paper No. 27, Ottawa.

———, ed. 1981. *Handbook of North American Indians, Vol. 6: Subarctic.* Washington: Smithsonian Institution.

———. 2000. *The People of Denendeh: Ethnohistory of the Indians of Canada's Northwest Territories.* Montreal and Kingston: McGill-Queen's University Press.

Helmer, J.W., S. Van Dyke, and F.J. Kense, eds. 1977. *Problems in the Prehistory of the North American Subarctic: The Athapaskan Question.* Calgary: Department of Archaeology, University of Calgary.

Honigmann, John J. 1946. *Ethnography and Acculturation of the Fort Nelson Slave.* Yale University Publications in Anthropology No. 33, Yale University Press, New Haven, CT.

———. 1954. *The Kaska Indians: An Ethnographic Reconstruction.* Yale University Publications in Anthropology No. 51, Yale University Press, New Haven, CT.

Ives, John W. 1990. *A Theory of Northern Athapaskan Prehistory.* Calgary: Westview Press/University of Calgary Press.

Jenness, Diamond. 1937. *The Sekani Indians of British Columbia.* National Museum of Canada, Bulletin No. 84, Ottawa.

———. 1943. *The Carrier Indians of the Bulkley River: Their Social and Religious Life.* Bureau of American Ethnology Bulletin 133: 469–586. Washington.

Jones, T.E.H. 1981. *The Aboriginal Rock Paintings of the Churchill River.* Saskatchewan Museum of Natural History, Anthropological Series No. 4, Regina.

Krech, Shepard, III. 1976. "The Eastern Kutchin and the fur trade, 1800–1860." *Ethnohistory* 23(3): 213–35.

———. 1978. "Disease, starvation, and Northern Athapaskan social organization." *American Ethnologist* 5(4): 710–32.

———. 1984. "The trade of the Slavey and Dogrib at Fort Simpson in the early nineteenth century." In *The Subarctic Fur Trade: Native Social and Economic Adaptations,* ed. Shepard Krech III, 99–146. Vancouver: UBC Press.

Leechman, Douglas. 1954. *The Vanta Kutchin.* Ottawa: Department of Northern Affairs and National Resources.

Legros, Dominique. 1985. "Wealth, poverty, and slavery among 19th-century Tutchone Athapaskans." *Research in Economic Anthropology* 7: 37–64.

Mackenzie, Alexander. 1971. *Voyages from Montreal on the River St. Lawrence through the Continent of North America to the Frozen and Pacific Oceans in the Years 1798 and 1793.* Edmonton: Hurtig.

McClellan, Catherine. 1975. *My Old People Say: An Ethnographic Survey of Southern Yukon Territory* (2 vols.). National Museums of Canada, Publications in Ethnology No. 6, Ottawa.

———. 1975. "Feuding and warfare among northwestern Athapaskans." In *Proceedings: Northern Athapaskan Conference, 1971,* ed. A. McFadyen Clark, 181–258. National Museum of Man Mercury Series, Canadian Ethnology Service Paper No. 27, Ottawa.

———. 1987. *Part of the Land, Part of the Water: A History of the Yukon Indians.* Vancouver: Douglas & McIntyre.

McKennan, Robert A. 1965. *The Chandalar Kutchin.* Arctic Institute of North America, Technical Paper No. 17, Montreal.

Mason, J. Alden. 1946. *Notes on the Indians of the Great Slave Lake Area.* Yale University Publications in Anthropology No. 34, Yale University Press, New Haven, CT.

Meyer, David. 1983. "The prehistory of northern Saskatchewan." In *Tracking Ancient Hunters,* ed. Henry T. Epp and Ian Dyck, 141–70. Regina: Saskatchewan Archaeological Society.

Morice, Rev. Father A.G. 1893. *Notes Archaeological, Industrial and Sociological on the Western Denes with an Ethnological Sketch of the Same.* Transactions of the Canadian Institute Vol. 4, Toronto.

Morlan, Richard E. 1973. *The Later Prehistory of the Middle Porcupine Drainage, Northern Yukon Territory.* National Museum of Man Mercury Series, Archaeological Survey of Canada Paper No. 11, Ottawa.

Morrison, William R. 1992. "Aboriginal land claims in the Canadian north." In *Aboriginal Land Claims in Canada,* ed. Ken Coates, 167–94. Toronto: Copp Clark Pitman.

Nash, Ronald J. 1975. *Archaeological Investigations in the Transitional Forest Zone: Northern Manitoba, Southern Keewatin, N.W.T.* Manitoba Museum of Man and Nature, Winnipeg.

Nelson, Richard K. 1973. *Hunters of the Northern Forest.* Chicago: University of Chicago Press.

Osgood, Cornelius. 1932. "The ethnography of the Great Bear Lake Indians." *National Museum of Canada Bulletin* 70: 31–97.

———. 1936a. "The distribution of the Northern Athapaskan Indians." *Yale University Publications in Anthropology* 7: 3–23. New Haven, CT.

———. 1936b. "Contributions to the Ethnography of the Kutchin." *Yale University Publications in Anthropology.* 14, New Haven, CT.

———. 1971. "The Han Indians." *Yale University Publications in Anthropology.* 74, New Haven, CT.

Ridington, Robin. 1968. "The medicine fight: an instrument of political process among the Beaver Indians." *American Anthropologist* 70(6): 1152–160.

———. 1971. "Beaver dreaming and singing." *Anthropologica* 13: 115–28.

———. 1978. *Swan People: A Study of the Dunne-za Prophet Dance.* National Museum of Man Mercury Series, Canadian Ethnology Service Paper No. 38, Ottawa.

———. 1979. "Changes of mind: Dunne-za resistance to empire." *BC Studies* 43: 65–80.

———. 1988. *Trail to Heaven: Knowledge and Narrative in a Northern Native Community.* Vancouver: Douglas & McIntyre.

Rushforth, E. Scott. 1986. "The Bear Lake Indians." In *Native Peoples: The Canadian Experience,* ed. R.B. Morrison and C.R. Wilson, 243–71. Toronto: McClelland and Stewart.

Russell, Dale R. 1991. *Eighteenth-Century Western Cree and Their Neighbours.* Hull, QC: Canadian Museum of Civilization.

Ryan, Joan. 1995. *Doing Things the Right Way: Dene Traditional Justice in Lac La Martre, NWT.* Calgary: University of Calgary Press.

Savishinsky, Joel S. 1974. *The Trail of the Hare: Life and Stress in an Arctic Community.* New York: Gordon and Breach.

Slobodin, Richard. 1960. "Eastern Kutchin warfare." *Anthropologica* 2(1): 76–94.

———. 1962. *Band Organization of the Peel River Kutchin.* National Museum of Canada Bulletin No. 179, Ottawa.

————. 1966. *Metis of the Mackenzie District.* Ottawa: Canadian Research Centre for Anthropology, Saint Paul University.

Smith, David M. 1982. *Moose-Deer Island House People: A History of the Native People of Fort Resolution.* National Museum of Man Mercury Series, Canadian Ethnology Service Paper No. 81, Ottawa.

Smith, J.G.E. 1975. "The ecological basis of Chipewyan socio-territorial organization." In *Proceedings: Northern Athapaskan Conference, 1971,* ed. A. McFadyen Clark, 389–461. National Museum of Man Mercury Series, Canadian Ethnology Service Paper No. 27, Ottawa.

————, ed. 1976. "Chipewyan Adaptations: Papers from a Symposium on the Chipewyan of Subarctic Canada." *Arctic Anthropology* 13(1): 1–83.

Teit, J.A. 1956. "Field notes on the Tahltan and Kaska Indians: 1912-1915." *Anthropologica* 3: 39–193.

VanStone, James W. 1965. *The Changing Culture of the Snowdrift Chipewyan.* National Museum of Canada, Bulletin 209, Ottawa.

————. 1974. *Athapaskan Adaptations.* Chicago: Aldine.

Watkins, Mel, ed. 1977. *Dene Nation: The Colony Within.* Toronto: University of Toronto Press.

Workman, William B. 1974. "The cultural significance of a volcanic ash which fell in the upper Yukon Basin about 1400 years ago." In *International Conference on the Prehistory and Paleoecology of Western North American Arctic and Subarctic,* ed. S. Raymond and P. Schledermann, 239–61. Calgary: Archaeological Association, University of Calgary.

————. 1978. *Prehistory of the Aishihik-Kluane Area, Southwest Yukon Territory.* National Museum of Man Mercury Series, Archaeological Survey of Canada Paper No. 74, Ottawa.

Wright, J.V. 1975. *The Prehistory of Lake Athabasca: An Initial Statement.* National Museum of Man Mercury Series, Archaeological Survey of Canada Paper No. 29, Ottawa.

Yerbury, J.C. 1976. "The post-contact Chipewyan: trade rivalries and changing territorial boundaries." *Ethnohistory* 23(3): 237–63.

————. 1980. "Protohistoric Canadian Athapaskan populations: an ethnohistorical reconstruction." *Arctic Anthropology* 17(2): 17–33.

————. 1986. *The Subarctic Indians and the Fur Trade, 1680–1860.* Vancouver: University of British Columbia Press.

CHAPTER TEN *The Arctic*

Summary articles on all Arctic peoples are provided in the Arctic volume of the *Handbook of North American Indians* (Damas 1984).

Recommended sources on Arctic archaeology are by McGhee (1978) and Maxwell (1985).

General ethnographic treatments of the Inuit are given in Birket-Smith (1971) and Weyer (1932). Detailed ethnographies of the Central Inuit include Balikci (1970), Boas (1901, 1964), Jenness (1922, 1946) and the publications of the Fifth Thule Expedition (Birket-Smith 1929; Mathiasson 1928; Rasmussen 1929, 1930, 1931, 1932). Other regions are less well documented. Hawkes (1916) is the standard source for the Labrador Inuit. For the western Arctic, Pettitot (1981) gives important nineteenth-century observations and McGhee (1974) provides a useful summary.

Jenness (1964) gives a historical overview, focussing on the relationship between government and the Inuit. More recent historical summaries are given in Mitchell (1996) and Fossett (2001). The historical events leading to Nunavut are well covered in Duffy (1988) and Purich (1992).

Alunik, Ishmael, Eddie Dean Kolausok and David Morrison. 2003. *Across Time and Tundra: The Inuvialuit of the Western Arctic.* Vancouver: Raincoast Books.

Arnold, Charles D. 1981. *The Lagoon Site (OjRl-3): Implications for Paleoeskimo Interactions.* National Museum of Man Mercury Series, Archaeological Survey of Canada Paper No. 107, Ottawa.

Arnold, Charles D., and Carole Stimmel. 1983. "An analysis of Thule pottery." *Canadian Journal of Archaeology* 7(1): 1–21.

Balikci, Asen. 1970. *The Netsilik Eskimo.* New York: Natural History Press.

Bielawski, E. 1988. "Paleoeskimo variability: the early Arctic small-tool tradition in the central Canadian Arctic." *American Antiquity* 53(1): 52–74.

Birket-Smith, Kaj. 1929. *The Caribou Eskimos: Material and Social Life and Their Cultural Position.* Report of the Fifth Thule Expedition 1921–24, Vol. v, Pts. 1 & 2, Copenhagen. (Reprinted in 1976.)

———. 1971. *Eskimos.* New York: Crown.

Blodgett, Jean. 1985. *Kenojuak.* Toronto: Firefly Books.

Boas, Franz. 1901. *The Eskimo of Baffin Land and Hudson Bay.* Bulletin of the American Museum of Natural History, Vol. xv. (Reprinted in 1975.)

———. 1964. *The Central Eskimo.* Lincoln: University of Nebraska Press. (Originally published 1888.)

Brody, Hugh. 1975. *The People's Land: Eskimos and Whites in the Eastern Arctic.* Harmondsworth, UK: Penguin Books.

Burch, Ernest S., Jr. 1978. "Caribou Eskimo origins: an old problem reconsidered." *Arctic Anthropology* 15(1): 1–35.

———. 2004. "The Caribou Inuit." In *Native Peoples: The Canadian Experience.* 3rd ed., ed. R.B. Morrison and C.R. Wilson, 74–94. Don Mills, ON: Oxford University Press.

Canada, Indian and Northern Affairs. 1984. *The Western Arctic Claim: The Inuvialuit Final Agreement.* Ottawa.

———. 1993. *Agreement Between the Inuit of the Nunavut Settlement Area and Her Majesty the Queen in Right of Canada.* Ottawa.

Clark, Brenda. 1977. *The Development of Caribou Eskimo Culture.* National Museum of Man Mercury Series, Archaeological Survey of Canada Paper No. 59, Ottawa.

Damas, David. 1963. *Igluligmiut Kinship and Local Groupings: A Structural Approach.* National Museum of Canada Bulletin No. 196, Ottawa.

———. 1972a. "The Copper Eskimo." In *Hunters and Gatherers Today,* ed. M.G. Bicchieri, 3–50. New York: Holt, Rinehart and Winston.

———. 1972b. "Central Eskimo systems of food sharing." *Ethnology* 11(3): 220–40.

———, ed. 1984. *Handbook of North American Indians, Vol. 5: Arctic.* Washington: Smithsonian Institution.

Duffy, R. Quinn. 1988. *The Road to Nunavut: The Progress of the Eastern Arctic Inuit Since the Second World War.* Montreal and Kingston: McGill-Queen's University Press.

Dumond, Don E. 1987. *The Eskimos and Aleuts.* rev. ed. London: Thames and Hudson.

Finkler, Harold W. 1975. *Inuit and the Administration of Criminal Justice in the Northwest Territories: The Case of Frobisher Bay.* Ottawa: Indian and Northern Affairs.

Fossett, Renée. 2001. *In Order to Live Untroubled: Inuit of the Central Arctic, 1550–1940.* Winnipeg: University of Manitoba Press.

Freeman, Milton M.R., ed. 1976. *Inuit Land Use and Occupancy Project* (3 vols.). Ottawa: Indian and Northern Affairs.

Harp, Elmer, Jr. 1964. *The Cultural Affinities of the Newfoundland Dorset Eskimo.* National Museum of Canada, Bulletin No. 200, Ottawa.

Hawkes, E.W. 1916. *The Labrador Eskimo.* Department of Mines, Geological Survey Memoir 91, Ottawa. (Reprinted in 1970.)

Honigmann, John J., and Irma Honigmann. 1970. *Arctic Townsmen.* Ottawa: Canadian Research Centre for Anthropology, Saint Paul University.

Houston, Alma, ed. 1988. *Inuit Art: An Anthology.* Winnipeg: Watson & Dwyer.

Hughes, Charles C. 1965. "Under four flags: recent culture change among the Eskimos." *Current Anthropology* 6(1): 3–69.

Jenness, Diamond. 1922. *The Life of the Copper Eskimos.* Report of the Canadian Arctic Expedition 1913–18, Vol. xii, Pt. A. (Reprinted in 1970.)

———. 1946. *Material Culture of the Copper Eskimo.* Report of the Canadian Arctic Expedition 1913–18, Vol. xvi, Ottawa.

———. 1964. *Eskimo Administration: ii. Canada.* Arctic Institute of North America, Technical Paper No. 14, Montreal.

———. 1965. *Eskimo Administration: iii. Labrador.* Arctic Institute of North America, Technical Paper No. 16, Montreal.

Linnamae, Urve. 1975. *The Dorset Culture: A Comparative Study in Newfoundland and the Arctic.* Technical Papers of the Newfoundland Museum No. 1, St. John's.

McCartney, Allen P. 1977. *Thule Eskimo Prehistory along Northwestern Hudson Bay.* National Museum of Man Mercury Series, Archaeological Survey of Canada Paper No. 70, Ottawa.

———. 1980. "The nature of Thule Eskimo whale use." *Arctic* 33(3): 517–41

———. ed. 1979. *Thule Eskimo Culture: An Anthropological Perspective.* National Museum of Man Mercury Series, Archaeological Survey of Canada Paper No. 88, Ottawa.

McCartney, A.P., and D.J. Mack. 1973. "Iron utilization by Thule Eskimos of central Canada." *American Antiquity* 38: 328–39.

McCartney, Allen P., and James M. Savelle. 1985. "Thule whaling in the central Canadian Arctic." *Arctic Anthropology* 22(2): 37–58.

McCullough, Karen M. 1989. *The Ruin Islanders: Early Thule Culture Pioneers in the Eastern High Arctic.* Archaeological Survey of Canada Mercury Series Paper 141, Canadian Museum of Civilization, Hull.

McGhee, Robert. 1972. *Copper Eskimo Prehistory.* National Museums of Canada, Publications in Archaeology No. 2, Ottawa.

———. 1974. *Beluga Hunters: An Archaeological Reconstruction of the History and Culture of the Mackenzie Delta Kittegaryumiut.* St. John's: Institute of Social and Economic Research, Memorial University of Newfoundland.

———. 1978. *Canadian Arctic Prehistory.* Ottawa: National Museum of Man.

———. 1979. *The Paleoeskimo Occupations at Port Refuge, High Arctic Canada.*

National Museum of Man Mercury Series, Archaeological Survey of Canada Paper No. 92, Ottawa.

———. 1981a. *The Tuniit: First Explorers of the High Arctic.* Ottawa: National Museum of Man.

———. 1981b. *The Dorset Occupations in the Vicinity of Port Refuge, High Arctic Canada.* National Museum of Man Mercury Series, Archaeological Survey of Canada Paper No. 105, Ottawa.

———. 1984. *The Thule Village at Brooman Point, High Arctic Canada.* National Museum of Man Mercury Series, Archaeological Survey of Canada Paper No. 125, Ottawa.

———. 1996. *Ancient People of the Arctic.* Vancouver: UBC Press.

Mathiassen, Therkel. 1927. *Archaeology of the Central Eskimos.* Report of the Fifth Thule Expedition 1921–24, Vol. IV, Pts. 1 & 2, Copenhagen. (Reprinted in 1976.)

———. 1928. *Material Culture of the Iglulik Eskimos.* Report of the Fifth Thule Expedition 1921–24, Vol. VI, No. 1, Copenhagen. (Reprinted in 1976.)

Matthiasson, John S. 1992. *Living on the Land: Change among the Inuit of Baffin Island.* Peterborough, ON: Broadview Press.

Maxwell, Moreau S., ed. 1976. *Eastern Arctic Prehistory: Paleoeskimo Problems.* Memoirs of the Society for American Archaeology No. 31.

———. 1985. *Prehistory of the Eastern Arctic.* New York: Academic Press.

Meyer, David A. 1977. *Pre-Dorset Settlements at the Seahorse Gully Site.* National Museum of Man Mercury Series, Archaeological Survey of Canada Paper No. 57, Ottawa.

Mitchell, Marybelle. 1996. *From Talking Chiefs to a Native Corporate Elite: The Birth of Class and Nationalism among Canadian Inuit.* Montreal and Kingston: McGill-Queen's University Press.

Morrison, David A. 1983. *Thule Culture in Western Coronation Gulf, NWT.* National Museum of Man Mercury Series, Archaeological Survey of Canada Paper No. 116, Ottawa.

———. 1983. "Thule sea mammal hunting in the western central Arctic." *Arctic Anthropology* 20(2): 61–78.

Mowat, Farley. 1951. *People of the Deer.* Toronto: McClelland and Stewart.

———. 1959. *The Desperate People.* Toronto: McClelland and Stewart.

Nash, Ronald J. 1969. *The Arctic Small Tool Tradition in Manitoba.* Winnipeg: University of Manitoba Press.

Nelson, Richard K. 1969. *Hunters of the Northern Ice.* Chicago: University of Chicago Press.

Oswalt, Wendell H. 1979. *Eskimos and Explorers.* Novato, CA: Chandler and Sharp.

Park, Robert W. 1993. "The Dorset-Thule succession in Arctic North America: assessing claims for culture contact." *American Antiquity* 58(2): 203–34.

Patterson, Palmer. 1982. *Inuit Peoples of Canada.* Toronto: Grolier.

Petitot, Father Emile. 1981. *Among the Chiglit Eskimos.* Edmonton: Boreal Institute for Northern Studies, University of Alberta.

Purich, Donald. 1992. *The Inuit and their Land: The Story of Nunavut.* Toronto: James Lorimer.

Rasmussen, Knud. 1929. *Intellectual Culture of the Iglulik Eskimos.* Report of the Fifth Thule Expedition 1921–24, Vol. VII, No. 1, Copenhagen. (Reprinted in 1976.)

————. 1930. *Observations on the Intellectual Culture of the Caribou Eskimos.* Report of the Fifth Thule Expedition 1921–24, Vol. VII, No. 2, Copenhagen. (Reprinted in 1976.)

————. 1931. *The Netsilik Eskimos: Social Life and Spiritual Culture.* Report of the Fifth Thule Expedition 1921–24, Vol. VIII, Nos. 1-2, Copenhagen. (Reprinted in 1976.)

————. 1932. *Intellectual Culture of the Copper Eskimos.* Report of the Fifth Thule Expedition 1921–24, Vol. IX, Copenhagen. (Reprinted in 1976.)

————. 1942. *The Mackenzie Eskimos,* ed. H. Ostermann. Report of the Fifth Thule Expedition 1921–24, Vol. X, No. 2, Copenhagen. (Reprinted in 1976.)

Ross, W. Gillies. 1975. *Whaling and Eskimos: Hudson Bay 1860–1915.* National Museums of Canada, Publications in Ethnology No. 10, Ottawa.

Savelle, James M. 1981. "The nature of nineteenth century Inuit occupations of the High Arctic islands of Canada." *Etudes/Inuit/Studies* 5(2): 109–23.

Schledermann, Peter. 1975. *Thule Eskimo Prehistory of Cumberland Sound, Baffin Island, Canada.* National Museum of Man Mercury Series, Archaeological Survey of Canada Paper No. 38, Ottawa.

————. 1978. "Prehistoric demographic trends in the Canadian High Arctic." *Canadian Journal of Archaeology* 2: 43–58.

————. 1980. "Notes on Norse finds from the east coast of Ellesmere Island, NWT." *Arctic* 33(3): 454–63.

————. 1981. "Eskimo and Viking finds in the High Arctic." *National Geographic* 159(5): 574–601.

————. 1990. *Crossroads to Greenland: 3000 Years of Prehistory in the Eastern High Arctic.* Arctic Institute of North America, University of Calgary.

Stefansson, V. 1919. *The Stefansson-Anderson Arctic Expedition: Preliminary Ethnological Report.* Anthropological Papers Vol. 14, American Museum of Natural History, New York. (Reprinted in 1978.)

Swinton, George. 1972. *Sculpture of the Inuit.* Toronto: McClelland and Stewart.

Taylor, J. Garth. 1974. *Labrador Eskimo Settlements of the Early Contact Period.* National Museums of Canada, Publications in Ethnology No. 9, Ottawa.

————. 1985. "The Arctic whale cult in Labrador." *Etudes/Inuit/Studies* 9(2): 121–32.

Taylor, William E., Jr. 1968. *The Arnapik and Tyara Sites: An Archaeological Study of Dorset Culture Origins.* Memoirs of the Society for American Archaeology No. 22.

Taylor, William E., Jr., and George Swinton. 1967. "Prehistoric Dorset art." *The Beaver* 298: 32–47.

Tester, Frank J., and Peter Kulchyski. 1994. *Tammarniit (Mistakes): Inuit Relocation in the Eastern Arctic, 1939–63.* Vancouver: UBC Press.

Tuck, James A. 1976. *Newfoundland and Labrador Prehistory.* Ottawa: National Museum of Man.

Turner, Lucien M. 1979. *Indians and Eskimos in the Quebec-Labrador Peninsula.* Quebec: Presses Comeditex.

Usher, Peter. 1971. "The Canadian Western Arctic: a century of change." *Anthropologica* 13(1–2): 169–83.

Valentine, Victor F., and F.G. Vallee, eds. 1968. *Eskimo of the Canadian Arctic.* Toronto: Carleton Library, McClelland and Stewart.

Vallee, F.G. 1967. *Kabloona and Eskimo in the Central Keewatin.* Ottawa: Canadian Research Centre for Anthropology, Saint Paul University.

Wenzel, George. 1991. *Animal Rights, Human Rights: Ecology, Economy and Ideology in the Canadian Arctic.* Toronto: University of Toronto Press.

Weyer, Edward M. 1932. *The Eskimos: Their Environment and Folkways.* New Haven, CT: Yale University Press.

Yorga, Brian W.D. 1980. *Washout: A Western Thule Site on Herschel Island, Yukon Territory.* National Museum of Man Mercury Series, Archaeological Survey of Canada Paper No. 98, Ottawa.

CHAPTER ELEVEN *The Métis*

The major historical source on the Métis is the massive two-volume work by Giraud (published in French in 1945, reprinted in English translation in 1986). A spate of more recent books has appeared on the Métis; Purich (1988), Harrison (1985) and Sealey and Lussier (1975) provide useful and readable summaries; see also the articles in Peterson and Brown (1985). The important role of women in the fur trade has been examined by Van Kirk (1980) and Brown (1980). A number of eyewitness accounts exist for the Red River colony and the buffalo hunt, but perhaps the best is given by Ross (1856), a prominent member of the colony. A number of Métis writers, such as Campbell (1973), Adams (1975) and Redbird (1980), provide their perspective on Métis culture and history.

Numerous studies on Riel and the rebellions exist. For somewhat different viewpoints see the works of Stanley (1960, 1963), Howard (1952), Flanagan (1979, 1983) and Siggins (1994). Woodcock (1975) provides a useful biography of Gabriel Dumont.

Adams, Howard. 1975. *Prison of Grass: Canada from the Native Point of View.* Toronto: General Publishing.

Barron, F. Laurie, and J.B. Waldram, eds. 1986. *1885 and After: Native Society in Transition.* Saskatoon: Canadian Plains Research Center, University of Regina.

Brown, Jennifer S.H. 1980. *Strangers in Blood: Fur Trade Company Families in Indian Country.* Vancouver: University of British Columbia Press.

Burley, David V., G.A. Horsfall, and J.D. Brandon. 1992. *Structural Considerations of Métis Ethnicity: An Archaeological, Architectural, and Historical Study.* Vermillion: University of South Dakota Press.

Campbell, Maria. 1973. *Halfbreed.* Toronto: McClelland and Stewart.

Chartrand, Paul L.A.H. 1991. *Manitoba's Métis Settlement Scheme of 1870.* Saskatoon: Native Law Centre, University of Saskatchewan.

Daniels, Harry W. 1979. *The Forgotten People: Métis and Non-Status Indian Land Claims.* Ottawa: Native Council of Canada.

Dempsey, Hugh A. 1984. *Big Bear: The End of Freedom.* Vancouver: Douglas & McIntyre.

Dickason, Olive P. 2002. "Metis." In *Aboriginal Peoples of Canada*, ed. Paul R. Magocsi, 189–213. Toronto: University of Toronto Press.

Driben, Paul. 1983. "The nature of Métis claims." *The Canadian Journal of Native Studies* 3(1): 183–96.

Flanagan, Thomas. 1979. *Louis "David" Riel: "Prophet of the New World."* Toronto: University of Toronto Press.

———. 1983. *Riel and the Rebellion: 1885 Reconsidered.* Saskatoon: Western Producer Prairie Books.

————. 1991. *Metis Lands in Manitoba.* Calgary: University of Calgary Press.

Foster, John E. 2004. "The Plains Metis." In *Native Peoples: The Canadian Experience.* 3rd ed., ed. R.B. Morrison and C.R. Wilson, 297–319. Don Mills, ON: Oxford University Press.

Giraud, Marcel. 1986. *The Métis in the Canadian West* (2 vols.). Edmonton: University of Alberta Press.

Harrison, Julia D. 1985. *Metis.* Vancouver: Glenbow-Alberta Institute, with Douglas & McIntyre.

Howard, Joseph Kinsey. 1952. *Strange Empire: The Story of Louis Riel.* Toronto: Swan.

Lussier, A.S., ed. 1979. *Louis Riel & the Métis.* Winnipeg: Pemmican.

Lussier, Antoine S., and D. Bruce Sealey. 1978. *The Other Natives: The Métis* (3 vols.). Winnipeg: Manitoba Métis Federation Press.

MacLeod, Margaret A., and W.L. Morton. 1963. *Cuthbert Grant of Grantown.* Toronto: McClelland and Stewart.

Martin, Fred V. 1989. "Federal and provincial responsibility in the Metis settlements of Alberta." In *Aboriginal Peoples and Government Responsibility,* ed. D.C. Hawkes, 243–96. Ottawa: Carleton University Press.

Metis Association of Alberta, Joe Sawchuk, Patricia Sawchuk, and Theresa Ferguson. 1981. *Metis Land Rights in Alberta: A Political History.* Edmonton: Metis Association of Alberta.

Morton, W.L., ed. 1956. *Alexander Begg's Red River Journal and Other Papers Relative to the Red River Resistance of 1869–1870.* Toronto: Champlain Society.

Pannekoek, Frits. 1991. *A Snug Little Flock: The Social Origins of the Riel Resistance of 1869–70.* Winnipeg: Watson & Dwyer.

Pelletier, Emile. 1977. *A Social History of the Manitoba Métis.* Winnipeg: Manitoba Métis Federation Press.

Peterson, Jacqueline. 1978. "Prelude to Red River: a social portrait of the Great Lakes Métis." *Ethnohistory* 25(1): 41–67.

Peterson, Jacqueline, and Jennifer S.H. Brown, eds. 1985. *The New Peoples: Being and Becoming Métis in North America.* Winnipeg: University of Manitoba Press.

Pocklington, T.C. 1991. *The Government and Politics of the Alberta Metis Settlements.* Saskatoon: Canadian Plains Research Center, University of Regina.

Purich, Donald. 1988. *The Metis.* Toronto: James Lorimer & Co.

Redbird, Duke. 1980. *We Are Métis.* Willowdale, ON: Ontario Métis & Non Status Indian Association.

Ross, Alexander. 1856. *The Red River Settlement: Its Rise, Progress, and Present State.* London: Smith, Elder.

Sawchuk, Joe. 1978. *The Metis of Manitoba.* Toronto: Peter Martin Associates.

Sealey, D. Bruce, and Antoine S. Lussier. 1975. *The Métis: Canada's Forgotten People.* Winnipeg: Manitoba Métis Federation Press.

Siggins, Maggie. 1994. *Riel: A Life of Revolution.* Toronto: HarperCollins.

Sprague, D.N. 1988. *Canada and the Métis, 1869–1885.* Waterloo, ON: Wilfrid Laurier University Press.

————. 1992. "Métis land claims." In *Aboriginal Land Claims in Canada,* ed. Ken Coates, 195–213. Toronto: Copp Clark Pitman.

Spry, Irene M., ed. 1963. *The Palliser Expedition.* Toronto: Macmillan.

Stanley, George F.G. 1960. *The Birth of Western Canada: A History of the Riel Rebellions.* Toronto: University of Toronto Press.

————. 1963. *Louis Riel.* Toronto: Ryerson Press.

Taylor, John L. 1983. "An historical introduction to Métis claims in Canada." *The Canadian Journal of Native Studies* 3(1): 151–81.

Tremaudan, A.H. de. 1982. *Hold High Your Heads (History of the Métis Nation in Western Canada).* Winnipeg: Pemmican.

Van Kirk, Sylvia. 1980. *Many Tender Ties: Women in Fur-Trade Society in Western Canada, 1670–1870.* Winnipeg: Watson & Dwyer.

Woodcock, George. 1975. *Gabriel Dumont.* Edmonton: Hurtig.

CHAPTER TWELVE *Aboriginal People and Canada: Emerging Relations*

Frideres and Gadacz (2001) provide a useful overview on contemporary Aboriginal issues in Canada. Aboriginal legal issues are extensively reviewed by Morse (1985) and Woodward (1989). Coates (1992) provides summaries on the state of land claims in Canada. The Royal Commission on Aboriginal Peoples (1993) has released the reports of several National Round Tables on modern issues. Perspectives of Aboriginal politicians are given in Cardinal (1969, 1977), Manuel and Posluns (1974), Mercredi and Turpell (1993) and contributors to the volume edited by Richardson (1989).

Useful Internet sites providing links for Aboriginal topics include Aboriginal Canada Portal (www.aboriginalcanada.gc.ca), Aboriginal Connections: First Nations (www.aboriginalconnections.com), Indian and Northern Affairs Canada (www.inac.gc.ca), Bill's Aboriginal Links (www.bloorstreet.com/300block/aborcan.htm) and Native Law Centre of Canada (www.usask.ca/nativelaw).

Asch, Michael. 1984. *Home and Native Land: Aboriginal Rights and the Canadian Constitution.* Toronto: Methuen.

————, ed. 1997. *Aboriginal and Treaty Rights in Canada.* Vancouver: UBC Press.

Barman, Jean, Yvonne Hebert, and Don McCaskill, eds. 1987. *Indian Education in Canada (Vol. 2: The Challenge).* Vancouver: University of British Columbia Press.

Barron, F. Laurie, and Joseph Garcea, eds. 1999. *Urban Indian Reserves: Forging new relationships in Saskatchewan.* Saskatoon: Purich Publishing.

Bartlett, Richard H. 1990. *Indian Reserves and Aboriginal Lands in Canada: A Homeland.* Saskatoon: University of Saskatchewan Native Law Centre.

Battiste, Marie, and Jean Barman, eds. 1995. *First Nations Education in Canada: The Circle Unfolds.* Vancouver: UBC Press.

Boldt, Menno. 1993. *Surviving as Indians: The Challenge of Self-Government.* Toronto: University of Toronto Press.

Boldt, Menno, and J.A. Long, eds. 1985. *The Quest for Justice: Aboriginal Peoples and Aboriginal Rights.* Toronto: University of Toronto Press.

Brown, George, and Ron Maguire. 1979. *Indian Treaties in Historical Perspective.* Ottawa: Research Branch, Department of Indian and Northern Affairs.

Canada, House of Commons. 1983. *Indian Self-Government in Canada: Report of the Special Committee.* Ottawa.

Canada, Indian and Northern Affairs. 1980. *Indian Conditions: A Survey.* Ottawa.

————. 1985a. *Living Treaties: Lasting Agreements: Report of the Task Force To Review Comprehensive Claims Policy.* Ottawa.

———. 1985b. *Task Force on Indian Economic Development*. Ottawa.

Canadian Education Association. 1984. *Recent Developments in Native Education*. Toronto.

Cardinal, Harold. 1969. *The Unjust Society: The Tragedy of Canada's Indians*. Edmonton: Hurtig.

———. 1977. *The Rebirth of Canada's Indians*. Edmonton: Hurtig.

Cassidy, Frank, ed. 1991. *Aboriginal Self-Determination*. Lantzville, BC: Oolichan Books.

Cassidy, Frank, and Robert L. Bish. 1989. *Indian Government: Its Meaning in Practice*. Lantzville, BC: Oolichan Books.

Castellano, Marlene Brant, Lynne Davis, and Louise Lahache, eds. 2000. *Aboriginal Education: Fulfilling the Promise*. Vancouver: UBC Press.

Chartrand, Paul L.A.H., ed. 2003. *Who Are Canada's Aboriginal Peoples?: Recognition, Definition, and Jurisdiction*. Saskatoon: Purich Publishing.

Coates, Ken. 1992. *Aboriginal Land Claims in Canada: A Regional Perspective*. Toronto: Copp Clark Pitman.

Comeau, Pauline, and Aldo Santin. 1990. *The First Canadians: A Profile of Canada's Native People Today*. Toronto: James Lorimer.

Corrigan, Samuel W., and Lawrence J. Barkwell, eds. 1991. *The Struggle for Recognition: Canadian Justice and the Métis Nation*. Winnipeg: Pemmican Publications.

Cumming, Peter A., and Neil H. Mickenberg, eds. 1972. *Native Rights in Canada*. 2nd ed. Toronto: General.

Cummins, Bryan D., and John L. Steckley. 2003. *Aboriginal Policing: A Canadian Perspective*. Toronto: Prentice-Hall.

Daniels, H.W. (commissioner). 1981. *Native People and the Constitution of Canada*. The Report of the Métis and Non-Status Indian Constitutional Review Commission. Ottawa: Mutual Press.

Dosman, Edgar J. 1972. *Indians: The Urban Dilemma*. Toronto: McClelland and Stewart.

Dyck, Noel. 1991. *What is the Indian "Problem": Tutelage and Resistance in Canadian Indian Administration*. St. John's: Institute of Social and Economic Research, Memorial University of Newfoundland.

Engelstad, Diane, and John Bird, eds. 1992. *Nation to Nation: Aboriginal Sovereignty and the Future of Canada*. Concord, ON: House of Anansi Press.

Frideres, James S., and René R. Gadacz. 2001. *Aboriginal Peoples in Canada: Contemporary Conflicts*. 6th ed. Scarborough, ON: Prentice-Hall.

Gaffney, R.E., G.P. Gould, and A.J. Semple. 1984. *Broken Promises: The Aboriginal Constitutional Conferences*. Fredericton: New Brunswick Association of Métis and Non-Status Indians.

Gosse, Richard, James Youngblood Henderson, and Roger Carter. 1994. *Continuing Poundmaker & Riel's Quest: Presentations Made at a Conference on Aboriginal Peoples and Justice*. Saskatoon: Purich Publishing.

Green, Ross Gordon. 1998. *Justice in Aboriginal Communities: Sentencing Alternatives*. Saskatoon: Purich Publishing.

Hamilton, A.C. 2001. *A Feather Not a Gavel: Working Towards Aboriginal Justice*. Winnipeg: Great Plains Publishers.

Hamilton, A.C., and C.M. Sinclair. 1991. *Report of the Aboriginal Justice Inquiry of Manitoba, Volume 1: The Justice System and Aboriginal People*. Winnipeg: Queen's Printer.

Hawkes, David C., ed. 1989. *Aboriginal Peoples and Government Responsibility: Exploring Federal and Provincial Roles.* Ottawa: Carleton University Press.

Hawley, Donna L. 1993. *The Annotated Indian Act 1993.* Toronto: Carswell.

Hawthorn, H.B., ed. 1966. *A Survey of the Contemporary Indians of Canada: Economic, Political, Educational Needs and Policies* (2 vols.). Ottawa: Indian Affairs Branch.

Jamieson, Kathleen. 1978. *Indian Women and the Law in Canada: Citizens Minus.* Ottawa: Advisory Council on the Status of Women.

Johnston, Basil H. 1988. *Indian School Days.* Toronto: Key Porter Books.

Johnston, Patrick. 1983. *Native Children and the Child Welfare System.* Toronto: James Lorimer.

Krotz, Larry. 1980. *Urban Indians: The Strangers in Canada's Cities.* Edmonton: Hurtig.

———. 1990. *Indian Country: Inside Another Canada.* Toronto: McClelland & Stewart.

Kuhlen, Daniel J., and Anne Skarsgard. 1985. *A Layperson's Guide to Treaty Rights in Canada.* Saskatoon: University of Saskatchewan Native Law Centre.

Little Bear, Leroy, Menno Bolt, and J.A. Long, eds. 1984. *Pathways to Self-Determination: Canadian Indians and the Canadian State.* Toronto: University of Toronto Press.

Long, David Alan, and Olive Patricia Dickason. 2000. *Visions of the Heart: Canadian Aboriginal Issues.* 2nd ed. Toronto: Harcourt Canada.

McCullum, Hugh, and Karmel McCullum. 1975. *This Land is Not For Sale.* Toronto: Anglican Book Centre.

Manuel, George, and Michael Posluns. 1974. *The Fourth World: An Indian Reality.* Don Mills, ON: Collier-Macmillan.

Maracle, Brian. 1993. *Crazywater: Native Voices on Addiction and Recovery.* Toronto: Viking.

Mercredi, Ovide, and Mary Ellen Turpel. 1993. *In the Rapids: Navigating the Future of First Nations.* Toronto: Viking.

Miller, J.R. 1996. *Shingwauk's Vision: A History of Native Residential Schools.* Toronto: University of Toronto Press.

Milloy, John. 1997. *"A National Crime": The Canadian Government and the Residential School System, 1879 to 1986.* Winnipeg: University of Manitoba Press.

Monture-Angus, Patricia. 1999. *Journeying Forward: Dreaming First Nations' Independence.* Halifax: Fernwood Publishing.

Morse, Bradford W., ed. 1985. *Aboriginal Peoples and the Law: Indian, Metis and Inuit Rights in Canada.* Ottawa: Carleton University Press.

Paquette, Jerry. 1986. *Aboriginal Self-Government and Education in Canada.* Kingston, ON: Institute of Intergovernmental Relations.

Ponting, J. Rick, ed. 1986. *Arduous Journey: Canadian Indians and Decolonization.* Toronto: McClelland and Stewart.

Ponting, J. Rick, and Roger Gibbons. 1980. *Out of Irrelevance: A Socio-Political Introduction to Indian Affairs in Canada.* Toronto: Butterworths.

Purich, Donald. 1986. *Our Land: Native Rights in Canada.* Toronto: Lorimer.

Richardson, Boyce. 1993. *People of Terra Nullius: Betrayal and Rebirth in Aboriginal Canada.* Vancouver: Douglas & McIntyre.

———, ed. 1989. *Drum Beat: Anger and Renewal In Indian Country.* Toronto: Assembly of First Nations and Summerhill Press.

Royal Commission on Aboriginal Peoples. 1993a. *Partners in Confederation: Aboriginal Peoples, Self-Government, and the Constitution.* Ottawa: Canada Communication Group.

————. 1993b. *Aboriginal Peoples in Urban Centres: Report of the National Round Table on Aboriginal Urban Issues*. Ottawa: Canada Communication Group.

————. 1993c. *The Path to Healing: Report of the National Round Table on Aboriginal Health and Social Issues*. Ottawa: Canada Communication Group.

————. 1993d. *Aboriginal Peoples and the Justice System: Report of the National Round Table on Aboriginal Justice Issues*. Ottawa: Canada Communication Group.

————. 1995. *Choosing Life: Special Report on Suicide Among Aboriginal People*. Ottawa: Canada Communication Group.

Schmeiser, Douglas A. 1974. *The Native Offender and the Law*. Law Reform Commission of Canada.

Silverman, Robert A., and Marianne O. Nielsen, eds. 1992. *Aboriginal Peoples and Canadian Criminal Justice*. Toronto and Vancouver: Butterworths.

Smith, Dan. 1993. *The Seventh Fire: The Struggle for Aboriginal Government*. Toronto: Key Porter Books.

Stanbury, W.T., assisted by Jay H. Siegel. 1975. *Success and Failure: Indians in Urban Society*. Vancouver: University of British Columbia Press.

Tanner, Adrian, ed. 1983. *The Politics of Indianness: Case Studies of Native Ethnopolitics in Canada*. St. John's: Institute of Social and Economic Research, Memorial University of Newfoundland.

Tennant, Paul. 1990. *Aboriginal Peoples and Politics: The Indian Land Question in British Columbia, 1849–1989*. Vancouver: University of British Columbia Press.

Waldram, James B. 1997. *The Way of the Pipe: Aboriginal Spirituality and Symbolic Healing in Canadian Prisons*. Peterborough, ON: Broadview Press.

Weaver, Sally M. 1981. *Making Canadian Indian Policy: The Hidden Agenda 1968–70*. Toronto: University of Toronto Press.

Whitehead, Paul C., and Michael S. Hayes. 1998. *Insanity of Alcohol: Social Problems in Canadian First Nations Communities*. Toronto: Canadian Scholars' Press.

Woodward, Jack. 1989. *Native Law*. Toronto: Carswell.

Wotherspoon, Terry, and Vic Satzewich. 1993. *First Nations: Race, Class, and Gender Relations*. Scarborough, ON: Nelson Canada.

York, Geoffrey. 1989. *The Dispossessed: Life and Death in Native Canada*. Toronto: Lester & Orpen Dennys.

INDEX

. . . . .